Bone, Bronze, and Bamboo

SUNY series in Chinese Philosophy and Culture

Roger T. Ames, editor

Bone, Bronze, and Bamboo

Unearthing Early China with Sarah Allan

Edited by

CONSTANCE A. COOK,
CHRISTOPHER J. FOSTER,
and SUSAN BLADER

Associate Editor

AMY MATTHEWSON

Assistant Editor

GAIL PATTEN

Cover Credit: From *Old Pines* 歲寒圖 (2023). Six images from a folding album. Ink on rice paper. © 2023 Wang Mansheng.

Published by State University of New York Press, Albany

© 2024 State University of New York

For information, contact State University of New York Press, Albany, NY
www.sunypress.edu

Library of Congress Cataloging-in-Publication Data

Names: Cook, Constance A., editor. | Foster, Christopher J., editor. | Blader, Susan, 1943– editor. | Matthewson, Amy, editor. | Allan, Sarah, honoree.
Title: Bone, bronze, and bamboo : unearthing early China with Sarah Allan / edited by Constance A. Cook, Christopher J. Foster, Susan Blader, and Amy Matthewson.
Description: Albany : State University of New York Press, [2024] | Series: SUNY series in Chinese philosophy and culture | Includes bibliographical references.
Identifiers: LCCN 2023042746 | ISBN 9781438499000 (hardcover : alk. paper) | ISBN 9781438499017 (ebook)
Subjects: LCSH: China—History—To 221 B.C.—Historiography. | Folklore and history—China. | Mythology, Chinese. | Allan, Sarah.
Classification: LCC DS741.25 .M98 2024 | DDC 931—dc23/eng/20240208
LC record available at https://lccn.loc.gov/2023042746

To Sarah Allan

Photo of Sarah Allan by C. A. Cook, Yantai, China, 2014.

Contents

Preface   ix

Acknowledgments   xvii

1. The Owl in Oracle-Bone Inscriptions and on Early
   Ritual Bronzes   1
   Wang Tao

2. A Study of the Décor on a Shang Dynasty Architectural
   Object from the Site of Xiaoshuangqiao in Zhengzhou   23
   Han Ding

3. Respecting Heaven and Sacrificing to the Ancestors:
   Social Order and Ritual Reflected in Early Western Zhou
   Bronze Drinking Vessel Sets   37
   Lu Liancheng

4. The Cheng Wang *Fangding*   61
   Colin Mackenzie

5. The Western Zhou Court and Hedong Salt Lake: Revelations
   from the Newly Excavated Ba Bo (Elder Ba) Bronze Vessels   77
   Han Wei

6. Changing Ideas about *De*, the Lineage, and the Individual in
   Fifth- and Fourth-Century BCE China as Reflected in the
   Wenxian Covenant Texts   119
   Crispin Williams

7. The Editing and Publication of Ancient Books Written on
   Bamboo and Silk   163
   Li Ling

8. The Philological Value of the Tsinghua Bamboo-Slip
   Manuscripts   191
   Zhao Pingan and Wang Tingbin

9. A Brief Look at the Shanghai Museum Manuscript "The State
   of Lu Suffered a Great Drought"   215
   Scott Cook

10. An Introduction and Preliminary Translation of the *Jiaonü*
    (Instructions for Daughters), a Qin Bamboo Text   233
    Anne Behnke Kinney

11. The Shape of the Text: *Gu* Prisms and Han Primers   259
    Christopher J. Foster

12. Sanjiaowei M1: Hand Tools from the Grave of a
    Hobbyist Woodworker?   293
    Charles Sanft

Afterword. Wandering Mt. Song, Chatting in Friendship:
Exploring Mt. Song in Oracle-Bone Inscriptions   311
    Qi Wenxin

List of Contributors   319

Index   321

Preface

The advent of scientific archaeology and the discovery of oracle bones more than one hundred years ago opened up the field of early China studies in dramatic ways. The constant unveiling of new archaeological discoveries, including inscriptions and manuscripts, has forced scholars of early China to broaden the scope of their research beyond the traditional sources of our received corpus. At the same time, novel theoretical approaches and methodologies have been brought to bear alongside this wave of new data. The field has been bursting with innovation and recalibration ever since.

There has been no scholar more attuned to these developments than Sarah Allan. Over the past fifty years, she has published path-breaking scholarship on early China. Utilizing both received texts and archaeological discoveries as her sources, she has helped mold early Chinese studies with pioneering research on a remarkable range of topics and time periods—from the Neolithic up through the Han—in disciplines as varied as paleography and conceptual metaphor theory.

Bone, Bronze, and Bamboo is part of a three-book series, with *Myth and the Making of History* and *Metaphor and Meaning*, that celebrates Allan and the integral role she has played in the immense growth and development of early China as a field. Scholars throughout the world, who have collaborated with her as mentors, colleagues, and students, were invited to contribute essays in her honor, which we have compiled into these three books. While the range of specialist essays presented here testifies to the expanding boundaries of the study of early China, we believe that, as with Allan's scholarship from the very beginning, there is a compelling and overlapping concern: to understand early China on its own terms. Whether through uncovering the root metaphors of the culture, articulating the interplay between myth and history, or examining newly discovered artifacts, Allan has sought to detach from our modern vantage, to enter into the minds of the ancient peoples of China, understand how they thought, and discern how they communicated those ideas.

∾

Bone, Bronze, and Bamboo pays homage to Sarah Allan's signature contributions to the study of artifacts, manuscripts, and other archaeological data. Insights from archaeological discoveries have become central to our understanding of early China. One of the hallmarks of Allan's scholarship is her commitment to working directly with these materials. In *The Shape of the Turtle: Myth, Art, and Cosmos in Early China*, one of her earliest monographs, Allan, for instance, draws upon the design of royal tombs and bronze vessel décor to argue convincingly that the Shang conceived of their cosmos as *ya* 亞-shaped, akin to the turtle plastrons that served as the primary tool for state divination.[1] In her most recent and much acclaimed book, *Buried Ideas: Legends of Abdication and Ideal Government in Recently Discovered Early Chinese Bamboo-Strip Manuscripts*, Allan unearths a lost discourse surrounding abdication among newly discovered bamboo-strip manuscripts, bolstering her prior explication of the tensions ingrained within the heavenly mandate and dynastic-cycle model that legitimated Zhou rule.[2] These are but two of countless examples where Allan has employed the latest archaeological finds to reimagine early China.

Beyond the central role excavated artifacts have played in her own scholarship, we wish to highlight Allan's unwavering dedication to making these sources accessible to a broader community of interested researchers. This has included, for instance, the publication of collections of oracle bones (*Yingguo suocang jiagu ji* 英國所藏甲骨集 and *Ruidian Sidegeermo Yuandong Guwu Bowuguan cang jiagu wenzi* 瑞典斯德哥爾摩遠東古物博物館藏甲骨文字), bronze vessels (*Ouzhou suocang Zhongguo qingtongqi yizhu* 歐洲所藏中國青銅器遺珠), and Dunhuang manuscripts (*Ying cang Dunhuang wenxian* 英藏敦煌文獻) held in various European institutions.[3] Similarly, Allan has organized numerous international conferences dedicated to understanding the latest discoveries, including hosting several at Dartmouth College, which has facilitated the translation of newly unearthed manuscripts and helped synthesize China's archaeological finds of the past century.[4] Her contributions have spawned many further investigations, including those by the scholars found within these pages.

Bone, Bronze, and Bamboo proceeds in a roughly chronological order, while also paralleling the title of the book itself in its treatment of unearthed artifacts. Within this chronological procession, however, larger themes emerge. The first half of *Bone, Bronze, and Bamboo* concerns the religious, political, and economic interests of the Shang and Zhou ruling elite. Through the paleographic analysis of terms for birds on oracle-bone inscriptions, Wang Tao raises the importance of owls in royal Shang sacrifices linked to weather divination. In time the divine powers the Shang associated with owls came to be reinterpreted in a much harsher light, with the once mysterious but rather benign owl transformed into an evil omen by the Han period. It is a process Wang documents through the close reading of shifting bronze vessel motifs and literary allusions. A similar close reading is conducted by Han Ding for the so-called "dragon and tiger wrestling with elephant motif" (龍虎搏象圖) on Shang architectural ornaments found in Zhengzhou. Han identifies in this motif a human with plumes of feathers and birdlike claws, featured alongside a tiger and snake, whom he connects to Shang shamanistic rituals.

The Zhou overthrow of the Shang was a major historical event that dramatically altered the political landscape of early China. Lu Liancheng examines the aftermath of the Zhou conquest through the lens of mortuary rites, specifically the composition of entombed bronze-vessel assemblages. Lu shows how sets of drinking vessels bearing one *zun* 尊 with two *you* 卣 were an important signifier of Zhou status that spread throughout the Central Plains region. The curious mixture of foreign vessels—some of Shang provenance—alongside the one-*zun* and two-*you* sets leads Lu to intriguing insights into how the Zhou incorporated Shang allies, resources, and technologies into their own society during this time of political transition. In his study of the King Cheng *fangding* vessel 成王方鼎 held by the Nelson-Atkins Museum of Art and the inscription that it bears, Colin Mackenzie highlights a rare example of a vessel cast on behalf of a Zhou king by a close royal relative. Noting the paucity of such vessels, Mackenzie further wonders about the complete absence of inscribed vessels cast by the Zhou kings themselves. It is a curious anomaly that may speak to the political institutions responsible for and social meanings invested in the production of bronze vessels and their inscriptions early in the Zhou reign.

Control over natural resources is an important facet of governance as well. In antiquity, salt was an especially valuable natural resource, as a vital food preservative and ingredient. Han Wei analyzes evidence from the newly discovered Elder Ba 霸伯 *gui* 簋- and *xu* 盨-vessel inscriptions to explicate how the Zhou court managed salt harvests at the critical Hedong Salt Lake site. Immense wealth was at stake in the salt industry, while the production, transportation, and distribution of salt was logistically complex, forcing the Zhou court to carefully navigate relationships with local Jin 晉 lords. Taking the salt industry as his lens, Han traces a shifting power dynamic between the Zhou and Jin, where the Zhou court eventually concedes control over the Hedong Salt Lake to Jin, enriching and empowering this state.

Power dynamics of a different sort are addressed in Crispin Williams's reading of early Warring States stone covenant tablets. Expanding upon Sarah Allan's observations about the historical transformations of the concept *de* 德 (inner power, virtue), Williams examines the use of this term among the oaths sworn to Han 韓 lineage leaders on the Wenxian 溫縣 tablets. While the concept of *de* in these oaths retains archaic associations of a collective lineage-based power, externally preserved through sacrifice, the oaths themselves move away from the ancestral cult by addressing individuals as the basic unit of state administration. It is a juxtaposition, Williams notes, of ideological conservatism with political practicality, in the face of a deteriorating traditional lineage system and at a time when the Han sought separation from the ruling Jin house. It also, Williams argues, laid the groundwork for a new understanding of *de*—seen in Warring States philosophical treatises—as an internal virtue of individuals preserved through self-cultivation. Williams's study anticipates several themes found in later chapters, including an interest in intellectual history and in social actors beyond the ruling elite, thereby serving as a wonderful transition to the second half of *Bone, Bronze, and Bamboo*.

The remaining chapters of *Bone, Bronze, and Bamboo* concern bamboo and wood strips that date from the Warring States to Han periods. Li Ling offers methodological preliminaries by surveying the history of these manuscript discoveries and how they have prompted development of a new specialist field of study over the course of the past century. Li's main concern is with establishing best practices for the editing and publication of ancient manuscripts today. He discusses fundamental first steps, including how manuscripts are categorized, titling, the arrangement of strip order, printing images, transcription, referencing, supplying a graph index, and page formatting.

As Sarah Allan has shown convincingly in her research, the newly unearthed manuscripts "give us our first glimpse of the broader intellectual and literary environment" out of which the received corpus was formed.[5] Understanding this environment in full demands consideration of how texts were transmitted in early China, a topic that Allan explores in-depth in

Buried Ideas.[6] This theme is continued by Zhao Pingan and Wang Tingbin, who discuss the origin, transmission, and editing of *shu* 書 "documents" and similar works among the Tsinghua bamboo strips. The presence in the Tsinghua collection of duplicate manuscripts of *Zheng Wen Gong wen Taibo* 鄭文公問太伯 (Lord Wen of Zheng Questions Tai Bo) and of the preservation of regional features in *Houfu* 厚父 (Houfu [Questioned by the King]) allow for an examination of scribal copying practices. Zhao and Wang show how *She ming* 攝命 (Command to She) and other Tsinghua texts struggled to edit archaic language and argue that the *Yue ming* 說命 ([Fu] Yue's Command) and *Rui Liangfu bi* 芮良夫毖 (Rui Liangfu's admonition) manuscripts include prefaces, revealing a process whereby old documents were transformed into "classics" proper.

The intertextuality of excavated manuscripts and received texts points not only to processes of transmission but also to the evolution of intellectual history. Scott Cook analyzes the Shanghai Museum's *Lu bang da han* 魯邦大旱 (The State of Lu Suffered a Great Drought) bamboo-strip manuscript, recording a dialogue between a Lord of Lu, Confucius, and one of his disciples, Zigong 子貢. Based on parallels between this text and the *Yanzi chunqiu* 晏子春秋 (Master Yan's Spring and Autumn Annals), Cook argues that the *Lu bang da han* derived from the *Master Yan* materials but was adapted to serve a Confucian agenda, demonstrating how rich dialogue took place among Warring States thinkers. Moreover, he notes a shared pedagogical strategy between *Lu bang dahan* and *Zigao* 子羔, another manuscript in the Shanghai Museum collection, with both employing a strategy of using popular "irrational" beliefs as foils for higher-order Confucian values.

The next two chapters explore primary education in early imperial China, shedding light on textual practices reaching other segments of early Chinese society beyond the ruling elite, including women and low-level bureaucratic officials. In a newly unearthed Qin bamboo-strip manuscript from the Peking University collection titled *Jiaonü* 教女 (Educating Women), Di 帝 instructs his daughter on the proper behavior of young women. Anne Behnke Kinney translates this rhyming lesson book and contextualizes it in terms of other, more familiar early moral instruction manuals and admonitions for women, such as the Han-period *Lienüzhuan* 列女傳 (Categorized Biographies of Women) or *Nüjie* 女誡 (Lessons for Daughters). Through Kinney's close reading of the *Jiaonü*, we learn not only about women's education in early China but also about the structure of Qin society and roles played by women within it.

During the Han dynasty, multisided prisms called *gu* 觚 were utilized for the study of primary education works. Christopher J. Foster argues that the materiality of this unique writing support profoundly impacted primers like the *Cang Jie pian* 蒼頡篇 (Cang Jie Volumes), on which low-level scribes were trained and tested to gain positions in the Han bureaucracy. By comparing different editions of the *Cang Jie pian*, and bringing in manuscript evidence for the later *Jijiu pian* 急就篇 (Swift Employ Volumes), Foster demonstrates how the physical constitution of *gu* writing supports transformed these primers, from dictating new chapter divisions and title conventions to strengthening their overall textual identity.

The final essay of *Bone, Bronze, and Bamboo*, by Charles Sanft, likewise considers the training and skill sets of officials and, in the process, challenges our expectations for class domains in early imperial China. Sanft introduces the tomb of Huan Ping 桓平, a treasury official from the Han kingdom of Guangling 廣陵, found in the cemetery of Sanjiaowei 三角圩, near Tianchang 天長, modern-day Anhui. Within the tomb, in close proximity to Huan Ping, was a lacquer toolbox with a complete set of woodworking tools, including some of the earliest known exemplars of certain tool types, such as the wood plane. Why was such a rich set of tools entombed alongside an official, ostensibly of a separate class than the artisans with whom we might usually associate their use? Sanft suggests that the presence of these tools reflects Huan Ping's interest in woodworking as a hobby, showing his individual penchant for the artistry of craftwork. Sanft's study is reminder that—despite immense separations in time, space, and culture—ultimately we deal with *people* who participated in our shared humanity, and we should not be afraid to populate antiquity with personalities.

The archaeological discoveries of the past century have opened exciting new avenues for the study of early China, while also raising new methodological challenges. Whether interpreting the meanings behind artistic motifs and curated assemblages of burial goods, or conducting a close reading of long-lost philosophical treatises and other more ephemeral genres, these finds allow scholars to move past the limited corpus of disembodied received texts. Doing so demands the cross-disciplinary integration of multiple complex types of data, an arduous task but one that promises a more holistic and nuanced appreciation of China's past. It is for this reason that Sarah Allan's work is both so remarkable and so important. In *Bone, Bronze, and Bamboo*, the fruits of this scholarly effort are likewise on full display and, being inspired by Allan, are offered in her honor.

—Constance A. Cook, Christopher J. Foster, and Susan Blader

Notes

1. Sarah Allan, *The Shape of the Turtle: Myth, Art, and Cosmos in Early China* (Albany: State University of New York Press, 1991).

2. Sarah Allan, *Buried Ideas: Legends of Abdication and Ideal Government in Early Chinese Bamboo-Slip Manuscripts* (Albany: State University of New York Press, 2015).

3. Li Xueqin 李學勤, Qi Wenxin 齊文心, Ai Lan 艾蘭 (Sarah Allan), et al., *Yingguo suocang jiagu ji* 英國所藏甲骨集 (Beijing: Zhonghua, 1985); Li Xueqin and Ai Lan (Sarah Allan), *Ouzhou suocang Zhongguo qingtongqi yizhu* 歐洲所藏中國青銅器遺珠 (Beijing: Wenwu, 1995); Zhongguo shehui kexue yuan lishi yanjiusuo 中國社會科學院歷史研究所, et al., *Ying cang Dunhuang wenxian: Hanwen Fojing yiwai bufen* 英藏敦煌文獻: 漢文佛經以外部分, 15 vols. (Chengdu: Sichuan renmin, 1990–2009); Li Xueqin, Qi Wenxin, Ai Lan (Sarah Allan), *Ruidian Sidegeermo* [Stockholm, Sweden] *Yuandong Guwu Bowuguan cang jiagu wenzi* 瑞典斯德哥爾摩遠東古物博物館藏甲骨文字 (Beijing: Zhonghua, 1999).

4. For conference proceedings, see for example: Sarah Allan and Crispin Williams, eds., *The Guodian Laozi: Proceedings of the International Conference, Dartmouth College, May 1998* (Berkeley: Society for the Study of Early China, Institute of East Asian Studies, University of California, Berkeley, 2000); Xing Wen 邢文, ed., "*The X Gong Xu* 曰䢼火公盨: A Report and Papers from the Dartmouth Workshop," special issue *International Research on Bamboo and Silk Documents Newsletter* (2003); Ai Lan (Sarah Allan) and Xing Wen, *Xinchu jianbo yanjiu: Xinchu jianbo guoji xueshu yantaohui wenji, 2000 nian 8 yue, Beijing* 新出簡帛研究: 新出簡帛國際學術研討會文集, 2000 年 8 月, 北京 (Beijing: Wenwu, 2004). For a synthesis, see: Sarah Allan, *The Formation of Chinese Civilization: An Archaeological Perspective* (New Haven: Yale University Press, 2005).

5. Allan, *Buried Ideas*, 321.

6. Allan, *Buried Ideas*, especially chaps. 3, 7, and 8.

Acknowledgments

We would like to express our most heartfelt appreciation to our colleagues for their enthusiastic engagement with this project, their insightful scholarly outputs, and their extraordinary patience. We are certain that, as a result of their care and attention, the essays in the three books—*Myth and the Making of History: Narrating Early China with Sarah Allan*; *Bone, Bronze, and Bamboo: Unearthing Early China with Sarah Allan*; and *Metaphor and Meaning: Thinking Through Early China with Sarah Allan*—will be welcomed by scholars and students in the China field, as well as by individuals interested or involved in the study of any ancient civilization.

These three books could never have been brought to completion without the editing expertise of four colleagues. Gail Patten[1] did the first complete editing and compilation of the pieces. The editorial and computer expertise of Ehud Z. Benor[2] was indispensable in creating the template required by SUNY Press to unify the formatting of each chapter. William N. French III,[3] at an exceptionally busy and stressful time, took on the huge task of finalizing *Metaphor and Meaning*, for which we are immensely grateful. Amy Matthewson[4] beautifully finalized both *Myth and the Making of History* and *Bone, Bronze, and Bamboo*. We also wish to express our gratitude to James Peltz[5] for his support of this massive project, and to the two anonymous reviewers of *Bone, Bronze, and Bamboo*, who offered much helpful advice.

Our thanks go to Lehigh University for providing Constance A. Cook[6] with research funding as part of her position as an NEH Distinguished Professor. The project began when Cook was an active member of the Institute for Advanced Study in Princeton, New Jersey, whose support is much appreciated. Christopher J. Foster[7] is grateful for the support he received from Pembroke College, University of Oxford, when Stanley Ho Junior Research Fellow; and from the British Academy and SOAS University of London, during his British Academy Postdoctoral Fellowship.

Finally, Connie and Chris both wish to acknowledge the profound contribution of Susan Blader,[8] who conceived of the project as a felicitous tribute to Sarah, nurtured it constantly, and ensured—through all manner of trials and tribulations—that it grew to adulthood.

Notes

1. Administrator Department of History, Dartmouth College, Retired.
2. Emeritus, Department of Religion, Dartmouth College.
3. PhD ABD, Chinese History, East Asian Languages and Civilizations, Harvard University; Dartmouth College '08.
4. PhD, History, SOAS University of London.
5. Associate Director and Editor in Chief at SUNY Press.
6. Professor and Chair, Modern Languages and Literatures, Lehigh University.
7. PhD Chinese History, East Asian Languages and Civilizations, Harvard University; Dartmouth College '06.
8. Associate Professor Emerita, Asian and Middle Eastern Languages and Literatures, Dartmouth College.

1

The Owl in Oracle-Bone Inscriptions and on Early Ritual Bronzes

Wang Tao

Bird Graphs in Oracle-Bone Inscriptions and Their Significance

In June 1936, during an excavation at the late Shang capital Yinxu, today's Anyang in Henan Province, archaeologists from the Institute of History and Philology, Academia Sinica, retrieved over seventeen thousand inscribed oracle bones from a storage pit (YH127), the largest single discovery of oracle-bone inscriptions (hereafter: OBI) at Yinxu.[1] Among the inscribed bones, two turtle plastrons bear similar inscriptions (figs. 1.1a and b).[2] Deeply incised

Figures 1.1a–b. *Heji*: 11497, Plastron Front (left) and Back (right). *Source:* Images after *Yinxu wenzi yibian* 殷墟文字乙編 (Taipei: Academia Sinica, 1956), 6664 and 6665, and *Jiaguwen heji* 甲骨文合集 (Beijing: Zhonghua, 1978–1983), 11497 and 11498, with citation to Li Zongkun 李宗焜, *Dang jiagu yushang kaogu—daolan YH127 keng* 當甲骨遇上考古—導覽YH127坑 (Taipei: Academia Sinica, 2006).

with bold strokes imitating brushwork and filled in with red pigments, the distinctive "ceremonial style" is in sharp contrast to the cursive-style inscriptions that appear side by side on the same plastrons. The contents of the inscriptions were obviously significant to the Shang king Wu Ding 武丁 (reign ca. 1250–1192 BCE) under whom the divination was made.[3]

The inscriptions on these plastrons represent a complete formula of Shang divinatory records, consisting of preface, charge, prognostication, and verification. There is no great difficulty in deciphering the inscriptions—they are about ancestral worship, weather, and sacrifices. But, the identification of several of the bone graphs poses challenges. Among them, there is a pictograph depicting a beaked bird with round eyes and plump torso, 鳥, which has been interpreted by scholars in different ways.

First, let us look at the transcription and decipherment of *Heji*: 11497. The English translation is rendered by David Keightley:[4]

[1] *Heji*: 11497

(Plastron front) 丙申卜㱿貞來乙巳酒下乙王占曰酒唯有祟其有設乙巳酒明雨伐既雨咸伐亦雨施卯鳥星

(Plastron back) 乙巳夕有設于西

Translation:

(Preface:) Crack-making on *bingshen* (day 33), Que divined:

(Charge:) "On the following *yisi* (day 42), offer wine libation to Xia Yi."

(Prognostication:) The king, reading the cracks, said: "When we offer wine libation, there will be harm. There will perhaps be an X natural phenomenon."

(Verification:) On *yisi* (day 42), we offered wine libation. In the early morning it rained; at the *fa* sacrifice, it stopped raining; at the *fa* sacrifice to Xian (= Cheng), it also rained. We offered *shi* and *mao* sacrifice to the Bird Star(s).

(Plastron back) On the evening of *yisi* (day 42), there was an X natural phenomenon in the west.

In this inscription, the graph 𝔛, which Keightley did not decipher but translated as "natural phenomenon," should be read as *she* 設, or *zhuo* 鑿, or *yi* 異, meaning an abnormal omen in the sky;[5] *fa* 伐 means human sacrifice; both *shi* 施 and *mao* 卯 refer to the specific methods in which sacrificial victims were slaughtered and dismembered.[6] The bird pictograph is read as *niao* 鳥, and, together with the character *xing* 星, written as 𝔞, they have been interpreted as *niaoxing* 鳥星, referring to the constellation.[7] The inscription is thus understood as certain sacrifices being made to ancestors and to the Bird Star in order to influence the weather. This interpretation is widely accepted and has been used by many scientists and historians to demonstrate the astronomical developments of the Shang dynasty.[8]

However, questions have been raised about the decipherment of the character *xing* 星. As Yang Shuda 楊樹達 argued, a more plausible reading of the character is *qing* 晴 (clear sky), not *xing* (star).[9] In an article published in 1981,[10] Li Xueqin 李學勤 reinforced this decipherment by referencing further examples in which the character *xing* is clearly understood as *qing*. He tentatively proposed that the character *niao* could be a loan graph for the particle *shu* 倏, meaning "swiftly," and read together, the two characters, *niao xing* 鳥星, should be *shu qing* 倏晴 (swiftly the sky lightened). To support his argument, Li cited another example from the same pit YH127. The following translation follows Li's interpretation:

[2] *Heji*: 11499

癸卯卜爭貞下乙其侑鼎王占曰侑鼎唯大示王亥亦㘝 [乙巳] 酒明雨伐 [既] 雨咸伐既 [雨] 施卯鳥大啟易 [暘]

Translation:

(Preface) Cracking made on *guimao* (day 40), Zheng, divining:

(Charge) "Onto Xia Yi we perhaps offer a *ding*-tripod."

(Prognostication) The king read the cracks and said: "To offer a *ding*-tripod to the greater ancestor Wang Hai who should receive fragrant wine."

(Verification) On *yisi* (day 42), wine-offering was performed, it rained in the morning; at human sacrifice the rain stopped, but once human sacrifice was finished, rain started again; *at the slaughtering and cutting sacrifices, swiftly the sky lightened and became sunny.*

In terms of its content, this inscription is very similar to *Heji*: 11497, but with a different diviner, Zheng 爭, who also worked under King Wu Ding. The divination is also about the weather; the sacrifices were made to the ancestor Xia Yi 下乙 and other important ancestors, such as Wang Hai 王亥. But, in this example, the character *niao* appears by itself, and the character *qing* is replaced by *da qi yang* 大啟暘, which allows the sentence to be understood as "the sky is lightened and sunny." Compared to the "Bird Star" theory, this new reading seems to make better sense and has gained support from many scholars.[11] However, this interpretation cannot completely rule out the alternative explanation—as Li admitted that the reading of *niao* 鳥 as *shu* 倏 was tentative and needs further evidence.[12] In fact, on whether the characters are interchangeable, the phonetic relationship between these two characters in Old Chinese is not as close as we would normally take for granted; and we find little evidence of them being used as loan characters in early texts.[13]

In a more recent study of Shang dynasty astronomy, Feng Shi 馮 時 argues that the *niao* 鳥 in this case is better understood as a bird deity (*niaoshen* 鳥神) who receives sacrifices from the Shang people.[14] This explanation is much more convincing in my opinion; and, moreover, I would suggest that the pictograph can be deciphered as *xiao* 鴞 <*tjagw (or *jiao* 梟<*kiagw), meaning owl. This decipherment is based on both graphic and phonological grounds, as well as examples found in OBI.

The inscribers of OBI often tried to make graphic distinctions between different pictographs. There are many bird graphs that are basically derived from two pictographs: 隹 and 隹, both represent a bird, but the first is more stylized and the second simply pictographic. Scholars have conventionally read the former as *zhui* 隹 <*tjəd and the latter as *niao* <*tiəgwx.[15] In early lexicon dictionaries, such as Xu Shen's 許慎 *Shuowen jiezi* 說文解 字 (2nd c., hereafter: *Shuowen*), *zhui* refers to birds with short tails (鳥之 短尾總名也), and *niao* are birds with long tails (鳥長尾禽總名也). But, as Luo Zhenyu 羅振玉 observed, this differentiation is not always reflected in early epigraphy and in many cases the two elements are interchangeable.[16] Thus, in OBI, the character *niao* may be read as *xiao* or *jiao*, representing the owl, and the same reading could apply to the character *zhui*, which may also be understood as the owl. In the *Shuowen*, *xiao* 鴞 is simply explained as *chixiao* 鴟鴞—an alternative name for the owl. In his annotation to the *Shuowen*, the Qing dynasty scholar Duan Yucai 段玉裁 (1735–1815) proposed that *chixiao* is disyllabic and the two characters should not be read separately. He also notes that the character *xiao* imitates the screech call the bird makes and, more importantly, a variation of *chi* 鴟 <*thjid, also written as *zhi* 鳷, is interchangeable with another character *zhi* 雉 <*drjidx.[17]

In fact, there are a number of bone graphs representing birds, but some may refer to the owl as well. For instance, Cai Yunzhang 蔡運章 argues that the bone graph 𤤩 could refer to the owl.[18] There is another bone graph, 𤰃, depicting a bird with horns, which is identified with *huan* 雚, and, according to the *Shuowen*, it refers to a type of owl whose screech call will bring disaster to the people (所鳴其民有既).[19]

The character *jiao* 梟 is a pictograph representing a bird on a tree, which may suggest an owl that is sacrificed and hanged on a tree. The definition found in the *Shuowen* for *jiao* is more meaningful; it is defined as an "unfilial bird" (不孝鳥也), as there is a general belief that the owl devours its own mother. The *Shuowen* goes on to state, "When the sun rises (or when summer begins), the owl is captured and slaughtered" (故日至捕梟磔之). This indicates that the owl was used especially in a ritual context and the pronunciation of the character *jiao* again has something to do with the screech call of the owl.[20]

Indeed, we find a number of OBI examples in which divinations were made about the "crying owl":

[3] *Heji*: 17366 (reverse):

. . . 之日夕有鳴鳥

Translation:

"... in the evening of the day there is the crying owl."

[4] *Heji*: 4725

辛未卜鳴獲井鳥 / 鳴不其[獲]井鳥

Translation:

"On xinwei (day 8), ming captures the owl at Jing."

"... Ming perhaps cannot capture the owl at Jing."

As previously mentioned, the character *zhi* 雉 stands for the pheasant in later texts, but it may refer to the owl in OBI. Here, we find a number of examples in which the *zhi* bird appears in a context very similar to that of the owl:

[5] *Heji*: 522 (reverse):

[乙]卯有[設] . . . X庚申亦有設有鳴雉 . . . 疛圍羌或

Translation:

> "On *yimao* (day 52) there was a strange omen, . . . on *gengshen* (day 57) there was again a strange omen, and the crying owl . . . sick . . . human sacrifice of the Qiang-tribe man/ . . ."

In some cases, the Shang people attempted to capture the owl for ritual sacrifices:

[6] *Heji*: 10514:

甲寅卜呼鳴网雉獲鳳丙辰獲五之夕風

Translation:

> Cracking made on *jiayin* (day 51): "To call Ming to set up nets (used to capture the owl)[21] to capture the peacock." On *bingchen* (day 53), five [peacocks] were captured, and that evening was very windy.

Here, the graph 🐦 (*feng* 鳳) depicts a crowned long-tailed bird that is understood to be a peacock; later on, a phonetic sign (*fan* 凡) is added, written as 🐦. It is also used as *feng* 風, meaning the wind.

[7] *Tunnan*: 51:[22]

丁卯貞己巳登鳥于祖辛暨父丁茲用

Translation:

On *dingmao* (day 4), divining: "On *yisi* (day 6) we make an offering of the owl to Grandfather Xin and Father Ding." This was used.

Having discussed all the examples, we may now return to the inscription (*Heji*: 11497) cited at the beginning of this chapter and translate it as follows:

Cracking made on *bingshen* (day 33), Que, divining: "On the following *yisi* (day 42) we will perform a wine rite to Xia Yi." The king read the cracks and said: "In performing the wine rite, there will be harm, perhaps some strange omen appearing in the sky." The wine rite was performed on *yisi* (day 42) and it was raining in the morning; and at human sacrifice the rain stopped, but once human sacrifice was ended, the rain started again; at the *slaughtering and cutting of the owl, the sky lightened.* On the evening of *yisi*, there was a strange omen appearing in the west.

The preceding example clearly shows that the owl was an important sacrifice in Shang rituals—the bird seemed to possess a certain magical power that could influence the weather; Yu Xingwu has observed that, in OBI, many weather-related characters all have the bird element as their semantic, probably because certain birds (in this case, the owl) and their crying sounds could predict and influence the weather.[23]

Now, the question is: Why the owl? In the natural world, there are over thirty different subspecies in the owl family and, among them, the most familiar ones are the long-eared Eurasian eagle owl and short-eared tawny owl, best known as the screech owl and the horned owl in China. In its natural habitat, the owl is an extraordinary nocturnal bird, with binocular vision and binaural hearing. The owl makes a screech call and catches prey in the dark, which fits perfectly with the perception of abnormity in ritual and magic; the owl's physical appearance also reminds people of a warrior. In ancient Greece, the owl was a sacred bird associated with Athena, the goddess of war, wisdom, and the crafts, and for the Etruscans, the owl was regarded as some kind of deity who received human sacrifices.[24] As Liu Dunyuan 劉敦願 argued, it is possible that the Shang people perceived the owl as the god of night and dreams, as well as the messenger between the human and the spirit world, on account of its silent flight and hunting in darkness.[25] If so, this would explain why the owl is mentioned repeatedly in

Shang divination records and is found on ritual bronzes, another important piece of evidence for understanding Shang religion and art.

It is not difficult to imagine that the owl might have played a similar role in Shang religion. An investigation into Shang mythology throws new light on the question of owl worship. Several scholars recently proposed a theory that the mythical black bird (*xuanniao* 玄鳥) from which the Shang people originated is, actually, the owl. We find an ancient hymn in the *Shijing* 詩經, the earliest anthology of Chinese poetry, which reads:[26]

> 天命玄鳥, 降而生商, 宅殷土芒芒; 古帝命武湯, 正域彼四方.
> 方命厥后, 奄有九有; 商之先后, 受命不殆, 在武丁孫子.
> 武丁孫子, 武王靡不勝; 龍旂十乘, 大糦是承.
> 邦畿千里, 維民所止, 肇域彼四海.
> 四海來假, 來假祁祁, 景員維河; 殷受命咸宜, 百祿是何.

> Heaven ordered the black bird to descend and bear the Shang; he dwelt in the great land of Yin that was very vast; of old, God gave the appointment to the martial Tang, he regulated and set boundaries for those (states of the) four quarters.

> And then it (Heaven) charged the sovereign extensively to hold the nine possessions; Shang's first sovereign received an appointment never imperiled.

> When it rested with the descendant of the Martial King (i.e., Tang), the descendant of the Martial King, Wu Ding, had none whom he did not vanquish; with dragon banners and ten chariots he (went and) presented the great sacrificial grain.

> The royal domain was of a thousand *li*, that was where the people (of our tribe) settled; but he (also) delimited and set boundaries for those (states between the) four seas.

> The (states between the) four seas came (in homage), they came in crowds; the great (circle =) encircling boundary was the river; that Yin received the appointment was entirely right; a hundred blessings they bore.

This hymn is an origin myth of the Shang people likely transmitted orally and continued into the Zhou period. In classical lexicography, the character *xuan* 玄 can be understood as "mysterious" or "divining." In OBI, the bird pictograph is often combined with ancestral names such as Wang Hai 𩿅. On a Shang bronze *hu* vessel, we find a pictograph depicting a long-eared owl above the name *fu* 婦 (figs. 1.2a and b),[27] which can be deciphered as

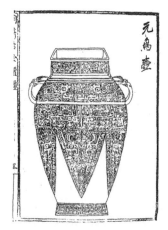 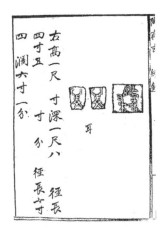

Figures 1.2a–b. Yuanniao *Hu* 元鳥壺 Vessel and Its Inscription Recorded in the *Taozhai jijin xulu. Source:* Duanfang 端方, *Taozhai jijin xulu* 陶齋吉金續錄 (Shanghai: You zheng shu ju, Xuan Tong ji you, 1909), 2:5.

"lady of the black bird clan" (*xuanniao fu* 玄鳥婦), probably the emblem of a lineage. Thus, evidence from Shang archaeology and historical literature render it quite possible that the Shang people believed in some mythical relationship with the owl. For instance, according to Sun Xinzhou 孫新周 and several other scholars, owl worship existed in the Shang dynasty and the mythical ancestor Di Jun 帝俊 (also known as Di Ku 帝嚳 or Shun 舜) can be identified with the black bird deity who was also the productive god, agriculture protector, and solar god for the Shang people.[28] Although Sun's argument is grounded in the old totemic theory, the point about the owl being the black bird is certainly worthy of note.

The conventional explanation is, however, that the *xuanniao* or black bird is not the owl but a swallow (*yanzi* 燕子), and this was the popular view among Han dynasty scholars. Indeed, the swallow is presented as the black bird that appears both in Han mythology and in visual art as the sunbird, and, at the same time, the owl becomes the bird of the underworld. For example, the famous silk funerary banner unearthed from the Mawangdui No. 1 Han tomb depicts a swallowlike black bird in the sun, and an owl near the entrance of heaven. Moreover, two owl-on-turtle images are positioned on the left and right side of the earth platform. According to Eugene Wang, the visual meaning of the painting on the left is to signify "the sun setting at dusk in the west and re-emerging from the east at dawn."[29] Han ideology favored the association of the swallow with filial piety (*xiao* 孝) since the swallow faithfully returns every year, whereas the owl was conversely portrayed as an evil bird that ate its own parent. We, however, do not find such opposition in the earlier period and, in Shang archaeology, though there are a few references to the swallow, the owl is clearly more prominent.

The Owl Motif on Shang Bronzes— Prominent, yet Most Mysterious

The main decoration on Shang bronzes is a two-eyed motif, commonly known as the *taotie*. It is difficult to identify the *taotie* with any real animal. As Sarah Allan has observed, the motif is always bifurcated and dissolved "prevent[ing] any single reading and mutability of the imagery of the *taotie* cannot be imagined as a depiction of any particular creature, real or imagined."[30] Allan further explains, "Not only are the motifs of Shang bronze art continually transformed, their primary allusions are to transformations of states of being—eating and sacrifice, the watery underworld of the dead, the dragon that is also a bird, snakes that slough their skins, deer that shed their antlers, the cicada that emerges winged from the earth."[31] Wu Hung has argued in a similar way: "These varying images seem to attest to a painstaking effort to create metaphors for an intermediate state between the supernatural and reality—something that one could depict but not portray."[32] There are, however, exceptions. A few real animals, notably the elephant, the tiger, and the owl, are sometimes represented in Shang art in a more naturalistic way than other animals.

Among the many animal motifs used in Shang art, the representation of the owl is one of the most prominent yet most mysterious images. Robert Bagley has observed that for a period of time, the owl is probably the only real animal that competes successfully with the *taotie* as the principle motif on Shang ritual bronzes. Owl representations can be divided into three types. (1) Owl motifs that occur as surface decoration on round and square vessels, usually on *you*, *zhi*, and *gong*. (2) Two owls, back to back, on a round wine bucket, as a double-owl *you* in a semi-sculptural form. This type is the most popular during the late Shang period and many examples exist. And finally, (3) a wine container, usually a *zun*, in a three-dimensional, owl-shaped vessel. Bagley thinks that the last type, the owl-shaped vessels, are the earliest among the three, probably introduced in the beginning of the Anyang period, and he listed more than a half dozen similar examples in various collections.[33] The one featured in his detailed discussion is the small owl *zun* in the Sackler collection, which entered the collection of the celebrated collector Wang Yirong 王懿荣 as early as 1881.[34] These objects are all of the late Shang period and have attracted a great deal of scholarly discussion because of their rarity as well as their outstanding artistic quality.

However, the identification of the owl motif on Shang bronzes is not so straightforward. For example, the Song dynasty catalog *Xuanhe bogutu* 宣和博古圖 called the owl-shaped bronze bucket a "four-legged *you*" (*sizu you* 四足卣).[35] The Qing dynasty catalog *Xiqing gujian* 西清古鑑, compiled under Emperor Qianlong's patronage (18th c.), recorded a double-owl *you* (cover missing) but called it a "phoenix vessel of the Zhou dynasty" (Zhou feng *yi* 周鳳彞),[36] and, in another imperial catalog *Xiqing xujian Jiabian* 甲編, there is an owl-shaped vessel that was named a "rooster vessel of the Zhou dynasty" (Zhou ji *yi* 周雞彞).[37] Even in the nineteenth century, the learned antiquarian scholar Wu Dacheng 吳大澂 (1835–1902) did not distinguish this particular form; he called the small owl-shaped *zun* in the Wang Yirong collection a "*zun* in the form of a sacrificial animal" (*xixing zun* 牺形尊).[38] He also misidentified a double-owl bucket in his own collection as the "elephant *zun*" (*xiang zun* 象尊).[39] In his publications, these bronzes were also frequently wrongly attributed to the Zhou instead of the Shang period.

The advancement of modern archaeology has dramatically changed our understanding of Shang ritual and art. In the 1930s, Academia Sinica excavated the Shang royal cemetery at Xibeigang in Anyang, on the northern bank of the Huan River. In tomb M1885, archaeologists found a bronze wine vessel made in the shape of a standing owl,[40] missing its cover and somewhat naturalistically modeled, with hooked claws and a wide tail. From another tomb, M1001, they also found a marble owl (fig. 1.3),[41] 17.1 cm

Figure 1.3. Marble Owl from Tomb 1001 at Yinxu. *Source:* Gao Quxun 高去尋, *Houjiazhuang: 1001 hao damu* 侯家莊: 1001 號大墓 (Taipei: Academia Sinica, 1962), pl. 88.

in height, in a standing pose, with round eyes, hooked beak, large raised horns, and split tail; its torso was decorated with stylized patterns and two facing birds (owls) on the chest, two *kui* dragons on its head, and a cicada on its back. Also found in this tomb was another larger owl-like animal (fig. 1.4),[42] 34.1 cm in height, carved in marble, but with very different decoration from the previous one: it had a pointed beak, two flat horns, and humanlike ears; and its torso is covered with featherlike patterns, with its wings turned into the coiled snake and *kui* dragon patterns. The larger owl also has an open channel on its back, suggesting that it may originally have been attached to a wooden pole, as a guardian spirit placed at the entrance of the tomb. A marble tiger in kneeling position was also found in this tomb, with a similar channel on its back, perhaps with the same function. According to archaeologists, tomb M1001 belonged to the most powerful king, Wu Ding of the late Shang dynasty.

In 1976, archaeologists from the Institute of Archaeology, Chinese Academy of Social Sciences, discovered an intact royal tomb in Anyang, which belonged to Fu Hao 婦好, one of King Wu Ding's consorts. A number of small jade owls were found in her tomb, together with a pair of large bronze wine vessels (*zun*) made in the shape of a standing owl (fig. 1.5).[43] These two vessels are among the most impressive bronzes ever discovered at Anyang. They bear a close resemblance to the marble owls: they have long hooked beaks, short ears, and high horns in dragon form, their necks and chests decorated with *kui* dragons and *taotie* motifs, their wings transformed into coiled snakes, and their backs and tails fashioned into another owl. On the covers, two small knobs are in the form of a dragon and an owl sculpted

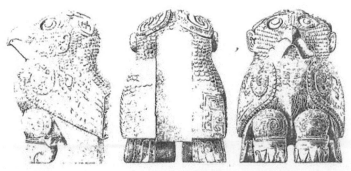

Figure 1.4. Marble Owl-Like Figure from Tomb 1001 at Yinxu. *Source:* Gao, *Houjiazhuang*, pl. 74.

Figure 1.5. Bronze Owl-Shaped *Zun* Vessel from the Tomb of Fu Hao. *Source:* Zhongguo shehui kexueyuan kaogusuo, *Yinxu Fu Hao mu* 殷墟婦好墓 (Beijing: Wenwu, 1980), 55, fig. 36.

in the round. The owl-like motif also appears on several other large bronze vessels from the tomb of Fu Hao; for instance, the large *fangyi*, *fangzun*, and *fanghu*,[44] as three-dimensional sculpted small owls placed on the shoulders of the vessels, as well as being a register of their surface decoration; in these cases, the owl seems to have a hooked beak and a long tail.

The Owl Motif on Western Zhou Bronzes—A Transformation

In the early Western Zhou period, the owl motif underwent a transformation from the naturalistic representation of a real bird to a more mythical birdlike phoenix. How did the change happen? Could new meaning(s) of the owl influence the production and interpretation of ancient bronzes? It is indeed with these examples and questions in mind that two owl-shaped vessels of the Western Zhou period become significant in our inquiry. The first example is the Da Bao *you* 大保卣, which is said to have been found in Shandong Province and is now in the collection of the Hakutsuru Fine Art Museum in Japan.[45] The bronze *you* is a rare example made in the round and in the shape of a similar bird, with a strong beak and long plumage on its head; though impressive in volume, its bold shape and simplified décor indicate a clear departure from the Shang tradition. Most scholars have avoided identifying the species of the bird, but a close comparison suggests it could be a stylized owl motif; with the hooked beak and round eyes, it closely resembles the owl on the Fu Hao bronzes. But the main difference between the Zhou bird motif and the Shang dynasty prototype lies with its elongated plumage and long tail, which are the attributes of the mythical phoenix (*fenghuang* 鳳凰). The phoenix became the major motif on Zhou bronzes and as the counterpart of the *taotie*, the divine bird is associated with the birth myth of the Zhou people. In terms of stylistic development, we can see that the *fenghuang* motif derives from the owl and pheasant; its artistic representation probably enhances the mythical character of the bird, as seen on the Hakutsuru owl-shaped *you* and a unique *zun* vessel.

The owl-shaped *zun* in the Shen Zhai 慎齋 collection in Singapore (formerly in the Idemitsu Museum of Arts in Tokyo) is unusual in terms of its configuration.[46] It is modeled in the round with a realistic approach, showing open rounded eyes, small pointed ears, and a hooked beak, and its short body is supported by clawed feet and a tressed tail—all these allude to a real owl. Unlike any other known example, however, it has a back-to-back double head, perhaps inspired by the illusion created by the owl's ability to turn its head vigorously. High-raised notched flanges divide the two heads while similar flanges appear on its chest, wings, and tail. The same decoration appears on both sides of the vessel: on the right is a *kui* dragon and on the left a large bird with a hooked beak and long plumage, all set against a dense spiral background. The bronze is covered with a light green patina and patches of malachite encrustation. This owl-shaped vessel is conceived as a wine container. It originally had a lid, now missing, leaving an opening on the back of the vessel. Judging by its shape, decoration, and inscription, the owl *zun* is a product of the early Western Zhou period, probably in the transition from the Shang tradition to the Zhou innovation. The modeling and execution demonstrate a superb technique seen on pieces made by the hands of skilled Shang casters, but the notched flanges and the combination of the dragon and bird decoration are typical of early Western Zhou bronzes.

A close examination of the owl *zun* reveals an inscription cast onto the bottom of the interior. Due to corrosion, the inscription is partially illegible. However, the first line mentions both King Wen and King Wu (曰文王武王), who are the founders of the Zhou dynasty, and at the end of the inscription there is a signed name of the patron of the vessel, "Xing" 井 (= 邢). In terms of epigraphic evidence, the name of King Wen (文王)

and King Wu (武王) are written in *hewen* or combined graphs, an archaic style of writing commonly seen in the late Shang and early Western Zhou periods. A comparison between this owl-shaped *zun* and other well-known examples may help us arrive at a more accurate conclusion of its date. The patron of this bronze is Xing, who was the son of the Duke of Zhou. The Duke of Zhou was the younger brother of King Wu and acted as regent until his nephew King Cheng came of age. The Duke of Zhou's son was later enfeoffed as Lord of Xing (Xing Hou 邢侯), with a principality at today's Xingtai in Hebei Province (another theory places this at Wenxian in Henan). The famous Xing Hou *gui* 邢侯簋, now in the British Museum, bears a sixty-eight-character inscription that records the enfeoffment ceremony of the Lord of Xing by King Cheng (r. 1042–1021 BCE). The other bronze is the Mai *fangzun* 麦方尊, which was first recorded in the now-lost *Xiqing gujian* (named Zhou Xing Hou *zun* 周邢侯尊),[47] also mentions the Lord of Xing performing a libation rite and the archery ritual (*sheli* 射禮) with the Zhou king at Biyong 璧雍 in Chengzhou; he was awarded many gifts and even offered the use of the king's own chariot. His scribe, Mai, was awarded metal and this precious vessel was made by Mai to commemorate the event.

The other noticeable change is that on many bronze vessels produced during the King Cheng period, the bird motif became more prominent, taking over the central position of the *taotie*, such as the Yan Hou *yu* 郾侯盂 that was found in Lingyuan in Liaoning Province and the Er Shu *gui* 鄂叔簋, now in the Shanghai Museum collection. The most striking example is the Ran *fangding* 冉方鼎 in the San Francisco Asian Art Museum, Avery Brundage collection, which is a square cauldron with four large birds facing out from the corners of the vessel and with the body supported by four bird-formed feet.

According to Tang Lan 唐蘭, the Xing Hou *gui* dates to King Kang's 康王 reign (r. 1020–996 BCE) and the Mai *fangzun* is later, probably during the early period of King Zhao's 昭王 reign (995–977 BCE).[48] But Chen Mengjia 陳夢家 thinks that both bronzes are of the Cheng-Kang 成康 period.[49] In comparing the Mai *fangzun* with the current example, we see that their style and decoration, in addition to the inscriptions, share many common features. For instance, the main motifs of the dragon and phoenix are of a peculiar style with flowing bodies; the dragon with projecting snout, horns, and limbs, and the phoenix with a long beak and trailing plumage. The distinctive hooked flanges are also similar. Based on such a comparison, we can attribute the owl-shaped *zun* to the King Cheng period or the early years of King Kang's reign, around 1000 BCE. Thus, this owl *zun* may offer us a chance to further explore the significant changes of the very early Western Zhou bronze industry, as well as the development of a belief system in that particular historical moment.

In the early Western Zhou period, the mythic power of the owl seemed to continue to play in people's minds. Here, allow me to cite a well-known poem that is recorded in the *Shijing*:[50]

《鴟鴞》

鴟鴞鴟鴞, 既取我子, 無毀我室.
恩斯勤斯, 鬻子之閔斯.
迨天之未陰雨, 徹彼桑土, 綢繆牖戶.
今女下民, 或敢侮予.
予手拮据, 予所捋荼, 予所蓄租, 予口卒瘏, 曰予未有室家.
予羽譙譙, 予尾翛翛, 予室翹翹, 風雨所漂搖, 予維音嘵嘵.

The Owl

Oh, kite-owl, kite-owl,
You have taken my young.
Do not destroy my house.
With such love, such toil
To rear those young ones I strove!
Before the weather grew damp with rain
I scratched away the bark of that mulberry-tree
And twined it into window and door.
"Now you people down below,
If any of you dare affront me . . ."
My hands are all chafed
With plucking so much rush flower;
With gathering so much bast
My mouth is all sore.
And still I have not house or home!
My wings have lost their gloss,
My tail is all bedraggled.
My house is all to pieces,
Tossed and battered by wind and rain.
My only song, a cry of woe!

In translating this poem into English, Arthur Waley debuted the traditional interpretation that it was associated with the story of King Cheng 成王 and his protector the Duke of Zhou 周公, in which the kite-owl symbolizes the wicked, rebellious uncles of the king, and the persecuted bird (the speaker in the poem) refers to the Duke of Zhou who looks after the young king with love and care. Waley pointed out that the allegory does not make sense and the poem must have derived from an earlier legend.[51] In a new study, Ye Shuxian 葉舒憲 has reinterpreted this lyric, treating it as a ritual prayer, and argued that the poem can be read as an oral exchange between the worshiper and the owl deity.[52] Thus, the owl is no longer a wicked bird but the personified bird goddess.

From Artistic Motif to Ill Omen—
A Question of Meaning

It is difficult to reconstruct how the meaning(s) of the owl motif developed and changed over a very long period of time, from the Shang to the Zhou dynasties. Many scholars have tried to interpret the meaning of early ritual bronzes and their decorations. Bagley, however, rejects any symbolic interpretations of the motifs and insists that the explanation of the bronze decoration should follow a décor scheme.[53] It is true that a design or motif has its own invention and development; nonetheless, employed in the form of a vessel or in surface decoration, the animal motif gives the impression that the vessel is an important object. The motifs may not refer to any particular category of imagined fantastic creatures nor to animals in the real world; instead, we should regard these as completely new configurations. When a ritual bronze was specially designed and created, the intention was to create some function and to refer to a particular visual experience; thus, the significance would have been understood in that context. There is no doubt whatsoever that Shang artisans had the knowledge and skills to make bronzes in any form they wanted. When they chose to present animals in a specific way, it is likely that the reasons lay not only with the program of design but were also conditioned by the social and religious system of the Shang people.

For instance, the owl continued to feature in literature and art, usually with mysterious powers. The poem cited earlier shows that art and old legend could be transmitted in later times but were easily misinterpreted.

Over time, the particular mythical associations surrounding owls in ancient times were lost. We can still find a few eighth to seventh century BCE examples in which the owl motif was used decoratively. However, from the sixth century BCE onward, the owl gradually disappeared from mainstream visual art. The radical intellectual movement of the Eastern Zhou period led to the reorganization and schematization of early beliefs and myths. The owl was still associated with special powers but there was a shift in attitude. No longer thought of as benign, the owl was portrayed as a threat, an ill omen, and the harbinger of unwelcome death. A well-known example is the rhyme-prose *Rhapsody on the Owl* (*Pengniao fu* 鵩鳥賦), written by the Han dynasty statesman and poet Jia Yi 賈誼 (220–168 BCE) after he was banished to Changsha, a remote region in the south, formerly the territory of the Chu state. One day, he was visited by an owl:[54]

單閼之歲, 四月孟夏, 庚子日斜, 鵩集余舍, 止於坐隅, 貌甚閒暇. 異物來萃, 私怪其故, 發書占之, 讖言其度. 曰 "野鳥入室, 主人將去." 問於子鵩: "余去何之? 吉虖告我, 凶言其災. 淹速之度, 語余其期."

　　鵩乃太息, 舉首奮翼, 口不能言, 請對以意. 萬物變化, 固亡休息. 斡流而遷, 或推而還. 形氣轉續, 變化而嬗. 沕穆亡間, 胡可勝言! 禍兮福所倚, 福兮禍所伏; 憂喜聚門, 吉凶同域. . . . 其生兮若浮, 其死兮若休. 澹虖若深淵之靚, 氾虖若不繫之舟. 不以生故自保, 養空而浮. 德人無累, 知命不憂. 細故蒂芥, 何足以疑!

The year was *chanye*, it was the fourth month, summer's first, the thirty-seventh day of the cycle, at sunset, when an owl alighted in my house. On the corner of my seat it perched, completely at ease. I marveled at the reason for this uncanny visitation and opened a book to discover the omen. The oracle yielded the maxim: "When a wild bird enters a house, the master is about to leave." I should have liked to ask the owl: "Where am I to go? If lucky, let me know; if bad, tell me the worst. Be it swift or slow; tell me when it is to be."

　　The owl sighed; it raised its head and flapped its wings, but could not speak.—Let me say what it might reply: All things are in flux, with never any rest, whirling, rising, advancing, retreating; body and breath do a turn together—change form and slough off, infinitely subtle, beyond words to express. From disaster fortune comes, in fortune lurks disaster. Grief and joy gather at the same gate, good luck and bad share the same abode . . . Let your life be like a floating, your death like a rest. Placid as the peaceful waters of a deep pool, buoyant as an unfastened boat, find no cause for complacency in life, but cultivate emptiness and drift. The Man of Virtue is unattached; recognizing fate, he does not worry. Be not dismayed by petty pricks and checks!

Here, Jia Yi used the owl to express his Daoist belief of life and death. In his eyes, the owl was some kind of spirit or prophet who told the philosophy of life and death, as well as the Mandate of Heaven. Clearly, by Jia Yi's time, the owl was perceived very differently from the time of the Shang and Zhou dynasties. It was generally regarded as an inauspicious creature, a strange and menacing being. But in Jia Yi's writing, we detect the very idea and imagery of the owl as derived from the deep-rooted tradition of the Shang and Zhou religions.

Notes

1. For a brief introduction to YH127, see Li Zongkun 李宗焜, *Dang jiagu yushang kaogu—daolan YH127 keng* 當甲骨遇上考古——導覽YH127坑 (Taipei: Academia Sinica, 2006).

2. The inscriptions were first published in the *Yinxu wenzi yibian* 殷墟文字乙編 (Taipei: Academia Sinica, 1956), 6664 and 6665. In the *Jiaguwen heji* 甲骨文合集 (Beijing: Zhonghua, 1978–1983, hereafter: *Heji*), they are renumbered as 11497 and 11498. Whenever OBI are cited, I will refer only to the *Heji* number in this chapter. Figure 1.1 is after Li, *Dang jiagu yushang kaogu*, 68–69.

3. The OBI from YH127 largely belong to the Bin 賓 diviner group, with some from the Shi 師, Zi 子, and Wu 午 diviner groups. All these diviner groups worked under King Wu Ding.

4. David N. Keightley, *Sources of Shang History: The Oracle-Bone Inscriptions of Bronze Age China* (Berkeley: University of California Press, 1978), 88. I have converted the Wade-Giles romanization into pinyin.

5. Yu Xingwu 于省吾 first deciphered it as *she* 設 in *Jiagu wenzi tanlin* 甲骨文字探林 (Beijing: Zhonghua, 1979), 103–07; Liu Zhao 劉釗 reads it as *zhuo* 鏨 in "Tan jiaguwen 'zhuo' de yizhong yongfa" 談甲骨文 "鏨" 的一種用法, *Shixue jikan* 1992.1, 62–63, 76. More recently, Chen Jian 陳劍 has proposed that this graph is a variation of *zhi* 戠 and can be read as *yi* 異 in "Yinxu buci de fenqi fenlei dui jiaguwenzi kaoshi de zhongyaoxing" 殷墟卜辭的分期分類對甲骨文字考釋的重要性, in *Jiagu jinwen kaoshi lunji* 甲骨金文考釋論集 (Beijing: Xianzhuang, 2007), 414–27.

6. See Zhao Cheng 趙誠, *Jiaguwen jianming cidian* 甲骨文簡明詞典 (Beijing: Zhonghua, 1988), 239, 241.

7. This decipherment was first offered by Dong Zuobin 董作賓 in his *Yin lipu* 殷曆譜(Chongqing: Academia Sinica, 1945), *xiabian, juan* 3, 1–2, and Hu Houxuan 胡厚宣 in his "Yindai tianshen zhi chongbai" 殷代天神之崇拜, in *Jiaguxue Shangshi luncong* 甲骨學商史論叢, vol. 2 (Chengdu: Qilu daxue guoxue yanjiusuo, 1945), 300–01.

8. For example, *Zhongguo tianwenxue shi* 中國天文學史 (Beijing: Kexue, 1981), 16.

9. See Yang Shuda, *Jiweiju jiawen shuo, buci suoji* 積微居甲文說, 卜辭瑣記 (Beijing: Zhongguo kexueyuan, 1954), 10–11.

10. Li Xueqin, "Yinxu buci de xing" 殷墟卜辭的星, in *Zhengzhou daxue xuebao* 1981.4, 89–90.

11. For example, in their book *Yinxu buci yanjiu—kexue jishu pian* 殷墟卜辭研究——科學技術篇 (Chengdu: Sichuan shehui kexueyuan, 1983), 54–55, Wen Shaofeng 溫少峰 and Yuan Tingdong 袁庭棟 dismissed the old "Bird Star" theory and followed Li's argument.

12. Li Xueqin, "Yinxu buci de xing."

13. The two characters belong to the different rhyme groups in Old Chinese, *niao* 鳥, 端母蕭韻 (Duan Initial, Xiao Final); *shu* 倐, 書母屋韻 (Shu Initial, Wu Final), and their phonetic reconstruction can vary substantially. For the various proposed phonetic reconstructions, see the online dictionary 漢典 http://www.zdic.net/.

14. See Feng Shi, "Yin buci ershibasu zhi jiantao" 殷卜辭二十八宿之檢討, in his *Guwenzi yu gushi xin lun* 古文字與古史新論 (Taipei: Shufang, 2007), 176–81.

15. I use Li Fang-kuei's system in this chapter. See his *Shangguyin yanjiu* 上古音研究 (Beijing: Shangwu, 2015 [1971]), and Axel Schuessler, *A Dictionary of Early Zhou Chinese* (Honolulu: University of Hawai'i Press, 1987).

16. See *Jiaguwenzi gulin* 甲骨文字詁林 (Beijing: Zhonghua, 1996), 1667.

17. *Zhi* 雉 (OBI 🐦) stands for the pheasant in late lexicography. But, because its pronunciation is very close to *chi* 鴟, and their phonetic and semantic elements are often interchangeable, I think that it may also refer to the owl in OBI.

18. Cai Yunzhang, *Jiaguwen jinwen yu gushi yanjiu* 甲骨文金文與古史研究 (Zhengzhou: Zhongzhou guji, 1993), 109–14.

19. This character is pronounced as *zhui* <*tjəd or *huan* <*gwan, is used interchangeably with *guan* 觀 <*kwan and *jiu* 舊 <*gwjəgh, and sometimes interpreted as a recipient of sacrifices but was wrongly interpreted as *huo* 獲 (capture). See Chen Jian, "Yinxu buci de fenqi fenlei," 381–89.

20. One variation of *jiao* 叫 (噭) <*k iəgwh is interchangeable with *dao* 禱 <*təgwx, meaning "religious prayers." See Sun Yirang 孫詒讓, *Zhouli zhengyi* 周禮正義, vol. 8 (Beijing: Zhonghua, 1987), 1987.

21. Yu Xingwu reads 网雉 as *luo* 羅, a *hewen* 合文 or combined character, meaning "to catch birds with a net"; see *Jiaguwenzi tanlin*, 323–24.

22. *Tunnan* is an abbreviation for *Xiaotun nandi jiagu* 小屯南地甲骨 (Beijing: Zhonghua, 1980).

23. *Jiaguwenzi tanlin*, 107–33.

24. James Hall, *Illustrated Dictionary of Symbols in Eastern and Western Art* (Boulder: Westview Press, 1996), 360–67.

25. Liu Dunyuan, "Ye yu meng zhi shen de chixiao" 夜與夢之神的鴟鴞, in *Liu Dunyuan wenji* 劉敦願文集 (Beijing: Kexue, 2012), 159–71.

26. Translation follows Bernhard Karlgren, *The Book of Odes* (Stockholm: Museum of Far Eastern Antiquities, 1950), 263, slightly adapted with the Wade-Giles romanization also converted into pinyin.

27. See Duanfang 端方, *Taozhai jijin xulu* 陶齋吉金續錄 (1909), 2:5, where it is named as Yuanniao *hu* 元鳥壺.

28. Sun Xinzhou, "Chixiao chongbai yu huaxia lishi wenming" 鴟鴞崇拜與華夏歷史文明, *Tianjin shifan daxue xuebao* 2004.5, 31–37. See also Ma Yinqin 馬銀琴, "Lun Yin Shang minzu de chixiao chongbai jiqi lishi yanhua" 論殷商民族的鴟鴞崇拜及其歷史演變, in *Tianwen, Bingxu juan* 天問, 丙戌卷, ed. Cheng Gongrang 程恭讓 (Nanjing: Jiangsu renmin, 2006).

29. Eugene Y. Wang, "Why Pictures in Tombs? Mawangdui Once More," *Orientations* (March 2009): 27–34.

30. Sarah Allan, "The *Taotie* Motif on Early Chinese Ritual Bronzes," in *The Zoomorphic Imagination in Chinese Art and Culture*, ed. Jerome Silbergeld and Eugene Y. Wang (Oxford: Oxford University Press, 2016), 30.

31. Allan, "The *Taotie* Motif," 32.

32. Wu Hung, *Monumentality in Early Chinese Art and Architecture* (Stanford: Stanford University Press, 1995), 48, 53.

33. Robert W. Bagley, *Shang Ritual Bronzes in the Arthur M. Sackler Collections* (Washington DC: Arthur M. Sackler Foundation, 1987), 31–32, figs. 146, 147, 150, 152, 153, 154, 155, and 156.

34. Bagley, *Shang Ritual Bronzes in the Arthur M. Sackler Collections*, 406–11.

35. *Xuanhe bogutu*, 11:35–37. Facsimile in Liu Qingzhu 劉慶柱, Duan Zhihong 段志宏, and Feng Shi 馮時, eds., *Jinwen wenxian jicheng* 金文文獻集成 (Beijing: Xianzhuang, 2005), hereafter JWWXJC.

36. *Xiqing gujian*, 14:26, JWWXJC.

37. *Xiqing xujian Jiabian*, 5:53, JWWXJC.

38. Wu Dacheng, *Hengxuan suojian suocang jijinlu* 恆軒所見所藏吉金錄 (1885), 1:47, JWWXJC.

39. See Zhou Ya 周亞, *Kezhai jigutu jianzhu* 愙齋集古圖箋註 (Shanghai: Shanghai guji, 2012), 55.

40. Bagley illustrated this vessel in *Shang Ritual Bronzes in the Arthur M. Sackler Collections*, 410, figure 72.3.

41. Gao Quxun 高去尋, *Houjiazhuang: 1001 hao damu* 侯家莊: 1001號大墓 (Taipei: Academia Sinica, 1962), pl. 88.

42. Gao, *Houjiazhuang*, pl. 74.

43. Zhongguo shehui kexueyuan kaogusuo, *Yinxu Fu Hao mu* 殷墟婦好墓 (Beijing: Wenwu, 1980), 55, figure 36.

44. Zhongguo shehui kexueyuan kaogusuo, *Yinxu Fu Hao mu*, *fangyi* (791) color pl. 6, *fangzun* (792) color pl. 8:1, *fanghu* (794) color pl. 8:2.

45. Zhongguo qingtongqi quanji bianji weiyuanhui 中國青銅器全集編輯委員會, ed., *Zhongguo qingtongqi quanji* 中國青銅器全集 (Beijing: Wenwu, 1996), vol. 5, no. 176.

46. Patrick K. M. Kwok, *Dialogue with the Ancients: 100 Bronzes of the Shang, Zhou, and Han Dynasties—The Shen Zhai Collection* (Singapore: Select Books, 2018), no. 11.

47. *Xiqing gujian*, 8:33, JWWXJC.

48. Tan Lang, *Xi Zhou qingtongqi mingwen fendai shizheng* 西周青銅器銘文分代史徵 (Beijing: Zhonghua, 1986), 159–63, 249–54.

49. Chen Mengjia, *Xi Zhou tongqi duandai* 西周銅器斷代 (Beijing: Zhonghua, 2004), 81–84.

50. Translation follows Arthur Waley, *Book of Songs* (New York: Grove Press, 1957 [rpt.]), 275–76. Wade-Giles romanization of Chinese names has been converted to pinyin.

51. Waley, *Book of Songs*, 275–76.

52. Ye Shuxian, "Jingdian de wudu yu zhishi kaogu—yi *Shijing* 'Chixiao' weili" 經典的誤讀與知識考古——以 "詩經" 鴟鴞為例, *Shaanxi shifan daxue xuebao* 35, 2006.4, 56–64.

53. Robert Bagley, "Meaning and Explanation," *Archives of Asian Art* 46 (1993): 6–26.

54. Translation follows Robert Hightower with slight adaptations; see V. H. Mair, ed., *The Shorter Columbia Anthology of Traditional Chinese Literature* (New York: Columbia University Press, 2000), 209–11.

2

A Study of the Décor on a Shang Dynasty Architectural Object from the Site of Xiaoshuangqiao in Zhengzhou

Han Ding

Translated by Constance A. Cook

In 1985 and 1989, archaeologists found U-shaped bronze architectural decorations near the Xiaoshuangqiao 小雙橋 site in Zhengzhou 鄭州.[1] The 1989 example (89ZX.2, see fig. 2.1a) is composed of three sides, with a *taotie*-style mask design in the center and patterned side pieces composed of essentially the same three-part décor but in opposition. The side pieces have facing rectangular holes. The three parts include dragons, tigers, and what seems to be a squatting figure with elephant and humanistic features.

The three parts, which the excavation report understood as a "dragon and tiger wrestling with elephant motif" (龍虎搏象圖), are the subject under discussion in this essay (see figs. 2.1b and 2.2a). The excavation report describes the mask as the protruding head of a "curly dragon" (*panlong* 蟠龍) with cloudlike eyebrows over two symmetrical eyes and a diamond shape in between. Around the rectangular holes on the side pieces, the dragon stretches

Research and writing for this chapter has been supported by the National Social Science Foundation of China (18BKG015). This chapter is based on Han Ding 韓鼎, "Zhengzhou Xiaoshuangqiao Shang dai qingtong jianzhu shijian wenshi yanjiu" 鄭州小雙橋商代青銅建築飾件紋飾研究, in *Sandai kaogu* 三代考古 (Beijing: Kexue, 2017), 91–99.

23

Figures 2.1a–b. Photo (a) of Bronze Architectural Decoration from Xiaoshuangqiao and Rubbing (b) of the Decoration. *Source:* Henansheng wenwu kaogu yanjiusuo 河南省文物考古研究所, ed., *Zhengzhou Xiaoshuangqiao—1900–2000 nian kaogu fajue baogao* 鄭州小雙橋——1990–2000年考古發掘報告 (Beijing: Kexue, 2012), vol. 1, 17 (rubbing), vol. 2, 17 (pl. 26).

up the outside around the hole along the top edge, its body decorated with geometrical shapes in squares and triangles. Around the edges are cloud lines. The tails are curled. The tigers are stretched below the holes, looking fierce with staring eyes and open mouths and with something like a frog or piece of meat in between the jaws. Distinctly drawn lines pattern the bodies and their striped tails are slightly curled and just below the dragon tails. In the surrounding cloud lines, the tigers' front claws grip the ground as if about to pounce. The third figure, in between the dragon and tiger mouths, is a stylized crouching animal, somewhat similar to an elephant but with clear differences. Besides the long nose, we see that the eyes, four limbs, and the body are misarranged and malformed with unrealistic cloud décor.[2] This description by the archaeologists will be reevaluated here. Most particularly the so-called "elephant" motif is analyzed to answer the question of why it would be stylized and mutated in form in such direct contrast to the realistic styles of the dragons and tigers.

The Elephant Argument

The primary identifier that the third animal is an elephant is its long and curly nose. The problem is that making the rest of the body fit with this identification is forced and thus it is described as deformed and misaligned. For the sake of analysis, we will divide the body of this animal into two parts in figure 2.2, with the upper section black and the lower section gray (see fig. 2.2b). We compare it to a famous Shang jade of a squatting humanoid figure from Fu Hao's tomb (M5:470, see fig. 2.2c).[3] Immediately, we see a correspondence between the lower halves of the mystery third animal on the

Figure 2.2a. Side of the Architectural Decoration with the Three Animals (rubbing). *Source:* After Henansheng wenwu kaogu yanjiusuo 河南省文物考古研究所, ed., *Zhengzhou Xiaoshuangqiao—1900–2000 nian kaogu fajue baogao* 鄭州小雙橋——1990–2000年考古發掘報告 (Beijing: Kexue, 2012), vol. 1, 17 (rubbing).

Figure 2.2b. Detail of Third Animal. *Source:* After Henansheng wenwu kaogu yanjiusuo 河南省文物考古研究所, ed., *Zhengzhou Xiaoshuangqiao—1900–2000 nian kaogu fajue baogao* 鄭州小雙橋——1990–2000年考古發掘報告 (Beijing: Kexue, 2012), vol. 1, 17 (rubbing).

Figure 2.2c. Rubbing of Fu Hao Jade (M5:470). *Source:* Zhongguo shehui kexueyuan kaogu yanjiusuo 中國社會科學院考古研究所, *Yinxu Fu Hao mu* 殷墟婦好墓 (Beijing: Wenwu, 1980), 154–55. For M5:470, see 154.

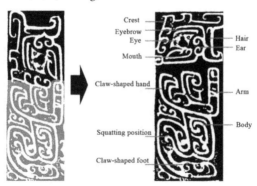

Figure 2.2d. Repositioning of Head and Body of Third Animal on Architectural Decoration. *Source:* After Henansheng wenwu kaogu yanjiusuo 河南省文物考古研究所, ed., *Zhengzhou Xiaoshuangqiao—1900–2000 nian kaogu fajue baogao* 鄭州小雙橋——1990–2000年考古發掘報告 (Beijing: Kexue, 2012), vol. 1, 17 (rubbing).

architectural decoration and the Shang jade. Both have inwardly curled bird claw hands on bent, chest-level arms and the legs are in a squatting position.

In the architectural piece, the eye, a typical Shang-style eye, is sideways, providing the hint that the entire head is facing downward. If we rotated it clockwise (see fig. 2.2d) to better correspond with the Fu Hao jade, the humanoid face becomes clear. Above the eye is the eyebrow and around the head is hair with feathers. An ear and mouth are also obvious.

The detailed features and overall structure of the profile can be compared to a marble carving discovered in a pit in Xiaotun 小屯 in Anyang (see fig. 2.3), which also has a feather design in front of the forehead. This head is called a "marble spirit-man decoration" (大理石神人面飾, R000932).[4] It should be compared with the décor of the "spirit-man double bird drum" (神人紋雙鳥鼓) presently stored in the Senoku Hakuko Museum 泉屋博古館 in Kyoto, Japan (see fig. 2.5c). This figure also has a feather on its head in between the two horns.[5]

Before discussing the feather décor further, we must consider why the head of the crouching human on the architectural piece is facing downward. It seems likely that this is related to the direction of the dragon's mouth. To understand this, we examine an early Shang pottery shard from Shangcheng 商城 in Zhengzhou 郑州 (C8T62:9).[6] The part illustrated in gray has been reconstructed.[7] It depicts a bifurcated crouching person with a dragon or snake (indicated by the forked tongue) "biting" it at the side of its head. Whether the person is being consumed is a matter of debate. Shang art features many figures in the mouths of tigers and often they seem to be smiling. Further, it is questionable whether this human-shaped figure is actually a person. Increasingly, scholars believe that these images represent shamanistic-style sacrifices or communication rituals with gods and ancestors.[8]

The mouths of the dragons in both the architectural piece and in the ceramic shard are facing the ears of the sacrificial human's, or perhaps shaman's, face. Interestingly, the shape of the dragon or snake's mouth on the architectural piece, in particular, is remarkably similar to the shape of the person's ear. These two shapes are inverse to each other. It is quite possible that the artistic decision to face the head downward reflected this stylistic parallelism or the idea that the dragon was facing the ear.

Feathers and Hair

The feathery lines around the face of the figure on the architectural decoration are not easily interpreted. Only by comparing it to other figures can we understand that the curly lines represent feathers, and that the straight line with a wave in the back of his head must depict hair. This identification also clarifies the ornaments in the remarkable bronze face mask discovered in Sanxingdui 三星堆, Sichuan (K2②:144, fig. 2.3c).[9] The forehead of this face was also decorated with a tall, curly plume. Hayashi Minao 林巳奈夫 called the plume a symbol of rank, a *jue* 蕤.[10]

Figures 2.3a–c. Forehead feather plume.

Figure 2.3a. Forehead Feather Plume: Architectural Decoration Head. *Source:* After Henansheng wenwu kaogu yanjiusuo 河南省文物考古研究所, ed., *Zhengzhou Xiaoshuangqiao—1900–2000 nian kaogu fajue baogao* 鄭州小雙橋——1990–2000 年考古發掘報告 (Beijing: Kexue, 2012), vol. 1, 17 (rubbing).

Figure 2.3b. Marble Spirit-Man Head from Xiaotun (R000932). *Source:* Collection of the Zhongyuan yanjiuyuan lishi yuyan yanjiusuo [https://openmuseum.tw/muse/digi_object/3df549d53412d556b2c8b bf87db1aa3e#96] (May 20, 2023). Public domain. CC BY-NC-SA 3.0 TW.

Figure 2.3c. Sanxingdui Bronze Mask (K2②:144). *Source:* Sichuansheng wenwu kaogu yanjiusuo 四川省文物考古研究所, *Sanxingdui jisikang* 三星堆祭祀坑 (Beijing: Wenwu, 1999), 197.

While the feather plumes are curly, the hair, when it is depicted on these faces, is in fact flat. It tends to drape back behind the ears. While not that common in Shang art, scholar Deng Shupin 鄧淑蘋 has shown that it was commonly depicted on the heads of spirit-men in Neolithic art (see figs. 2.4a–b).[11] We see the same style on the Shang architectural ornament figure. What this hairstyle indicated—whether or not it was related to the person's role in shamanic ritual—remains to be seen.

Figure 2.4a. Neolithic Spirit-Man Head. Shanghai Museum jade knife rubbing. *Source:* Teng Shu-p'ing 鄧淑蘋, "Lun diao you Dongyixi wenshi de you ren yuqi" 論雕有東夷系紋飾的有刃玉器, part 1 and part 2, *Gugong xueshu jikan* 故宮學術季刊 3 (1999): 1–34; 4 (1999): 135–61.

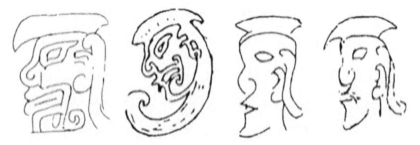

Figure 2.4b. Neolithic Spirit-Man Head. Drawings of four heads from jade staffs, one from the National Palace Museum, Taipei; one from the Freer Gallery; and two from Yangde Gallery 養德堂, Christie's, Hong Kong (left to right, respectively). *Source:* Teng Shu-p'ing 鄧淑蘋, "Lun diao you Dongyixi wenshi de you ren yuqi" 論雕有東夷系紋飾的有刃玉器, part 1 and part 2, *Gugong xueshu jikan* 故宮學術季刊 3 (1999): 1–34; 4 (1999): 135–61.

Squatting with Bird Claws

Squatting figures, especially carved into jade, are not uncommon. Besides the example from Fu Hao discussed earlier, there are other Fu Hao examples (M5:518, fig. 2.5a),[12] and Shang examples from Xibeigang 西北岡 in Houjiazhuang 侯家莊 (M1550.40, R001339, fig. 2.5b),[13] as well as examples dating later to the Western Zhou period. Some scholars describe it as an Anyang style with "a human figure, carved in relief, which is squatting with raised arms" (浮雕人像多作側視蹲踞形，雙臂上舉).[14] The feathered and horned spirit-man on the double bird drum is also depicted as squatting with arms outstretched. Yu Weichao 俞偉超 (1939–2003) suggested that this figure represented "a deity with nine bends" (jiuqu shenren 九屈神人), such as tubo jiuyue 土伯九約 as described in the Chu ci 楚辭 song "Zhao hun" 招魂: occupying the "dark city of the dead/ The Earl of the Earth is there with his nine tails/ And his horns are sharp as pikes./ And humpbacked and bloody clawed. He'll come charging after you,/ With his three eyes in his tiger's head . . ."[15] This identification of the Shang spirit-man with the later Earl of the Earth with nine tails is very thought-provoking.

The squatting posture with the bent arms and clawed hands are, as Sarah Allan has pointed out, to imitate that of birds.[16] Shamans, like birds, were supposed to fly and in many cultures wore feathers or mimicked birds.[17] That the hands are in fact bird claws can be determined by comparing the images of the spirit-men with that on the architectural decoration as well as with other images in figures 2.5a–d. The "half man, half bird" image was particular to shamanistic practice.[18] There was also the "half man, half snake" image.[19]

Human, Tiger, Snake

We have seen that the three animals on the architectural decoration consist of a person, a tiger, and a dragon or snake. One immediately thinks of the famous early Neolithic site with the burial of a man in between a dragon and a tiger formed out of clam shells in Puyang 濮陽, tomb 45 in Xishuipo 西水坡.[20] However, the many millennia difference in dating makes any connection between that site and the later image extremely speculative.[21]

The argument for seeing the "dragon" as actually a "snake" on the architectural piece is reinforced by the tiny horns and lack of feet or claws. This suggests an earlier dating than images of full-fledged dragons with claws.

Figures 2.5a–d. Spirit-men, squatting with bird claws.

Figure 2.5a. Fu Hao. *Source:* Zhongguo shehui kexueyuan kaogu yanjiusuo 中國社會科學院考古研究所, *Yinxu Fu Hao mu* 殷墟婦好墓 (Beijing: Wenwu, 1980), 154–55. u 殷墟婦好墓 (Beijing: Wenwu, 1980), 154–55. For M5:470, see 154.

Figure 2.5b. Caved Jade Figure, Xibeigang. *Source:* Collection of the Zhongyuan yanjiuyuan lishi yuyan yanjiusuo [https://openmuseum.tw/muse/digi_object/fc69dd3dabc2215d48a4f0b6d36348eb#80] (May 20, 2023). Public domain. CC BY-NC-SA 3.0 TW.

Figure 2.5c. Double Bird Drum, Senoku Hakuko Museum, Kyoto. *Source:* Zhongguo qingtongqi quanji editorial group, *Zhongguo qingtongqi quanji* 中國青銅器全集, vol. 4 (Beijing: Wenwu, 1998), 172, fig. 179.

Figure 2.5d. Dahe Human Face Bronze *Fangding* 大禾人面方鼎 detail. *Source:* Shanghai bowuguan qingtongqi yanjiuzu, ed., 上海博物館青銅器研究組, *Shang Zhou qingtongqi wenshi* 商周青銅器紋飾 (Beijing: Wenwu, 1984), 343.

Figure 2.6. Human, Tiger, Snake-Dragon. Tiger *you* and details of arm and leg décor, photo. *Source:* Zhongguo qingtongqi quanji editorial group, *Zhongguo qingtongqi quanji*, vol. 4 (Beijing: Wenwu, 1998), 148.

In the tiger *you* bronze vessel, stored at the Senoku Hakuko Museum in Kyoto (fig. 2.6),[22] we see snakes running up and down the human figures' arms and legs. The snakes represented seem to be of different types. The one on his thigh seems to be exactly like that depicted in the architectural piece, thus confirming that this early "dragon" was in fact a snake.

Besides the position of the snakes' mouths and the humans' heads in the architectural piece and in the ceramic shard from Zhengzhou discussed earlier, there is another similarity. Both figures are crouching. If we orient the figure in the ceramic shard upright, it would be in the familiar squatting position. The fact that it is a bifurcated image, like many Shang bifurcated images, especially those associated with *taotie*-like masks or including tigers and dragons, means that it was an attempt to represent a three-dimensional object in two dimensions.[23]

A bronze knife in the Freer Gallery in Washington, DC, brings up the debate over whether the tiger image with an open mouth does or does not represent devouring the human. This knife has the triad of human, tiger, and snake.[24] On the back of the knife, the snake goes up from the shoulder of the figure and opens its mouth around the top of the man's head. The man is squatting with arms bent up and his mouth open, showing teeth. While we cannot confirm the relationship between the tiger and the man, we can say that the image is similar to that of a fierce open-mouthed tiger creeping toward the squatting man on the architectural piece as if about to pounce. The image of the human head inside the tiger's mouth is seen on the foot of a bronze *guang* vessel, also in the Freer Gallery. We see it too in the famous bronze *you* vessel stored in Kyoto, mentioned earlier, and a carved bone in the Minneapolis Institute of Art.[25] In the latter case, the man is also holding a snake that is coiling up from below. If the human figure is a shaman, then the ability to control tigers and snakes may indicate his abilities to transcend death and communicate with the spirits and ancestors.[26] The late K. C. Chang, Sarah Allan, and others see the mouth of the tiger as symbolizing death.[27] It seems likely that a human wearing a tiger skin and handling snakes in shamanistic ritual ceremonies was seen as having magical abilities. While not all Shang examples include each element—human, tiger, snake—the underlying theme is prevalent.

Conclusion

The decoration on the Shang architectural piece from Xiaoshuangqiao in Zhengzhou was not an image of a dragon and tiger wrestling with an elephant. The décor was consistent with the common Shang theme of "human, tiger, snake." The human figure is typically squatting with bird claws but the head was facing downward. The feather plume decorating its head is typical of spirit-man depictions dating as early as the late Neolithic. The image seems to represent a shamanistic ritual.[28]

Notes

1. Henansheng wenwu kaogu yanjiusuo 河南省文物考古研究所, ed., *Zhengzhou Xiaoshuangqiao—1900–2000 nian kaogu fajue baogao* 鄭州小雙橋——1990–2000 年考古發掘報告 (Beijing: Kexue, 2012), vol. 1, 17 (rubbing), vol. 2, 17 (pl. 26).

2. Henansheng wenwu kaogu yanjiusuo, *Zhenghzhou Xiaoshangqiao*, 18.

3. There are four examples from Fu Hao's tomb. See Zhongguo shehui kexueyuan kaogu yanjiusuo 中國社會科學院考古研究所, *Yinxu Fu Hao mu* 殷墟婦好墓 (Beijing: Wenwu, 1980), 154–55. For M5:470, see 154.

4. Li Yongdi 李永迪, ed., *Yinxu chutu qiwu xuancui* 殷墟出土器物選粹 (Taipei: Zhongyuan yanjiuyuan lishi yuyan yanjiusuo 中央研究院歷史語言研究所, 1999), 178. Figure 2.3b is after: Marble spirit-man head from Xiaotun (R000932), collection of the Zhongyuan yanjiuyuan lishi yuyan yanjiusuo [https://openmuseum. tw/muse/digi_object/3df549d53412d556b2c8bbf87db1aa3e#96] (May 20, 2023), under the Creative Commons license CC BY-NC-SA 3.0 TW.

5. Hayashi Minao 林巳奈夫, *In Shū jidai seidōki monyō no kenkyū* 殷周時代青銅器紋様の研究, in *Shū jidai seidōki sōran* 殷周青銅器綜覽, part 2 (Tokyo: Yoshikawa Kōbunkan 吉川弘文館, 1986), 304.

6. Henansheng wenwu kaogu yanjiusuo, *Zhengzhou Shangcheng—1953–1985 nian kaogu fajue baogao* 鄭州商城——1953–1985年考古發掘報告 (Beijing: Wenwu, 2001), 267.

7. Tang Wei 湯威 and Zhang Wei 張巍, "Zhengzhou Shangcheng 'ren shou muti' taopian tuan fuyuan ji xiangguan wenti tantao" 鄭州商城 "人獸母題" 陶片圖案復原及相關問題探討, *Zhongguo lishi wenwu* 中國歷史文物 2008.1, 39.

8. Zhang Guangzhi 張光直, "Shang Zhou qingtongqi shang de dongwu wenyang" 商周青銅器上的動物紋様, *Kaogu yu wenwu* 考古與文物 1981.2, 53–68; Xu Lianggao 徐良高, "Shang Zhou qingtongqi 'ren shou muti' wenshi kaoshi" 商周青銅器 "人獸母題" 紋飾考釋, *Kaogu* 考古 1991.5, 446; Elizabeth Childs-Johnson, "The Ghost Head Mask and Metamorphic Shang Imagery," *Early China* 20 (1995): 79–92; "The Metamorphic Image: A Predominant Theme in Shang Ritual Art," *Bulletin of Museum of Far Eastern Antiquities* 70 (1998): 5–171; Chen Xingcan 陳星燦, "'Hu shi ren you' ji xiangguan tuxiang de shiying lice" "虎食人卣" 及相關圖像的史影蠡測, in *Yu Weichao xiansheng jinian wenji* 俞偉超先生紀念文集 (Beijing: Wenwu, 2009), 232–40; Shi Jinsong 施勁鬆, "'Hu shi ren' muti zhong de renwu Xinxiang" "虎食人" 母題中的人物形象, *Zhongguo wenwu bao* 中國文物報, September 16, 2011, 6.

9. Sichuansheng wenwu kaogu yanjiusuo 四川省文物考古研究所, *Sanxingdui jisikang* 三星堆祭祀坑 (Beijing: Wenwu, 1999), 197.

10. Linsi Naifu 林巳奈夫 (Hayashi Minao), *Shen yu shou de wenyang xue—Zhongguo gudai zhushen* 神與獸的紋様學——中國古代諸神, trans. Chang Yaohua 常耀華 et al. (Hong Kong: Sanlian, 2009), 8.

11. Teng Shu-p'ing 鄧淑蘋, "Lun diao you Dongyixi wenshi de you ren yuqi" 論雕有東夷系紋飾的有刃玉器, part 1 and part 2, *Gugong xueshu jikan* 故宮學術季刊 1999.3, 1–34; 4 (1999): 135–61.

12. Zhongguo shehui kexueyuan kaogu yanjiusuo, *Yinxu Fu Hao mu*, 154.

13. Liang Siyong 梁思永 and Gao Quxun 高去尋, *Houjiazhuang dibaben: 1550 hao damu* 侯家莊第八本·1550 號大墓 (Taipei: Zhongyang yanjiuyuan lishi yuyan yanjiusuo, 1976), pl. 44. Figure 2.5b after Carved Jade Figure, collection of the Zhongyuan yanjiuyuan lishi yuyan yanjiusuo [https://openmuseum.tw/muse/digi_object/fc69dd3dabc2215d48a4f0b6d36348eb#80] (May 20, 2023), under the Creative Commons license CC BY-NC-SA 3.0 TW.

14. Zhongguo shehui kexueyuan kaogu yanjiusuo, *Yinxu de faxian yu yanjiu* 殷墟的發現與研究 (Beijing: Kexue, 1994), 339.

15. Yu Weichao, "'Shenmian you' shang de ren gehua 'tiandi' tuxiang" "神面卣" 上的人格化 "天帝" 圖像, in *Gushi de kaoguxue tansuo* 古史的考古學探索 (Beijing: Wenwu, 2002), 148. For the translation of the *Chuci*, see *The Songs of*

Chu; An Anthology of Ancient Chinese Poetry by Qu Yuan and Others, ed. and trans. Gopal Sukhu (New York: Columbia University Press, 2017), 173.

16. Ai Lan 艾蘭, "Shangdai taotiewen ji xianguan wenshi de yiyi" 商代饕餮紋及相關紋飾的意義, trans. Han Ding 韓鼎, *Jiaguwen yu Yin Shang shi* 甲骨文與殷商史 7 (2017): 339.

17. Sarah Allan, "He Flies Like a Bird; He Dives Like a Dragon; Who Is That Man in the Tiger Mouth? Shamanic Images in Shang and Early Western Zhou Art," *Orientations* 41, no. 3 (2010): 45–51. On the role of birds, see also Elizabeth Childs-Johnson, "The *Jue*-Vessel and Its Ritual Use in the Ancestor Cult of Shang China," *Artibus Asiae* 48, nos. 3–4 (1987): 171–96.

18. Han Ding 韓鼎, "Dahe renmian fangding wenshi yanjiu" 大禾人面方鼎紋飾研究, *Zhongyuan wenwu* 中原文物 2015.2, 57–61, 67.

19. Han Ding 韓鼎, "Zaoqi 'renshe' zhuti yanjiu" 早期 "人蛇" 主題研究, *Kaogu* 3 (2017): 82–93. The author disagrees with Elizabeth Childs-Johnson's argument in "The Metamorphic Image" that it was the Shang king that took on an animal form to communicate with the spirits but agrees with the idea of using animals to do so.

20. Henansheng wenwu kaogu yanjiusuo et al. *Puyang Xishuipo* 濮陽西水坡 (Zhengzhou: Zhongzhuo guji, 2012), 113.

21. The Xishuangqiao site is dated to around 3400 BCE (and the Puyang site to around 6400 BCE). See Henansheng wenwu kaogu yanjiusuo, *Zhengzhou Xiaoshuangqiao*, 723.

22. Zhongguo qingtongqi quanji editorial group, *Zhongguo qingtongqi quanji*, vol. 4 (Beijing: Wenwu, 1998), 148.

23. Ai Lan, "Shangdai taotiewen," 337; Sichuan wenwu kaogu yanjiusuo, *Sanxingdui*, 36; Zhongguo qingtongqi quanji editorial group, *Zhongguo qintongqi quanji* 1 (1996): 118; Han Ding 韓鼎, "Shang Zhou wenshi zhong pouzhan biaoxian moshi yanjiu" 商周紋飾中剖展表現模式研究, in *Zengguo kaogu faxian yu yanjiu* 曾國考古發現與研究, ed. Hubeisheng wenwu kaogu yanjiusuo 湖北省文物考古研究所 (Beijing: Kexue, 2018), 333–44.

24. John Alexander Pope, Rutherford John Gettens, James Cahill, and Noel Barnard, *The Freer Chinese Bronzes*, vol. 1 (Washington, DC: Smithsonian Institution, 1967), 258, pl. 34. Compare to the *guang* vessel, where the snake runs up the back of the body of the vessel and the lid is composed of a human face, 227.

25. Hayashi Minao 林巳奈夫, Chang Yaohua 常耀華 (trans.), *Shen yu shou de wenyang xue: Zhongguo gudai zhu shen* 神與獸的紋樣學: 中國古代諸神 (Beijing: Shenghuo, dushu, xinzhi sanlian shudian, 2009), 172.

26. Han Ding, "Zaoqi 'ren she.'"

27. See, for example, Zhang Guangzhi, *Zhongguo qingtong shidai* 中國青銅時代 (Hong Kong: San Lian, 1983), 313; K. C. Chang, *Art, Myth, and Ritual: The Path to Political Authority in Ancient China* (Cambridge, MA: Harvard University Press, 1983); Sarah Allan, *The Shape of the Turtle: Myth, Art, and Cosmos in Early China* (Albany: State University of New York Press, 1991), revised in Ai Lan, *Gui zhi mi:*

Shangdai shenhua, jisi, yishu he yuzhouguan yanjiu 龜之謎: 商代神話, 祭祀, 藝術和宇宙觀研究 (Beijing: Shangwu, 2010), 181. For the mouth and these Shang images as a symbol of birthing, see C. A. Cook and Luo Xinhui, *Birth in Ancient China: A Study of Metaphor and Identity in Pre-Imperial China* (Albany: State University of New York Press, 2017), 15–19.

28. In fact, the image could be termed a "human-tiger-snake-bird" given the additional bird imagery, but the basic meaning remains the same.

3

Respecting Heaven and Sacrificing to the Ancestors

Social Order and Ritual Reflected in Early Western Zhou Bronze Drinking Vessel Sets

Lu Liancheng

Translated by Constance A. Cook

In the 1970s, the Gansu Museum Antiquities Team 甘肅省博物館文物隊 excavated the Baicaopo 白草坡 site in Lingtai District 靈臺縣, Gansu Province. The most important tombs at the site were M1 and M2.[1]

Of the twelve inscribed ritual bronze vessels in M1, most belong to the late Shang period. The "clan signs" (*huihao* 徽號) were a mix of eight different types, including four different "sun signs" or calendrical stem signs (*rigan* 日干) used to name ancestral figures. Of these, Fu Ding 父丁 received cult on two vessels but the rest were completely unrelated. It is obvious that this collection of vessels came from many time periods and places and thus cannot be used to determine early Western Zhou elite mortuary ritual. However, there is one complete ritual set in M1, consisting of one *zun* and two *you* (一尊二卣) (both are vessels for storing alcoholic beverages), each with the inscription: "Jing Bo made precious ritual vessels to pay his respects" (涇伯作寶尊彝). The two *you* are different sizes but exactly the same in terms of manufacture and ornament. These must be the tomb occupant's personally manufactured set of ritual bronzes.[2]

37

Baicaopo M2 contained ten inscribed vessels, also including a set with one *zun* and two *you*. The surfaces of these three vessels are covered with curly tailed phoenix ornaments (卷尾鳳鳥紋). The two *you*, bucket shaped with handles, were manufactured and ornamented the same but also different in size. The inscription on all three vessels was the same: "Xi Bo made precious ritual vessels for expressing reverence" (鄨伯作寶尊彝).[3] As in the case with M1, it is clear that the sociopolitical rank and lineage identity (身份和國別, 族邑) of the tomb occupant can be determined from this set. The occupant of M1 was Jing Bo and that of M2 was Xi Bo. From the large numbers of weapons found in their tombs—axes of various types (*fu* 斧, *yue* 鉞, and *ge* 戈) and so forth—Jing Bo and Xi Bo must have been leaders in their state armies. The set of alcohol vessels, made up of one *zun* and two *you*, found in Jing River valley 涇水流域 burials signified aristocratic rank.

It is obvious from the excavations of the Yu 弓魚 state burial ground at Zhuyuangou 竹園沟 in Baoji 寶雞, Shaanxi, that the one-*zun*-two-*you* set was an important feature of early Western Zhou tombs.[4] For example, in BZM7 tomb, that of a Yu aristocrat and a sacrificed female servant, there was a set.[5] The three vessels were decorated with two sets of monster masks (*taotie dashou mian* 饕餮大獸面) with high curly horns. The two *you* of different sizes had handles decorated with water buffalo and ram heads. The inscription shared by these unique and lively vessels is: "Bo Ge made treasured ritual vessels for expressing reverence" (伯各作寶尊彝). This tomb also produced a lot of weapons, including a bronze axe with a tiger mouth biting down (虎紋鋬口銅鉞) and short sword revealing that the tomb occupant had been a military figure of high rank in the state of Yu.[6] Yu Bo Ge was most likely a ruler of the early state of Yu.

Zhuyuangou BZM13 of the Yu state cemetery is a large tomb also with accompanying sacrificial burials of female servants.[7] Of the nine inscribed bronze vessels there are nine different clan sign and stem sign named ancestors indicated, similar to the situation in Baicaopo M1 at Lingtai, Gansu. Obviously, these vessels are military booty that originated in other places. But BZM13 also contained a one-*zun*-two-*you* set, with the *you* in graduated sizes but with the same décor and bucket shape with handles. The most eye-catching aspect of this set is the fact that the tomb occupant had personally cast a set of ritual vessels, including a range of other vessel types, such as drinking vessels *jue* 爵, *gu* 觚, *zhi* 觶 and the food vessel *dou* 斗, that were arranged on a rectangularly shaped lacquer tray and placed prominently next to the occupant's head. The number of weapons also included in BZM13, along with the tiger-décor axe, suggests that the occupant was a powerful figure of military stature in the Yu state.

Another set of one-*zun*-two-*you* vessels was found in Zhuyuangou tomb BZM8. The *zun* and the two *you* of different sizes had been manufactured as a set and inscribed with "made precious ritual vessels to express reverence" (作寶尊彝).[8] This set, along with the other two, show that they were used in early Western Zhou aristocratic male tombs as key markers of rank.

This fact is confirmed by the contents of early Western Zhou tombs at Shigushan 石鼓山 in Baoji excavated in 2013. Once again, the one-*zun*-two-*you* set appears as a marker of rank.[9] Shigushan M3 was larger than either Zhuyuangou tomb, BZM7 or BZM13, and contained thirty-one bronze vessels of fourteen different types. The most notable were the three alcohol vessels: a large square *yi*-style ritual vessel (*fangyi* 方彝) and the two *you*, which typically were two different sizes but with the exact same décor and style.[10] The *fangyi* was 63.7 cm tall and weighed 35.55 kg, making it the largest Western Zhou alcohol vessel seen yet. The three vessels, magisterial and elegant in style, all bear the clan sign Hu 戶. This set was clearly the result of careful manufacturing by the Hu clan.

The Hu vessel set of Shigushan M3 was even more grand than that of Zhuyuangou BZM7's Bo Ge set. The *fangyi* and the *zun*-type vessels were distinct in form but both were used for storing alcoholic beverages. A *fangyi* matched with two *you* is similar in function to a *zun* with two *you*, however it is possible that a distinction in rank was intended. The purposeful choice of the *fangyi*, the *fanglei* 方罍, or the *zun* may have indicated different ranks in early Western Zhou ritual.

Further, it should be noted that the vessel set at Shigushan M3 was matched with two bronze rectangular altar tables (*fangjin* 方禁) of different sizes.[11] Upon reconstruction, it is clear that the large one was rectangular with no feet and measured 94.5 by 45 cm. Placed on it were the Hu *fangyi* vessel, the large and the small Hu *you* vessels, and two ladles. The small Hu *you* was further distinguished by having been placed on a small rectangular altar table. Both altar tables were specially made for the presentation of the Hu alcohol set. This unique arrangement was a clear sign of the aristocratic rank of the occupant when he participated in ancestral sacrifices and important ceremonies. The fact that the vessels sets of Zhuyuangou BZM7, BZM13, and BZM8 and that of Baicaopo M1 and M2 were simply placed on lacquer trays suggests that these tomb occupants were lower in status than those of Shigushan M3.

The recently published monograph *Baoji Daijiawan yu Shigushan chutu Shang Zhou qingtongqi* 寶雞戴家灣與石鼓山出土商周青銅器 brings together pictures and writings concerning bronzes plundered from two tombs in Daijiawan 戴家灣 and Shigushan in 1901 and during the years 1926–1928. This is a tremendously valuable contribution.[12] There were three one-*zun*-two-*you* sets at Daijiawan. In the first set, the *zun* and two graduated in size *you* carried the name Ding 鼎. Underneath the smaller *you* is a small rectangular altar table (*jin*). The entire set along with ladles were placed on a large bronze altar table. The arrangement is the same as the Hu set found at Shigushan M3. The Ding set was first collected during the late Qing by the Two Rivers viceroy Duanfang 兩江總督端方 and later passed from one person to another until it reached the collection of the Metropolitan Museum in New York.[13]

The second set consists of one *fangyi* with four protruding flanges (四出戟直棱紋) and two *you* of different sizes with four protruding phoenix designs (四出戟鳳鳥紋). This set is large in size, thick in core, unusual in shape, and elegant in décor. The flanges soar upward. The three vessels are finely crafted and a rare example of Western Zhou bronze art.[14] Plundered from the tomb by warlord Yu Kun 毓琨, these vessels were dispersed and passed around until now, where they are found in the collections of Harvard's Sackler Art Museum, the Freer Gallery in Washington, DC, and the Museum of Fine Arts in Boston. The History Museum in Tianjin collected a large altar table plundered from Daijiawan during the years 1926–1928. It is 126 by 46.6 cm large. There are three slightly protruding oval-shaped holes on the surface, suggesting where the set of vessels had originally been placed.[15] Whether the missing set was the second one from Daijiawan is unknown as there are no inscriptions to indicate ownership, rank, or state affiliation.

The three vessels of the third set include a *kui*-dragon pattern (*kuilong wen* 夔龍紋) decorated *zun* and two *kui*-dragon patterned *you* of different sizes with the exact same manufacture and decorative style.[16] The *zun* and the large *you* are found in the Hakutsuru 神戶白鶴 Fine Art Museum in Kobe, Japan, and the smaller *you* is found in the Minneapolis Institute of Art. Since the vessel type and décor are almost exactly like the vessels in the Zhuyuangou BZM8 set, it seems likely that they were manufactured in the same foundry.

If we compare all the sets hitherto discussed, we see the typical combination of one *zun* or *yi* and two differently sized *you*, but with variations in the overall sizes, elegance, décor, and craftsmanship. These variations reflect differences in the sociopolitical status of the tomb occupants. The second set from Daijiawan with the protruding flanges and bird décor can be taken as prime examples of fine Western Zhou bronzeware. Their owner was perhaps the King of Ze 夨王, a ruler of an ancient kingdom on the western periphery of the Western Zhou polity.[17]

Crafted as a set, the one *zun* and two *you* combined the most important ritual vessels in elite ancestor worship and mortuary ritual. This phenomenon was not isolated to the Baoji or western region of the early Western Zhou. In fact, it was common throughout the central region as well.

For example, in Henan, an early Western Zhou tomb, Taiqinggong 太清宮 M1 in Luyi 鹿邑, included a one-*zun*-two-*you* set belonging to Zhangzi Kou 長子口.[18] Another set with the inscription: "Kuo made a precious ritual vessel for expressing reverence to Father Ding" 㝬作父丁寶尊彝 was found in Waliucun 窪劉村 99M1 in Zhengzhou 鄭州.[19] Unprovenanced sets include: one said to come from Xun District 濬縣 belonging to Mo Bo Yi 沬伯逸,[20] one from Luoyang Mangshan Mapo 洛陽邙山馬坡 belonging to Shi Shang 士上,[21] and one belonging to a Qing 卿, also from Luoyang.[22] In Hubei, Yuanshi District 元氏縣, a set belonging to Shu Quan Fu 叔趯父 was found in Xizhangcun 西張村.[23] Sets have also been found in Western Zhou tombs in the Jianghan 江漢 region. In Hubei, Sui District 隨縣, a set belonging to E Hou 噩侯 was found in Yangzishan 羊子山 M4. Also from this tomb, a set with "spirit face" (神面) décor was discovered.[24] Yejiashan 葉家山 M28, also in Sui District, produced a set belonging to Zeng Hou Jian 曾侯諫.[25] It is likely that even more sets will become evident, either via future archaeological discoveries, or upon the closer examination of unprovenanced examples handed down through history.

Shared Archaeological and Cultural Features of Western Zhou Tombs with One-*Zun*-Two-*You* Sets

Feature one: they have an early Western Zhou dating, with sets from the reigns of Kings Wu 武 and Cheng 成, or sets from the reigns of Kings Cheng and Kang 康.

When the Zhou overthrew the Shang mandate and a new royal order replaced the old, battles were intense and society was in upheaval. Many lords and princes entered the fray to set up and stabilize the Western Zhou court. These sets signify the status of the Zhou elite during this period.

The latest example of a tomb with a one-*zun*-two-*you* set belonged to Tan Ji Jufu 憻季遽父 buried in Liujiacun 劉家村, Fufeng District 扶風縣, Shaanxi. The *zun* and the two *you* of different sizes each bore the same décor and inscriptions: "Tan Ji Jufu made this precious ritual vessel to express reverence for Feng Ji" 憻季遽父作豐姬寶尊彝. The tomb is dated to King Zhao 昭, toward the end of the early Western Zhou era.[26] Lord Tan was an important ally of the Zhou court and Tan Ji was a descendant of his. The Tan lord named Li was an officer during King Wu's reign and had participated in the key battle at Muye 牧野 against the Shang. His merit was awarded with an inscription upon the bronze vessel known as the Li *gui* 利簋.[27]

Feature two: these sets indicate sociopolitical and lineage status of the tomb occupant.

We see that political allegiance and social status are clearly indicated in the sets belonging to Jing Bo and Xi Bo of Baicaopo in Gansu, three tombs in Shaanxi (Yu Bo Ge of Zhuyuangou, Hu of Shigushan, and Ding of Daijiawan), two tombs in Hubei (E Hou of Yangzishan M4 and Zeng Hou Jian of Yejiashan M28), Mo Bo Yi of Jun District in Henan, and so forth. While the inscribed dedications clearly indicate occupants' sociopolitical identity (for example, Jing, Yu, E, Zeng) and their rank (for example, *bo*, *hou*), the prominent placement of uninscribed sets within the tomb played a similar role. They were obviously not purposefully cast by the occupant and not gifts or war booty from elsewhere.

Feature three: foreign vessels are often found alongside these sets.

Many vessels placed in the same tombs with these special sets came from other locations and were probably war booty or gifts. They sported numerous unrelated clan signs and dedications to ancestors with stem sign names seemingly of no relation to the tomb occupant. Of the thirty-one vessels excavated from Shigushan M3 in Baoji, there were about ten different clan sign names and ten different stem sign named ancestors.[28] Only the set of one *zun* and two *you* referenced the tomb occupant, a man named Hu, out of the twenty or so vessels obtained by Duanfang from Daijiawan. Besides the set with the Ding clan sign, the other vessels had six different clan sign and ancestral names. They were Shang-style vessels and, based on Zhang Maorong's 張懋鎔 research, they belonged to the Shang.[29]

The fact that vessels bearing the marks of different states, clans, owners, and ancestors have been discovered together in the same tomb presents interesting questions regarding mortuary ritual and secular relationships. These vessels suggest both beneficial and antagonistic relationships. Polities and lineages of people within those polities traded gifts as signs of mutual appreciation and aid. But these vessels could also be the results of violent takeovers, in which the ancestral treasures, wealth, land, and slaves of one group of people, perhaps aligned with the Shang, had been redistributed. Huang Mingchong 黃銘崇, Chen Zhaorong 陳昭容, and others have discussed this "dividing of the vessels" (fenqi 分器).[30]

Feature four: the vessels composing a set are cast as a single casting event and represent a new style.

The *zun* and *you* vessels were manufactured and decorated with care, exhibiting an exquisite sense of majesty and mystery—representing a new Zhou style of simple elegance. A number of the *zun* and *you* are decorated with ox heads in relief and round carved ram heads, adding an earthly element to contrast with the fine lines of phoenixes, which fluidly trace upward in the form of dramatic flanges.

This new style included bronze forms not seen before. These included a large rectangular bronze altar table (*jin*) with a square-shaped small bronze altar table along with four-eared and double-eared square *gui* 簋 vessels (a type of food tureen). The fine craftsmanship reflects a well-supplied workshop employing highly skilled designers and casters. The final products represented the match of artisan technique with ceremonial function. Mortuary ritualists placed these critical vessels in the tomb either by the head, feet, or right hand and arranged the *gui* on a bronze or lacquerware altar table.

Feature five: the sets accompanied high-level aristocrats associated with the military.

The tombs in which these sets appeared were large and rich with mortuary goods of all types. The occupants were buried with a range of weapons, including three types of axes, swords, spears, and shields that were placed next to the bodies. This expressed military power and rank. Many of them are also buried with female servants, further enhancing the image of virility. The inscriptions on some of the *zun* and *you* verify the status of the occupants as protector lords (*hou*), as we see with Zeng Hou Jian, E Hou, and others. In other cases, they were state leaders or lineage heads (*bo*), such as Yu Bo Ge, Jing Bo, and Xi Bo, or as Mo Bo Yi, Shi Shang, and so forth. It is possible that the military elite not only functioned as local leaders but also joined Zhou King Wu's march against the Shang and served in the early Western Zhou battles to settle the Eastern Yi 東夷 and Southern Huaiyi 南淮夷 peoples.

Feature six: the sets are found in early Western Zhou tombs that also feature bronze ding *and* gui *vessels.*

The *ding* and *gui* vessels (both are vessels for presenting grain and meat offerings, one a caldron and the other a tureen) tend to have rather thin bases and be cast in a cruder fashion, suggesting local manufacture in a lesser workshop. Some of the "earless" (no handles) *gui* are decorated with large nipples and some with small and sharp ones. The bellies of the *ding* vessels are decorated with a single animal face. Another local and new feature was the manufacture of many *ding* of multiple sizes with the same shape and décor. Placed in a single tomb, this array began the Zhou trend of display-ing arrays of *ding* vessels (*lieding* 列鼎). However, from the standpoint of craftsmanship and décor, these vessels are clearly inferior to the vessels in the one-*zun*-two-*you* sets, produced at higher-quality workshops.

A famous example of a locally produced *ding* and confirmation of the military role of the owner is the Ran *fangding* 塱方鼎 from Daijiawan, a Ze 夨 state burial ground in Baoji. It has the following inscription:[31]

> It is when the campaign against the Eastern Yi, Feng Bo, and Fu Gu led by Zhou Gong was finished that (Zhou) Gong returned and presented offerings in the Zhou temple. On day *wuchen* (day 5), the drinking ritual was performed. (Zhou) Gong awarded Ran a hundred cowry shells to use to have made a *ding* for expressing his reverence.
>
> 佳周公于征伐東夷, 豐伯, 尃古 (薄姑) 咸哉. 公歸, 荐于周廟, 戊辰. 畲 (飲) 秦畲. 公賞塱貝百朋, 用作尊鼎.

Ran seemed to be an important official in the Ze court in the Doujitai 鬥雞台–Daijiawan 戴家灣 area of Baoji. He had achieved military merit while accompanying Zhou Gong on the expedition east and was thus honored.

Conclusion

It is noteworthy that in such a short time over such a vast area so many one-*zun*-two-*you* sets were placed in early Western Zhou tombs of the military elite. The most important historical event of the eleventh century BCE was King Wu's attack on the Shang, symbolizing the Zhou revolution against the Shang mandate. It was followed by the eastern campaigns led by Zhou Gong to certify Zhou control over "All Under Heaven" (*tianxia* 天下). Approximately two hundred thousand men were engaged in the battle at Muye 牧野 between the Shang and the Zhou, probably one of the largest battles on earth during the late second millennium BCE. This was followed by three years of pacification campaigns led by members of the Ji 姬 lineage, King Wu, and Zhou Gong. The two great tribal groups, the Ji and the Jiang 姜, allies in government and military affairs, formed the backbone of the revolution. Over eight hundred local lords joined the Ji-Jiang alliance ensuring that the Muye battle would be decisive. The "Zhou benji" 周本紀 of the *Shiji* records:[32]

> (Thereupon) King Wu announced to all the lords: "Yin has committed a grave crime and must be fully punished." So then following King Wen, he subsequently led 300 war-chariots, 3,000 Tiger Troops, 40,500 armored men east to punish the Shang.
>
> 武王徧告諸侯曰: "殷有重罪, 不可以不畢伐." 乃遵文王, 遂率戎車三百乘, 虎賁三千人, 甲士四萬五千人, 以東伐商.

And the "Mu shi" 牧誓 of the *Shangshu* 尚書 records:[33]

> The time was dawn on a *jiazi* day (day 1) when the king met up (with his allies) at the Shang suburb Muye and made an oath. Grasping a yellow *yue*-axe in his left hand and waving a white pennant in his right, he said: "So alienated are we men of the west!" . . . The king said: "Ah! Allied Leaders, Ministers of Affairs, Supervisors of Troops, Supervisors of Horses, and Supervisors of Works, Descendant-Official Corps, Collected Masters (of military and ritual affairs), leaders of units of one thousand, leaders of units of one hundred, and peoples of Yong, Shu, Qiang, Mao, Wei, Lu, Peng, and Pu, raise up your dagger-axes, align your

shields side by side, and stand your spears up; I thereby make this oath.

時甲子昧爽, 王朝至於商郊牧野, 乃誓. 王左杖黃鉞, 右秉白旄以麾曰: 逖矣西土之人! . . . 王曰: 嗟! 我友邦冢君, 御事, 司徒, 司馬, 司空, 亞旅, 師氏, 千夫長, 百夫長, 及庸, 蜀, 羌, 髳, 微, 盧, 彭, 濮人, 稱爾戈, 比而幹, 立爾矛, 予其誓.

These records vividly describe the battle scene at Muye.

The occupants of tombs with sets of *zun* and *you* were all local rulers, lords, lineage heads, and members of Zhou aristocratic families. They joined their forces for King Wu to prevail over the Shang at Muye. They also participated in Zhou Gong's pacification campaigns against the Eastern Yi and Southern Huaiyi peoples. After Muye, King Wu issued several important government edicts, the most important of which was "to grant land to the local lords, give awards by rank of ritual vessels for ancestral shrines, and distribute the Shang vessels" (封諸侯, 班賜宗彝, 作分殷之器物).[34]

The tombs with the sets of one *zun* and two *you* described earlier all contained numerous Shang bronze ritual vessels, many of which bear clan signs and the stem signs used by the Shang and their allies to categorize their ancestors.[35] After the destruction of the Shang state, these ancestral treasures became war loot, which was awarded by rank and military merit to the newly formed military elite of the Zhou court. This is what is meant by "distribute the Yin (Shang) vessels" (*fen Yin zhi qi* 分殷之器). After the revolution, the wealth and treasures were redistributed as rewards to the new military elite and buried with them.

The transfer of government power and wealth impacted and altered the prior Shang social organizational structure. The capital of Shang (Dayi Shang 大邑商) and its satellite regions were divided up and ruled by the Western Zhou royal house and its allied lineages. The *Zuo zhuan* 左傳 records for Ding 定 Year 4 make note that Zhou Gong had Bo Qin 伯禽 of Lu 魯 take charge of six lineages of the Shang peoples, and Kang Shu 康叔 of Wei 衛 took charge of seven lineages after the Shang lost. Large numbers of Shang refugees were moved to central sites, such as Luoyi 洛邑, and to western sites, such as Fenghao 豐鎬 and Zhouyuan 周原. Those with specialized technical knowledge, such as craftsmen and their kin, had to work for the newly risen Western Zhou aristocrats at the central and local courts. The Zhou preserved the Shang peoples' lineage organization and customs for administrative purposes. Thus, the *Zuo zhuan* Ding Year 4 records: "(These six houses) were made to lead those who shared their ancestral lineages, to gather together their collateral houses, and to aid their many dependents (in following Zhou Gong's models)" (帥其宗氏, 輯其分族, 將其類醜).[36] As long as these Shang groups accepted Zhou rule, they could enjoy a certain amount of power. It is possible that the Shang vessels discovered in the Zhou tombs with one-*zun*-two-*you* sets were produced by these established lineages.

The material discovered in the Western Zhou elite tombs at Baoji, including the sites of Doujitai, Shigushan, and Zhuyuangou, date to this time of political transition. The Ji and Jiang lineage heads and elite soldiers of the western area of the Guanzhong 關中 Plains, along with their peoples, who amassed in support of King Wu and Zhou Gong's campaigns, formed the main conquering force. From the Baicaopo material in the tombs of Jing Bo and Xi Bo in Gansu, we know that the Jiang-Rong 戎 and Western Rong peoples of the Jing River 涇水 and Qian River 汧水 valleys also allied with the Zhou against the Shang. We even see that the former Shang subordinate, E Hou, whose tomb was found in the lower Han River 漢水 valley, in Yangzishan, Sui District in the Sui-Zao 隨棗 corridor, also allied with the Zhou against the Shang. The inscriptions on the vessels in the one-*zun*-two-*you* set from E Hou's tomb say: "E Hou made this ritual vessel for display" (噩侯作旅彝).[37] E 噩 is the same as E 鄂, recorded as Ji 姞 lineage, and one of the twelve tribes descended from the Yellow Emperor (Huangdi 黃帝) according to the *Guoyu* 國語.[38] E 鄂 was a Shang land grant, and during Shang times, the Lord of E was killed for remonstrating with evil Shang king Zhou 紂, which made the people sympathetic to King Wu's attack. As a reward, the Lord of E was granted land in the modern Sui District in Hubei, the southern edge of the Zhou world.

Thirty kilometers from Yangzishan is Yejiashan, an early Western Zhou burial ground for the Zeng elite. Archaeological material from this site seems to preserve the tombs of three generations of Zeng rulers.[39] From M28, Zeng Hou Jian's 曾侯諫 tomb, in a set of one-*zun*-two-*you* vessels, each bears the inscription: "Zeng Hou Jian makes a precious ritual vessel for reverence to Kui" (曾侯諫作媿寶尊彝).[40] This vessel set was manufactured for Zeng Hou Jian's wife of the Kui 媿 people. Zeng Hou Kang 曾侯犺 was the Zeng lord buried in M111. An inscription on a bronze *gui* in his tomb says:[41] "Kang made this treasured ritual vessel for reverence to his Glorious Deceased-Father Nan Gong" (犺作烈考南公寶尊彝). The reference to Nan

Gong 南公 turns up elsewhere, in a Wenfengta 文峰塔, Suizhou 隨州, in
a late Chunqiu tomb, M1, and on an inscribed set of bells belonging to a
Zeng Hou Yu 曾侯與. Its inscription says:[42]

> Bo Kuo, up above with Wen and Wu on either side of Di, beat
> down the Shang mandate and soothed the world below Heaven.
> The king commissioned him as Nan Gong, building his residence
> on lands at the river bend, he ruled the Huai River Yi peoples,
> overseeing the Xia (people) of the Jiang River.
>
> 伯适 (括) 上帝, 左右文武, 撻殷之命, 撫定天下. 王遣命南公, 縈
> 宅汭土, 君庀淮夷, 臨有江夏.

Zeng Hou Yu, eulogizing his ancestor Bo Kuo 伯括, referred to him as Nan
Gong. The eulogy praises his work helping Kings Wen and Wu to complete the attack on the Shang mandate and to settle the Zhou world. The
Zhou king had sent him to the southern states to manage the borderlands,
warn off the Huaiyi, and monitor the Jiang Xia peoples 江夏. Bo Kuo was
Nangong Kuo, one of the four friends of King Wen, and is recorded as an
important Ji lineage minister. He aided Kings Wen and Wu in attacking
the Shang and in setting up the Zhou, establishing outstanding merit. The
"Zhou Benji" in the *Shiji* records that just as the battle at Muye came to
a close, King Wu commanded:[43]

> Nangong Kuo disperses the goods of the Lutai, distributes the
> grain of the Juqiao, so as to raise up the poor, weak, and sub-
> servient. He commanded Nangong Kuo to record and display
> the nine *ding* and precious jades of those who fled.
>
> 南宮适 (括) 散鹿台之財, 發巨橋之粟, 以振貧弱萌隸. 命南宮适,
> 史佚展九鼎寶玉.

After things settled down, Zhou king Wu granted Nangong Kuo land and
power to act as the protective lord of the Zeng state, controlling the Huaiyi
for the Zhou court and supervising the Jiang Xia. The Zeng tombs at Yejiashan held large numbers of ritual Shang bronzes inscribed with clan signs
and stem sign ancestral names, many bearing the Shang royal family Zi 子
lineage name. No doubt these were booty brought back by Nangong Kuo
as his share after "dividing up the Yin (Shang) goods."

One important branch of the Nangong Kuo lineage stayed back in the western area of Zhouyuan, continuing to aid the royal house. The well-known Western Zhou bronze, Da Yu *ding* 大盂鼎, was owned by a man named Yu 盂, who was a descendant of Nangong Kuo. Yu aided Zhou king Kang 康 as a high-ranked minister. He and his descendants enjoyed wealthy lives in Zhouyuan and owned many servants.[44]

Scholars have pointed out that the one-*zun*-two-*you* set actually started in the late Shang era. A set was recovered from a tomb in Anyang 安陽, in southeastern Dasikongcun 大司空村 M303. The vessels in this set, including two *you* of different sizes, were inscribed with the words *ma wei* 馬危.[45] Outside of Anyang, in a Shang tomb in Shanxi 山西, Lingshijingjie 靈石旌 介 M1, there were two *you* of different sizes with the sign 𠃌.[46] In Shaanxi, at Gaojiabao 高家堡 in Jingyang 涇陽 District, tomb M4 had two *you* of different sizes each with the sign 𠬝.[47] However, the *zun* bronzes in the latter arrangements did not have the same clan signs. Clearly these sets had been put together from mismatched vessels. Only when the inscriptions and décor are the same can we consider it a purposeful and complete set, cast at the same time and sharing a style, such as we see in the purposeful casting events after King Wu destroyed the Shang and established the Western Zhou state. Then the set was cast and presented as a recognized symbol of acknowledgment and respect for high-ranking military elite.

The set made for Yu Ji was discovered in the Yu state burial ground tomb BZM4, which dates to around the time of King Zhao, the end of the early Western Zhou era.[48] By this time, the integrity of the set had begun to erode. After King Mu and with the beginning of the middle Western Zhou era, they had disappeared. It is no coincidence that the classic set (one *zun* with two *you* of different sizes) appeared in elite Zhou tombs in different regions during the same early time period. This configuration should be understood to represent a ritual standard that was enforced by the Zhou royal family and obeyed by regional lords, princes, and lineage heads as part of their participation in ceremonial activities. The set was an elite badge of honor for participating in the war against the Shang and in the eastern pacification campaigns.

After the war, the royal house and the participating lords made oaths and the Zhou king promulgated laws and announcements granting titles and awards. These are preserved in the chapters of the *Shangshu*: "Mu shi" 牧誓, "Dagao" 大誥, "Weizi zhi ming" 微子之命, "Jiu gao" 酒誥, "Kang gao" 康誥, "Zicai" 梓材, "Luo gao" 洛誥, "Wuyi" 無逸, "Jun Shi" 君奭, "Duofang" 多方, "Cao Zhong zhi ming" 蔡仲之命, and so forth. They all explain why the Shang lost their state. The last Shang ruler, King Zhou, and the Shang aristocracy "did not revere the Lord on High" (不恭上帝), "sacrifices were performed irreverently" (禋祀不寅), "the suburban and altar of soil and millet had fallen into disrepair; the ancestral shrines received no offerings" (郊社不修, 宗廟不享). The Shang aristocracy loved to drink and play to the extent that "the scent of crowds lost in alcohol was detected on high" (庶羣匄酒, 腥聞在上) resulting in their Heavenly Mandate being cut off; they were fated to lose their state. King Wu, King Cheng, and Zhou Gong earnestly warned the members of their family, their court, and all the regional lords and rulers of allied polities to avoid the Shang fate. They must respect and obey the Mandate of Heaven, behave elegantly and morally, and properly present fragrant and pure sacrifices to the Lord on High and to the ancestors. The sacrifices must be timely and serious, performed with propriety and refinement. Only this way could the Mandate of Heaven be preserved.

The Da Yu *ding* records:[49]

> We heard of the fall of the Shang mandate; it was due to the Shang border lords, the managers of the suburbs, and the Shang regulators, the one hundred aides, who all lined up for ale, so they lost the army.
>
> 我聞殷述 (墜) 令 (命), 隹殷邊侯, 田 (甸), 雫殷正百辟, 率肆於酒, 故喪師.

When Zhou king Kang awarded Yu, he used the Shang loss of the mandate given by Heaven as a warning against lords expecting to come to court and get drunk. The *Shangshu* "Jiugao" 酒誥 records:[50]

> My grave and deceased-father King Wen, who began our state in the western territory, admonished the regional lords and the aristocrats, going as far as the minor regulators and business managers; day and night, he said: when presenting alcoholic sacrifice . . . do not indulge in ale . . . [and] when drinking the ritual ale, behave morally with no drunkenness.
>
> 穆考文王, 肇國在西土厥誥毖庶邦, 庶士, 越少正, 御事, 朝夕曰: 祀茲酒. . . . 無彝酒 . . . 飲惟祀, 德將無醉.

It was not that they could not drink at all; only when presenting alcohol during sacrifices to Heaven and the ancestors, they had to behave morally and refined. Drunken behavior like that of the Shang would not be tolerated under any circumstances.

The prominent placement of the one-*zun*-two-*you* drinking vessel sets on altar tables within the tombs of the early Western Zhou elite certainly had the effect of a warning. This new military elite must remember not to lose the state through bad behavior but to revere and obey the Heavenly Mandate, respect the ancestors, and behave in a moral and refined manner in order to protect the Zhou state and to enjoy descendants.

Bronze Manufacturing in the Early Western Zhou

The square *yi* or bronze *zun* vessels paired with the two *you* of different sizes in various places are generally the most exquisitely made ritual vessels found in the tombs. They retain Shang features but also reveal lively stylistic innovation. Scholars debate where the workshops that produced them were located. This was particularly the case after the vessels from the two burial sites in Baoji, Shigushan and Daijiawan, came to light. Some scholars felt that the casting expertise points to a large-scale foundry, such as those maintained at Anyang in southeastern Xiaomintun 孝民屯 or northern Miaopu 苗圃.[51] These foundries did not cease operating after the fall of the Shang and there is some evidence that they produced vessels for the new Zhou elite. Other scholars are convinced that the Anyang artisans were all forced westward to the Shaanxi area after the war and applied their skills in service to the newly emergent aristocracy of the Guanzhong region.[52] Jessica Rawson pointed out that some of the features on the bronzes reveal a southern artistic influence.[53] This topic remains a serious point of academic interest and debate.

The Li *gui* 利簋, discovered in 1976 in Lintong District 臨潼縣 of Shaanxi, provides additional fuel to the debate. It is a new-style, square-based *gui*, representing the fusion of a deep basined, two-eared *gui* and a square bronze altar table—a type not seen among Shang-manufactured *gui*. The inscription on this innovative piece reads as follows:[54]

> When King Wu rectified the Shang, it was on *jiazi* (number
> 1) day at dawn. Jupiter was correctly in a favorable position.

Accordingly, we were able to learn of the securing of the Shang. On *xinwei* (number 8) day, the king was at Lan garrison; he bestowed on me, Li, Scribe of the Right, bronze used to cast for my honored forebear Tan this treasured ritual vessel for expressing reverence.

珷征商, 隹甲子朝, 歲鼎, 克昏夙有商, 辛未, 王才闌自, 賜有事利金 (銅), 用作檀公寶尊彝.

The vessel maker, Li, was an important member of the Tan Gong 檀公 family lineage. As a Zhou officer he personally participated in the battle at Muye on the morning of the first day of the sexagenary ritual calendar. King Wu rewarded his valor and merit, most likely with smelted bronze ingots. On the eighth day of the battle, at Lan garrison where he attacked the Shang army, this unique vessel was cast. Lan may have been located in the countryside outside of the Shang secondary capital of Chaoge 朝歌. The Shang king Zhou had often performed sacrifices, feasts, and award ceremonies at Lan during the last years of the Shang; therefore, it must have been the location of a secondary Shang palace.[55] The Li *gui* was cast there on the eighth day after the battle at Muye, no doubt using Shang booty. The foundry must have been near Anyang and not near the ancestral town of Tan Gong in Lintong, Shaanxi.

This situation suggests that after the victory over the Shang, the military elite of the allied Zhou armies received prizes and awards from King Wu and, in consequence, cast ritual vessels to commemorate and display their merits to their ancestors and descendants. An inscription on the Ban *gui* 班簋 records:[56] "The king commanded Mao Gong to attack the starving Rong peoples in the eastern states with the local rulers, foot and chariot soldiers, and people of Die" (王令毛公以邦冢君, 徒馭, 戜人伐東國痟戎). The Zhou king Cheng ordered Mao Gong to attack the starving Rong people of the eastern states, so he commanded an army made up of clan groups, including local rulers and soldiers. The Die people 戜人 may have been an outside clan that included artisans with special skills used in support of the army. Skilled support staff was necessary during wars to not only keep war chariots and weapons in good order but also to maintain roads and river crossings.

Bronze casting molds discovered in the foundry site of southeastern Xiaomintun in Anyang are similar in style to ritual vessels found in Western Zhou tombs in Shigushan, Baoji. These include mold pieces for a large rectangular bronze altar table with *kui*-dragon décor and open holes on four sides. There is also an outer mold sidepiece for a square-based *gui* as well as pieces from flanges that would arc upward or trail downward like the phoenix tails on a *you*. This material suggests that once the Zhou occupied the Shang capital, the large-scale foundries were still operating and served the needs of the new military elite.[57]

The four-eared *gui* and *you* with protruding phoenix décor from the Baoji foundries (found in Shigushan and Daijiawan) reveal a technique whereby the flanges were cast first and then later smelted on, causing them to stick out. Some scholars point out that the casting on these vessels may have been adapted by early Western Zhou artisans from southern bronze casting arts and styles.[58]

Within three years, King Wu gathered over eight hundred lords to attack the Shang and Zhou Gong led the Zhou army and allied clans against the east, putting down all Shang rebellion. During this period of struggle between the old and new regimes, the Zhongzhou 中州 larger area included a mix of peoples—Shang, Zhou, Jiang Rong 姜戎, Western Rong 西戎, Northern Di 北狄, Eastern Yi 東夷, Southern Huaiyi 南淮夷, and so forth. These clans, lords, and cultures melded and clashed, forming new groups and boundaries, and their artisans learned new techniques. The Zhou royal house, with its new power and control over the economy, could improve technical production, such as in casting, jade work, weaving, lacquerware, architecture, and other arts; these skills had once lagged behind during the Shang. During the war and subsequent years as the Zhou elite swept through cities and seized and controlled territories, they acquired not only great wealth in manufactured goods but also many Shang and Eastern Yi refugees, with artisans and skilled casting artisans among them.

Two completely different sets of bronze ritual drinking vessels came out of E Hou's tomb in Yangzishan, Sui District, Hubei, which reveal divergent manufacturing skills. In the first set of three vessels, each is inscribed: "E Hou made ritual vessels for display" (噩侯作旅彝). These vessels reveal a heavy Central Plains 中原 stylistic flavor. The other set has a *you* with the inscription "made a treasured vessel for expressing reverence" (作寶尊). The three vessels are plain on the surface, except for the exaggerated animal faces that cover them. The first set is the product of Central Plains artisans and the second set is most likely from local artisans of the lower Han River valley, a Southern Huaiyi peoples region.[59]

During the Shang era, the art of bronze casting was a tightly organized and highly specialized, complex process managed by the royal family, local lords, and administrative officials. The process included seeking out mining operations, mining, smelting, casting ingots, transportation, and setting up foundries at the capital and elsewhere. Foundries required large numbers of skilled artisans and administrators to manage them and their families. Foundries also relied on being able to design and execute the designs of different types of vessels and décor according to government, ideological, and ceremonial specifications. In addition, local lords and aristocrats of various ranks might order certain vessels. Then, the final products had to be shipped out in all directions. In sum, without a strong administrative structure, it would be impossible to maintain large-scale production of bronze ritual vessels.

During the time of transition, the smaller polities and local lords would not have been able to arrange for a full-fledged foundry to cast ritual vessels. During the period before the end of the Shang and the early years of the Zhou, the vessels cast in areas outside the capital were of inferior quality. There was no way to sustain the large-scale process. But the surge in fine-quality casting, vessel type variety, and beautiful décor after King Wu's victory required taking advantage of the Shang foundries, their equipment, and select artisans. Shang capitals and cities such as Chaoge, Zhengzhou 鄭州, Luoyang 洛陽, Bogu 薄姑, and Shanghe 商盍 would still retain some foundries, even after being pillaged. It is possible that these remaining foundries still produced exquisite bronze ritual vessels.

Large amounts of bronze ingots must have been captured by the Shang royal house as well as by the Eastern Yi and Southern Huaiyi peoples and then used by the victorious Zhou military elite to cast their vessels. After Zhou Gong settled the east, the Zhou court was relatively stable. After the new Zhou center, Chengzhou 成周, was built in Luoyi 洛邑, Shang refugees along with artisans and their families were moved to Luoyang, Fenghao, and Zhouyuan in the west. With stability came economic growth, which allowed for the rise of bronze foundries and jade and bone workshops in these areas.[60] Foundry sites have also been discovered in polities of local outstanding lineages and regional lords.[61] However, the influence of Shang bronze features slowly retracted over time.

The Zhou revolution was an eleventh century BCE political collision between two cultural groups, the Shang and the Zhou, that resulted in the improved, elevated, and refined civilization of the Western Zhou bronze age. The blending of local Zhou arts with metropolitan Shang artisans synergistically produced a golden age of Western Zhou bronze culture.

Notes

1. Gansusheng bowuguan wenwudui 甘肅省博物館文物隊, "Gansu Lingtai Baicaopo Xi Zhou mu" 甘肅靈臺白草坡西周墓, *Kaogu xuebao* 考古學報 1977.2, 99–130.

2. Yan Yiping 嚴一萍, *Jinwen zongji* 金文總集 (Taipei: Yiwen, 1983), 4758.1, 4758.2, 5362.1; Ma Chengyuan 馬承源, ed., *Shang Zhou qingtongqi mingwen xuan* 商周青銅器銘文選 (Beijing: Wenwu, 1986), 154 (lid).

3. Yan Yiping, *Jinwen zongji*, 5361; Ma Chengyuan, *Shang Zhou qingtongqi*, 155.

4. Lu Liancheng 盧連成 and Hu Zhisheng 胡智生, *Baoji Yuguo mudi* 寶雞 強國墓地 (Beijing: Wenwu, 1988).

5. Lu Liancheng and Hu Zhisheng, *Baoji Yuguo mudi*, 92–127, figs. 73, 379, 82, 83, 85, 88, 90, color pls. 1, 12.1; Zhang Tianen 張天恩, ed., *Shaanxi jinwen jicheng* 陝西金文集成 (Xian: San Qin, 2016), juan 8, 867.

6. Lu Liancheng and Hu Zhisheng, *Baoji Yuguo mudi*, color pl. 13.2.

7. Lu Liancheng and Hu Zhisheng, *Baoji Yuguo mudi*, 45–91, figs. 34, 47–51, 59, 60, color pls. 8.1, 9.1, 13.1.

8. Lu Liancheng and Hu Zhisheng, *Baoji Yuguo mudi*, 173–85, figs. 130, 134, color pls. 8.1, 93, 94; Zhang Tianen, *Shaanxi jinwen jicheng*, juan 8, 867.

9. Shigushan kaogudui 石鼓山考古隊, *Shaanxi Baoji Shigushan Xi Zhou muzang fajue jianbao* 陝西寶雞石鼓山西周墓葬發掘簡報, *Wenwu* 2013.2, 4–54.

10. Chen Zhaorong 陳昭容, ed., Zhongyang yanjiuyuan lishi yuyan yanjiusuo 中央研究院歷史語言研究所, and Shaanxisheng kaogu yanjiuyuan 陝西省考古研究 院, *Baoji Daijiawan yu Shigushan chutu Shang Zhou qingtongqi* 寶雞戴家灣與石鼓 山出土商周青銅器 (Taipei: Zhongyang yanjiuyuan lishi yuyan yanjiusuo, 2015), nos. 2, 13, 14.

11. Chen Zhaorong, *Baoji Daijiawan yu Shigushan chutu Shang Zhou qing-tongqi*, nos. 68, 69.

12. Chen Zhaorong, *Baoji Daijiawan yu Shigushan chutu Shang Zhou qing-tongqi*, nos. 2, 13, 14.

13. Chen Zhaorong, *Baoji Daijiawan yu Shigushan chutu Shang Zhou qing-tongqi*, 27–29, nos. 4, 15, 16, 66, 70.

14. Chen Zhaorong, *Baoji Daijiawan yu Shigushan chutu Shang Zhou qing-tongqi*, 29–33, nos. 1, 11, 12.

15. Tianjinshi wenwu guanlichu 天津市文物管理處, "Xi Zhou kuiwen tong-jin" 西周夔紋銅禁, *Wenwu* 1975.3, 47–48; Chen Zhaorong, *Baoji Daijiawan yu Shigushan chutu Shang Zhou qingtongqi*, 255–257, no. 67.

16. Chen Zhaorong, *Baoji Daijiawan yu Shigushan chutu Shang Zhou qing-tongqi*, nos. 6, 24, 25.

17. Lu Liancheng, "Xi Zhou Zeguo shiji kaolüe ji xiangguan wenti" 西周夨國史蹟考略及相關問題, *Xi Zhou shi yanjiu* 西周史研究 Renwen zazhi 人文雜誌 special monograph 3, ed. Wang Guo 王果 and Zhang Yulang 張玉良 (Xi'an: Renwen zazhi bianjibu, 1984), 232–48.

18. Henansheng wenwu kaogu yanjiusuo 河南省文物考古研究所 and Zhoukoushi wenhuaju 周口市文化局, *Luyi Taiqinggong Zhangzi Kou mu* 鹿邑太清宮長子口墓 (Zhengzhou: Zhongzhou, 2000), 98, 107–10.

19. Zhengzhoushi wenwu kaogu yanjiusuo 鄭州市文物考古研究所, "Zheng-zhoushi Waliucun Xi Zhou zaoqi muzang ZGW99M1fajue jianbao" 鄭州市窪劉村西周早期墓葬ZGW99M1發掘簡報, *Wenwu* 2001.6, 28–44; see also, Zhong Bosheng 鍾柏生, Chen Zhaorong 陳昭容, Huang Mingchong 黃銘崇, and Yuan Guohua 袁國華, *Xinshou Yin Zhou qingtongqi mingwen ji qiying huibian* 新收殷周青銅器銘文暨器影彙編 (Taipei: Yiwen, 2006), nos. 594, 595, 0597. The twelve vessels from this tomb do not share the same clan signs or ancestral names. Only the three vessels in the set are the same.

20. Zhongguo shehui kexueyuan kaogu yanjiusuo 中國社會科學院考古研究所, *Yin Zhou jinwen jicheng* 殷周金文集成 (Beijing: Zhonghua, 1984–1994), nos. 5954, 5363, 5364.

21. Zhongguo shehui kexueyuan kaogu yanjiusuo, *Yin Zhou jinwen jicheng*, nos. 5999, 5451, 5422. Presently the *zun* and the small *you* are preserved in the Hakutsuru Art Museum and the large *you* is in Harvard's Sackler Museum.

22. Zhongguo shehui kexueyuan kaogu yanjiusuo, *Yin Zhou jinwen jicheng*, nos. 5889, 5258, 5259. Presently the *zun* and the large *you* are preserved in Harvard's Sackler Museum and the small *you* is in a private American collection.

23. Hebeisheng wenwu guanlichu 河北省文物管理處 and Tang Yunming 唐雲明, "Hebei Yuanshixian Xizhangcun de Xi Zhou yizhi he muzang" 河北元氏縣西張村的西周遺址和墓葬, *Kaogu* 1979.1, 23–26, figs. 7–8.

24. Suizhoushi bowuguan 隨州市博物館 and Shenzhou bowuguan 深圳博物館, *Liyue Handong* 禮樂漢東 (Beijing: Wenwu, 2012), 32–39, 42–47.

25. Hubeisheng bowuguan 湖北省博物館, Hubeisheng wenwu kaogu yanjusuo 湖北省文物考古研究所, and Suizhoushi bowuguan 隨州市博物館, *Suizhou Yejiashan—Xi Zhou zaoqi Zengguo mudi* 隨州葉家山—西周早期曾國墓地 (Beijing: Wenwu, 2013), 76–77, 82–83, 85–87.

26. Cao Wei 曹瑋, ed., *Zhouyuan chutu qingtongqi* 周原出土青銅器, vol. 6 (Chengdu: Bashu, 2005), 1170, 1176, 1180.

27. Zhao Kangmin 趙康民, "Shaanxi Lintong faxian Wu Wang zheng Shang gui" 陝西臨潼發現武王征商簋, *Wenwu* 1978.8, 2, fig. 2; Zhang Tianen, *Shaanxi jinwen jicheng, juan* 13, 1439.

28. Chen Zhaorong, "Baoji chutu qingtong jin ji qi xiangguan wenti" 寶雞出土青銅禁及其相關問題, *Guwenzi yu gudaishi* 古文字與古代史, vol. 4 (Taipei: Zhongyang yanjiuyuan lishi yuyan yanjiusuo, 2015), 314–17.

29. Zhang Maorong 張懋鎔, "Zhouren bu yong riming shuo" 周人不用日名説, *Lishi yanjiu* 歷史研究 1993.5, 173–77; Zhang Maorong, "Zhouren bu yong zuhui shuo" 周人不用族徽説, *Kaogu* 1995.9, 835–40.

30. Huang Mingchong 黃銘崇, "Cong kaogu faxian kan Xi Zhou muzang de 'fen qi' xianxiang yu Xi Zhou shidai liqi zhidu de leixing yu jieduan" 從考古發現看西周墓葬的 "分器" 現象與西周時代禮器制度的類型與階段, *Zhongyang yanjiuyuan lishi yuyan yanjiusuo jikan* 中央研究院歷史語言研究所集刊 83, 2012.4, 1–82, 607–70; 84, 2013.1, 1–82; see also Chen Zhaorong, "Baoji chutu qingtong jin ji qi xiangguan wenti," 291–336.

31. Zhang Tianen, *Shaanxi jinwen jicheng*, *juan* 7, 798. For a discussion on how Baoji doujitai and Daijiawan both belonged to the Ze state, see Lu Liancheng, "Xi Zhou Ze guo shi ji kaolüe ji xiangguanwenti."

32. "Zhou benji" 周本紀, *Shiji* 史記 (Beijing: Zhonghua, 1959), *juan* 4, 121.

33. "Mu shi" 牧誓, *Shangshu zhengyi* 尚書正義 11.70–71, in *Shisanjing zhushu* 十三經注疏, vol. 1 (Beijing: Zhonghua, 1979), 182–83.

34. "Zhou Benji," *Shiji*, 126–27.

35. See n. 30 in this chapter.

36. *Chunqiu Zuo zhuan Zhengyi* 春秋左傳正義 54.432–33 in *Shisanjing zhushu*, vol. 2 (Beijing: Zhonghua, 1979), 2134; cf. Stephen Durrant, Li Wai-yee, and David Schaberg, *Zuo Tradition / Zuozhuan: Commentary on the "Spring and Autumn Annals"* (Seattle: University of Washington Press, 2016), vol. 3, 1748–49.

37. Suizhoushi bowuguan and Shenzhou bowuguan, *Liyue Handong*, 32–39.

38. For the twelve *xing* 姓 including Ji of Huangdi, see *Guoyu*, "Jinyu, si" 晉語四, in Sibu beiyao edition (Taipei: Zhonghua, 1975), 10.7–8. E is linked to the Ji lineage group in the set of late Western Zhou *gui* tureens made by a lord of E as dowry vessels for a Ji lineage woman; see Zhongguo shehui kexueyuan kaogu yanjiusuo, *Yin Zhou jinwen jicheng*, nos. 3928–30.

39. See n. 25 in this chapter. Hubeisheng bowuguan et al., *Suizhou Yejiashan—Xi Zhou zaoqi Zengguo mudi*. The occupants of M28, M65, and M111 were likely three generations of Zeng rulers.

40. Hubeishen bowuguan et al., *Suizhou Yejiashan—Xi Zhou zaoqi Zengguo mudi*, 62, 65, 77.

41. Hubeishen bowuguan et al., *Suizhou Yejiashan—Xi Zhou zaoqi Zengguo mudi*, 124.

42. Hubeisheng wenwu kaogu yanjiusuo 湖北省文物考古研究所 and Suizhoushi bowuguan 隨州市博物館, "Suizhou Wenfengta M1 (Zeng Hou Yu mu), M2 fajue jianbao" 隨州文峰塔 M1 (曾侯與墓), M2 發掘簡報, *Jianghan kaogu* 江漢考古 2014.4, 3–51.

43. "Zhou beji," *Shiji*, 126.

44. For an illustration of the Da Yu *ding*, see Zhang Tianen, *Shaanxi jinwen jicheng*, *juan* 1, 47.

45. Yue Hongbin 岳洪彬, Yue Zhanwei 岳佔偉, and He Yuling 何毓靈, "Yinxu Dasikong M303 fajue baogao" 殷墟大司空 M303 發掘報告, *Kaogu xuebao* 考古學報2008.3, 353–94; Chen Zhaorong, "Baoji chutu qingtong jin ji qi xiangguan wenti," 318.

46. Shanxisheng kaogu yanjiusuo 山西省考古研究所, *Lingshijingjie Shang mu* 靈石旌介商墓 (Beijing: Kexue, 2006), 36, 39, 45; Chen Zhaorong, "Baoji chutu qingtong jin ji qi xiangguan wenti," 318–19, fig. 15.

47. Shaanxisheng kaogu yanjiusuo 陝西省考古研究所, ed., *Gaojiabao Geguo mudi* 高家堡戈國墓地 (Xian: Sanqin, 1995), 81–84; Zhong Bosheng et al., *Xinshou Yin Zhou qingtongqi mingwen ji qiying huibian*, nos. 792, 793, 794.

48. Lu Liansheng and Hu Zhisheng, *Baoji Yuguo mudi*, 141–72, figs. 110, 116, color plate 16.

49. See n. 43 in this chapter.

50. *Shangshu zhengyi* 14.93–94, *Shisanjing zhushu*, vol. 1, 205–06.

51. Li Yongdi 李永迪 and Yue Zhanwei 岳佔偉, "Yinxu Xiaomintun dongnandi chutu de taofan yu Daijiawan Shigushan tongqiqun" 殷墟孝民屯東南地出土的陶範與戴家灣石鼓山銅器群, in *Baoji Daijiawan yu Shigushan chutu Shang Zhou qingtongqi*, ed. Chen Zhaorong (Taipei: Zhongyang yanjiuyuan lishi yuyan yanjiusuo, 2015), 506–12.

52. Zhang Tianen 張天恩, "Shang Zhou zhi ji qingtong zhizao chongxin xiyi de guancha" 商周之際青銅制造重心徙移的觀察, in *Jinyu jiaohui—Shang Zhou kaogu, yishu, yu wenhua lunwenji* 金玉交輝——商周考古，藝術與文化論文集, ed. Chen Guangzu 陳光祖 (Taipei: Zhongyang yanjiuyuan lishi yuyan yanjiusuo, 2013), 235–55.

53. Jessica Rawson, *Western Zhou Bronzes from the Arthur M. Sackler Collections*, vol. 2B (Cambridge, MA: Harvard University Press, 1990), 155–60.

54. See n. 27 in this chapter. Translation adapted from David W. Pankenier in *A Source Book of Ancient Chinese Bronze Inscriptions*, rev. ed., ed. Constance A. Cook and Paul R. Golding (Berkeley: Society for the Study of Early China, 2020), 11.

55. For a discussion of the Li *gui*, see Tang Lan 唐蘭, "Xi Zhou shidai zuizao de yi jian tongqi Li gui mingwen jieshi" 西周時代最早的一件銅器利簋銘文解釋, *Wenwu* 1977.8, 9; Yu Shengwu 于省吾, "Li gui mingwen kaoshi" 利簋銘文考釋, *Wenwu* 1977.8, 12; Zhang Zhenglang 張政烺, "Li gui shiwen" 利簋釋文, *Kaogu* 1978.1, 59; Zhong Fengnian 鐘鳳年, Xu Zhongshu 徐中舒, Qi Guiyan 戚桂宴, Zhao Cheng 趙誠, Huang Shengzhang 黃盛璋, and Wang Yuxin 王宇信, "Guanyu Li gui mingwen kaoshi de taolun" 關於利簋銘文考釋的討論, *Wenwu* 1978.6, 79.

56. For the illustration and inscription of the Ban *gui* 班簋, see Zhongguo qingtongqi quanji bianji weiyuanhui 中國青銅器全集編輯委員會, *Zhongguo qingtongqi quanji* 中國青銅器全集 (Beijing: Wenwu, 1993), *juan* 5, 58.

57. Li Yongdi, Yue Zhanwei, and Liu Yu 劉煜, "Cong Xiaomintun donnandi chutu taofan tan dui Yinxu qingtongqi de jidian xin renshi" 從孝民屯東南地出土陶范談對殷墟青銅器的幾點新認識, *Kaogu* 2007.3, 52–63; Li Yongdi and Yue Zhanwei,

"Yinxu Xiaomintun dongnandi chutu de taofan yu Daijiawan Shigushan tongqiqun," 506–12, see also appendix 2, 482–85.

58. Su Rongyu 蘇榮譽, "Lun Xi Zhou chunian de niushoushi qingtongqi sier gui" 論西周初年的牛首飾青銅四耳簋, in *Baoji Daijiawan yu Shigushan chutu Shang Zhou qingtongqi*, ed. Chen Zhaorong (Taipei: Zhongyang yanjiuyuan lishi yuyan yanjiusuo, 2015), 513–23.

59. See n. 24 in this chapter.

60. Zhang Tianen, "Shang Zhou zhi ji qingtong zhizao Chongxin xiyi de guancha"; Shaanxisheng kaogu yanjiuyuan 陝西省考古研究院, Beijing daxue wenbo kaogu xueyuan 北京大學文博考古學院, Zhongguo shehui kexueyuan kaogu yanjiusuo 中國社會科學院考古研究所, and Zhouyuan kaogudui 周原考古隊, *Zhouyuan—2002 nian Qijia zhijue zuofang he Licun yizhi kaogu fajue baogao* 周原——2002年齊家制玦作坊和禮村遺址考古發掘報告 (Beijing: Kexue, 2010); Zhouyuan kaogudui 周原考古隊, "Fufeng Yuntang Xi Zhou guqi zhizao zuofang yizhi shijue jianbao" 扶風雲塘西周骨器制造作坊遺址試掘簡報, *Wenwu* 1980.4, 27–38; Zhouyuan kaogudui, "Shaanxi Zhouyuan yizhi faxian Xi Zhou muzang yu zhutong yizhi" 陝西周原遺址發現西周墓葬與鑄銅遺址, *Kaogu* 2004.1, 3–6; Luoyangshi wenwu gongzuodui 洛陽市文物工作隊, "1975–1979 nian Luoyang Beiyao Xi Zhou zhutong yizhi de fajue" 1975–1979 年洛陽北窯西周鑄銅遺址的發掘, *Kaogu* 1983.5, 430–41.

61. Xu Tianjin 徐天進, "Zhou Gong miao yizhi de kaogu suohuo ji suosi" 周公廟遺址的考古所獲及所思, *Wenwu* 2006.8, 55–62; Zhong Jianrong 種建榮 and Lei Xingshan 雷興山, "Xian Zhou wenhua zhutong yicun de queren ji qi yiyi" 先周文化鑄銅遺存的確認及其意義, *Zhongguo wenwubao* 中國文物報, November 30, 2007, 7.

4

The Cheng Wang *Fangding*

Colin Mackenzie

The Cheng Wang *fangding* 成王方鼎 in the Nelson-Atkins Museum of Art (figs. 4.1–4.2) is a rare example of a Western Zhou bronze naming King Cheng. The brevity of its inscription—only three characters—and its unusual formulation (Cheng Wang *zun* 尊) have, however, raised doubts about its

Figure 4.1. Cheng Wang *Fangding*. Chinese, Western Zhou dynasty (1045–771 BCE), late eleventh-century BCE bronze, 11 by 6 by 7¼ in. (27.9 × 15.2 × 18.4 cm). *Source:* Nelson-Atkins Museum of Art, Kansas City, Missouri. Purchase: William Rockhill Nelson Trust, 41–33.

Figure 4.2a. Rubbing of Inscription on the Cheng Wang *Fangding*. After rubbing in Nelson-Atkins Chinese Department object file. *Source:* Nelson-Atkins Museum of Art, Kansas City, Missouri. Purchase: William Rockhill Nelson Trust, 41–33.

Figure 4.2b. Inscription on the Cheng Wang *Fangding*. *Source:* Nelson-Atkins Museum of Art, Kansas City, Missouri. Purchase: William Rockhill Nelson Trust, 41–33. Photograph by Colin Mackenzie.

authenticity in the minds of a minority of scholars, notably Yu Xingwu 于省吾.[1] This chapter discusses the authenticity of the inscription, its significance for dating the vessel, and the questions it raises about royal Zhou bronzes.

The vessel is recorded as having been in the collection of Shen Bingcheng 沈秉成 (1823–1895), a noted collector resident in Suzhou.[2] Its subsequent history is not known until 1939, when it came into the possession of C. T. Loo (Lu Qinzhai 盧芹齋), who exhibited it at his New York galleries.[3] While in the possession of Loo, it was part of a loan exhibition at the Detroit Institute of Arts accompanied by a catalog authored by James M. Menzies.[4] It was purchased from Loo by the Nelson-Atkins in 1941, probably at the instigation of Laurence Sickman, Curator of Oriental Art, since he chose it as the "Masterpiece of the Month" for October of that year.[5] Sickman, despite not claiming to be a specialist in Chinese bronzes, was responsible for some excellent acquisitions of bronzes for the Nelson-Atkins. He was also a scholarly and insightful writer, with a gift for placing the objects in their broad historical and aesthetic contexts. A passage from his description of the *ding* is worth quoting:[6]

> In the great majority of the vessels datable to the earliest years of Chou [Zhou] rule, an interesting and highly suggestive process of selection appears to be at work. The elements of Shang design that are the more striking in effect, such as fully modeled animal heads and protruding flanges, are seized upon and emphasized. The treatment of the usual motifs—like birds and dragons—undergoes a change and becomes more flamboyant, more obviously vigorous, and less subtle in their linear rhythms. In a word, the conceptions are more consciously dramatic, more obviously striking and keyed to a higher emotional pitch.

This description succinctly sums up the style of the *fangding* 方鼎 (rectangular *ding*). In his article, Sickman also discusses the short inscription, which he interprets as indicating that King Cheng used the *ding* for sacrifices to his ancestors. As we shall see, this reading is probably not correct. Prior to discussing the inscription, it is worth considering further the form and decoration of the vessel in the context of the history of the vessel type.

The *fangding* is a well-known type of tetrapod that appears during the Erligang 二里崗 period (ca. 1500–1300 BCE). Already at this time, examples are of considerable size; indeed, the largest known Erligang vessel is a *fangding*, one of two discovered in 1974 in a pit at Zhangzhai Nanjie 張寨南街, Zhengzhou 鄭州. It reaches a height of 100 cm. Two other finds at Zhengzhou have also yielded massive *fangding*.[7] One of these, a hoard at Nanshunchengjie 南順城街 in 1996, yielded a set of four graduated *ding*, ranging in height from 59 to 83 cm, the earliest example of a graduated set of ritual vessels.[8] The dominance of *fangding* continued into the Anyang period, as illustrated by examples such as the Hou (Si) Mu Wu *fangding*

后 (司) 母戊方鼎 from Wuguancun 武官村, the pair of Hou (Si) Mu Xin *fangding* 后 (司) 母辛方鼎 from the tomb of Fu Hao 婦好, and the Deer and Buffalo *fangding* from tomb 1004.[9] Clearly *fangding* commanded a central place in the rituals, which often required that they were cast on a huge scale. Not all *fangding* were monumental, however. Some examples are almost miniature in scale; the Cheng Wang *fangding* is modest, reaching a height of approximately only 28.5 cm, and many are smaller.

Although the highly sculptural appendages produce an effect that is dramatic compared with Shang versions, precedents for the individual elements of its decoration abound. The pointed bosses that decorate its vertical surfaces are developments of the bosses that decorated the earliest *fangding* and which, lacking any zoomorphic reference, are purely abstract. The earliest examples occur on the two most primitive of the large *fangding* from the Zhengzhou hoard (fig. 4.3). On these, the bosses are irregularly placed along a central band but also on raised vertical strips at the corners.

Figure 4.3. *Fangding* from Zhengzhou Nanshunchengjie (H1 上 3). Height 64 cm. *Source:* After Henan sheng wenwu kaogu yanjiiusuo et al., *Zhengzhou Shangdai tongqi jiaocang* (Beijing: Kexue, 1999), pl. 5.

These strips seem to be reinforcements, so it is possible that the bosses originally performed some practical role in the casting process. During the Shang, the bosses are low rounded forms, but, in early Western Zhou, they become extended and more pointed, as on the Cheng Wang *fangding*, in keeping with the flamboyant styles in vogue. The most famous example of these "prickly" bosses is the four-handled *gui* in the Freer Gallery of Art.[10]

On the early Zhengzhou *ding*, a horizontal register of bosses runs midway across each face, but in all subsequent iterations, the horizontal panel is moved up near the mouth and the bosses are replaced with a *taotie* (mask) or a row of birds. The long-tailed birds on the Cheng Wang *fangding* were an innovation of the late Shang, gradually replacing the more compact birds previously in vogue. Below this panel, the central zone came to be filled either with a diagonal textile design or vertical ribbing as on the Cheng Wang *fangding*. The ribbing occurs on a number of different vessel types and seems to have been purely decorative, devoid of any symbolic meaning, and may possibly have originated in basketry.[11]

The sculptural dragon or tigerlike animals applied to the handles are translations into three dimensions of the tiger forms that decorate the handles of the Hou (Si) Mu Wu *fangding*.[12] This innovation seems to have happened in early Western Zhou in keeping with Sickman's observation on the exaggeration of features already present. The same dragon appendages decorate the handles of the *fangding* in the Asian Art Museum of San Francisco, on the famous Tai (or Da) Bao *fangding* 太保方鼎 in the Tianjin Museum, one of a set of seven vessels linked by inscription to Tai Bao, who is known to have been active during the reigns of Kings Cheng and Kang.[13]

Two interesting technical features of the Cheng Wang *fangding* should be pointed out: Each of the two curled horns of the mask on each leg was cast on using separate molds (fig. 4.4a). Although casting on is a common technique during the Shang and Western Zhou, the fact that a total of eight molds were used for these small features reflects the complexity of the casting of the vessel as a whole. Second, a careless slash across the model for one of the leg masks was not repaired and is preserved in the final bronze (fig. 4.4b).

Unlike the stylistic elements of the vessel itself, which can be linked with the many other precedents and parallels previously described, the inscription of three characters—Cheng Wang *zun* 成王尊—is unusual for its brevity, at least for an inscription naming a king, and grammatical peculiarity. It is probably this grammatical anomaly alone that made Yu

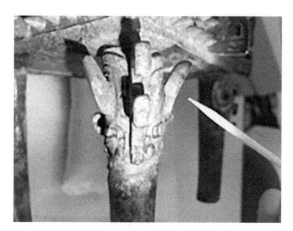

Figure 4.4a. View of a Leg of the Cheng Wang *Fangding*, Showing Slash on Original Clay Model Transferred to Bronze Casting. *Source:* Nelson-Atkins Museum of Art, Kansas City, Missouri. Purchase: William Rockhill Nelson Trust, 41–33. Photograph by Colin Mackenzie.

Figure 4.4b. View of Animal Mask on Leg Showing Cast-On Horns. *Source:* Nelson-Atkins Museum of Art, Kansas City, Missouri. Purchase: William Rockhill Nelson Trust, 41–33. Photograph by Yayoi Shinoda.

Xingwu suspicious, since we do not know that he ever examined the vessel itself. As for these three characters, they are well written and fall within an acceptable degree of variation exhibited by these characters when they occur

on other bronzes of the same period. The character for Cheng is similar
to that used for the capital city Chengzhou 成周 on the De *fangding* 德
方鼎 (fig. 4.5a); the character for *wang* is somewhat more rounded at the
base than other examples of *wang* but is still similar. The character for *zun*
is virtually identical to that on the Kang Hou Feng *fangding* 康侯 丰 (封)
方鼎 (fig. 4.5b). Close examination of the inscription in the conservation
laboratory at the Nelson-Atkins confirmed that it is cast, not incised, and

Figure 4.5a. Rubbing of Inscription on De *Fangding. Source:* After Wu Zhenfeng,
Shang Zhou qingtongqi mingwen ji tuxiang jicheng (Shanghai: Shanghai guji, 2012),
vol. 5, 4, no. 02266.

Figure 4.5b. Rubbing of Inscription on Kang Hou Feng *Ding. Source:* After Wu
Zhenfeng, *Shang Zhou qingtongqi mingwen ji tuxiang jicheng*, vol. 3, 250, no. 01575.

therefore coeval with the vessel. Assuming, as we should, that the vessel itself is authentic, the inscription must also be ancient. One somewhat puzzling technical feature is that the wall of the vessel is slightly thicker where the inscription is located, possibly because the inscribed panel that carried the inscription in relief was inlaid slightly deeper into the core than the surrounding area.

Although the inscription is undoubtedly genuine, its meaning is not initially clear. What is the grammatical relationship between Cheng Wang and *zun*? *Zun* is usually an adjective "sacrificial" or "used for sacrifices" that qualifies the noun following it, usually either the generic *yi* 彝 (ritual vessel) or sometimes more specific names of vessels such as *ding*. In other short inscriptions, the commissioner of the vessel might inscribe it using the phrase "X made a precious sacrificial vessel" (X *zuo bao zun yi*, X作寶尊彝), or sometimes "X made a precious sacrificial vessel for or in honor of Y" (X *zuo* Y *bao zun yi*). In these cases, *zun* is an adjective that describes *yi*. X is the subject of the sentence, that is, the commissioner of the bronze, while Y is the object and recipient or dedicatee. In the case of the Cheng Wang *fangding* the *yi* character is omitted, an almost unparalleled occurrence. However, the inscription on the Shi X *yan* 師X甗, excavated from Mapo 馬坡 at Luoyang 洛陽, includes a similarly unconventional use of *zun*: Shi X *zuo lü yan zun* 師X作旅甗尊 (fig. 4.6a). In this case, the character *zun* follows *yan*. The inscription perhaps should be interpreted: "Shi X commissioned this *yan* for traveling; may he use it for sacrifices." Or possibly, the character was just misplaced by the craftsman who inscribed it. Another anomalous example is the inscription on the late Shang-period Xiao Chen Fou *fangding* 小臣缶方鼎 (fig. 4.6b), the second half of which reads: "Fou used [the gift] to commission [the *ding*] to feast Taizi Yi Jia and to use for sacrifices" (缶用作享太子乙家祀尊).

These two inscriptions might at first seem to support Menzies's and Sickman's readings. Menzies interprets *zun* as a verb "to ascend steps and present in the temple" and translates the inscription as "King Cheng presents his sacrifices in this *ting* [*ding*]."[14] Sickman, presumably following Menzies's interpretation, translates the inscription as "King Ch'eng [Cheng] uses this cauldron for offerings."

These interpretations, however, are not persuasive, since the two inscriptions cited earlier are the only two examples that I have encountered where *zun* might possibly function as a verb. It seems more likely in the case of the Cheng Wang *fangding* that *zun* is a qualifier for the character *yi* vessel that has been omitted. But since there is no verb present, it is

Figure 4.6a. Rubbing of Inscription on Shi X *Yan*. *Source:* After Wu Zhenfeng, *Shang Zhou qingtongqi mingwen ji tuxiang jicheng*, vol. 7, 151, no. 03273.

Figure 4.6b. Rubbing of Inscription on Xiao Chen Fou *Fangding*. *Source:* After Wu Zhenfeng, *Shang Zhou qingtongqi mingwen ji tuxiang jicheng*, vol. 4, 442, no. 02224.

not immediately clear whether Cheng Wang is the subject or object of the implied verb. Did King Cheng make [i.e., commission] the vessel—Cheng Wang [*zuo*] *zun* [*yi*]—or did someone else commission it for the king—[*zuo*] Cheng Wang *zun* [*yi*]?

Although Western Zhou ritual bronzes with inscriptions mentioning an unspecified king are plentiful, and those naming a specific king such as Wu, Cheng and Kang, Zhao, and Mu are not infrequent, Li Chaoyuan 李朝遠 has shown that the king, whether named or unnamed, is almost always referred to in the third person.[15] Usually, the king is mentioned in passing as the benefactor of the commissioner of the vessel or simply as a way of dating the event to a particular year. Instead, the commissioner is usually an official or regional lord who casts the vessel to sacrifice to his ancestors or as a gift to another person. In only a few inscriptions is the king mentioned as the person who seems to be the commissioner of the bronze. However, Li argues that, even in these cases, the person who is named as recipient was probably in fact the caster of the bronze, and that the king was only the bestower of the gift that led to the casting.[16]

Menzies's and Sickman's interpretation also assumes that Cheng Wang is the name of a living king rather than a posthumous title. Earlier scholars such as Wang Guowei and Guo Moruo argued that the honorific titles (*shihao* 謚號)—Wu, Cheng, Kang, among others—were used during the lifetime of the respective kings.[17] Until recently, this was still accepted by most Chinese scholars. However, Chang Jincang 常金倉 has convincingly argued that this is unlikely, pointing out that, whenever a king mentioned in an inscription is clearly alive, his honorific title is never mentioned.[18] Moreover, vessels such as the Qiang *pan* 墙盘 and Lai *pan* 逨盘 list former kings with their honorific titles, whereas the reigning king is referred to not by his title but as "Son of Heaven" (*tianzi* 天子).[19]

Edward Shaughnessy, nevertheless, still questions whether the *shihao* has necessarily to be posthumous: "There is certainly nothing wrong with the [authenticity of] the Cheng Wang *fangding*, but it presents a big problem for those who are convinced that the *shihao* have to be posthumous."[20] Shaughnessy alerted me to his discussion of the famous Zuoce Da *fangding* 作冊大方鼎 inscription, which states that "the duke came to cast the King Wu and King Cheng cultic cauldrons" (公來鑄武王成王異鼎).[21] Shaughnessy, citing Shirakawa Shizuka, raises the intriguing possibility that the latter actually refers to the Cheng Wang *fangding*.[22] If this theory is correct, this would be a unique instance where an identified existing vessel is referenced in another inscription. If the unnamed duke is identified with Zhou Gong Dan 周公旦, King Wu's most famous brother, it implies that Cheng was alive when it was cast, since Zhou Gong Dan was older than Cheng—who is said to have reigned for thirty years—and probably passed away before him.[23] However, I think it unlikely that a duke would have cast a vessel for a living king who was his superior and master—after all, what would have been the point of so doing? Instead, it is more likely that the unnamed duke refers to an almost equally famous brother of Wu Wang—Shao Gong Shi 召公奭—who held the title Tai Bao mentioned later in the inscription and who outlived Cheng by many years.[24]

Although the Zuoce Da *fangding* cannot be taken as evidence of the *shihao* being employed during the lifetime of a king, another inscribed vessel naming King Cheng implies more persuasively that he was alive when that vessel was cast. This is the Xian Hou *li-ding* 獻侯鬲鼎, which appears to state that King Cheng gave cowries to Xian, who used them to cast a vessel (fig. 4.7): "It was when Cheng Wang held the Great Fu Exorcism at Zong Zhou, [he] bestowed *zhu* cowries on Marquis Xian, who used [or exchanged] them to cast the sacrificial vessel for Marquis Ding" (唯成王大祓在宗周, 賞獻侯佇貝, 用作丁侯尊彝). If this interpretation is correct, then Cheng Wang was certainly alive when the vessel was cast.

This is the way Tang Lan interpreted the inscription, which would support Menzies's and Sickman's readings of the Cheng Wang inscription.[25] However, Chang Jincang argues that the event recorded in the Xian Hou *li-ding* inscription had actually taken place sometime previously, and that the caster of the vessel was not Xian but a descendant.[26] This interpretation is, in my view, rather forced, but Chang's general point—that the casting of a bronze can postdate an event mentioned in the inscription by a number of years—is certainly valid.

Figure 4.7. Rubbing of Inscription on Xian Hou *Li-ding. Source:* After Wu Zhenfeng, *Shang Zhou qingtongqi mingwen ji tuxiang jicheng,* vol. 4, 378, no. 02181.

We should therefore interpret Cheng Wang *zun* as a shortened version of the typical formula "X commissioned the sacrificial vessel in honor of Y" (X *zuo* Y *wang zun yi*) and that the deceased Cheng was the person to receive sacrifices using the *ding*. This raises the question: Who commissioned the vessel? If, as Tang Lan and Shirakawa believe, the Zuoce Da *fangding* inscription does in fact refer to the Cheng Wang *fangding*, then the commissioner was Shao Gong Shi. Tang Lan believes that this event took place in the third year of Kang's reign.[27] This is certainly possible, but it is also possible that the Zuoce Da *fangding* inscription refers to a different bronze, since it is likely that a number of bronzes were cast for Cheng Wang after his death, perhaps by his brothers.[28] But it seems unlikely that the Cheng Wang *fangding* was cast by Cheng's son, since (on more than one occasion) inscriptions from the Shang and Western Zhou indicate that sons commonly used the formula "made a sacrificial vessel for father X" (*zuo fu* X *yi*, 作父丁彝). They would have been unlikely to refer to their deceased fathers as "king" (*wang*). The balance of evidence does therefore suggest that the *ding* was commissioned by a relative (but not a son) of Cheng, perhaps Shao Gong Shi himself. What was the circumstance of the casting of the vessel? Was it cast to offer sacrifices to Cheng at his funeral? Or was it cast sometime later, for use in the ancestral temple in connection with some later sacrifice, as Tang Lan believes? At any rate, it is unlikely to have been cast after the reign of King Kang, since we have little evidence that vessels were cast in honor of long-deceased kings. Nor could it have been commissioned by a nonrelative.

The implication, therefore, is that the Cheng Wang *fangding* may be one of the very few vessels that we can confidently identify as having been cast by a Zhou royal family member—either an uncle or a brother—for a Zhou king. This, however, raises another issue: Why are there no bronzes with inscriptions stating that they were cast *by* Zhou kings? This absence has sometimes been explained by the fact that the royal Zhou tombs have not been discovered either by archaeologists or tomb robbers. However, not all royal Zhou bronzes would have been buried in tombs; many, we may assume, were kept in the ancestral temples. When the Zhou royal family fled their homelands in 771 BCE, they might have buried some of these in hoards, as did some of their officials, but they surely would have taken some with them to Luoyang. The fact that none of these have come to light is puzzling. In the Shang, for instance, Fu Hao's tomb contained bronzes that were cast in her honor as "mother" (*mu* 母), presumably by her sons. We do not know whether any of them became kings, but, in any case, they did not inscribe their names as kings on the bronzes they cast for their mother. The tombs of the Shang kings at Xibeigang yielded bronzes undoubtedly cast in royal Shang foundries, yet none of these bronzes name the king as commissioner. It therefore seems possible, as Jenny So has suggested, that the Shang and Zhou kings, unlike their officials and relatives, felt no need to inscribe the bronzes that they commissioned with lengthy inscriptions.[29] If this is the case, it is remarkable that they ignored the potential of their most impressive monuments as vehicles for proclamations, even while their officials and relatives vied with each other in composing long and elaborate inscriptions on their own bronzes. The absence of inscribed royal Zhou bronzes is even more surprising, given the fact that the kings of a number of Eastern Zhou regional states such as Chu, Wu, Yue, and Zhongshan did inscribe their bronzes. In their reticence to inscribe their bronzes, the Zhou kings seem thus to have been fundamentally different from rulers in other parts of the ancient world, who used inscriptions in their own names on monuments to make pronouncements and promulgate laws.

Notes

1. See Wu Zhenfeng 吳鎮烽, *Shang Zhou qingtongqi mingwen ji tuxiang jicheng* 商周青銅器銘文暨圖像集成, vol. 2 (Shanghai: Shanghai guji, 2012), 316, no. 01064. Rong Geng 容庚 did not include it in his list of ninety-one bronzes that he attributes to the reign of Cheng Wang, nor among the thirty bronzes he attributes to the subsequent reign of Kang Wang. See Rong Geng 容庚, *Shang Zhou yiqi tongkao* 商周彝器通考, *Yenching Journal of Chinese Studies*, Monograph Series no. 17, no. 1 (1941): 42–49. Zou Heng examined the piece at the Nelson-Atkins on April 28, 1983, and opined that "he could not swear to its authenticity but found absolutely nothing wrong with it" (note in the Nelson-Atkins Chinese Department's object file).
2. Wu Zhenfeng, *Shang Zhou qingtongqi mingwen*, vol. 2, 316. A brief note on Shen Bingcheng's collection is given in Rong Geng, *Shang Zhou yiqi tongkao*, vol. 1, 249.
_3. J. Leroy Davidson (introduction), *An Exhibition of Chinese Bronzes* (New York: C. T. Loo, 1939), pl. 3, catalog no. 17.
4. See the Detroit Institute of Arts, *An Exhibition of Ancient Chinese Ritual Bronzes Loaned by C. T. Loo & Co.*, catalog by James M. Menzies (New York: William Bradford, 1940), catalog no. 30, pl. 18.
5. The Nelson-Atkins Museum of Art, accession no. 41-33. Sickman's text for "Masterpiece of the Month" is preserved in the object file for the *ding* kept in the Chinese department at the Nelson-Atkins.

6. See n. 5.

7. These three finds are published in Henansheng wenwu kaogu yanjiiusuo 河南省文物考古研究所 and Zhengzhoushi wenwu kaogu yanjiusuo 鄭州市文物考古研究所, ed., *Zhengzhou Shangdai tongqi jiaocang* 鄭州商代銅器窖藏 (Beijing: Kexue, 1999), pls. 1–6; see also Elizabeth Childs-Johnson, "Big *Ding* 鼎 and China Power: Divine Authority and Legitimacy," *Asian Perspectives* 51, no. 2 (Fall 2012): 164–220.

8. The original excavation reports on the earlier two finds are published in Henan bowuguan 河南博物館, ed., "Zhengzhou xin chutu de Shangdai qianqi da tong ding" 鄭州新出土的商代前期大銅鼎, *Wenwu* 1975.6, 64–68, pl. 1, and Henansheng wenwu yanjiusuo and Zhengzhoushi bowuguan, ed., "Zhengzhou xin faxian de Shang dai jiaocang qingtongqi" 鄭州新發現的商代青銅器, *Wenwu* 1983.3, 49–59, pl. 4. They are also discussed by Robert Bagley, "Erligang Bronzes and the Discovery of the Erligang Culture," in *Art and Archaeology of the Erligang Civilization*, ed. Kyle Steinke and Dora C. Y. Ching (Princeton: Princeton University Press, 2014), 19–48, esp. 32–37.

9. For the Hou (Si) Mu Wu *fangding*, see Zhongguo qingtongqi quanji bianji weiyuanhui 中國秦通緝全集編輯委員會, ed., *Zhongguo qingtongqi quanji* 中國青銅器全集 (Beijing: Wenwu, 1997), vol. 2, no. 47; for the Hou (Si) Mu Xin *fangding*, see vol. 2, no. 39; for the Ox and Deer *fangding*, see vol. 2, nos. 41 and 42.

10. John Alexander Pope, Rutherford John Gettens, James Cahill, and Noel Barnard, *The Freer Chinese Bronzes*, vol. 1 (Washington, DC: Smithsonian Institution, 1967), no. 66, pl. 66.

11. A *zhi* from Anyang period 4 tomb (GM 907) is decorated mainly in this style. See Zhongguo shehui kexueyuan kaogu yanjiusuo, ed., *Yinxu qingtongqi* 殷墟青銅器 (Beijing: Wenwu, 1985), pl. 74. An early Western Zhou rectangular vessel decorated with ribbing in the Palace Museum, Beijing, seems to be modeled on imitating a basketry form. See Jessica Rawson, *Western Zhou Ritual Bronzes from the Arthur M. Sackler Collections*, vol. 2A: *Ancient Chinese Bronzes from the Arthur M. Sackler Collections* (Washington, DC: Arthur M. Sackler Foundation and Arthur M. Sackler Museum, Harvard University, 1990), part 1, 107, fig. 151a.

12. Robert W. Bagley, *Shang Ritual Bronzes in the Arthur M. Sackler Collections*, vol. 1: *Ancient Chinese Bronzes in the Arthur M. Sackler Collections* (Washington, DC: Arthur M. Sackler Foundation and Arthur M. Sackler Museum, Harvard University, 1987), 107, fig. 133.

13. For the Tai Bao *fangding*, see Zhongguo qingtongqi quanji bianji weiyuanhui, ed., *Zhongguo qingtongqi quanji* (Beijing: Wenwu, 1997), vol. 5, no. 4. The Tai Bao bronzes are discussed in Edward L. Shaughnessy, "The Role of Grand Protector Shi in the Consolidation of the Zhou Conquest," *Ars Orientalis* 19 (1989): 51–77. A *fangding* with similar dragon-surmounted handles is in the Asian Art Museum. See Zhongguo qingtongqi quanji bianji weiyuanhui, *Zhongguo qingtongqi quanji*, vol. 5, no. 7.

14. Detroit Institute of Arts, *An Exhibition of Ancient Chinese Ritual Bronzes*, catalog no. 30, pl. 18.

15. Li Chaoyuan 李朝遠, "Xi-Zhou jinwen zhong de 'wang' yu 'wang qi' " 西周金文中的 "王" 與 "王器," in Li Chaoyuan, *Qingtongqi xuebuji* 青銅器學步集 (Beijing: Wenwu, 2007), 353–58, esp. 354–55.

16. The most famous of these inscriptions is the Hu *gui* unearthed from Qicun 齊村 in Fufeng 扶風. An early Western Zhou *fangding* from Licun 禮村 in Qianshan County 岐山縣 is inscribed: "The king made this precious vessel for Zhong Ji" (*Wang zuo Zhong Ji bao yi*, 王作中姬寶彝), this might be taken as a rare example of a king casting a bronze for another person. See Wu Zhenfeng, *Shang Zhou qingtongqi mingwen*, vol. 3, 199, no. 01519. Another from a hoard at Qinghua gongshe Youfangbao 青化公社油坊堡 in Meixian 眉縣 is inscribed with *Wang zuo Zhong Jiang bao ding* 王作中姜寶鼎. See Wu Zhenfeng, *Shang Zhou qingtongqi mingwen*, vol. 3, 200, no. 01520. Additional examples are discussed by Li Chaoyuan, who argues that these were in fact cast not by the king but by the recipients of gifts mentioned in their inscription. See Li Chaoyuan, "Xi-Zhou jinwen zhong de 'wang' yu 'wang qi,' " 353–58.

17. For a discussion of this question, see Li Chaoyuan, "Xi-Zhou jinwen zhong de 'wang' yu 'wang qi,' " 353–58, esp. 353–54, and Liu Yu 劉雨, "Jinwen zhong de wangcheng" 金文中的王稱, *Gugong bowuguan yuankan* 故宮博物院院刊 2006.4, 6–29, reprinted in Liu Yu, ed., *Jinwen lunji* 金文論集, *Gugong bowuyuan xueshu wenji wenku* (Beijing: Zijincheng, 2008), 445–72.

18. Chang Jincang 常金倉, "Xi-Zhou qingtongqi duandai yanjiu de jige wenti" 西周青銅器斷代研究的幾個問題, *Kaogu yu wenwu* 考古與文物 2006.2, 36–40, 45.

19. Chang Jincang, "Xi-Zhou qingtongqi duandai," 37–38. For the Qiang *pan*, see Zhongguo qingtongqi quanji bianji weiyuanhui, ed., *Zhongguo qingtongqi quanji* 中國青銅器全集 (Beijing: Wenwu, 1997), vol. 5, no. 198. For the Lai *pan*, see Shaanxisheng kaogu yanjiusuo, Baojishi kaogu gongzuodui 寶雞市考古工作隊, Yangjiacun lianhe kaogudui 楊家村聯合考古隊, and Meixian wenhuaguan 眉縣文化館, "Shaanxi Meixian Yangjiacun Xi-Zhou qingtongqi jiaocang fajue jianbao" 陝西眉縣楊家村西周青銅器窖藏發掘簡報, *Wenwu* 2003.6, 4–42, figs. 1–53, esp. figs. 37–42.

20. Edward Shaughnessy, email communication, January 19, 2019. Shaughnessy implies that Wen Wang was a title adopted by Chang 昌 during his lifetime. See Edward L. Shaughnessy, "Western Zhou History," in *The Cambridge History of Ancient China: From the Origins of Civilization to 221 B.C.*, ed. Michael Loewe and Edward L. Shaughnessy (Cambridge: Cambridge University Press, 1999), 307.

21. The inscription appears on four vessels, one of which is in the Freer Gallery of Art, Washington, DC. See John Alexander Pope et al., *The Freer Chinese Bronzes*, vol. 1, 190–95, no. 34.

22. Edward L. Shaughnessy, *Sources of Western Zhou History* (Berkeley: University of California Press, 1991), 53–54.

23. Shaughnessy, "Western Zhou History," 310–16.

24. The reign of Cheng Wang and the roles of Zhou Gong Dan and Shao Gong Shi are exhaustively discussed in Edward L. Shaughnessy, "The Role of Grand Protector Shi"; see also Shaughnessy, "Western Zhou History," 309, 317.

25. Tang Lan 唐蘭, *Tang Lan quanji: Xi-Zhou qingtongqi mingwen fen dai shi zheng* 唐蘭全集: 西周青铜器铭文分代史徵7, ed. Liu Yu 劉雨 (Shanghai: Giji guji, 2015), 85–87.

26. Chang Jincang, "Xi-Zhou qingtongqi duandai," 37.

27. Tang Lan, *Tang Lan quanji*, vol. 7, 150–55, esp. 155.

28. For a discussion of Wu's and Cheng's siblings, see Shaughnessy, "Western Zhou History," 310–12.

29. Jenny F. So, "Where Are the Royal Zhou Bronze Vessels?," unpublished paper delivered at a workshop at the University of Chicago in 2010.

5

The Western Zhou Court and Hedong Salt Lake

Revelations from the
Newly Excavated Ba Bo (Elder Ba) Bronze Vessels

HAN WEI

TRANSLATED BY CHRISTOPHER J. FOSTER

Excavation of the large-scale tomb, M1017, from the Western Zhou cemetery at Dahekou 大河口, Yicheng 翼城, Shanxi, yielded rich burial goods.[1] Included among them are over fifty bronze vessels and three chime-bells, varied in type, decoration style, and set arrangement, revealing that they were cast at different times over the course of a long chronological span. The inscriptions on the bronzes also indicate that not only were these pieces owned by more than a single person, they were potentially the property of multiple different families. In a previous study, I sorted this cache of bronzes into three "groups" based on their dating.[2] Group A, the earliest pieces, date approximately to the reign of King Zhao 昭王 (early 10th c. BCE), bridging the early and mid-Western Zhou period. Group B vessels are slightly later and date to the reign of King Mu 穆王 (mid-10th c. BCE) in the early mid-Western Zhou period. Group C vessels are the latest and date to the late mid-Western Zhou period, around the time of King Gong 恭王 (late 10th c. BCE). Early and mid-Western Zhou elite tombs often contain objects handed down from previous generations, whose origins can be quite complex, with some pieces, for instance, given as gifts by other families, or others taken as the spoils of war.[3] It is not surprising, therefore, that the bronzes found in M1017 appear so mixed.

The vast majority of Group C bronzes, the latest dating pieces in the tomb, carry inscriptions naming a "Ba Bo" 霸伯 or "Elder Ba." This includes two *gui* 簋 tureens with short walls, contracted mouths, and circular feet; two *xu* 盨 containers, which the archaeological report calls "mountain[-shaped] *gui*" (*shan gui* 山簋) based on the names by which they self-identify in their inscriptions. Also in Group C is a vessel with a rectangular body and circular foot (self-identified as *yi* 釴 but referred to as a "square *gui*" [*fanggui* 方簋] in the report). In addition, this group includes four *dou* 豆 serving dishes; one *yu* 盂-style caldron; one *lei* 罍 vat; one *pan* 盘 basin; and one *he* 盉 pot. Judging by their types and decoration, as well as the calligraphy of their inscriptions, all of these bronzes were cast at roughly the same time. Moreover, most of the vessels in Group C are "millet bearing" (*zicheng* 粢 盛) vessels used for storing food. The next most common category is the *pan* basin and *he* pot, which are for storing liquids. There is only a single alcohol vessel, the *lei* vat. Among the earlier Group A and B pieces, there are numerous examples of alcohol vessels like the *zun* 尊 and *you* 卣-type storage vessels and the *jue* 爵, *zhi* 觶, and *gu* 觚-type drinking cups, none of which appear in Group C. This disappearance of alcohol vessels reflects one of the key shifts that took place during the ritual reforms of King Gong's reign.[4] The name Elder Ba 霸伯 refers to the family head of the Ba clan (the *shi* 氏). From the inscription on the Elder Ba *yu* vessel, we know that the name of this "Elder Ba" was Shang 尚. He is most likely the occupant of M1017.

These four vessels all bear the same inscription, and as the archaeological report has already pointed out, they were likely cast at the same time.[5] The Elder Ba *gui* (fig. 5.1a) each have short walls, a contracted mouth, and circular foot, with one set of semicircular handles decorated with animal heads on top, and the entire vessel decorated with a "tile ridge" (*waling* 瓦棱) pattern of horizontal lines. This style of *gui* first appears in the early mid-Western Zhou, which is to say, during the reigns of King Zhao and King Mu. Other representative pieces include the Xian *gui* 賢簋 (*Jicheng* 集成 4104–4105; *Mingtu* 銘圖 5070–5071); You *gui* 友簋 (*Jiecheng* 4194; *Mingtu* 5204); and Marquis of Jin *gui* 晉侯簋 (*Mingtu* 4736–4737).[6] These *gui* tureens all have paired, semicircular handles, with animal heads decorating the top part of the handles. When it comes to the slightly later reigns of King Gong and King Yi 懿王, the handle for this type of *gui* vessel popularly becomes an

Figure 5.1a. Elder Ba *Gui* (Excavation Label M1017:8). *Source:* After Shanxi sheng kaogu yanjiu yuan, *Ba jin jicui*, 277, 279.

Figure 5.1b. Rubbing of the Inscriptions on Its Lid. *Source:* After Shanxi sheng kaogu yanjiu yuan, *Ba jin jicui*, 277, 279.

Figure 5.1c. Rubbing of the Inscriptions on Its Body. *Source:* After Shanxi sheng kaogu yanjiu yuan, *Ba jin jicui*, 277, 279.

animal head in its entirety, with a ring dangling from its mouth. Exemplars include the Doubi *gui* 豆閉簋 (*Jicheng* 4276; *Mingtu* 5326); Shihu *gui* 師虎簋 (*Jicheng* 4316; *Mingtu* 5371); and Guai Bo *gui* 乖伯簋 (*Jicheng* 4331; *Mingtu* 5385). The Elder Ba *gui* are unusually short and wide in body, more so than the other *gui* of this type previously discovered, suggesting a slightly later date for them.

The Elder Ba *xu* containers (fig. 5.2a) have an especially unique shape that has never been seen before. They are rectangular, with rounded corners, deep bellies, and straight walls. Thick knobs in the form of dragon heads are placed on either side of the vessel. The outer edges of the lids have eight upward protrusions shaped like "mountain peaks," which alternate between tall and short peaks, with spaces in-between. On the top surfaces of the lids there is a "large bird" (*daniao* 大鳥) pattern, with four birds set in pairs facing one another. This pattern evidently evolved from the large bird patterns popular during the reigns of Zhao and Mu; however, in this case, the bird's body, crest, and tail feathers are already depicted via elongated, slim lines. The large bird patterns, with facing pairs of birds, decorate the outer edges of the lids and underneath the lips of the vessels, though here the bodies of the birds are simplified, while their crests and tails are extended, which when taken altogether reflects a development toward the curvilinear pattern called *qiequ* 竊曲. The outsides of the vessels' bodies are decorated with large "wavy band" (*bodai* 波帶) patterns, akin to the "mountain peaks" that jut upward on top of the lids. In their inscriptions, the *xu* vessels self-identify as "treasured mountain *gui*" (*bao shan gui* 寶山簋), which is the first appearance of this type of vessel name. Following the traditional classification of bronze vessels, this "mountain *gui*" should actually be regarded as a *xu*-style container. This type of food vessel is first attested toward the end of the mid-Western Zhou period, between the reigns of King Mu and King Gong. To date, our earliest examples include the Marquis Cheng of Ying *xu* 應侯再盨 (*Mingtu* 5639), excavated from Pingdingshan 平頂山 tomb M84; Cheng *xu* 再盨 (*Mingtu* 5666), held in a private collection; and the Neishi *xu* 內史盨, recently acquired by the National Museum of China 中國國家博物館.[7] Two major types of *xu* were known early on: those with four legs, and those with a single circular foot. The former type evolved out of small, rectangular *ding* cauldrons with rounded corners, appended handles, and lids. The latter type of *xu* must have branched off from the *gui*-style tureen with single circular foot, while at the same time being influenced by the form of small, rectangular *ding* vessels.[8] Because *xu* containers served a similar function as *gui* tureens, and there was an affinity between their forms, *xu* initially were often classified as *gui*.[9] The reason why these particular vessels were called "mountain *gui*" must be to describe the upward protrusions shaped like mountain peaks on the lids and large wavy-band patterns on the bodies.

The wavy-band pattern, also called the "wavy curves" (*boqu* 波曲), is one of the most popular decorations employed during the late Western

Zhou and early Spring and Autumn periods, however because of a lack of data, previous scholarship has not been able to identify its origins. The King Zhao period Qi *zun* 啓尊 (*Jicheng* 5983; *Mingtu* 11778) and Qi *you* 啓卣 (*Jicheng* 5410; *Mingtu* 13321) have decoration on their necks that alternates between wavelike lines and circles, but this is still very different from the true wavy-band pattern popular later, therefore we really cannot assert a definite relationship between the two. By the King Gong period, Lu *gui* 親簋 (*Mingtu* 5362) and Marquis Cheng of Ying *xu* (*Mingtu* 5639) vessels already feature circular feet with openwork wavy-band pattern designs. The wavy-band pattern began to appear widely as the primary decoration on the body of bronze vessels in the mid- and late Western Zhou. Even later, toward the end of the late Western Zhou, vessels with lids bearing upward protrusions with wavy-band designs, like on the Elder Ba *xu* under discussion, seem to appear. Late examples include the Jin Hou Jin *hu* 晉侯斷壺 (*Mingtu* 12396–12397) and Liang Qi *hu* 梁其壺 (*Jicheng* 9716–9717; *Mingtu* 12420–12421). The wavy-band pattern on the Elder Ba *xu* is already very close in its appearance to the archetypical wavy-band pattern seen in the late Western Zhou, which pushes the arrival of this design back to King Gong's reign. Moreover, as the name "mountain *gui*" implies, the wavy-band pattern perhaps originates in depictions of mountain peaks.[10] The names "mountain *zun*" 山尊 and "mountain *lei*" 山罍 are found in reference to vessels in the *Zhou li* 周禮 "Chunguan" 春官 entry for "Si Zunyi" 司尊彝, and the *Liji* 禮記 chapter "Mingtang wei" 明堂位. Commentators have interpreted these names as describing decorations on the vessels' bodies that depict mountain ranges. In the *Xunzi* 荀子, chapter "Dalue" 大略, there is a mention of "the Son of Heaven's mountain crown" (*tianzi shanmian* 天子山冕), which quite possibly denotes a royal crown that was either itself shaped like mountains or carried decorations resembling mountains.[11] Indeed, traditional studies on ancient bronzes and inscribed stones (*jinshi xue* 金石學) in the past have referred to the wavy-band pattern as the "mountain pattern" (*shanwen* 山 紋). The Elder Ba *xu* vessels finally help us solve this longstanding riddle.[12]

The excavation report has published rubbings of the inscriptions on the two Elder Ba *gui* vessels and for one of the Elder Ba *xu* containers. The inscriptions are repeated on each vessel's lid and body, making for six rubbings altogether. The inscriptions not only repeat the same content but also the calligraphic style of the writing and orthography of their characters is very similar, suggesting that they were produced by the same scribal hand. A transcription of the text on the Elder Ba *gui*, into modern (traditional) forms so far as possible, is as follows:

Figure 5.2a. Elder Ba *Xu* (Excavation Label M1017:35). *Source:* After Shanxi sheng kaogu yanjiu yuan, *Ba jin jicui*, 284, 287.

Figure 5.2b. Rubbings of the Inscriptions on Its Lid. *Source:* After Shanxi sheng kaogu yanjiu yuan, *Ba jin jicui*, 284, 287.

Figure 5.2c. Rubbings of the Inscriptions on Its Body. *Source:* After Shanxi sheng kaogu yanjiu yuan, *Ba jin jicui*, 284, 287.

In the eleventh month, Younger Jing arrived and requested salt. He offered Elder Ba enticements and had him vaunt his merits. He gave him two hundred covers (for carriage sideboards), two *liang* measures of cinnabar, and two tiger skins. Elder Ba clapped his hands together and bowed, extolling the grace of Younger Jing and taking this opportunity to make a precious *gui* tureen. May [we, Elder Bo's family,] for ten thousand years of sons of sons and grandsons eternally treasure and use it.

唯十又一月，井叔來求鹽，蔑霸伯懋，事伐，用壽 (幬) 二百、丹
二量、虎皮二．霸伯拜稽首，對揚井叔休，用作寶簋．其萬年子子
孫其永寶用．

The inscriptions on the Elder Ba *xu* container are the same, with the sole exception being that the phrase "treasured *gui*" is replaced with "treasured mountain *gui*."

It is important to note that the writing in these inscriptions is very idiosyncratic and irregular. Often a single character is written in multiple ways, with the addition or removal of strokes and whole components, the substitution of different components instead, or even downright errors. Take for example the character *ba* 霸 in the Elder Ba *gui* inscriptions. Its bottom component is written with the components *shi* 事 on the left, and *ge* 各 on the right. In the Elder Ba *xu* inscriptions however, these components are replaced with *dong* 東 on the left and *yue* 月 on the right. As another example, consider how, in some of these inscriptions, the two horizontal strokes of "cinnabar" (*dan* 丹) traverse its vertical lines, making the character indistinguishable from "well" (*jing* 井). Moreover, the "two" (*er* 二) in the phrase "two tiger skins" (*hupi er* 虎皮二) is miswritten as "one" (*yi* 一) in the inscriptions on the lid and body of the other Elder Ba *gui* (M1017:8; figs. 5.1b, 5.1c), the body of the second Elder Ba *gui* (M1017:40), and on the lid of the Elder Ba *xu* (M1017:35; fig. 5.2b). Additional examples could be raised, but I will not elaborate on them here, as the focus of this chapter lies elsewhere.

Crucial to my argument is the line from these inscriptions that "Younger Jing arrived and requested salt" (井叔來求鹽). Jing Shu 井叔, or Younger Jing, is the name of a person. This name has appeared in other inscriptions as well, such as those on the Hu *ding* (*Jicheng* 2838; *Mingtu* 2515), Chi *zun* 趩尊 (*Jicheng* 6516; *Mingtu* 10659), Mian *gui* 免簋 (*Jicheng* 4240; *Mingtu* 5268), Mian *zun* 免尊 (*Jicheng* 6006; *Mingtu* 11805), and Mi Shu Shi Cha *gui* 弭叔師察簋 (*Jicheng* 4253–4254; *Mingtu* 5291–5292). According to my previous research, Younger Jing refers to the primary branch head (*zongzi* 宗子) of the Jing Shu clan 井叔氏 (Younger Jing clan), which was an elite family that held office in the Western Zhou court. As part of a derivative family line, Younger Jing was also head of a collateral lineage (*xiaozong* 小宗) to the Jing Bo clan 井伯氏 (Elder Jing clan). The Younger Jing clan branched off from the Elder Jing clan toward the end of King Gong's reign. The first generation Younger Jing was likely a brother (from the same mother) of Elder Jing Lu 井伯娹. Elder Jing Lu was an important

1 figure, having served the Zhou court as Grand Commander (*zhong sima*
2 冢司馬). This particular Younger Jing would have served at roughly the
3 same time as Elder Jing Lu, namely from the end of King Gong's reign
4 to the early part of King Yi's reign. In the inscription on the Yu *ding* 禹
5 鼎 (*Jicheng* 2833; *Mingtu* 2498), cast during the reign of King Li 厲王, he
6 is addressed by the honorific Youtai Shu 幽大叔 or (literally) "Remote and
7 Lofty Younger." This is because he served as the first primary branch head
8 for the Younger Jing clan.
9   In the winter of 1980, the family cemetery of the Jing Shu clan was
10 discovered at the Zhangjiapo 張家坡 site, near Chang'an 長安, Shaanxi.[13]
11 Three generations of men, all titled Younger Jing, were buried in this cem-
12 etery, with the earliest tomb, M170, likely belonging to the first generation,
13 the one known as Youtai Shu or "Remote and Lofty Younger."[14] In light of
14 the dating for the Elder Ba *gui* and Elder Ba *xu* vessels, the Younger Shu
15 mentioned in their inscriptions can only be the first generation Younger Shu,
16 namely the same individual appearing on the inscriptions on the Hu *ding*,
17 Chi *zun*, Mian *gui*, Mian *zun*, among others, listed earlier.[15] Conversely,
18 because of the appearance of Younger Shu in their inscriptions, the Elder
19 Ba *gui* and *xu* vessels must date no earlier than the reign of King Gong. In
20 the archaeological report for the Dahekou cemetery, tomb M1017 is said
21 to belong to "the early phase of the mid-Western Zhou" (西周中期偏早階
22 段), but clearly it should be dated slightly later.[16]
23   Before the formal publication of the rubbings to the Elder Ba *gui* and
24 *xu* inscriptions, some scholars relied on photographs of the inscriptions to
25 transcribe the text. The inscriptions were not always clear in these photo-
26 graphs, however, and led to a few mistakes. For example, the two characters
27 I give as *qiu yan* 求鹽, were transcribed by other scholars initially as "wheat"
28 (*mai* 麥) and "then" (*nai* 迺 >乃) and read with a sentence break inserted
29 between them.[17] With the data now available from the rubbings, it is clear
30 that this interpretation is incorrect. The first graph is written in the inscrip-
31 tions as ![glyph] or ![glyph], the latter being a more complex form that adds a hand
32 component (*you* 又). Huang Yifei 黃益飛 and Xie Yaoting 謝堯亭 transcribe
33 the character as *hui* 桒 and argue that to *hui* salt was akin to the phrases
34 "to offer *hui*-prayers for grain" or "to offer *hui*-prayers for the harvest" seen
35 often in the Yin [Shang] oracle-bone inscriptions, namely, it means to pray
36 for an abundant yield of salt.[18] In oracle-bone and bronze inscriptions, the
37 verb *hui* usually means "to pray for" (*qiqiu* 祈求), and many scholars read it
38 as the word "to pray" (*dao* 禱).[19] Yet in Western Zhou bronze inscriptions,
39 *hui* is a specific type of sacrifice that, grammatically speaking, only appears
40

on its own and never takes a direct object. In the oracle-bone divinations, the seeming objects, the words "grain" (*he* 禾) and "harvest" (*nian* 年) can be verbal, meaning "to bring in an abundant yield [of grain or harvest]." But it is clear that in Western Zhou bronze inscriptions, "salt" (*yan* 鹽) or "crude salt" (*lu* 鹵) are only used as nouns, and cannot carry the further meaning of "to bring in an abundant yield [of salt]." For these reasons, interpreting the phrase *hui yan* as "to pray for an abundant yield of salt" does not make sense grammatically.

In my opinion, the character *hui* in the Elder Ba *gui* and *xu* inscriptions should be read as "to seek out" (*qiu* 求).[20] Drawing on pertinent examples from the Guodian 郭店 bamboo-strip manuscripts, Chen Jian 陳劍 has argued that in Western Zhou bronze inscriptions, the character written from the components *chuo* 辵 and *hui* 羍 should be transcribed as *qiu* 逑 (match, mate) and could also be read as the word *qiu* 仇 (companion), in the sense of "to marry, join together" (*pipei* 匹配).[21] Following this line of thought, directly transcribing *hui* as *qiu* should be unproblematic. *Hui* often appears in the formulaic "benedictions" (*guci* 嘏辭) that conclude many Western Zhou bronze inscriptions, such as in the phrase "use [this vessel] to seek out longevity" (*yong hui shou* 用羍壽) found on the Wei *ding* 衛鼎 (*Jicheng* 2733; *Mingtu* 2346), "use [this vessel] to entreat [the ancestors] and seek out ten thousand years 用祈羍萬年" from the Bo Hao *gui* 伯椃簋 (*Jicheng* 4073; *Mingtu* 5078), and "use [this vessel] to seek blessings 用羍福" on the Ji Ning *zun* 季宁尊 (*Jicheng* 5940; *Mingtu* 11715). Previously, *hui* 羍 has been read as meaning "to pray [to a spirit]" (*dao* 禱). In these instances, however, taking it as the word "to seek out" (*qiu*) is actually more appropriate.[22]

The character for "salt" (*yan* 鹽) in the Elder Ba *gui* inscriptions is written as ▨, with *lu* 鹵 as the upper component, and *kou* 口 as the lower component. In the Elder Ba *xu* inscriptions, it is given as ▨, with *lu* again as the upper component but *min* 皿 as the lower component instead. These are clearly variants of the same word, with either the *kou* component serving as a simplification of *min* or *min* as an embellishment upon *kou*. Before the Elder Ba *gui* and *xu* vessels were discovered, the only word for salt seen in the Western Zhou bronze inscriptions was *lu* 鹵 (more on this later). In the *Shuowen jiezi* 說文解字, under the *Lu* 鹵 classifier, the entry for the head word *lu* reads: "A salty region in the west. . . . In Anding [Commandery] there is a Lu County. In the east it is referred to as *chi* 㢟, in the west it is referred to as *lu*" (西方鹹地也. . . . 安定有鹵縣, 東方謂之㢟, 西方謂之鹵).[23] Duan Yucai 段玉裁 (1735–1815), in his *Shuowen jiezi zhu* 說文解字注, under the *Yan* 鹽 classifier, writes: "*Yan* is *lu*. When it is produced naturally, we call it *lu* (crude salt); when it is produced by man, we call it *yan* (salt)" (鹽，鹵也。天生曰鹵，人生曰鹽).[24] Thus, in antiquity the word *lu* referred to a place in the west that was either a salt lick or an area where salt was produced. It was also used as a more general reference for salt itself. If we are to specify further, then naturally precipitated pieces of crude salt were called *lu*, while salt refined by man through heating processes was called *yan*. In antiquity, salt in the Central Plain region primarily came from the salt lake in Hedong 河東 (in modern-day Yuncheng 運城, Shanxi). One of the defining characteristics of such a salt lake is that, during the summer season, crude salt naturally precipitates here (further details to follow). Since people in these early periods referred to the crude salt produced from salt lakes as *lu*, in the *Shiji* 史記 chapter "Huozhi liezhuan" 貨殖列傳, it states that "in Shandong (lit., east of the mountains) they eat sea salt, in Shanxi (lit., west of the mountains) they eat *yanlu* (lake salt)" (山東食海鹽山西食鹽鹵).[25] On slip no. 147 in the mid–Warring States period Baoshan 包山 Chu strips, there is the line: "Chen Bao and Song Xian, on behalf of the king, boiled *yan* 'salt' from the sea" (陳憊宋獻為王煮鹽於海).[26] Scholars such as Lin Yun 林澐, Liu Zhao 劉釗, and Zhao Pingan 趙平安 have all transcribed the graph 鹽 as *yan* 鹽. Zhao Pingan, moreover, has further argued that the character is a "syssemantograph, associated ideas character" (*huiyi* 會意). Its original meaning was "to boil (and make) salt," with the lower component, from *min* 皿, representing a utensil used in the boiling to make salt. Zhao provides a number of examples of graphs composed of the components *min* 皿 and *lu* 鹵 found on Warring States–period seal inscriptions as well. He transcribes these as "salt" (*yan* 鹽).[27] The graph 鹽 in the Elder Ba *xu* inscriptions is identical to the Warring States examples with *min* and *lu*; there is absolutely no doubt that *yan* is the correct transcription. This latest discovery, therefore, pushes the earliest appearance of the character *yan* back to the mid-Western Zhou. In light of the inscriptional data, it appears that *lu* and *yan* both referred to table salt, and, specifically, to the crude salt produced from the Hedong Salt Lake. There is, moreover, no indication of any distinction in these terms between salt that was "naturally produced" versus being "manmade."

The line "Younger Jing arrived and requested salt" (井叔來求鹽) thus describes how Younger Jing arrived in the Ba clan's territory and requested salt from Elder Ba. The Ba clan were enfeoffed in the land around Yicheng County 翼城, Shanxi. This area lacks salt resources of its own, but, located about one hundred kilometers directly to the southwest, is the celebrated

Hedong Salt Lake. As such, the salt possessed by Elder Ba could only have come from this salt lake. In the inscription on the Jin Jiang *ding* 晉姜鼎 (*Jicheng* 2826; *Mingtu* 2491), which dates to the early Spring and Autumn period, there is the line: "With fanfare I dispatched a thousand carts of salt reserves that had been awarded to us" (嘉遣我賜鹵積千輛). Because of the geographic location of Jin, scholars early on understood *luji* 鹵積 in the inscription to refer to salt produced from the Hedong Salt Lake. The discovery of the Elder Ba *gui* and *xu* vessels offer even earlier direct textual evidence for the production of salt at the Hedong Salt Lake dating back to the mid-Western Zhou.

The Hedong Salt Lake is located in modern-day Yuncheng 運城 city, Shanxi. In antiquity, it was also called Gu 盬.[28] In the *Shuowen jiezi*, under the *Yan* 鹽 classifier, it describes *gu* 盬 as: "Hedong Salt Lake, which has a length of 51 *li* (half-kilometers), a width of 7 *li*, and a perimeter of 116 *li*" (河東鹽池, 袤五十一里, 廣七里, 周百十六里).[29] In the *Zhou li* "Tianguan" 天官, for the entry on *yanren* 鹽人 ("salt stewards"), it declares: "When conducting sacrifices, [salt stewards] furnish bitter salt and powdered salt" (祭祀共其苦鹽散鹽).[30] According to Zheng Xuan's 鄭玄 (127–200) commentary, "Du Zichun 杜子春 read *ku* 苦 [bitter] as *gu* 盬, referring to using salt directly after its harvest, without being refined through boiling" (杜子春讀苦為鹽, 謂出鹽直用, 不湅治). In his subcommentary to this line, Jia Gongyan 賈公彥 (fl. 650) argues: "The character *ku* 苦 [bitter] should be *gu* 盬. This *gu* is [salt] that comes from the salt lake, this is our granulated salt today" (苦當為鹽, 鹽謂出於鹽池, 今之顆鹽是也).[31] When the *Shiji* chapter "Huozhi liezhuan" mentions that "Yi Tun used *guyan* [salt] to grow wealthy" (猗頓用鹽鹽起), what it refers to as *guyan* 鹽鹽 is the same as *kuyan* 苦鹽 found in the *Zhou li*, namely coarsely granulated salt produced in a salt lake. Because the water of a salt lake contains sodium sulfate (Na_2SO_4), the crude salt it produces has an extremely bitter taste, therefore it was given a technical name of *gu* 盬. This type of crude salt is naturally precipitated (via evaporation), and for this reason Du Zichun notes that it was "not prepared via boiling," which means that this type of salt does not require further refining. The *Shuijing zhu* 水經注 entry on Su Shui 涑水 includes the following record:[32]

> Hedong Salt Lake is called Gu 盬. Today the lake is seventy *li* east to west and seventeen *li* north to south. (The water) is of a purple hue, it is clear and still, forming a pool that does not flow onward. The water produces rock salt, naturally imprinted

(upon the shore), if taken in the morning it returns again at night, without ever diminishing in quantity.

河東鹽池謂之鹽. 今池水東西七十里, 南北十七里, 紫色澄渟, 潭 而不流. 水出石鹽, 自然印成, 朝取夕復, 終無減損.

This exceptional feature encouraged large-scale exploitation of the salt lake, the earliest such harvesting of a natural salt resource in North China. Its bountiful reserves were almost inexhaustible, extracted continuously from the Neolithic period all the way to the twentieth century. Because this type of crude salt is formed naturally, it only needs to be filtered out from the water and does not require any further processing. There are, however, rigid seasonal restrictions to its production, which depends upon the intense sunlight and sweltering heat of the summer and scorching southerly winds. Even in the Tang and Song periods, when the "embankment fields method" (*qizhong fa* 畦種法) had already been adopted widely for the creation of lake salt dried in the sun, climatic conditions still impacted production cycles: "On the first day of the second month of the year, till the land and build the embankments; begin planting in the fourth month; then cease in the eighth month" (歲二月一日墾畦, 四月始種, 八月乃止).[33] In other words, the production of lake salt was primarily concentrated in the summer, between the fourth and fifth months (of the Song calendar).[34]

Considering the seasonal nature of salt production, note how the inscriptions on the Elder Ba *gui* and *xu* vessels begin with the date: "In the eleventh month . . ." The Zhou calendar is known to have been "established upon the *zi* month" (*jian zi* 建子), which means that it takes the eleventh month of the Xia calendar as the beginning of the year. For this reason, in the Zhou calendar, the "eleventh month" is actually the ninth month of the Xia calendar, which is precisely when the season for producing lake salt would have just concluded. It cannot be merely a coincidence, therefore, that Younger Jing chose to come at this time to "request salt."

The next question that needs to be asked then, is whether Younger Jing's "requesting salt" of Elder Ba was a private trade between aristocratic lords, or if he was acting as a representative of the royal court in state-sponsored dealings. Was Younger Jing acting on behalf of his and his family's self-interest? Or was he sent by the Zhou king, completing a mission assigned to him as an official of the court? Was the salt that Elder Ba handed over to Younger Jing produced by his family and regarded as their own possession? Or was Elder Ba acting as an official of the court as well, authorized by the Zhou king to supervise the salt's production, and now he was required to deliver it to court?

To answer these questions, let us turn our attention back to the inscriptions, and specifically to the line: "(He) offered Elder Ba enticements and had him vaunt his merits" (蔑霸伯懋事伐).[35] The phrase *miemao* 蔑懋 refers to a type of ritual act, though scholars are divided in their opinion of what, precisely, it entails. Tang Lan 唐蘭 argued that "*mie* 蔑 should be read as *fa* 伐, 'to extol or boast of,' and X 厤 read as *li* 歷, 'past merits,' with the phrase *mie* X meaning 'to extol his merits'" (蔑讀為伐厤讀如歷蔑厤是伐其經歷).[36] This explanation has been very influential, and many scholars now read these two words directly as "to extol the past merits" (*mieli* 蔑歷 or *fali* 伐歷).[37] Recently, however, Chen Jian 陳劍 has proposed that X 厤 be transcribed as *mao* 懋, with a meaning of "encouragement, enticement" (*mianli* 勉勵). He explains that the word *mie* marks a passive, literally meaning "to cover (with)" (*fubei* 覆被).[38] At present, there is greater evidence in support of Chen Jian's interpretation. When *miemao* 蔑懋 is mentioned in Western Zhou bronze inscriptions, it is always the case that the person conducting the action is of a higher status than the recipient. Most often, the Zhou king is the actor, while an aristocratic lord is acted upon. There are, however, a number of examples where an aristocratic lord conducts *miemao* toward a person of lower status. This occurs in three types of situations:

1. Between the head of a family (*zongzi* 宗子) and an ordinary person who belongs to his clan. For example, the inscription on the Fan *you* 繁卣 vessel (*Jicheng* 5430; *Mingtu* 13343) records how the duke (*gong* 公, a family head), after offering a "*rong* sacrifice" 肜祀, proceeded to "offer Fan enticements" 蔑繁懋. In this case, Fan 繁 was probably a member of the duke's clan.

2. Between the head of a family and a retainer. For example, the inscription on the Ci *zun* 次尊 vessel (*Jicheng* 5994; *Mingtu* 11792) bears the lines: "Duchess Ji ordered Ci to manage the hunting entourage. Ci was enticed (to act)" (公姞命次司田人次蔑懋). Duchess Ji 公姞 was the head of the family, while Ci 次 was ordered to manage the "hunting entourage" 田人, suggesting that he served as a retainer.

3. Between a superior and his subordinate, following a hierarchy
   dictated by their respective official duties. For example, the
   inscription on the Yi *you* 稽卣 vessel (*Jicheng* 5411; *Mingtu*
   13322) states: "Yi followed Commander Yong Fu and pro-
   tected the borders at You garrison, he was enticed (to act)"
   (稽從師雍父戍于由𠂤, 蔑懋). As part of this military activity,
   Yi served as a subordinate of Commander Yong Fu 師雍父
   and received "enticements."

The relationship between Younger Jing and Elder Ba does not fit either
of the relationships outlined in 1 or 2, but is similar to what is found in
category 3. On this, we may also consult the Peng Bo Cheng *gui* 倗伯再
簋 vessel inscription, excavated from tomb M2 in Hengshui 橫水 cemetery,
which is not far from Dahekou, to its southwest. The inscription reads:

> In the twenty-third year, on the first auspicious day, *wushu* (35),
> Duke Yi offered Cheng, the Elder of Peng, enticements, (after
> which) an assistant made the announcement. He ordered (Cheng
> to receive) a bronze carriage and a pennant. Cheng clapped his
> hands together and bowed, extolling the duke's grace. I take this
> as an opportunity to cast this precious *zun* vessel for my father.

> 唯廿又三年初吉戊戌, 益公蔑倗伯再懋, 右告, 令金車旂, 再拜手
> 稽首, 對揚公休, 用作朕考寶尊.

The inscription documents how Duke Yi, a senior court official, "offered
enticements" to Cheng, the Elder of Peng, and bestowed gifts upon him. The
phrase "assisted to announce" (*you gao* 右告) is perhaps an abbreviation for
"some person who assisted and announced Cheng to Duke Yi" (某人右告再
于益公), which suggests that, following the "offering of enticements" 蔑懋,
a ceremony was held that resembled "appointments" (*ceming* 冊命, literally
"inscribing the orders"). This demonstrates that Cheng, the Elder of Peng,
must be regarded as a subordinate of Duke Yi. The Elder of Peng and the
Elder of Ba both occupied similar positions (discussed further later). For
this reason, it appears that the relationship between Younger Jing and Elder
Ba is likely also that of superior and subordinate, following the hierarchy
dictated by their respective official duties.

The compound *shifa* 事伐 is not seen elsewhere in our corpus of
bronze inscriptions, and no satisfactory interpretation of the phrase has

yet to be proposed. If I were to offer a conjecture, *shi* 事 here is perhaps read as the verb "to cause, to make X do Y" (*shi* 使), as in the Younger Jing "caused" Elder Ba to do something. The word *fa* 伐, when used as a noun, can mean "meritorious deeds" (*gonglao* 功勞). For example, in the *Zuo zhuan* 左傳, Duke Zhuang 莊公, year 28, there is the line "and also make your merit manifest" (且旌君伐), to which Du Yu 杜預 comments: "The word *fa* means merit" (*fa gong ye* 伐功也).[39] The phrase "meritorious deeds" (*gongfa* 功伐) also appears frequently in Pre-Qin and early imperial texts. The term *fa* is likewise used to express one's "level of merit" (*laogong dengji* 功勞等級). *Shiji*, *juan* 18, "Gaozu gong chenhouzhe nianbiao" 高祖功臣侯者年表, explains:[40]

> In antiquity, meritorious officials had five grades: To erect the ancestral temples and establish the altars of soil and grain through virtue is called "laudable" (*xun* 勛); (to do so) with (fine) speech is called "skillful" (*lao* 勞); the use of strength is called "industrious" (*gong* 功); exhibiting one's quality is called "estimable" (*fa* 伐); and to amass (many) days (of service) is called "experienced" (*yue* 閱).

> 古者人臣功有五品: 以德立宗廟定社稷曰勛, 以言曰勞, 用力曰功, 明其等曰伐, 積日曰閱.

Similarly, the term *fa* can also be used as a verb, meaning "to flaunt (one's) merits" (*kuayao gonglao* 誇耀功勞), and in particular "to boast about oneself" (*ziwo kuayao* 自我誇耀). For example, in the *Yupian* 玉篇, under the *Ren* 人 classifier, it states: "To brag about oneself is called *fa*" (*zi jin yue fa* 自矜曰伐).[41] The *Han shu* 漢書 also gives the line: "Boasted of his own merits" (*zi fa qi gong* 自伐其功).[42] Thus, the phrase *shifa* 使伐 in the Elder Ba bronze inscription must mean "(Younger Jing) had (Elder Ba) recount the extent of his merit." The "merit" in this context perhaps refers to Elder Ba's contributions from the salt harvest season that had just concluded.

The inscription continues by stating: "(He) gave (him) two hundred covers (for carriage sideboards), two *liang* measures of cinnabar, and two tiger skins." These were the rewards that Younger Jing bestowed upon Elder Ba, which can be viewed as a prize for his meritorious service. Most scholars read *shou* 壽 as "curtain, canopy" *chou* 幬, which refers to leather pieces that cover a carriage's sideboards. An amount of "two hundred" was fairly generous. The term *dan* 丹 is cinnabar, which was a red pigment used often in the Pre-Qin period. The compound "red lacquer" (*danqi* 丹漆), which incorporates cinnabar, was important raw material used in the production of lacquerware. The term *liang* 量 was likely both the name of a type of vessel used for measuring and also a unit of volume based on that measure. The term "tiger skin" (*hupi* 虎皮) refers to a precious animal hide. It is an item that appears in other inscriptions frequently, sometimes written as "tiger furs" (*huqiu* 虎裘). The rewards Elder Ba received are all items that possess real economic value, differing in nature from the "ornamental garments, mandated clothing (indicative of rank)" (*mingfu* 命服) in appointment inscriptions. This suggests that Elder Ba could receive fiscal remuneration from his superiors, for the expenditures he incurred completing his charge.[43]

In light of this, it appears that Elder Ba was an official dispatched by the Zhou court to southern Shanxi, to organize and oversee the production of salt from the salt lake. Younger Jing was his superior, an official from the court responsible for the production, transport, and distribution of salt. The *Zhou li* "Tianguan" entry for "Zhongzai" 冢宰 lists officials called "salt stewards" (*yanren* 鹽人) and states:[44]

> Salt stewards are in charge of (carrying out) government ordinances concerning salt, so as to provide salt for all events. When conducting sacrifices, they furnish bitter salt and powdered salt. For guests, they furnish "(tiger-)shaped" salt and powdered salt. For the king's meals, they furnish sweetened salt. The empress and crown prince are treated in the same fashion. Whenever a feast is held, boiled salt is used in accordance with the precepts and ordinances.

> 鹽人掌鹽之政令，以共百事之鹽。祭祀共其苦鹽、散鹽，賓客共其形鹽、散鹽，王之膳差共飴鹽，后及世子亦如之。凡齋事，鬻鹽以待戒令。

This excerpt is often cited as testimony for the production and consumption of salt during the Pre-Qin period. Although the *Zhou li* describes "salt stewards" as being "in charge of (carrying out) government ordinances concerning salt, so as to provide salt for all events," in fact, they were only responsible for providing various types of salt for ceremonies and daily meals held at the palace. These salt stewards, according to the *Zhou li*, moreover, only consisted of relatively low-status workers, "two eunuchs, twenty salt maids, and forty servants" (奄二人女鹽二十人奚四十人). For this reason, "salt stewards" are listed after the "spice stewards" (*hairen* 醢人) and "vinegar stewards" (*xiren* 醯人) in the list of subordinates to the minister of state (*zhongzai* 冢宰) and are nothing more than palace kitchen staff who handle condiments. Although Younger Jing's position in the court perhaps necessitated that he interact with such "salt stewards," his rank was far higher than the personnel described in the *Zhou li*.[45]

Mention of salt production and consumption from our received corpus of Pre-Qin works can be counted on one's fingers, while there are even fewer contemporaneous records preserved in our paleographic sources. Feng Shi 馮時 has argued that the character *lu* 鹵 seen in the Yinxu oracle-bone inscriptions should be read as "salt" (*yan* 鹽) and refers to the Hedong Salt Lake. Based on these materials, Feng believes that already in the Shang period, production at the salt lake was strictly managed. The title "petty salt officer" (*lu xiaochen* 鹵小臣) appears in the oracle-bone inscriptions (see *Heji* 5596), and therefore certain scholars contend that the Shang court established a position for overseeing the salt industry.[46] The reading of these inscriptions, however, is still largely uncertain, and the interpretations just presented are not yet adopted by scholarly consensus. Since the crude salt produced from the salt lake is naturally formed, and does not require additional refining, the situation is not analogous to that found in the Shang and Zhou salt production sites in the Three Gorges region or along the Northeast coastline, where an extraordinary number of "helmet-shaped" (*kuixing* 盔形) pottery vessels used for salt production have been excavated. Despite many years of searching, archaeologists have yet to discover any ancient remains related to the salt industry in the vicinity of the salt lake.[47] However, a little over ten kilometers to the south of the salt lake, there is the site of Qingliangsi 清涼寺, Ruicheng 芮城, in the southern foothills of Zhongtiao Mountains 中條山, where a Longshan-period cemetery was discovered featuring numerous sacrificial victims and rich with jade goods. Because the site is situated in the Zhongtiao Mountain Range, near what would have been an important route for the transportation of salt in antiquity, and moreover, because this particular cemetery is so exceptional, archaeologists believe that it belonged to a tribe that amassed a large amount of wealth by controlling the trade of salt.[48] This is certainly a reasonable hypothesis. The site of Dongxiafeng 東下馮, in Xia County 夏縣, is located approximately thirty kilometers to the northeast of the salt lake. It is the largest Erlitou culture residential site discovered in southern Shanxi to date and was continually occupied until the early Shang period.[49] In the southwest corner of the wall in the site's fifth phase (which is equivalent to the early Shang, Erligang 二里崗 lower strata), over forty circular building foundations were discovered, forming seven rows, with six to seven structures in each row. The shapes of these structures are all the same, consisting of circles with diameters 8.5–9.5 m in length. These are clearly not standard lodgings but were likely storerooms instead. Liu Li 劉莉 and Chen Xingcan 陳星燦 argue that these features match how ancient salt silos are described in the *Tiangong kaiwu* 天工開物 (published in 1637) and therefore suggest that they may be storerooms used to keep salt during the Shang dynasty.[50] Dongxiafeng was an important Xia- to early Shang-period settlement in the Yuncheng Basin and served as a strategically positioned stronghold by which the Xia and Shang courts could control the copper and lake salt resources in southern Shanxi (also known as "southern Jin" 晋南).[51]

For the Western Zhou dynasty, records concerning lake salt appear from the middle of King Mu's reign to those of King Gong and King Yi. The *Mu tianzi zhuan* 穆天子傳, *juan* 6, documents: "On the day *yiyou* (22), the Son of Heaven headed west, crossing [Mount] Xing, and then headed southwest. On the day *wuzi* (25), he arrived at the salt (harvesting locale)" (乙酉天子西絕鈃隥, 乃遂西南, 戊子至于鹽).[52] Based on the *Mu tianzi zhuan* account, the *Jinben zhushu jinian* 今本竹書紀年 writes: "In winter (of the fifteenth year of King Mu's reign), the king surveyed the salt marshes" (冬王觀于鹽澤).[53] During King Mu's tour, he made a special point to survey the salt lake, revealing how much he valued this important natural resource. The large-scale exploitation of the salt lake by the Western Zhou court perhaps started at this point, although the mention of salt in bronze inscriptions occurs on later vessels dating to the reigns of King Gong and King Yi. The inscription on the Mian *pan* 免盤 (Jicheng 10161; Mingtu 14515) vessel reads:

> In the fifth month, on the first auspicious day, the king was in Zhou. He commanded the document maker and inner court archivist to award Mian a hundred measures of salt. Mian offered Jing Nü (enticements, giving a portion of) the king's grace. I take this as an opportunity to cast this *panhe* basin. May (my progeny) for ten thousand years treasure and use it.
>
> 唯五月初吉, 王在周, 命作册內史賜免鹵百隥. 免蔑静女王休, 用作盤盉, 其萬年寶用.

Other vessels cast by this same individual include the Mian *gui* 免簋 (*Jicheng* 4240; *Mingtu* 5268), Mian *hu* 免瑚 (*Jicheng* 4626; *Mingtu* 5974),

Mian *zun* 免尊 (*Jicheng* 6006; *Mingtu* 11805), and Mian *you* 免卣 (*Jicheng* 5418; *Mingtu* 13330). Guo Moruo 郭沫若 and Chen Mengjia 陳夢家 both date the Mian vessels to the reign of King Yi, and this is followed by most scholars.[54] The inscriptions on the Mian *gui*, Mian *zun*, and Mian *you* mention a Younger Shu serving as "court guarantor" (*youzhe* 右者). This should be the same Younger Shu who appears in the Elder Ba *gui* and *xu* inscriptions. Following the general rules for appointment inscriptions, Mian was perhaps a subordinate of Younger Shu. Guo Moruo proposes that the term 隬 from the phrase "a hundred measures of salt" 鹵百隬, refers to "a vessel that holds salt" (*cheng lu zhi qi* 盛鹵之器), while Tang Lan 唐蘭 suspects that it stands for a "square basket" (*kuang* 筐) or a "jar" (*fou* 缶).[55] Regardless of what sort of container this was, a hundred's worth of them is no small number. Therefore, Mian was able to take a portion of the salt awarded to him by the Zhou king, "the king's grace" (*wang xiu* 王休), and regift it to Jing Nü 靜女, who was likely a member of the same tribe as Mian.

New evidence for the awarding of salt during the Western Zhou period may be found on the Dian *gui* 典簋 (*Mingtu xu* 422) recently acquired by the National Museum of China.[56] Its inscription reads:

> In the twenty-fourth year, after the full moon, on the day *dingsi* (54), in the eighth month, (the Zhou king) awarded a hundred carriages worth of salt from the silos. Dian takes this as an opportunity to cast a precious *gui* vessel for his resplendent deceased father.

唯廿年又四年, 在八月既望丁巳, 賜廩鹵百車. 典用作厥文考寶簋.

The Dian *gui* is a *yu* 盂-style caldron-shaped *gui* tureen that has appended handles and a lid. Its morphology is very similar to that of the Jin *gui* 新簋 (*Mingtu* 5295), which is also held by the National Museum of China.[57] The only difference is that the handles on the Dian *gui* extend further up beyond the rim of the vessel, and the top-half of the body is decorated with just a few simple "cord-line patterns" (*xianwen* 弦紋), whereas the Jin *gui* features the "dragons with heads looking backward pattern" (*gushoulong wen* 顧首龍紋). The date on the Jin *gui* inscription reads: "In the twenty-eighth year, after the growing brightness, on the day *dingmao* (4), in the first month" (廿又八年正月既生霸丁卯), which I believe refers to the twenty-eighth year of King Gong's reign.[58] The year recorded in the Dian *gui* is in fact "the twenty-fourth year" (二十四年). As luck would

Figure 5.3a. Dian *Gui*. *Source:* After Zhongguo guojia bowuguan, *Zhongguo guojia bowuguan guancang wenwu yanjiu congshu, Qingtong qi juan (Xi Zhou)*, 204, 205.

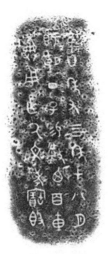

Figure 5.3b. Rubbings of the Inscriptions on Its Lid. *Source:* After Zhongguo guojia bowuguan, *Zhongguo guojia bowuguan guancang wenwu yanjiu congshu, Qingtong qi juan (Xi Zhou)*, 204, 205.

Figure 5.3c. Rubbings of the Inscriptions on Its Body. *Source:* After Zhongguo guojia bowuguan, *Zhongguo guojia bowuguan guancang wenwu yanjiu congshu, Qingtong qi juan (Xi Zhou)*, 204, 205.

have it, the National Museum of China holds yet another vessel, the Lu *gui* 親簋 (*Mingtu* 5362), which dates to the mid-Western Zhou period and likewise bears a date with "the twenty-fourth year." The day notation given on this Lu *gui* reads, "after the full moon, on the day *gengyan* (27), in the ninth month" (九月既望庚寅). This is exactly thirty-three days after the day recorded on the Dian *gui*, "after the full moon, on the day *dingsi* (54), in the eighth month" (八月既望丁巳). The events documented in these two inscriptions undoubtedly occurred in the same year. Zhu Fenghan 朱鳳瀚 dates the Dian *gui* to the reign of King Mu.[59] Yet, many years ago, I pointed out that the Lu *gui* should actually date to the twenty-fourth year of King Gong's reign.[60] Since the events in the Dian *gui* and Lu *gui* took place during the same year, then the Dian *gui* could only date to the reign of King Gong as well. As such, the "awarding of a hundred carriages worth of salt from the silos" 賜廩鹵百車 documented on the Dian *gui* happened at a time not too distant from the events found in the Elder Ba *gui* and *xu*, and Mian *pan* inscriptions.

In the Dian *gui* inscription, the subject is missing for the line: "Awarded a hundred carriages worth of salt from the silos." This is fairly rare for this type of "reward" (*shangci* 賞賜) inscription. Considering that "a hundred carriages" was probably an even greater volume of salt than the "hundred X-containers" found on the Mian *pan*, I believe that it must be the Zhou king who awarded the salt documented on the Dian *gui*.[61] Measuring salt by means of "carriages" is also found in the inscription on the Jin Jiang *ding* 晉姜鼎, where it records "salt reserves (in the amount of) one thousand carts" (鹵積千輛). The words *liang* 輛 and *che* 車 have the same meaning, namely "a cart, carriage." The phrase "silo salt" (*linlu* 廩鹵) on the Dian *gui* inscription also deserves our close attention. The original meaning of the word *lin* 廩 is "a storeroom for keeping grain." The circular buildings discovered at the Dongxiafeng site in Xia County, introduced before, were quite possibly "granaries" (*lin* 廩). Of course, a storeroom for grain could also be used for salt, and the "salt from the silos" likely refers to salt that was kept within such storerooms. During the Song dynasty (960–1279), facilities installed in the vicinity of the Hedong Salt Lake that used to temporarily store crude salt were called "huts" (*an* 庵). The term *an* 庵 was then also used as a unit of measure for calculating volumes of crude salt.[62] The term *an*, taken literally, was probably similar to the salt silos described in the *Tiangong kaiwu*, which were simply constructed warehouses, built out of brushwood and logs, with a cylindrical base and a rounded top that comes to a point. The *lin*-style silos used to store salt in the Western Zhou were probably similar facilities.

We should also note the timing for the award of salt recorded in the Dian *gui*. It states that this occurred in the eighth month of the Zhou calendar, while the Elder Ba *gui* and *xu* inscriptions both mention that "Younger Jing arrived and requested salt" in the eleventh month. In the eighth month, the salt newly produced from the Hedong Salt Lake would not yet have been transported to the capital region. Therefore, the Zhou king could only award Dian with the salt that was kept in the storerooms at the capital, which is why the inscription makes a point to specify that this was "salt from the silos."

Even though the inscriptions on the Mian *pan* and Dian *gui* do not mention where the salt (*lu*) was produced, nearly all scholars agree that it came from the Hedong Salt Lake. This is a reasonable assumption, since the Hedong Salt Lake served as the principle source of salt for the Central Plains region through most of China's antiquity. During the Tang and Song periods, salt lakes in Ningxia, Northern Shaanxi, and the Ordos region of Inner Mongolia were exploited, with the lake salt produced by them supplying the lands "Within the Pass" (Guanzhong 關中, Central Shaanxi). During the Western Zhou, however, these regions did not fall within the Zhou court's sphere of influence. The only salt pool in Central Shaanxi seen in our textual records is the Lianshao Salt Pool (Lianshao lu 蓮勺鹵).[63] It is possible that some salt production occurred here.[64] Even if so, this production was on a very small scale and certainly unable to satisfy the needs of the entire population of Central Shaanxi. The Elder Ba *gui* and *xu* inscriptions now conclusively prove that in the mid-Western Zhou, it was the Hedong Salt Lake that supplied salt to the Zhou capital area.

Bringing together the bronze inscription evidence discussed previously, we are able to outline the supply chain for salt resources in the Zhou capital area during the mid-Western Zhou period. This supply chain entailed three principle steps: production, transportation, and distribution. Elder Ba was the local official responsible for organizing salt production at Hedong Salt Lake. During the summer season, when salt could be harvested, Elder Ba led members of his tribe and other subordinates, which may have included workers temporarily conscripted from neighboring polities and families, in the collection of naturally precipitated crude salt from along the shores of the salt lake. That salt was then temporarily stored in simply constructed silos nearby. Younger Jing was an official of the Zhou court, responsible for overseeing the production and transportation of salt. At the end of the salt harvest season, he traveled to the salt lake, and his retinue likely included a large number of carriage teams to aid in transportation.[65] After examining the fruits of Elder Ba's labor, and rewarding him appropriately, Younger Jing then transported the salt back to the capital in Central Shaanxi and delivered it to special silos there. The Zhou king then held ultimate authority over the final distribution of the salt. Through the distribution of "awards" (*shangci* 賞賜), salt was issued to the aristocratic lords retained by the court. In the Mian *pan* and Dian *gui* inscriptions, the phrase "offering enticements" (*miemao* 蔑懋) does not appear. This suggests the Zhou king is not awarding salt as a reward for meritorious service. Rather, this is a type of routine distribution of resources. The aristocratic lords Mian and Dian do not enjoy an especially high social standing but are mid-level officials in the court. Since the salt awarded to them by the Zhou king far exceeded their daily needs, they could then "redistribute" this salt. This is revealed by the Mian *pan*, where a portion of salt was given by Mian to an ordinary member of his tribe. The salt could even be given out to lowly servants owned by the household, and we cannot exclude the possibility that extra salt was traded for different goods that may have been needed. Through this relatively straightforward supply chain, the salt produced by Hedong Salt Lake was able to reach the hands of any Zhou person who needed it. A similar salt supply chain can be imagined for the Eastern Zhou capital of Chengzhou as well. Senior aristocratic lords in the royal court, such as members of the Jing clan, and distant states, perhaps received special permission from the Zhou king to themselves oversee the transport of salt back to their own territories for redistribution.[66]

Salt is a staple good that is rather unwieldy to transport in large quantities. The long-distance transport of salt in antiquity would have been extremely difficult and entailed a significant amount of waste. For this reason, the main costs involved in the salt industry were accrued in the transportation of the salt, as opposed to its actual production. Trips to the salt lake to harvest salt demanded the organization of a sizeable amount of manpower, together with carriages for transporting the salt and beasts for pulling those carriages (generally oxen were employed to draw carriages of goods in antiquity). Adequate grain, fodder, and other provisions were also required to sustain the men and animals on their journey there and back. Furthermore, hostile Rong and Di peoples were active in southern Shanxi up to the Spring and Autumn period. During the Western Zhou, the road from Central Shaanxi to the salt lake must have been dangerous, in which case a military escort was needed to protect the transport teams. This sort of large-scale operation clearly was not something that minor or even mid-level aristocratic lords were capable of undertaking in the Western Zhou. Moreover, the salt harvest season at the salt lake was concentrated in just a few months during the summer. If the aristocratic lords from every polity all dispatched their own teams to the salt lake for this harvest, it would have inevitably placed a strain on the natural resources, leading to clashes.

Thus, following the emergence of dynastic rule in the Central Plains region, special officials were established by the central government to manage salt production at the salt lake and arrange for its transport. This was an essential task, and one of the most important functions of the state.[67] Although the salt supply chain arranged by the Western Zhou court may seem simplistic, it was able to ensure, so far as possible, that every member of society could satisfy their daily needs. This was done not only through the investment of relatively few resources but also despite the fact that, at that time, the productive forces and system of government administration were still archaic and underdeveloped.[68]

Furthermore, a tradition of communal clan ownership continued to prevail from prehistoric times, which always saw products from the "mountains, forests, rivers, and marshes" (*shanlin chuanze* 山林川澤) as public property. The Zhou king stood as representative of the Altar to Soil and Grain (*she* 社). He was entrusted with the authority to manage and distribute these goods and therefore could possibly abuse his authority to seek private gain for himself.[69] Yet if one day he were to flout tradition and monopolize this wealth, it would incite rebellion from both the aristocratic lords and commoners alike. Recall how King Li of Zhou 周厲王 (r. mid-9th c. BCE) implemented policies whereby the "mountains, forests, rivers, and marshes" were reserved for his "exclusive profit" (*zhuanli* 專利), which led the "people of the state" (*guoren* 國人) to remove him from the throne.[70]

Some readers may wonder: since Elder Ba was in charge of overseeing operations at the salt lake, why was he not enfeoffed nearby, as opposed to at Yicheng, which is over a hundred kilometers away? This question may be answered in two ways. First, in the Pre-Qin period, the environs around where the salt was harvested were not hospitable for human habitation and were especially unsuitable for agriculture. Liu Li and Chen Xingcan point out that the Yuncheng region was full of lakes in antiquity, with low-lying terrain, and belts of land suffering from salinization. During the Erlitou and Erligang periods, only a few archaeological sites are present here, and those are small in size.[71] These conditions did not change by the Western Zhou period, and we have discovered only a few Western Zhou sites and cemeteries in the Yuncheng Basin to date. According to our textual records, of the polities located in southern Shanxi, the one closest to the salt lake was the state of Xun 郇 (荀). Xun was established in modern-day Linyi County 臨猗縣, which is still twenty-five kilometers away. A historical anecdote from the *Zuo zhuan* sheds further light on this point: in the sixth year of Duke Cheng of Lu's 魯成公 reign (585 BCE), which was the fifteenth year of

Duke Jing of Jin's 晉景公 rule, Jin planned to move their capital. When debating where the new capital should be located, differing opinions were raised by senior officials. Some advocated moving the capital to "the land of the Xun and Xia clans" (郇瑕氏之地), which was the former site of the state of Xun. The reason they gave for picking this location was because "the soil is fertile and it is close to the salt (lake)" (沃饒而近鹽).[72] Another important minister, Han Xianzi 韓獻子 (Han Jue 韓厥), vehemently disagreed:[73]

> At Xun and Xia the soil is thin and the water is shallow, and foul substances can easily accumulate. If such accumulation is easy, the people will be miserable; if they are miserable, they will be enfeebled, and they will thus be sick with rheumatism and swollen limbs. That area does not compare to Xintian. There the soil is thick and the water is deep; living there does not cause sicknesses; and the Fen and Hui Rivers allow foul substances to flow away.

> 郇瑕氏土薄水淺, 其惡易覯, 易覯則民愁, 民愁則墊隘, 於是乎有沉溺重膇之疾。不如新田, 土厚水深, 居之不疾, 有汾澮以流其惡。

This debate demonstrates how, in antiquity, when selecting the site for a city, the soil and water conditions were important factors taken into consideration. Preference was given for high lands, with thick soil, ample groundwater, and rivers running nearby. The former site of the state of Xun, which was still a distance from the salt lake, in Han Xianzi's opinion, was a place where "the soil is thin and the water is shallow," and that since the land was low-lying, various hazardous pollutants could easily accumulate there, causing people to fall ill. Duke Jing of Jin ultimately adopted Han Xianzi's proposal and moved the capital to Xintian 新田 (New Fields), located in modern-day Houma City 侯馬, Shanxi. To date, the most important Western Zhou (and even late Shang) archaeological sites and cemeteries discovered in central and southern Shanxi are principally distributed among the middle reaches of the Fen River 汾河, to the north as far as Lingshi 靈石 and south down to Houma, which is in large part due to the natural terrain. Moreover, Han Xianzi also argued: "For mountains, marshes, forests, and salt are treasures of the domain. If the domain is rich in resources, the people will become arrogant and indolent. Being close to these treasures, the lord's house will be impoverished" (夫山澤林鹽國之寶也. 國饒則民驕佚, 近寶公室乃貧).[74] In other words, the produce of the "mountains, marshes, forests, and salt (lakes)" ought to be controlled by the state, specifically by the hand of the "lord's house." If the capital is too close to the salt lake, the people (including the aristocratic lords) will grow wealthy by directly harvesting the salt themselves and trading it. Because of this, the ruler and government will lose control over the salt lake and grow poor.[75] By placing the state at a distance from the salt lake, commoners and other ordinary aristocratic lords could not harvest the lake salt on their own. The Western Zhou court adopted this policy as a measure to maintain state control over the salt lake's resources.

The second reason that Elder Ba's home was far away is that Elder Ba was a subject of the state of Jin 晉. Based on the burial customs and inscriptions on the bronze vessels excavated from the two Western Zhou cemeteries of Hengshui, Jiang County 絳縣 and Dahekou, Yicheng, I have argued elsewhere that the Ba clan and Peng 倗 clan were among the "nine ancestral lines of the Huai surname" 懷姓九宗 (that is, the families with the surname of Kui 媿) under the founding ancestor of the Jin state, Tang Shu Yu 唐叔虞 (Younger Tang, Yu), when he was enfeoffed.[76] For a long period of time, these families maintained a dual identity as both "subjects of the royal court" (*wangchen* 王臣) and "subjects of the state of Jin" (*Jin chen* 晉臣), with both the Zhou king and the Jin lord enjoying a degree of sovereignty over them.[77] The Dahekou cemetery is located less than twenty kilometers to the east of the site of the Jin capital at Tianma 天馬-Qucun 曲村, while the Hengshui cemetery is thirty kilometers to the south of it. Recently, a Western Zhou cemetery has been discovered fifteen kilometers to the east of Hengshui, in Ju Village 雎村, Jiang County. One of the tombs belongs to a senior aristocratic lord. Although this tomb was looted and thus severely damaged, it is apparent that the burial was oriented east-west, included a "waist-pit" (*yaokang* 腰坑), and had sacrificial victims. These are all burial customs very similar to what we find with the graves in the Hengshui cemetery.[78] It is quite possible that this cemetery belonged to another one of the "nine ancestral lines of the Huai surname." Judging by these three cemeteries, it appears that the "nine ancestral lines of the Huai surname" were positioned near the Jin capital, encircling it like "satellites." In this way, on the one hand they served to protect the capital, while, on the other hand, the Jin state could more easily exert control over them. In the famous anecdote about the enfeoffment of the three polities of Lu 魯, Wei 衛, and Tang 唐 (Jin 晉) recorded in the *Zuo zhuan*, Duke Ding 定 公 year 4, after describing the precious items awarded to Tang Shu Yu, it mentions "nine ancestral lines of the Huai clan and the five regulators for overseeing official duties" (懷姓九宗職官五正).[79] In Western Zhou bronze inscriptions, "regulator" (*zheng* 正) refers to the senior official who was in charge of each administrative branch of the royal court. This line, therefore, relates how members of these nine families either held the post of senior official in charge of five different branches of royal court's government, or that they variously assumed five branch offices given to them by the Zhou king. Positions such as these were hereditary, thus in the *Zuo zhuan* passage from Duke Yin 隱公, year 6, we still see the following name and title: "Jiafu, the son of Qingfu of Yi, officer for the nine ancestral lines and five regulators" (翼九宗五正頃父之子嘉父).[80] At this point in time, the "nine lineages of the Huai surname" had long been annexed by Jin, yet descendants of the "nine lineages" were still powerful aristocratic lords in Jin, and the title of Five Regulators (*wuzheng* 五正) continued to be retained. Elder Ba's post, managing activities at the salt lake, was likely one of the offices constituting the Five Regulators. Whether this post was held by the Ba clan alone or was an office shared among all the families remains to be determined. Although the Peng and Ba clans fell under the authority of Jin, because they assumed an office given to them by the Zhou king, they were also subordinates of the senior aristocratic lords attached to the court, such as Duke Yi and Younger Jing. This helps to explain why, in the bronze inscriptions unearthed from these two cemeteries, astonishingly the Peng and Ba clans had closer affiliations to the Zhou court and its senior aristocratic lords than they did with the state of Jin, their ancestral lineage head. These senior aristocratic lords, and even the Zhou king, frequently awarded them precious goods and sent envoys for formal visits. The Peng and Ba clans, moreover, intermarried with noble families of other aristocratic polities and even the Zhou royal house.[81]

The upper limit for the dating of the Hengshui and Dahekou cemeteries is to the late stage of the early Western Zhou, which is contemporaneous with the Bang cemetery (Bang *mu* 邦墓) area of the Jin state in Qucun and the Beizhao 北趙 Marquis of Jin cemetery (Jin Hou *mudi* 晉侯墓地). This reveals that the "nine ancestral lines of the Huai surname" followed the Jin Marquis Xiefu 晉侯燮父, whose land grant was changed from Tang 唐 to Jin 晉. Shortly afterward, during the reigns of King Mu and King Gong, the Peng and Ba clans gradually grew powerful, attaining the height of their power at some point during King Gong's rule. The three large "*jia* 甲-shaped" tombs (M1, M2, and M1011) discovered in the Hengshui cemetery, each with a single tomb ramp and positioned in a row together, all date to this period. Although the Dahekou cemetery lacks large tombs with tomb ramps of this sort, the Elder Ba tomb M1017 was discovered here, and its construction is also impressive in its scale. The bronze inscriptions also reveal that, during the reign of King Gong, the Peng and Ba clans had frequent contact with the royal court. Interestingly, the three Western Zhou bronze inscriptions that mention salt all date to this period. This suggests that a close correlation may exist between the flourishing of the "nine ancestral lines of the Huai surname" and the Zhou court's increasing control over, and exploitation of, the Hedong Salt Lake. The Ba and other families, by fulfilling their duty in harvesting the lake salt, were rewarded generously by the Zhou king and his senior officials; at the same time, they quite possibly took a portion of the lake salt for themselves, to use in trade with other families and states. In this way, the "nine ancestral lines of the Huai surname" were able to accumulate a large amount of wealth in a short period of time, while also raising their political status.

Fortune is fleeting however, and immediately following King Gong's reign both the Hengshui and Dahekou cemeteries exhibit sharp decline, as indicated by the complete absence of any high-level aristocratic burials. King Yi's reign likewise marks a turning point when the Zhou court began to decline as well. In the *Shiji* chapter "Zhou Benji" 周本紀, it states that "during the reign of King Yi, the royal house grew feeble" (懿王之時王室遂衰).[82] Through an investigation of the families to which "court guarantors" (*youzhe*) mentioned in appointment inscriptions belong, I have argued that, beginning in the reign of King Gong, an oligarchy formed where a small number of powerful families appropriated the supreme authority of the royal court. This system of governance continued down to the reign of King Li.[83] Following the decline of the Zhou royal house's influence, the "nine ancestral lines of the Huai surname" lost the support provided to them by the court, and the increasingly powerful state of Jin perhaps directly annexed them. At the same time, the power to dispense public resources reaped from the "mountains, forests, rivers, and marshes," formerly under the purview of the Zhou court, now fell into the hands of a few aristocratic lords. This probably led to the salt lake's resources being exploited with abandon, bringing the old supply chain for salt to the brink of collapse. Thus, we no longer see any records of relating to the awarding of salt in bronze inscriptions that date after King Gong's reign. When King Li assumed the throne, he attempted to restore the power of his office, and an assault was launched against the sway of the senior aristocratic lords. The first measure he took was to regain control of the "mountains, forests, rivers, and marshes" (for "exclusive profit"). Although King Li lost his battle with the aristocratic lords, King Xuan 宣王 adopted all of his father's policies, centralizing power in the king.[84] In the inscription on the late King Xuan–period Qiu *pan* 逨盤 (*Mingtu* 14543), the term "for the palace's administration" (*yong gongyu* 用宮御) first appears. The vessel's owner, Shan Qiu 單逨, is charged with "supervising the foresters and woodlands of (all) four regions (of the realm)" 鞃司四方虞林, which is to say he oversaw the timber industry in each territory. Because of this, I believe that the phrase "for the palace's administration" suggests that the Zhou king appointed a trusted official to manage the vital natural resources of the "mountains, forests, rivers, and marshes," as well as the various industries related to them, and then to present the goods and revenue amassed through those industries back to the royal house and palace.[85] This was quite possibly an expansion of King Li's policy of "exclusive profit."[86] The financial system of China's early states at this point underwent a major transformation. The yield of the "mountains, forests, rivers, and marshes," which formerly belonged to the public domain of the "people of the state," now became the exclusive property of the royal house. That officials presented this yield "for the palace's administration" is in fact already quite similar to how the chamberlain for the palace revenues (*shaofu* 少府) managed the wealth of the imperial house during the Qin and Han dynasties: "he was in charge of taxes on (the yields from) the mountains, oceans, lakes, and marshes, to provide food support (for the realm)" 掌山海池澤之稅以給共 (供) 養.[87]

With this in mind, let us scrutinize once more the inscriptions on the early Spring and Autumn–period Jin Jiang *ding* and Rong Sheng *zhong* 戎生鐘 bells (*Mingtu* 15239–15246) and offer a new interpretation of their content. The Jing Jiang *ding* (fig. 5.4) was unearthed from Hancheng 韓城, Shanxi, during the Northern Song period.[88] Its inscription reads:

> With fanfare I dispatched a thousand carts of salt reserves that had been awarded to us, and not abandoning Marquis Wen's illustrious mandate, sent them through Hong (?), campaigning to Fanyang X, obtaining their auspicious metal. I use (this metal) to cast this precious *ding* vessel for expressing reverence.
>
> 嘉遣我易 (賜) 鹵積千两 (輛), 勿廢文侯顈 (顯) 命, 俾貫通弘 (?), 征繁湯 (陽) 𤿌, 取厥吉金, 用作寶尊鼎.

The Rong Sheng *zhong* fourth bell contains similar lines in its inscription: "With fanfare we dispatched salt reserves, and I joined them in campaigning to Fanyang, obtaining their auspicious metal. I use (this metal) to cast these chime bells" (嘉遣鹵積, 俾諳征繁湯, 取厥吉金, 用作寶協鐘). Li Xueqin 李學勤 very astutely saw that these two inscriptions were connected to one another and has provided a convincing reading for them both. Li argues that the Jin Jiang *ding* and Rong Sheng *zhong* bells should be dated to the sixth year of Marquis Zhao of Jin's 晉昭侯 reign (the thirty-first year of King Ping of Zhou 周平王, 740 BCE). Jin Jiang was the wife of Marquis Wen of Jin 晉文侯, and at this time, Marquis Wen had already passed away. Carrying out his final testament, Lady Jiang dispatched a thousand carriages transporting salt to Fanyang 繁湯 (陽), which is north of modern-day Xincai 新蔡, Henan, to trade for copper made in the south, the "auspicious metal" (*jijin* 吉金). Rong Sheng served as a high minister in the state of Jin and also participated in this mission. The *ding* vessel and *zhong* bells on which the inscriptions appear were cast from the copper obtained during this exchange.[89]

Very few scholars have commented on how to interpret the term "award" (*ci* 賜) as it appears on the Jin Jiang *ding*. Li Xueqin believes that

 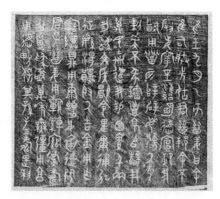

Figure 5.4. Jin Jiang *Ding* Image with a Hand Drawing of Its Inscription. *Source:* Eighteenth-century edition of *Yi Zhengtang chongxiu Bogu tu* 亦政堂重修博古圖 from the collection of the Harvard-Yenching Library of the Harvard College Library. Figure 5.4 is after Wang Fu 王黼 and Yi Zhengtang 亦政堂, eds., *Yi Zhengtang chongxiu Xuanhe bogu tu* 亦政堂重修宣和博古圖, *juan* 30, in Huang Cheng 黃晟 and *Sangu tu* 三古圖 (Tiandu: Huangshi Yi Zhengtang jiaokan ben, Qianlong renshen [1752]), vol. 2 (self-titled *Yi Zhengtang chongxiu Xuanhe bogu tulu juan di er* 亦政堂重修宣和博古圖錄卷第二), 6 (seq. 66–67). Available online: https://nrs.lib.harvard.edu/urn-3:fhcl:4909723?n=66.

this refers to "salt awarded by the state of Jin." At that time, however, Lady Jiang would have already assumed sovereignty over Jin's governance, so what need would there have been for Jin to "award" her with salt? This explanation is thus problematic. In fact, as we also saw with the mid-Western Zhou–period Mian *pan* and Dian *gui* inscriptions, the only person capable of "awarding" the state of Jin "a thousand carts of salt reserves" would be the reigning Zhou king, which in this case was King Ping. That King Ping would award Marquis Wen of Jin with this much salt must be because it was a gift in gratitude for his meritorious service on the king's behalf. The *Zuo zhuan*, Duke Yin, year 6, states: "In our Zhou (royal house) relocation to the east, it was upon Jin and Zheng that we relied" (我周之東遷晉鄭焉依).[90] During the long strife that occurred between the rival Zhou houses when there were "two kings reigning simultaneously," King Ping was able to defeat his opponent, King Xie 攜王, because of the support lent to him by Marquis Wen of Jin. This ultimately led to the relocation of the Zhou capital to Chengzhou, and the establishment of the Eastern Zhou dynasty. The *Xinian* 繫年 bamboo-strip manuscript acquired by Tsinghua University records on slips 8–9:[91]

> In the nine years during which Zhou was without a king, the state rulers and aristocratic lords began to not pay court to the Zhou. Marquis Wen of Jin then met King Ping at Shao'e and enthroned him in the capital. In the third year (following this), he moved the capital east, taking up residence in Chengzhou.

> 周亡(無)王九年, 邦君諸侯焉始不朝于周, 晉文侯乃逆平王于少鄂, 立之于京師. 三年乃東徙止于成周.

Supposing that "in the nine years during which Zhou was without a king" is best understood as "the nine years after King You of Zhou was murdered when there was no Zhou king generally recognized by the state rulers and aristocratic lords," then the date that Marquis Wen of Jin enthroned King Ping in the capital should be the year 761 BCE. This would make King Ping's relocation of the capital eastward to Chengzhou date to 758 BCE, which is the thirteenth year of King Ping's reign, and the twenty-third year of Marquis Wen of Jin's rule.[92] The grand appointment ceremony King Ping hosted in honor of Marquis Wen of Jin, recorded in the *Shangshu* 尚書 chapter "Wenhou zhi ming" 文侯之命, probably took place at this time. It was, moreover, in the twenty-first year of King Ping's reign (750 BCE, the thirty-first year of Marquis Wen's rule), that Marquis Wen finally deposed King Xie (who held power "Within the Pass"). This was only four years before Marquis Wen passed away (746 BCE). Based on the Jin Jiang *ding* inscription, Marquis Wen was awarded "a thousand carts of salt reserves" toward the end of his rule. Thus, I believe that the reason King Ping awarded Marquis Wen of Jin such a large quantity of salt on this occasion was to reward Marquis Wen for eliminating King Xie.

From the time of King Li's implementation of policies for "exclusive profit" to King Xuan's establishment of "palace administration," the Hedong Salt Lake must have seen the restoration of a system where dedicated officials oversaw its salt harvest. During the conflict between the two rival Zhou houses, the region in the southern Jin (southern Shanxi) would not have been greatly affected by the turmoil, and the production of salt at the salt lake during the summer seasons probably continued on each year. Yet the chaos wrought by this conflict may have impacted the ability of weak aristocratic lords to secure the transport of needed salt. For this reason, surplus salt was perhaps stored year round in silos by the lake, which was referred to as "salt reserves" (*luji* 鹵積), or, as in the Dian *gui* inscription, as the "salt from the silos" (*linlu* 廩鹵). After King Ping moved his capital eastward, the Zhou court continued to possess some measure of authority, therefore King Ping would have still held nominal control over production at the salt lake. Yet the Zhou were impoverished and weak upon settling in Chengzhou and would have lacked the means on their own to transport the salt reserves from storage back to the new capital. As such, awarding this salt to Marquis Wen of Jin was an ingenious plan that served dual purposes. On the one hand, it repaid the marquis for his services at little actual cost to the Zhou; on the other hand, it compelled the Jin instead to transport the salt to Fanyang, in the middle reaches of the Huai River 淮河, where it was exchanged for copper desperately needed by the various Central Plains states.[93] To move a thousand carriages full of salt would have required several thousand heads of oxen, at least five or six thousand conscripted workers, and up to a thousand soldiers for a protective escort as well. Even for a powerful state like Jin, completing a mission of such a grand scale must have demanded pouring all of the state's energy into its mobilization. Quite a few aristocratic lords from Jin likely participated in this mission, such as Rong Sheng. At the same time, the mission also required the cooperation of the aristocratic lords in the south. On the famous Zeng Bo Qi *hu* 曾伯漆瑚 (*Jicheng* 4631–4632; *Mingtu* 5979–5980) there is an inscription that reads: "Beating back the Huai Yi peoples, and pacifying (the way to) Fanyang, the road to metal and path to tin were brought back under submission" (克逊淮夷, 卬燮繁湯 (陽), 金道錫行具既俾方). Guo Moruo early on pointed out that this event was contemporaneous with the account in the Jin Jiang *ding*.[94] It thus appears that Zeng, an important Zhou polity located in the Han River valley, also took part in this mission, probably by the command of King Ping of Zhou, as was the case with Jin. The Eastern Zhou court, moreover, may have taken their share of the copper that was brought back.

This mission marks a transfer of power over control of the salt lake from the Zhou court to the state of Jin. Yet this transfer of power did not just occur in a single moment. Not long after this mission, a bitter war broke out between the Quwo clan 曲沃氏 (a collateral lineage of the Jin) and the Jin ducal house that lasted over six decades, greatly weakening the state of Jin; the Zhou court and its aristocratic lords supported the Jin ducal house at crucial moments and were an important factor throughout the many political reversals and internal upheavals that troubled Jin. This was the case until 679 BCE, when the last remaining forces of the Jin ducal house were eliminated by Duke Wu of Quwo 曲沃武公, and King Xi of Zhou 周釐王 had no choice but to finally grant Duke Wu the title Marquis of Jin. The Zhou court was no longer able to prevent Jin's expansion, and from this point onward Jin assumed complete control over the salt, starting a new page in the history of the salt lake.

Notes

1. Shanxi sheng kaogu yanjiusou 山西省考古研究所 et al., "Shanxi Yicheng Dahekou Xi Zhou mudi 1017 hao mu fajue" 山西翼城大河口西周墓地 1017 號墓發掘, *Kaogu xuebao* 考古學報 2018.1, 89–140, pls. 1–40; the bronze vessels from this site have also been published recently in Shanxi sheng kaogu yanjiu yuan 山西省考古研究院, *Ba jin jicui—Shanxi Yicheng Dahekou Xi Zhou mudi chutu qingtong qi* 霸金集粹——山西翼城大河口西周墓地青銅器 (Shanghai: Shanghai guji, 2021), 246–412.

2. Han Wei 韓巍, "Yicheng Dahekou M1017, M2002 liangmu de niandai ji xiangguan wenti" 翼城大河口M1017、M2002兩墓的年代及相關問題, in *Qingtongqi yu jinwen* 青銅器與金文, ed. Beijing daxue chutu wenxian yanjiusuo 北京大學出土文獻研究所, vol. 3 (Shanghai: Shanghai guji, 2017), 230–56.

3. This phenomenon changes dramatically in the late Western Zhou. Aristocratic burials from this period tend to contain bronzes that were all cast contemporaneously, mostly by the same family and specifically to serve as burial goods.

4. Han Wei 韩巍, "You xinchu qingtongqi zailun 'Gong Wang changnian shuo'—jianlun Xi Zhou zhongqi houduan qingtongqi de bianhua" 由新出青銅器再

論 "恭王長年說"——兼論西周中期後段青銅器的變化, *Zhejiang daxue yishu yu kaogu yanjiu* 浙江大學藝術與考古研究 2 (2015): 1–55, pls. 397–98.

5. For images of the Elder Ba *gui* and their inscriptions, see: Shanxi sheng kaogu yanjiusuo, "Shanxi Yicheng Dahekou Xi Zhou mudi 1017 hao mu fajue," 102, fig. 17, and pls. 9, 10; and Shanxi sheng kaogu yanjiu yuan, *Ba jin jicui*, 276–79, 290–93. For images of the Elder Ba *xu* and their inscriptions, see: Shanxi sheng kaogu yanjiusuo, "Shanxi Yicheng Dahekou Xi Zhou mudi 1017 hao mu fajue," 105, fig. 21, and pls. 13, 14; and Shanxi sheng kaogu yanjiu yuan, *Ba jin jicui*, 283–89, 298–302.

6. In this chapter, citations for data on bronze vessels and their inscriptions are placed in parenthesis immediately after the name of the vessel, giving the title of the reference work and the serial number for the piece found in that work. The following abbreviations will be adopted: *Jicheng* = Zhongguo shehui kexue kaogu yanjiusuo 中國社會科學院考古研究所, ed., *Yin Zhou jinwen jicheng* 殷周金文集成, 18 vols. (Beijing: Zhonghua, 1987–1994); *Mingtu* = Wu Zhenfeng 吳鎮烽, ed., *Shang Zhou qingtongqi mingwen ji tuxiang jicheng* 商周青銅器銘文暨圖像集成 (Shanghai: Shanghai guji, 2012); *Mingtu xu* = Wu Zhenfeng, ed., *Shang Zhou qingtongqi mingwen ji tuxiang jicheng xubian* 商周青銅器銘文暨圖像集成續編 (Shanghai: Shanghai guji, 2016).

7. For the Neishi *xu*, see Zhongguo guojia bowuguan 中國國家博物館, ed., *Zhongguo guojia bowuguan guancang wenwu yanjiu congshu, Qingtong qi juan (Xi Zhou)* 中國國家博物館館藏文物研究叢書, 青銅器卷 (西周) (Shanghai: Shanghai guji 2020), 294.

8. Han Wei, "You xinchu qingtongqi zailun 'Gong Wang changnian shuo,'" 293–94.

9. This point was first raised by Chen Mengjia 陳夢家, *Xi Zhou tongqi duandai* 西周銅器斷代 (Beijing: Zhonghua, 2004), 246.

10. Rong Geng 容庚 and Zhang Weichi 張維持 argue that the wavy-band pattern derives from what was originally a triangle pattern, which was then altered, with the triangles joining together with one another. See their *Yin Zhou qingtongqi tonglun* 殷周青銅器通論 (Beijing: Wenwu, 1984), 108. Ma Chengyuan 馬承源 believes instead that the wavy-band pattern imitates the bodies of dragons and snakes, therefore he classifies it under the category of "designs based on transformed animal bodies" 獸體變形紋類 in *Shang Zhou qingtongqi wenshi* 商周青銅器紋飾 (Beijing: Wenwu, 1984), 25–26. Zhu Fenghan 朱鳳瀚 likewise speculates that the wavy-band pattern originated in the single-headed, double-bodied dragon pattern and therefore lists it under "designs featuring simplified and transformed animals" 簡省和變形動物紋 in *Zhongguo qingtongqi zonglun* 中國青銅器總論 (2009; Shanghai: Shanghai guji, 2011 [rpt.]), 581. Based on the evidence now available, these hypotheses are incorrect.

11. Huang Yifei 黃益飛 and Xie Yaoting 謝堯亭, "Ba Bo gui mingwen kao" 霸伯簋銘文考, *Zhengzhou daxue xuebao* 鄭州大學學報 2018.1, 98; *Zhou li zhushu* 周禮注疏 27.135, in Ruan Yuan 阮元 (1764–1849), ed., *Shisanjing zhushu* 十三

經注疏 (Beijing: Zhonghua, 1987), vol. 1, 773; *Liji Zhengyi* 禮記正義 31.261 in *Shisanjing zhushu*, vol. 2, 1489; *Xunzi jijie* 荀子集解 19.27 in Wang Xianqian 王先謙 (1842–1917), ed., *Zhuzi jicheng* 諸子集成 (Shanghai: Shanghai shudian, 1991), vol. 2, 321.

12. In April 2017, Xie Yaoting invited Zhu Fenghan, Li Ling 李零, and myself to visit Shanxi Provincial Institute of Archaeology's 山西省考古研究所 Houma Work Station 侯馬工作站 to view the bronze vessels excavated from the Dahekou cemetery. At that time, the scholars there had also reached the same conclusion regarding the relationship between the decoration on the Elder of Ba *xu* vessels and their self-identified name of "mountain *gui*." Afterward, Fu Qiang 付強 published an article online espousing similar views, see: "Tantan Babo Shan gui de ziming he qingtongqi zhong jiucheng suowei de boquwen" 談談霸伯山簋的自名和青銅器中舊稱所謂的波曲紋, Fudan daxue chutu wenxian yu guwenzi yanjiu zhongxin wangzhan 復旦大學出土文獻與古文字研究中心網站, April 28, 2018, http://www.gwz.fudan.edu.cn/Web/Show/4245. Li Ling has also published his thoughts in: "Shanwen kao—Shuo huandai wen, bowen, boqu wen, bolang wen ying zhengming wei shanwen 山紋考——說環帶紋, 波紋, 波曲紋, 波浪紋應正名為山紋," *Zhongguo guojia bowuguan guankan* 中國國家博物館館刊 2019.1, 79–93.

13. Zhongguo shehui kexueyuan kaogu yanjiusuo 中國社會科學院考古研究所, *Zhangjiapo Xi Zhou mudi* 張家坡西周墓地 (Beijing: Zhongguo dabaike quanshu, 1999).

14. Han Wei 韓巍, "Xi Zhou jinwen shizu yanjiu" 西周金文世族研究, PhD dissertation, Peking University, Department of Chinese Literature, 2007, chap. 3, sec. 1, "Jing Clan" 井氏.

15. These vessels have been dated by scholars to the reign of King Yi. The Hu *ding* and Chi *zun* both record year numbers, giving the "first year" 元年 and "second year" 二年 respectively.

16. Shanxisheng kaogu yanjiusuo 山西省考古研究所 et al., "Mudi 1017 hao mu fajue," 138. Elsewhere, the primary author of the archaeological report, Xie Yaoting, explicitly claims that the Elder Ba *gui* dates to the reign of King Mu. See Huang Yifei 黃益飛 and Xie Yaoting 謝堯亭, "Ba Bo gui mingwen kao," 96.

17. Huang Jinqian 黃錦前 and Zhang Xinjun 張新俊, "Ba Bo gui mingwen xiaoyi" 霸伯簋銘文小議, *Jianbo* 簡帛 *Bamboo and Silk*, June 15, 2011, http://www.bsm.org.cn/ show_article. php?id=1470. In addition to this interpretation, Li Fa 李發 has transcribed the character I give as "to request" *qiu* 求 as "do obeisance" *bai* 拜 instead. See: *Fudan daxue chutu wenxian yu guwenzi yanjiu zhongxin wangzhan lunwen*, August 18, 2011, 1–10, http://www.gwz.fudan.edu.cn/Web/Show/1620.

18. Huang and Xie, "Ba Bo gui mingwen kao," 96.

19. Ji Xiaojun 冀小軍, "Shuo jiagu jinwen zhong biao qiqiuyi de hui zi—jian tan hui zi zai jinwen cheshi mingcheng zhong de yongfa" 說甲骨金文中表祈求義的羍字——兼談羍字在金文車飾名稱中的用法, *Hubei daxue xuebao* 湖北大學學報 1991.1, 35–44.

20. Li Ling suggested this reading during our visit to Houma, Shanxi, in April 2017, when we went to inspect the bronzes excavated from the Dahekou cemetery.

21. See Chen Jian 陳劍, "Ju Guodian jian shidu Xi Zhou jinwen yi li" 據郭店簡釋讀西周金文一例, *Jiagu jinwen kaoshi lunji* 甲骨金文考釋論集 (Beijing: Xianzhuang, 2007), 20–38.

22. In these closing formulaic auspicious wishes on Western Zhou bronze inscriptions, the word "to implore or beg for" (*gai* 匄) is found in similar contexts to *hui*.

23. Duan Yucai 段玉裁, *Shuowen jiezi zhu* 說文解字注 (Shanghai: Shanghai guji, 1981), 586.

24. Duan Yucai, *Shuowen jiezi zhu*, 586.

25. *Shiji* 史記 (Beijing: Zhonghua, 2014), 129.3967.

26. Hubeisheng Jingsha tielu kaogudui 湖北省荆沙鐵路考古隊, *Baoshan Chu jian* 包山楚簡 (Beijing: Wenwu, 1991), 28, pl. 67.

27. Zhao Pingan 趙平安, "Zhanguo wenzi zhong de yan zi ji xiangguan wenti yanjiu" 戰國文字中的鹽字及相關問題研究, *Kaogu* 考古 2004.8, 58–63.

28. In the medieval period, because the salt lake was located in Jie County 解縣, it was called Jie Lake 解池, and thus the salt produced from this lake was also labeled Jie salt 解鹽 or Lu salt 潞鹽.

29. Duan Yucai, *Shuowen jiezi zhu*, 586.

30. *Zhou li zhushu* 6.37, in *Shisanjing zhushu*, vol. 1, 675.

31. *Zhou li zhushu* 6.37, in *Shisanjing zhushu*, vol. 1, 675.

32. Li Daoyuan 酈道元 (466–527) et al., *Shuijing zhu* 水經注 (Beijing: Huaxia, 2007), Vol. 1, 129–130.

33. *Song shi* 宋史 (Beijing: Zhonghua, 1977), 181.4413.

34. Guo Zhengzhong 郭正忠, ed., *Zhongguo yanye shi (gudai bian)* 中國鹽業史 (古代編) (Beijing: Renmin, 1997), 111–12.

35. The second character in the phrase *miemao* 蔑懋 is often written with the graph 曆 in other bronze inscriptions. In the Elder Ba *gui* and *xu* inscriptions however, the lower component of this character is from *shui* 水 and *mu* 木. This is an extremely rare character form, and therefore this study opts to write *mao* 懋 directly.

36. Tang Lan 唐蘭 (1901–1979), " 'Mie X' xin gu" 蔑曆新詁, in Gugong bowuyuan 故宫博物院, ed., *Tang Lan xiansheng jinwen lunji* 唐蘭先生金文論集 (Beijing: Zijincheng, 1995), 224–35.

37. See discussion in Li Feng, *Bureaucracy and the State in Early China* (Cambridge: Cambridge University Press, 2008), 226–29.

38. Chen Jian 陳劍, "Jiantan dui jinwen 'miemao' wenti de yixie xin renshi" 簡談對金文蔑懋問題的一些新認識, in *Chutu wenxian yu guwenxi yanjiu* 出土文獻與古文字研究, ed. Fudan daxue chutu wenxian yu guwenzi yanjiu zhongxin 復旦大學出土文獻與古文字研究中心 (Shanghai: Shanghai guji, 2018), 91–117.

39. *Chunqiu Zuo zhuan zhengyi* 春秋左傳正義 10.79, *Shisanjing zhushu*, vol. 2, 1781; Stephen Durrant, Wai-yee Li, and David Schaberg, trans., *Zuo Tradition / Zuozhuan* 左傳 (Seattle: University of Washington Press, 2016), vol. 1, 212–13.

40. *Shiji*, 18.1049. The term *fa* 閥, which refers to "a gatepost announcing the merits of a family" or by association "a powerful individual or family," is derived from this sense of the word *fa* 伐.

41. Hu Jixuan 胡吉宣, *Yupian jiaoshi* 玉篇校釋 (Shanghai: Shanghai guji, 1989), 479.

42. *Han shu*漢書 (Beijing: Zhonghua, 1964), 94b.3806.

43. By comparison, in the inscription on the Elder Ba *yu* 霸伯盂 vessel (also called the Shang *yu* 尚盂) unearthed from tomb M1017, an emissary dispatched by the Zhou king "offered enticements" 蔑懋 to Elder Ba and bestowed upon him precious fine wine that had aromatic herbs steeped within it; and Elder Ba, in order to reciprocate this ritual gift, was required to host numerous grand ceremonies entertaining the emissary (and his guest), gifting to him a multitude of presents, including a horse-driven carriage, a horse, and jade items. It is clear in this case that the Zhou king's gift held symbolic value as a high honor but in itself was not of much economic value, whereas Elder Ba, as one of the regional aristocratic lords, was asked to pay a hefty price in the exchange.

44. *Zhou li zhushu* 6.37, in *Shisanjing zhushu*, vol. 1, 675.

45. Many inscriptions document Younger Jing serving as a "court guarantor" 右者 (see later discussion). Moreover, the tomb belonging to Younger Jing at Zhang-jiapo 張家坡, number M170, is a large "*zhong* 中-shaped" burial with a single tomb ramp. This indicates that Younger Jing enjoyed high status among the royals and aristocratic lords. It is possible that he was responsible for managing palace affairs and the royal family's finances, with the salt industry as only one of the domains under his charge. Of course, the Younger Jing mentioned in the Elder Ba *gui* and *xu* inscriptions would have been relatively young, and only at the beginning of his official career, therefore managing the salt industry was perhaps his primary duty at this time.

46. Feng Shi 馮時, "Guwenzi suojian zhi Shang Zhou yanzheng" 古文字所見之商周鹽政, *Nanfang wenwu* 南方文物 2009.1, 57–71.

47. Li Shuicheng 李水城, "Zhongguo yanye kaogu shinian" 中國鹽業考古十年, in *Kaoguxue yanjiu (jiu)* 考古學研究 (九), ed. Beijing daxue kaogu wenbo xueyuan 北京大學考古文博學院 (Beijing: Wenwu, 2012), 362–80.

48. Shanxi sheng kaogu yanjiusuo 山西省考古研究所, ed., *Qingliangsi shiqian mudi* 清涼寺史前墓地 (Beijing: Wenwu, 2016).

49. Zhongguo shehui kexueyuan kaogu yanjiusuo 中國社會科學院考古研究所, ed., *Xiaxian Dongxiafeng* 夏縣東下馮 (Beijing: Wenwu, 1988).

50. Note however that Cao Dazhi 曹大志 doubts that this is the case. He claims that Liu Li and Chen Xingcan's analysis of the chemical composition of the soil samples collected from the "storerooms" at Dongxiafeng is unreliable. Cao argues that these structures would not have been suitable for keeping salt but rather more closely resemble granaries. Moreover, he holds that the Dongxiafeng site was not really located along the main route for the transportation of salt in that period ("Lun Shangdai de liangchu sheshi—lin, xiang, jing" 論商代的粮儲設施向㐭京,

unpublished article provided by the author). Cao's interpretation has some merit; however, even if these features are not salt silos, this does not invalidate Liu Li and Chen Xingcan's judgment about the nature of the Dongxiafeng site.

51. Liu Li 劉莉 and Chen Xingcan 陳星燦, "Cheng—Xia Shang shiqi dui ziran ziyuan de kongzhi wenti" 城夏商時期對自然資源的控制問題, *Dongnan wenhua* 東南文化 2000.3, 45–60.

52. *Mu tianzi zhuan* 6.5b, Sibu beiyao ed. (Taipei: Zhonghua, 1978).

53. *Zhushu jinian* 竹書紀年, Sibu beiyao ed. (Taipei: Zhonghua, 1977), *zhuan xia* 下, 5a.

54. Guo Moruo 郭沫若, *Liang Zhou jinwen ci daxi tulu kaoshi* 兩周金文辭大系圖錄攷釋 (Shanghai: Shanghai shudian, 1999), vol. 2, 89–91; Chen Mengjia 陳夢家, *Liang Zhou tongqi duandai* 兩周銅器斷代 (Beijing: Zhonghua, 2004), 177–84.

55. Tang Lan 唐蘭, *Xi Zhou qingtongqi mingwen fendai shizheng* 西周青銅器銘文分代史徵 (Beijing: Zhonghua, 1986), 275.

56. Lü Zhangshen 呂章申 and Zhongguo guojia bowuguan 中國國家博物館, eds., *Jincang jicui* 近藏集粹 (Beijing: Beijing shidai huawen, 2016), 92–93; Zhongguo guojia bowuguan, *Zhongguo guojia bowuguan guancang wenwu yanjiu congshu, Qingtong qi juan (Xi Zhou)*, 205–06.

57. Zhongguo guojia bowuguan, *Zhongguo guojia bowuguan guancang wenwu yanjiu congshu, Qingtong qi juan (Xi Zhou)*, 209.

58. Han Wei, "You xinchu qingtongqi zailun 'Gong Wang changnian shuo,'" 283–84.

59. Lü Zhangshen and Zhongguo guojia bowuguan, eds., *Jincang jicui*, 76.

60. Han Wei, "Lu *gui* niandai ji xiangguan wenti" 虠簋年代及相關問題, in *Gudai wenming* 古代文明, ed. Beijing daxue Zhendan gudai wenming yanjiu zhongxin 北京大學震旦古代文明研究中心 (Beijing: Wenwu, 2007), vol. 6, 155–70.

61. The editors of *Jincang jicui* believe that the person who awarded the salt in the Dian *gui* was perhaps one of Dian's superiors or his family head, while Dian was then either a salt official working in the region of the salt lake or a retainer in a nearby polity. Yet the sheer scale of this gift, with a "hundred carriages" worth of salt, suggests to me that these interpretations may be misguided.

62. Guo Zhengzhong, *Zhongguo yanye shi (gudai bian)*, 269.

63. A sole mention of Lianshao Salt Pool is found in the *Han shu*, "Xuan Di ji" 宣帝紀 chapter, where it claims that Emperor Xuan, in his youth, "once ran into difficulties in (the environs of) Lianshao salt (pool)" (常困於蓮勺鹵中). To this, Ru Chun 如淳 comments: "Lianshao County had a salt lake, just over ten *li* half-kilometers in length and width. The local villagers called it 'Luzhong (Salt Containing Pool)' (蓮勺縣有鹽池, 縱廣十餘里, 其鄉人名為鹵中). See *Han shu*, 8.237. In the Western Han, Lianshao County was located on the northern bank of the Wei River 渭河 to the northeast of Chang'an 長安, which is to the south of Pucheng County 浦城縣 in modern-day Shaanxi.

64. Among Han period seal inscriptions, there is a "Seal of the Lianshao Salt Supervisor" (蓮勺鹵咸督印); see Luo Fuyi 羅福頤, *Han yin wenzi zheng* 漢印文字徵 (Beijing: Wenwu, 1978), vol. 12, 2. This was probably an official responsible for salt production assigned to the Lianshao Salt Pool. This office must have existed for only a short period of time, however, as the *Han shu* geographic treatise *Dilizhi* 地理志 does not list any "salt officials" under the entry for Lianshao County.

65. The Ba clan was enfeoffed in Yicheng, which was more than a hundred kilometers to the northeast of the salt lake. I cannot imagine that Elder Ba carried that salt back to Yicheng, which would have amounted to wasted effort once the salt was then sent back to the Zhou court. Instead, I believe that he must have stored the salt harvest in the vicinity of the salt lake, managing logistics "on site," while he awaited the court emissary to arrive and arrange for the salt's transport.

66. *Hou Han shu* 後漢書, "Jia Fu zhuan" 賈復傳, offers a good example of this: Jia Fu, in the last year of Wang Mang's reign, served as a county-level official in Guanjun County 冠軍縣, Nanyang Commandery 南陽郡. He and ten or so colleagues together "received salt from Hedong" (迎鹽河東), which means that they went to the Hedong Salt Lake and transported salt from there. While on the road, they encountered bandits, and Jia Fu's colleagues all abandoned the salt they were transporting. Jia Fu alone remained and carried out his duty faithfully, carrying the salt back to Guanjun County without suffering any loss. For this, the locals in the county all sung his praises. What this anecdote reveals is that, once the Salt and Iron Monopoly policies of Han were put into effect, the daily salt provisions required for a given locality were collected by individuals under the authority of that locality's government. They had to go to the production site themselves and then transport the salt back to their home territories. See *Hou Han shu* 後漢書 (Beijing: Zhonghua, 1973), 17.664–67.

67. As other scholars have suggested, it is likely that a system for controlling the salt lake resources was already in place from as early as the Xia and Shang periods, only we do not yet have clear textual evidence for this, as we do for the Western Zhou period.

68. At first glance, the Western Zhou system seems very similar to the Salt and Iron Monopoly model established during the reign of Emperor Wu of Han 漢武帝 (r. 141–87 BCE), but there is a fundamental difference between them, as the main purpose of the Salt and Iron Monopoly was to increase the state's revenue while weakening the position of private merchants.

69. For example, the king could leverage his control of natural resources to demand loyalty from his subjects, by giving greater amounts to senior officials whom he liked and trusted, while lashing out at any who failed to follow his commands.

70. The statement "Zhou King Li enjoyed his exclusive profit" 周厲王好專利 occurs in the *Qianfulun* 潛夫論, "E li" 遏利; see *Qianfulun jian jiaozheng* 箋校正, *zhuan* 3, in Xinbian zhuzi jicheng series, vol. 1 (Beijing: Zhonghua, 1985),

27. Accounts of conflicts with the *guoren* are first found in the *Guoyu*, "Zhou yu, shang," Sibu beiyao, 1.4b–6b, and in the *Shiji*, "Zhou Benji" chapter; see *Shiji*, 4.179–82. The earliest reference to "mountains, forests, rivers, and marshes" (*shanlin chuanze*) as a source of resources is in *Zuo zhuan*, "Yin Gong" 隱公, year 5, where it is argued they should not be the concern of the ruler (as in earlier practice); see Durrant, Li, and Schaberg, trans., *Zuo Tradition*, vol. 1, 34–35.

71. Liu Li and Chen Xingcan, "Cheng—Xia Shang shiqi dui ziran ziyuan de kongzhi wenti," 51.

72. Durrant, Li, Schaberg, trans., *Zuo Tradition*, vol. 2, 759, with translation modified.

73. Durrant, Li, Schaberg, trans., *Zuo Tradition*, vol. 2, 759, with translation modified.

74. Durrant, Li, Schaberg, trans., *Zuo Tradition*, vol. 2, 758–59.

75. Beginning in the mid-Tang period, the state prohibited stealing and selling salt (as a type of public property), installing moats and fences around the perimeter of the salt lake, even adding "preventative walls" (*jin qiang* 禁牆) later. Prior to this, however, it would have been difficult to prevent locals living beside the salt lake from illegally harvesting salt in secret.

76. In our textual records, the surname Kui 媿 is sometimes written as Huai 懷 or Kui 隗, but these all refer to the same families. While evidence from bronze inscriptions shows that the Peng clan did belong to the Kui surname, we do not yet have any clues about the Ba clan lineage surname. These two cemeteries, however, demonstrate similar burial customs that were markedly different from those in Zhou cemeteries for Ji 姬 surname families. For example, the burials are oriented in the east-west direction, with the tomb occupant's head positioned to the west, and many of the graves include "waist-pits" (*yaokang* 腰坑). Because of these shared features, most scholars believe that the Peng clan and Ba clan belonged to the same tribal group.

77. Han Wei, "Hengshui, Dahekou Xi Zhou mudi ruogan wenti de tantao" 橫水大河口西周墓地若干問題的探討, in *Liang Zhou fengguo lunheng—Shaanxi Hancheng chutu Ruiguo wenwu ji Zhoudai fengguo kaoguxue yanjiu guoji xueshu yantaohui lunwenji* 兩周封國論衡——陝西韓城出土芮國文物暨周代封國考古學研究國際學術研討會論文集, ed. Shanghai bowuguan 上海博物館 and Shaanxi sheng kaogu yanjiuyuan 陝西省考古研究院 (Shanghai: Shanghai guji, 2014), 388–406.

78. Excavation of the Jucun cemetery began in 2015, and more than four hundred tombs have been excavated to date. The data for this cemetery has yet to be formally published, however simple introductions are available online.

79. Durrant, Li, Schaberg, trans., *Zuo Tradition*, vol. 3, 1748–49.

80. Durrant, Li, Schaberg, trans., *Zuo Tradition*, vol. 1, 40–41.

81. According to the evidence currently available, the Peng clan intermarried with the Nangong 南宮, Rui 芮, and Hua 華 clans, which were of the Ji 姬 surname linked to the royal court. The Peng, moreover, once married an elder sister of a reigning Zhou king. The Ba clan intermarried with the state of Yan 燕.

82. *Shiji*, 4.178.

83. Han Wei, "Ceming tizhi yu shizu zhengzhi—Xi Zhou zhong wanqi wangchao zhengzhi jiexi" 冊命體制與世族政治西周中晚期王朝政治解析, in *Jiuzhou xuelin* 九州學林 (Spring 2011), Xianggang chengshi daxue Zhongguo wenhua zhongxin 香港城市大學中國文化中心, ed. (Shanghai: Shanghai renmin, 2012), 2–31.

84. The supposed "rebellion by the people of the state" (國人暴動) that occurred in King Li's reign may, in light of these historical developments, be interpreted instead as pushback orchestrated by the senior aristocratic lords, to fight back against the king's policies seeking to recentralize power.

85. The phrase "for the palace's administration" (用宮御) also appears in the inscription on the Song *ding* 頌鼎 (*Jicheng* 2827–2829; *Mingtu* 2492–2494), as is repeated on the Song *gui* 頌簋 and Song *hu* 頌壺 as well. These vessels' owner, Song, was in charge of supervising commerce at Chengzhou 成周.

86. Han Wei, "Ceming tizhi yu shizu zhengzhi," 2–31.

87. *Han shu*, 19a.731.

88. Figure 5.4 is after Wang Fu 王黼, Yi Zhengtang 亦政堂, ed., *Yi Zhengtang chongxiu Xuanhe bogu tu* 亦政堂重修宣和博古圖, *juan* 30, in Huang Cheng 黃晟, *Sangu tu* 三古圖 (Tiandu: Huangshi Yi Zhengtang jiaokan ben, Qianlong renshen [1752]), vol. 2 (self-titled *Yi Zhengtang chongxiu Xuanhe bogu tulu juan di er* 亦政堂重修宣和博古圖錄卷第二), 6 (seq. 66–67), available online: https://nrs.lib.harvard.edu/urn-3:fhcl:4909723?n=66.

89. Li Xueqin 李學勤, "Rong Sheng bianzhong lunshi" 戎生編鐘論釋, *Wenwu* 文物1999.9, 75–82.

90. After Durrant, Li, Schaberg, trans., *Zuo Tradition*, vol. 1, 42–43.

91. Li Xueqin, ed., *Qinghua daxue cang Zhanguo zhujian (yi)* 清華大學藏戰國竹簡(壹) (Shanghai: Zhongxi, 2011), part 2, 138.

92. A number of differing opinions have been raised concerning how to date the "two rival Zhou houses" period in light of evidence provided by the Tsinghua *Xinian* manuscript, but this debate is beyond the scope of the present chapter.

93. Based on the *Hou Han shu*, "Jia Fu zhuan," anecdote cited before, it appears that up to the end of the Western Han, the Hedong Salt Lake continued to supply salt for the Nanyang region. In the pre-Qin period then, it was common that the salt was transported to the Huai River and Han River 漢水 valleys in the south and exchanged for metals like copper or tin that were in short supply in the Central Plains. Indeed, a "Salt for Metal Road" certainly must have existed running from southern Shanxi to southern Henan and northwest Hubei. The chaos caused by the conflict between the two rival Zhou houses lasted more than two decades and quite possibly disrupted this trade route temporarily. Once order was restored again, it was in the best interests of both the north and south to trade with the other party.

94. Guo Moruo, *Liang Zhou jinwen ci daxi tulu kaoshi*, 186.

6

Changing Ideas about *De*, the Lineage, and the Individual in Fifth- and Fourth-Century BCE China as Reflected in the Wenxian Covenant Texts

CRISPIN WILLIAMS

In *The Way of Water and Sprouts of Virtue*, Sarah Allan describes how, from the period of the Western Zhou bronze inscriptions to that of the *Analects* of Confucius, "the concept of *de* 德 was transformed from an inner power or 'mana' which was particularly powerful among those of high social rank into an ethical term. Thus the 'adorned inner power' of the man of high hereditary position became the 'cultivated virtue' of the Confucian philosopher."[1] Allan explains how, in the bronze inscriptions, *de* is "transmitted to the worshipper from his ancestor," and is thus "hereditary and particular to the family or clan," whereas, as a later philosophical concept, it is "something

My research on the Wenxian Covenant Texts has been possible as a result of my collaboration on the publication project for these texts, and I would like to acknowledge my gratitude for the support in this from the excavators of these materials, Hao Benxing 郝本性 and Zhao Shigang 趙世綱 of the Henan Provincial Institute of Cultural Heritage and Archaeology, and to the former and current heads of the institute. I thank Susan Roosevelt Weld for inviting me to join the project she initiated with the excavators to photograph and digitalize the Wenxian texts. I am also very grateful to Constance A. Cook and Adam D. Smith for comments and suggestions during the revising of this chapter.

that people are born with and have the potential to develop."[2] Originally a concept tied directly to the lineage and ancestral rites, *de* loses these associations and becomes a quality the individual cultivates independently. This chapter discusses how the Wenxian 溫縣 (Wen County) Covenant Texts (*mengshu* 盟書) demonstrate the use of *de* in its archaic context, while also providing evidence for the changing significance of the lineage and individual, which correlates with the diversification of *de*'s meaning in philosophical texts.

The excavated Wenxian Covenant Texts comprise a number of oaths produced at different times during the late fifth and early fourth centuries BCE. They are particularly valuable in providing direct evidence of policy implementation by a ruling elite at this time. The oaths were used as a political tool by Han 韓 lineage leaders as the lineage grew increasingly independent of the Jin 晉 ruling house and finally seceded to form the Han state. The Wenxian oaths employ *de* only in the traditional context of lineage ritual, in two oaths focused on lineage sacrifice. However, the Wenxian texts, and the similar Houma 侯馬 Covenant Texts, are also characterized by their disregard for shared lineage affiliation as a qualification for participation in the oaths, instead treating individuals as independent political agents. The most common text from Wenxian is a basic oath of allegiance, found on over 11,600 personalized tablets. It reflects a governing model in which the individual, rather than the lineage, is treated as the basic unit for political participation in the nascent Han state.

This chapter discusses changing ideas about *de*, the lineage, and the individual in light of the Wenxian Covenant Texts. On the one hand, the Wenxian Covenant Texts employ the term *de* with its archaic lineage-based usage in the context of lineage sacrifice. On the other hand, their focus on the individual as political agent reflects the political and social developments that coincide with the transformation of *de* in philosophical texts into a personally cultivated, lineage-independent attribute. I begin with a brief overview of *de*'s changing usage, from its stable use in Western Zhou bronze inscriptions to the diversification of its meaning in different philosophical texts in the fourth century BCE. I then introduce and discuss relevant evidence from the Wenxian Covenant Texts, including the context and dating of the materials, the two oaths that use *de*, and the basic oath of allegiance.

I argue that the archaic use of *de* in the Wenxian Covenant Texts reflects an ideological conservatism on the part of the Han ruler, while his implementation of the individualized oath of allegiance in the consolidation of power as he seceded from Jin demonstrates his practical response to the reality of the breakdown of the traditional lineage system. In the discussion section, I provide related evidence to contextualize and support these claims. This allows us a fuller understanding of social and political changes during a period in which different thinkers redefined the term *de* to suit their own teachings. We may speculate that the weakening of traditional lineage-based sociopolitical and religious ideology, along with the recognition of greater individual autonomy, led to new ideas about the relative significance of the lineage and individual, and stimulated the development of these widely different interpretations of *de*.

A Brief Overview of *De*'s Changing Meaning from the Western Zhou to the Fourth Century BCE

The meaning of *de* varies considerably over time and between different texts. Rather like *dao* 道, it was a term embraced by all but also significantly redefined to serve the purposes of separate textual genres, contexts, and thinkers. These changes, "masked by a nominal continuity," make *de* a "keyword" in Raymond Williams's sense: a word significant in culture and society, that came "to express radically different or radically variable . . . meanings and implications of meaning."[3] This section briefly outlines the development of the concept of *de* from its origin in the Western Zhou period (1046–771 BCE) to the diversification of its meaning in the fourth century BCE. This provides context for the analysis of the Wenxian Covenant Texts' use of *de* and their focus on the individual as a political actor. This summary is based on an analysis of relevant passages in bronze inscriptions and the following eight texts: *Zuo zhuan* 左傳; *Lunyu* 論語; *Mencius* 孟子; the *Neiye* 內業 chapter of the *Guanzi* 管子; *Laozi* 老子; the "Inner Chapters" of the *Zhuangzi* 莊子; *Liude* 六德; and *Sande* 三德.[4] While acknowledging the significant challenges involved in dating early texts, a rough chronology is adopted here in order to trace the development of *de* and related concepts, and allow comparison with the Wenxian covenants. Broadly, I take the *Zuo zhuan* to reflect governing philosophies of the sixth to fifth centuries BCE, the *Lunyu* to reflect foundational Ruist ideas of the fifth century BCE, and the remaining works as texts that were produced or began to take form in the fourth century BCE.[5]

Throughout the Western Zhou period, bronze inscriptions portray *de* as a sacred power, bestowed by the high power Tian 天 / Shang Di 上帝 on the Zhou 周 royal house and necessary to successfully implement and maintain Tian's Mandate (*Tian ming* 天命) to govern.[6] Through investiture ceremonies, the Zhou incorporated multiple lineages, including many not sharing the Zhou's clan name, into their governing system.[7] In accepting Zhou's political supremacy and the Zhou king's divine ancestry (as Son of Tian 天子), these groups were granted a portion of *de* to ensure their own success in supporting Zhou's execution of Tian's Mandate.[8] *De* resided in the heart of individuals and was transferred to successive generations through individuals emulating the *de* of their ancestors, an emulation possibly enacted in ritual ceremony. *De* was maintained and strengthened through strict adherence to ancestral ritual to ensure continued blessings, along with other acts bringing renown to the lineage and its ancestors.[9] If not diligently maintained, *de*, like Tian's Mandate, could be lost. Thus, the bronze inscriptions praise those who "pay due attention" to their *de* (*shen jue de* 慎厥德) and "grasp" their *de* (*bing de* 秉德).[10] *De* was, then, critical to success in preserving Tian's Mandate through one's political service to the Zhou royal house, but it was also critical for the prestige of one's own lineage. The power of *de* was manifested in displays of *weiyi* 威儀 "awesome decorum" in ritual performance, and in the dazzling spectacle of arrayed ritual bronzes.[11]

With the fall of the Western Zhou, ruling lineages of some regional states began to claim their own divine legitimacy to rule, recording on bronzes that they received the Mandate directly from their own or other legendary founders.[12] However, *de* was still treated as essential to their governing success, and was still dependent on the modeling and support of ancestors, through emulation and ancestral ritual. Seeking *de* from the ancestors through ritual offerings and feasting continues to be recorded in bronze inscriptions into the late Spring and Autumn and early Warring States periods, overlapping with the time of received texts such as the *Zuo zhuan* and *Lunyu*.

In fifth- and fourth-century BCE texts, we generally see a significant development and diversification in the meaning of *de*. In the *Zuo zhuan*, as reflected in the later bronze inscriptions just mentioned, the focus turns from *de*'s role in political service to the Zhou kings, to its role as a crucial attribute of regional rulers and ministers, which ensures success in both the governing of their own states and interactions with other states.[13] As for the philosophical texts, *de*'s original meaning did not correspond neatly with new ideas being raised by thinkers at this time, but it was clearly too significant and useful a word to abandon, so these thinkers made it their own. As Alan Chan observes: "Attempts at providing a systematic account of *de* . . . may be said to constitute a major theme in the unfolding of early Chinese philosophy."[14] Nevertheless, these changes are, in almost all cases, clearly traceable to aspects of *de*'s original usage. For example, texts generally continue to associate *de* with governing to some degree. The idea of *de* as a force is also preserved in some way in the majority of texts from this period, probably also drawing on the association of *de* with awesome display in ritual performance. Thus, for the *Lunyu*, *de* is a power that affords one protection and, in governing, can bring others to submission, even at a distance, through the superhuman charisma it bestows.[15] In the *Laozi* and *Zhuangzi*, *de* becomes the life force, complementary to the Dao, guiding the development of and vitalizing all living things (not just humans).[16] In the *Laozi*, one with a full complement of *de* (as is found in a baby), becomes invulnerable and may possess a state and successfully rule. The *Zhuangzi* stresses that the aim of cultivating *de* is to experience the unity of all living things and become one with the Dao. This brings the power to rule successfully, extraordinary charisma regardless of appearance or status, awareness that allows political success (without endangering oneself), and a spirit-like state allowing transcendence of the human realm. The *Neiye*, notably not relating *de* to governing, treats *de* as a minor force associated with the guiding and preservation of *qi* 氣 (vital breath or vital energy) within the body, and it is *qi* instead that brings extraordinary powers.[17] In the *Mencius*, a humanistic and practical approach to life and governing equates *de* with exemplary moral and ritual behavior, essential qualities for the individual whether in government or not.[18] This development stems from *de*'s original links to ancestral ritual, as well as its embodiment in upright behavior in service and leadership, exhibited as moral qualities such as loyalty (*zhong* 忠), trustworthiness (*xin* 信), and benevolence (*ren* 仁). For the excavated *Liude* text, from the Guodian 郭店 site, a system based on clearly defined morals nullifies the need for a separate concept of *de*, and *de* becomes reduced to a classifying term for each of six listed morals.[19]

The concepts of Tian and Tian's Mandate, originally directly associated with *de*, come to be seen as a more naturalistic ordering of the world, in some cases encompassing standards of ritually correct human behavior, as well as the idea of destiny.[20] *De* is seen to be generated naturally (by Tian or as a complementary force to Dao) in all individuals. Thus, *de* loses its original close ties to political participation in the Zhou mandate, and the condition that it must be transferred within a lineage from ancestors to living descendants. *De* may now potentially be cultivated to the highest degree by a commoner or outcast. The *Sande* text, in the Shanghai Museum collection, is unusual in that it preserves the earlier concept of Tian as a deity responsive to human actions. This text uses *de* with its early sense of "divine gift," but in this case the gifts are the seasons, the bounty of the earth, and the strength of the people. The ruler and his ministers must harmonize with the natural cycles and order of these endowments, adhering to Tian's mandated ritual norms, otherwise Tian will send down disaster.[21]

As for the cultivation of *de*, emulation is still the primary method in the *Lunyu* and *Mencius*, but anyone can take King Wen 文王 as their model. One can also learn from non-kin living models in the form of worthy teachers and advisors, or even from the written words of the classics. The behaviors to be modeled and learned include correct ritual, exemplary moral behavior, and knowledge applicable to governing. In contrast, for the texts examined herein that we now classify as Daoist (*Neiye*, *Laozi*, and the "Inner Chapters" of the *Zhuangzi*), cultivation of *de* is a process of casting off one's learned knowledge and behaviors through the practice of breathing meditation.[22] This practice is unrelated to *de*'s earlier usage and presumably a result of the linking of *de* to the concepts of *qi* and *jing* 精 (vital essence).[23]

These developments in *de*'s meaning may also be observed in the changing metaphors and analogies used for the concept. Such an approach is, of course, inspired by Allan's *The Way of Water*, in which she examines root metaphors to analyze key philosophical concepts (including *de*). The bronze-inscription phrases "pay due attention to his *de*" (*shen jue de* 慎厥德) and "grasp his *de*" (*bing de* 秉德) use the metaphor of something that needs to be held tightly in the hand and attended to with constant vigilance, like a valuable object granted to one but with the understanding that it could be lost, or reclaimed. This accords with the idea of *de* as a divine gift, complementary to Tian's Mandate. The *de* of an ancestor was seen as a model to be emulated, suggesting a metaphor of a performance one learns and must remember. As Constance Cook suggests, this may reflect an actual choreographed ritual performance, symbolizing the handing over of *de* from ancestor to descendant, thus also including the "grasping" metaphor just discussed.[24] The concept of the modeling and emulation of *de* across generations perhaps develops into the idea of *de* as a force that influences at a distance. We thus have the metaphor of *de* as the wind that causes the grass to bend (*Lunyu* 12.19) and the attractive force that keeps stars circling the polestar (*Lunyu* 2.1).[25] This also explains the analogy made between the power of both *de* and music. It was observed that music was somehow able to move through space and cause a sympathetic response in other instruments, but also in humans. Similarly, the ruler's *de* could positively influence his subjects across great distances.[26]

The *Laozi* and *Zhuangzi* develop *de* as an independent animating force, or, perhaps, see *de* as the force that models the Dao in the myriad things, thus also reflecting the idea of emulation. As Allan discusses, these, and other texts, frequently apply the metaphor and imagery of water to *de*.[27] Thus, the *Laozi* uses the analogy of the valley, down to and in which water naturally flows, to describe the person always full of *de* (chap. 28).[28] As a vital force, essential to life, *de* "nourishes" (*xu* 畜) the myriad things, as water sustains all life (chap. 51).[29] As will be discussed later, the metaphor of fragrant sacrificial offerings is also used for *de* and perhaps relates to this idea of *de* as a nourishing force. "Mysterious *de*" (*xuan de* 玄德) is deep and distant, suggesting deep water in a ravine (chap. 65).[30] In the *Zhuangzi*, *de*'s not taking a specific shape is compared to still water being perfectly flat (chap. 5).[31] Allan sees this as a metaphor for the calm, reflective heart/mind of one with fully cultivated *de*.[32] The *Mencius* uses the metaphor of flowing water for the way *de*'s good example can spread through the land (4A.6).[33] However, Mencius's four-shoots analogy seems to be equated with the potential to develop *de*, suggesting the application of the plant-growth metaphor to *de*.[34] So, by this stage, we have multiple different metaphors applied to *de*. Allan brings these together, including the idea that *de* is particular to the lineage and the individual, and suggests: "At the level of root metaphor, the imagery of *de* is based on that of a seed, or, more precisely, water that contains the seed or essence of people (i.e., semen). Within this seed is the potential expression of each person's individuality and hereditary characteristics as a member of his lineage."[35]

Several aspects of the development in the meaning of *de* are particularly relevant for the following discussion on the excavated covenant texts. First, as discussed, Spring and Autumn bronze inscriptions reflect an understanding of *de* by the political elites that remains very conservative. This is true even in later examples contemporary with the early philosophers (5th c. BCE).[36] In the inscriptions, the lineage continues to be integral to the individual's cultivation of *de* for their political success. It is still emulation of and ancestral sacrifice to the lineage ancestors that leads to the transfer and preservation of *de*. The *de* so accumulated brings prestige to the lineage and maintains the political ties between the lineage and the Zhou king (or a regional ruler), and *de* could then continue to be passed down to future lineage generations.

In contrast, in the philosophical texts examined, *de* is very rarely discussed in the context of lineage and ancestors. *De* is directly generated in all individuals by Tian, or exists in a person as a complementary force to Dao: it does not have to be received from ancestors. Cultivation of *de* is not through ritual emulation of one's own ancestors but through modeling oneself on King Wen, other sage rulers, or on living models—worthy advisors unrelated to oneself. For the Daoist texts, it is the individual who cultivates themselves using breathing meditation. While several texts still mention ancestral ritual as a significant aspect of *de*'s cultivation, this is not stressed and the focus is on the world of the living, rather than the dead. This is a general trend, illustrated by the oft-cited *Lunyu* passage in which Confucius advises Ji Lu 季路 to focus on life and serving the living rather than death and the spirits (11.12).[37] The individual's purpose in cultivating *de* is still commonly for success in one's official duties, but it is also for personal moral and/or spiritual growth and fulfillment. It is not for the prestige of one's wider lineage.

We should note, however, that the lineage is not completely absent from philosophical texts from this period. For the Ruists, the lineage-related concepts of filial piety and devotion to elder brothers (*xiaoti* 孝悌) continue to be fundamental expectations. However, the aim is to extend moral behavior outward to everyone, and to treat others as one would wish to be treated oneself, so that, ultimately, "all within the four seas are brothers."[38] The *Laozi*'s idyllic settlement (chap. 80) must be kin based, but there is no hierarchy, no ritual, no use for bronze vessels, and no education or writing.[39] Thus, the Laozian *de* is completely removed from its original context and is, rather, a force that brings one into unity with the Dao and thus with all things.

These developments in *de*'s meaning and usage were taking place in the context of significant social and political changes in the fifth and fourth centuries BCE. The Wenxian Covenant Texts are political administrative materials, and their use reflects aspects of this sociopolitical transformation. They allow us insight into possible correlation between the sociopolitical and intellectual realms during this period. The following section introduces the Wenxian Covenant Texts, their dating, the two oaths that use *de*, and the oath most relevant to the issue of the political treatment of the individual.

The Wenxian Covenant Texts: *De* and Sociopolitical Change

The Wenxian Covenant Texts were excavated in 1980–1981 in the village of Xizhangji 西張計, in Wenxian (Wen County), Henan Province.[40] The site (approximately 135 × 50 m) was originally a raised earthen platform, still over 2 m in height during the first half of the twentieth century. It was then gradually leveled as the earth was dug out for use in construction projects. From what remained of the platform, 125 pits were excavated, the majority of which contained either a simple jade object or ovicaprine (i.e., sheep or goat) skeleton. On this basis, the site is identified as a sacrificial area that served an adjacent unexcavated city site, assumed to be a major Han 韓 settlement, and tentatively identified as the historical Zhou 州.

In sixteen pits, stone tablets were found, many of which still had legible brush-written texts in the form of oaths of allegiance to the leader of the Han lineage. Fragments of tablets, generally without legible text, were also found in other pits and areas of previously disturbed earth. The tablets are all under 29 cm in length and are categorized by shape and stone type. The most common type is *gui* 圭-shaped (i.e., flat and long with a level base and pointed top) and made of slate, although sandstone examples were also found, as well as a smaller number of tablets in the form of narrow slips of a finer stone (identified as carbonatite). The total number of tablets and large fragments excavated was about 13,700. The number of tablets in a single pit varied from a few dozen to over six thousand. Each legible tablet has a copy of one of nine different oath types, individualized with the name of the covenantor taking the oath. In most cases a single pit included just a single oath type. Some oath types were found in more than one pit. The oaths are highly formulaic: they begin with a name clause; this is generally followed by a stipulation demanding that the covenantor be loyal to the Han lineage leader; then a further stipulation making a specific demand or prohibition; a submission invoking the sanctioning spirit; and, finally, an imprecation to be triggered if the oath is violated (examples are given later).[41]

Dating of these texts is critical to align their use of *de* and related concepts to that of other fifth- and fourth-century BCE texts. The original short report on the discovery suggested a dating of the early fifth century BCE.[42] However, evidence discovered during later processing of the materials supports a reconsideration of this dating. I will briefly summarize my proposed new dating of the materials here, leaving a full discussion for a different venue.

Dating is complicated by the fact that every pit potentially represents a single covenant ceremony with a unique date. The sacrificial area was used over several decades. This is evident from the use of the personal names of two historically identifiable Han lineage leaders who ruled at different times, two different dates found on covenants in separate pits, and the stratigraphy of the pits (some cutting into earlier pits). The two Han lineage leaders' names are Qizhang 啟章, the name of Han Wu Zi 韓武子 (Viscount Wu of Han, whose traditional dates as lineage leader are 424–409 BCE), and Qu 取, the name of Han Lie Hou 韓烈侯 (Marquis Lie of Han, who led from 399 to 387 BCE).[43] Two dates have also been found, one from each of the two pits with the largest number of tablets, pits T1K1 and T1K14. All legible tablets from these pits are examples of the "Oath of Allegiance," which does not include the name of the covenant lord. Pit T1K1 had roughly 4,500 tablets, many of which include the following date: "Fifteenth year, twelfth month, *yiwei* was the first day of the month, [today is] *xinyou* [the twenty-seventh day of the month]" (十五年十二月乙未朔辛酉). More recently, a single tablet with a date was noticed among the over six thousand tablets from pit T1K14 (tablet T1K14-3381). That date is: "Sixteenth year, eleventh month, *gengshen* was the first day of the month" (十六年十一月庚申朔); there is no further *ganzhi* 干支 date given, so the intended date is the first day of the month.

The lunar months and new-moon day names in these dates match those in reconstructed calendrical tables for the corresponding (Julian calendar) dates of February 9th and December 5th, in the year 399 BCE.[44] I conjecture that the reign years in these dates (fifteenth and sixteenth years) are those of Jin Lie Gong 晉烈公 (Duke Lie of Jin), the leader, at that time, of the Jin state, in which Han was a ministerial lineage until its secession. However, there is a discrepancy of one or more years with the various extrapolated reign dates suggested for this ruler. Nevertheless, given that there are already at least four different reconstructed reign periods for this Jin lord, I would suggest such clear uncertainty about the dates of this reign gives leeway to consider this alternative as a possibility.[45] This is particularly true since the extrapolated dates for these two covenants correspond to the traditional dating for the first year of Han Lie Hou's rule, one of the two Han leaders named in other oaths. This strongly suggests that he was also the unnamed covenant lord of the "Oath of Allegiance," and he organized these covenant ceremonies during the first two years of his reign.

I believe that the roughly 11,650 participants in the "Oath of Allegiance" were swearing their loyalty to Han Lie Hou as Han was splitting from Jin to become an independent polity.[46] This also accords with passages found in many received texts stating that the Zhou king had recognized the leaders of the three Jin ministerial lineages of Han, Zhao 趙, and Wei 魏 as regional lords in 403 BCE.[47] Han Lie Hou, coming to power a few years later, wanted to clearly identify and consolidate a core group of the population within his polity, and the "Oath of Allegiance" was a tool with which to do this.[48] For the purposes of this chapter, it will be assumed that this was the case, and that the majority of the excavated covenants from Wenxian date to the reign of Han Lie Hou (r. 399–387 BCE). A very small number (from one pit) date to the reign of Han Wu Zi (r. 424–409 BCE), while some oath types have no evidence that lends itself to precise dating. Comparing this to the chronology adopted for the eight texts previously surveyed, these covenants were created toward the end of the period represented by the *Zuo zhuan* and *Lunyu*, that is, the late fifth century BCE, and the start of the period of the other texts, that is, the fourth century BCE.

Use of *De* in the Wenxian Covenant Texts

Two of the nine oath types identified among the Wenxian Covenant Tablets use the term *de*: the "Seeking Blessings" oath type (*jiaofu lei* 徼福類) and the "Prayers and Sacrifices" oath type (*daoci lei* 禱祠類).[49] The "Seeking Blessings" oath type was found only in pit T1K17 and has no covenant lord name or date, meaning accurate dating is not possible. I assume that, like those datable tablets, it was produced during the late fifth or early fourth century BCE. The "Prayers and Sacrifices" oath was found on tablets in two pits situated a few meters apart, T5K1 and T5K14, while a single example of the oath was found in pit T3K6 (tablet T3K6-16). Both pits T5K1 and T3K6 had tablets of other oath types in which the covenant lord was named as Qu 取, that is, the Han Lie Hou discussed earlier. Since we assume a single pit represents a single covenanting event, and that it is unlikely an identical oath would be used by two different leaders, we can be confident that the "Prayers and Sacrifices" oaths were all overseen by Han Lie Hou at some point during his reign (399–387 BCE).

Far fewer people participated in these two covenants, compared to the thousands that joined the "Oath of Allegiance." These two oaths were clearly targeted at select groups of people. Approximately 155 people participated in the "Seeking Blessings" covenant.[50] Around 140 covenantors participated in the "Prayers and Sacrifices" oath.[51] In both cases, the majority of the tablets were of *gui*-shaped slate, but slips of the finer stone were also found: seven in the case of the "Seeking Blessings" covenant; nine in one of the two main pits used for the "Prayers and Sacrifices" covenant. As Hao Benxing 郝本性 has conjectured, the slip-shaped tablets of finer stone, apparently placed first in the pit, and the slate tablets, placed next, can be taken to represent two different ranks of covenantor.[52] We may further speculate that, for each of these two covenants, the lower-ranked covenantors answered to those of higher rank in those official duties related to the stipulations of the oath.[53] Based on the content of the oaths, to be discussed later, the covenantors who participated in the "Seeking Blessings" oath type must all have had positions that entailed involvement in sacrifices to spirits who would bless the Han lineage leader. In the case of the "Prayers and Sacrifices" oath type, the covenantors must have had offices or responsibilities related to the supply of goods for sacrificial activity by the Han leader. The number of covenantors, and ratio between ranks, is close in both these oath types, and both are concerned with duties related to the Han leader's ancestral sacrifices. One might speculate, then, that the same set of people made up the majority of participants in both of these covenants.[54]

Examples of the full text of each oath type are given here:[55]

"Seeking Blessings" oath type (jiaofu lei 徼福類), Tablet T1K17-129

I. 自今以往, 強梁
II.A. 事其主, 敢不繩繩[56]焉判其腹心, 恪慎其德
II.B. 以徼主福者,
III. 嶽公大塚, 諦極視之,
IV. 靡夷彼氏.

I. From today onward, [if] Qiang Liang,
II.A. in serving his lord, dares to not vigilantly split open his guts and heart, and reverently pay due attention to his *de*,
II.B. in order to seek the lord's blessings [i.e., blessings for the lord],
III. resplendent Lord Yue, Great Mountain, attentively and tirelessly watching him [i.e., the covenantor],
IV. will wipe out that [i.e., the covenantor's] patriline [i.e., the covenantor and his direct male descendants].

"Prayers and Sacrifices" oath type (*daoci lei* 禱祠類), Tablet T5K14-32

I. 自今以往, □
II.A. 事主, 所敢不繩繩焉中心恪慎其德
II.B. 以勉供主禱祠者,
III. 嶽公大塚, 諦極視之,
IV. 靡夷彼氏.[57]

I. From today onward, [covenantor's name],

II.A. in serving [his] lord, if [he] dares to not vigilantly, [and in his] innermost heart, reverently pay due attention to his *de*,

II.B. in order to strive to supply the prayers and sacrifices of [his] lord,

III. resplendent Lord Yue, Great Mountain, attentively and tirelessly watching him [i.e., the covenantor],

IV. will wipe out that [i.e., the covenantor's] patriline [i.e., the covenantor and his direct male descendants].

The "Seeking Blessings" oath requires the covenantors to seek blessings for the covenant lord, that is, the Han lineage leader. The "Prayers and Sacrifices" oath requires the covenantors to supply the Han lineage leader with materials to be used in sacrificial ritual. Key aspects of these two oaths will be analyzed below.

The formulaic phrases in the first stipulation (II.A) of both oaths are contemporary equivalents of formulae found in bronze inscriptions. The phrase "reverently pay due attention to his *de*" (*ke shen qi de* 恪慎其德) is a modified version of the formulaic phrase *shen jue de* 慎厥德 "pay due attention to his *de*," commonly found in the inscriptions. In the bronze inscriptions, the phrase is often used in the context of praising ancestors who diligently served their lords, for example: "Resplendent, mighty father, Duke ___ , sublimely [he] was able to make clear his heart, paying due attention to his *de*, in this way serving the former king, . . ." (Shi Wang *ding* 師望鼎, mid-Western Zhou 976–878 BCE);[58] and also: "Sublime [was] my cultured ancestor, Shi Hua Fu, opening and yielding his heart, placid and quiet in his enterprise, properly paying due attention to his *de*, thus able to respectfully protect his lord, King Gong" (Ke *ding* 克鼎, late-Western Zhou 877–771 BCE).[59] Paying due attention to one's *de* was essential for successfully serving one's ruler. The same is true in the oaths, where the phrase translated as "in serving his lord" (*shi qi zhu* 事其主 or *shi zhu* 事主) refers to the covenantor serving the living leader of the lineage. The exhortation in the oaths that the covenantor "split open his guts and heart" (判其腹心) and act from his "innermost heart" (中心), that is, to show complete sincerity, are later interpretations of bronze-inscription phrases such as those used in the previous examples: "make clear his heart" (明厥心) and "opening and yielding his heart" (聰□(讓?)厥心).[60] Joern Grundmann argues that this is the case, suggesting that both the covenant texts and the

Western Zhou bronzes see the heart as the "seat of individual loyalty and political decision making."[61]

The choice to use the phrase "reverently pay due attention to his *de*" (*ke shen qi de* 恪慎其德) must have been motivated by the topic of these two oaths, that is, ritual sacrifice and prayer to the spirits. These are the only two Wenxian oath types that concern ritual prayer and sacrifice, and the only two that add this phrase to the highly formulaic first stipulation. Clearly, and in great contrast to philosophical texts from this period, for the Han lineage leader and the officials responsible for the text of the oath, *de* could still be treated as directly and narrowly associated with lineage sacrificial ritual in the context of service to one's lord.

The "Seeking Blessings" oath type requires each covenantor to swear to "seek the lord's blessings" (*jiao zhu fu* 徼主福), that is to say, "seek blessings [from the spirits] *for* the lord."[62] The oath explicitly links the act of "paying due attention to one's *de*" to this outcome (using the conjunction *yi* 以 "in order to"). Again, this is highly reminiscent of the bronze inscriptions, in which living descendants carefully cultivate and preserve the *de* transmitted from ancestors. They do so by regularly sacrificing to and feasting them, in order to receive blessings to further strengthen their *de*. The Qin Gong *bo* 秦公鎛, a post-Western Zhou bronze, tentatively dated to the end of the seventh, beginning of the sixth century BCE, gives a good example of this: "I am insignificant, [I] sublimely abide by and grasp bright *de*, wisely spread [the ancestors'] shining example, sincerely respect my sacrifices, in order to receive great blessings."[63] The Qin ruler here announces to his ancestors his emulation and maintenance of their *de* and their shining example, and his continuing sacrifices to them; all activities aimed at ensuring the ancestors will continue to bless him. However, while the language employed and the references to ancestral ritual in bronze inscriptions are so similar to the text of the oaths, the covenant texts utilize them for a different function, in a quite different context.

The covenant tablets were produced on the orders of the Han lineage leader, with the aim of consolidating a loyal group of subjects and coercing groups of subordinates to carry out or desist from specific actions. The tablets were produced for one-time use in a covenant ceremony at which a particular oath was sworn by the covenantors, each named on a personalized tablet. The sanctioning deity, a mountain spirit called Lord Yue (Yue Gong 嶽公), was invoked to witness the oath, the tablets then buried in a pit as a permanent record, always accessible to the spirit.[64] If a covenantor ever violated the oath, the all-seeing and ever-vigilant Lord Yue would know this and would kill him and all members of his immediate direct-patriline unit (sons, grandsons).[65] This is far removed from the function of the bronzes, which were permanently and proudly displayed in the lineage temple, their inscriptions functioning to memorialize and celebrate the glorious achievements of lineage members and their ancestors, often in the context of their positive relations with the Zhou king.

In contrast, in the "Seeking Blessings" oath, the Han lineage leader is requiring, on pain of death, a group of subordinates to engage in activities, in their service to him, that will bring him blessings. Their use of *de* in archaic formulaic language associated with lineage-based ancestor worship strongly suggests that these blessings are to be sought through ancestral sacrifice. The question is, why did the Han lineage leader find it necessary to use an oath to pressure this group of subordinates to take part in ancestral sacrifices to seek blessings for him? Traditionally, assisting in these sacrifices would have been the responsibility of his own lineage members.[66] If he really needed to coerce his own lineage members (or at least a large group of them) to participate in such basic lineage duties, this would suggest a complete breakdown in the lineage tradition. This seems to conflict with other evidence, such as the ongoing use of lineage cemeteries, that indicates the continued relevance of the lineage in at least some contexts.[67]

Another explanation might be that the covenanting group included people who were not members of the Han trunk lineage.[68] With the transition to a political structure based on allegiance of the individual, the Han ruler would have expected branch-lineage and non-Han members among his officials and followers to take on sacrificial activities that had previously been restricted to his own lineage. The *Zuo zhuan* stresses the importance for regional rulers to demonstrate to the spirits that they were maintaining *de*, so that they might receive the spirits' blessings in support of the state.[69] If support from the spirits for the leader of the state translated to divine support for the whole state, then the Han leader may have felt justified in expecting broad assistance with these rituals. However, it seems plausible that members of non-Han and branch lineages may have been reluctant to join the worship of ancestors other than their own. The call to "pay due attention to one's *de*" would feel particularly incongruous since *de* was traditionally considered to be passed down through, and identified with, one's own lineage. That this understanding of lineage sacrifice as exclusive to lineage members still prevailed at this time is evident from texts from the period. For example, the *Zuo zhuan* states: "The spirits do not savor non-kin [offerings], people do not sacrifice to non-lineage [ancestors]"; and: "If spirits are not of one's lineage, they do not savor one's sacrifices."[70] In the *Lunyu*, Confucius is recorded as saying: "If not one's [ancestral] spirits, yet one sacrifices to them, that is currying favor."[71] The Han leader, while no doubt acutely aware of this point, may well have expected that, by swearing allegiance to him, the covenantors had forsworn their prior loyalties and were now members of a quasi-Han lineage. The use of blood sacrifice that was part of the covenanting ceremony perhaps functioned partly to symbolize the creation of artificial blood ties.[72] The Han lineage leader would, then, have expected all who had sworn allegiance to him to take on the obligation to perform rites that were a traditional requirement of lineage membership. The "Prayers and Sacrifices" oath highlights a related aspect of sacrificial ritual activity that was causing further problems for the Han leader.

The "Prayers and Sacrifices" oath type demands, I have argued elsewhere, that the covenantor "strives to supply (*gong* 供) the prayers and sacrifices of his lord."[73] In practice, this would mean supplying the Han leader with the materials needed for him to conduct regular sacrifices, for example, sacrificial animals, grains, alcohol, and firewood. Pre-Qin received texts from all periods include passages describing such requirements, for instance:

Lüshi chunqiu 呂氏春秋 "Ji Dong 季冬" (text: 239 BC)[74]

乃命四監, 收秩薪柴, 以供寢廟及百祀之薪燎. . . . 乃命太史, 次諸侯之列, 賦之犧牲, 以供皇天上帝社稷之享. 乃命同姓之國, 供寢廟之芻豢. 令宰歷卿大夫至于庶民土田之數, 而賦之犧牲, 以供山林名川之祀. 凡在天下九州之民者, 無不咸獻其力, 以供皇天上帝社稷寢廟山林名川之祀.

Then he [the Son of Tian] orders the four supervisory officials to collect and organize firewood, in order to supply the sacrificial fires of the ancestral temple and the many sacrifices. . . . Then [the Son of Tian] orders the Grand Scribe to rank the feudal lords, to levy from them sacrificial animals to supply the offerings for mighty Tian, Shang Di, and the Earth and Grain altars. Then [he] orders the states with [rulers] of the same surname, to supply [sacrificial] animals for the ancestral temple. [He] orders the prime minister to rank, in order of number, the lands of the great ministers [and those of all ranks down] to the commoners, and levy from them sacrificial animals, to use to supply the sacrifices to the mountains, forests, and famed rivers. Among every person under the sky and within the nine lands, there is not one who does not contribute his strength in order to supply the sacrifices to mighty Tian, to Shang Di, to the Earth and Grain altars, the ancestral temple, the mountains, forests, and famed rivers.

While this example describes the organization of tributes to the Zhou king, a similar system would have been in place for regional lords and lineage heads. In the traditional lineage-based ruling system, tribute sustained the regular sacrifices carried out by a ruler to ancestors and nature spirits. The sacrifices, in turn, assured the continuing bestowal of *de* from the ancestors. Furthermore, after the sacrifices, the tradition of redistributing sacrificial meat to allies, subordinates, and subjects was critical to maintain their goodwill and support, making a sufficient supply of tributes a political necessity.[75] Tribute was simply another aspect of serving one's lord and supporting his ancestral and other sacrifices, all activities associated with the traditional concept of *de*. Thus, the use of the phrase *ke shen qi de* "reverently pay due attention to his *de*" is apt in this oath.

The suggestion that the use of *de* in this oath would have been associated with the sacrifices, which are the focus of the oath, finds support in the actual form of the graph used for *de* on some of the tablets. Among the tablets from pit T5K14, three examples of the graph that writes *de* add the *shi* 食 "food" component to the phonetic *zhi* 直.[76] This has not previously been seen as a variant for *de*. If, as would be most likely, the *shi* 食 "food" component was added by the scribe or scribes as a semantic component, this suggests an association between *de* and food sacrifice to ancestors in the minds of people at the time. This suggestion is supported by the *Shijing* 詩 經 poem "Ji zui" 既醉, in which the ancestral spirits speak to the descendants through a ritual specialist, praising their sacrifices and feasting, and blessing the descendants. The poem opens with "We are drunk with wine, we are sated with *de*," the *de* occurring where one would expect a word for food sacrifices of some sort.[77] Similarly, in the *Zuo zhuan*, an advisor emphasizing to a ruler the importance of *de* in the eyes of the spirits quotes the *Zhou shu* 周書 saying: "The [sacrificial] millet is not fragrant, it is only bright *de* that is fragrant."[78] This suggests that the sacrificial offerings were, at some level, thought to symbolize the *de* of the descendants, and it is this *de* that the ancestors truly appreciate and reward with blessings. Marcel Granet also links *de* to food received in tribute. The ruler's subordinates and subjects provided tributes that he both ate and used for sacrifice. The ruler thus assimilated "through [the tributes] the totality of sacred forces emanating from his domain." In turn, those ruled shared in the feast, and thus they "procured a small part of the Power realized by their common effort."[79] For a lineage leader, food received as tribute "nourished within him the Virtues [*de*] specific to his Line, and his Virtues passed to those who ate his leavings."[80] The power to obtain sacrificial offerings in the form of tributes and then redistribute sacrificial meat was, arguably, a measure of the strength and effectiveness of a leader's *de*, as utilized in governing his subordinates and subjects.

This oath makes it clear that the covenantors were not supplying the expected tribute that the Han lineage leader relied on to carry out his sacrifices and prayers to ancestors, and presumably also those to nature spirits (such as the Lord Yue of the oaths). In the case of this oath, we can be sure that not all the covenantors were members of the Han trunk lineage. Among the T5K14 examples, three tablets have legible covenantor names that give another character before the given name. One is Han 韓 (tablet T5K14-41), so this covenantor was a member of the Han lineage. One is *shi* 史 (tablet T5K14-40), so either the person's official title (i.e., Scribe), or an official title being used as a lineage name. And one is a variant form of Su 蘇 (tablet T5K14-38), an ancient state name that early glosses suggest was located in the area of modern-day Wenxian, so either the name of a completely separate lineage or possibly the name of a Han branch lineage that had adopted a local place name for their lineage name. Based on this occurrence of both a Han and at least one non-Han lineage name among the covenantors, it is evident that this tribute was expected from individuals both inside and outside the Han trunk lineage. That some form of tribute would have been expected from all subjects, regardless of lineage affiliation, is supported by evidence from received texts, such as the passage quoted earlier from the *Lüshi chunqiu*.[81] Nevertheless, those covenantors from different lineages might have felt that appeals to one's *de* were inappropriate, given *de*'s traditional association with one's own lineage. However, as will be discussed further, this reluctance to support the leader with tributes may also reflect a new economic framework in which the traditional redistribution of wealth through the lineage was undermined by a growing concept of private property. The Warring States period also saw an increase in localized sacrificial activity, which would then have competed for resources with the demand for state-level tribute.[82] Lothar von Falkenhausen notes how the lineage sacrifices of sublineages focused on several recent generations of ancestors, thereby weakening the link to ancestors of remote antiquity and concentrating attention on the living lineage: "The focus of ritual had shifted from the ancestral spirits to the living ritual community."[83] In such a context, appeals to these covenantors to consider their obligations arising from the shared *de* of the lineage may have seemed outmoded.

Overall, the "Seeking Blessings" and "Prayers and Sacrifices" oath types portray a Han lineage leader with a traditional view of the ritual requirements expected of him as head of a lineage (now also ruler of a regional state), and the expectation that his subordinates would adhere to these. They apparently were not doing so, leading the Han ruler to utilize the tool of covenant to persuade them to comply. The oaths of these covenants used archaic and formulaic language, employing the traditional concept of *de* in its original context of lineage-based ancestral sacrifice. This was taking place at the beginning of the fourth century BCE, yet philosophical texts from around this period have, in contrast, only passing reference to the lineage and little to say about ancestral rituals, particularly in the context of *de*. This may reflect a reduction in the significance attached to these institutions by the new class of low-ranking mobile elites. This class would have included the philosophers and many of their followers, and, we can conjecture, many of the covenantors taking part in these two oaths. To better understand the sociopolitical changes that seem to correlate with these changing attitudes, we will now consider the most common oath found at Wenxian, the "Oath of Allegiance."

THE WENXIAN "OATH OF ALLEGIANCE"

This is a basic oath of allegiance to the Han lineage leader, found on approximately 11,650 tablets, distributed among five pits, with an additional single example found in a sixth pit. An example is given here:[84]

"Oath of Allegiance" (*xiaozhong lei* 效忠類), Tablet T1K1-3705

I.   十五年十二月乙未朔辛酉, 自今以往, 雷瘱

II.A. 敢不繩繩焉中心事其主,

II.B. 而敢與賊為徒者,

III.   丕顯嶽公大塚, 諦極視汝,

IV.   靡夷彼氏.

I.   Fifteenth year, twelfth month, *yiwei* was the first day of the month, [today is] *xinyou* [the twenty-seventh day of the month]. From today onward, [if] Lei Biao

II.A. dares to not vigilantly [and] with his innermost heart serve his lord,

II.B. and dares to join with the enemy as a follower,

III. resplendent Lord Yue, Great Mountain, attentively and tirelessly watching you [i.e., the covenantor],

IV. will wipe out that [i.e., the covenantor's] patriline [i.e., the covenantor and his direct male descendants].

The oath states that, from the date given in the first clause, the covenantor will be completely loyal to the Han lineage lord and not join any enemy or renegade group (*zei* 賊) as a "follower" (*tu* 徒).[85] As stated earlier, I believe Han Lie Hou used this oath at the start of his rule, on at least two occasions in 399 BCE. He did this to consolidate the covenanting group of around 11,650 people as loyal followers, clearly demarcating them from enemies, renegade Han lineage members, and others not willing to accept his authority.[86] While not mentioning *de*, this oath provides key evidence for the increased focus on individual agency as the lineage-based sociopolitical system was breaking down.

The composition and nature of the covenanting group for this oath illustrates the increasing political significance of the individual. This seems to coincide with or anticipate the focus on the individual in the philosophical texts discussed earlier and their reinterpretation of *de* to fit this new construct. Susan Roosevelt Weld, writing on the similar Houma Covenant Texts, considers "one of the most important revelations of the find" to be that "the covenants emphasize the individual, as opposed to the collective, liability of the separate covenantors, and that breach by one covenantor did not affect the obligations of all the others."[87] Covenantors were entering into this relationship with the Han leader on an individual basis for, as we know, each tablet is personalized with a single name. There is now an assumption that each individual has political agency, independent of their personal lineage affiliation. In the Western Zhou, links between the Zhou and other lineages were based on individual relationships, but the extended lineage was also allied with the royal house. However, as the Houma and Wenxian covenants themselves make very apparent, over the course of the fifth century BCE, lineages had broken into warring factions and lineage affiliation was not a guarantee of political allegiance.[88] As a result, anyone willing to swear their loyalty to the Han leader was welcome to join the new Han polity, regardless of their original lineage affiliation. This is clearly borne out in examples of non-Han lineage names on tablets with this oath type.

These include Zhao, the name of one of the rival Jin ministerial families and a lineage completely unrelated to Han, not even sharing the same clan name (Zhao's was Ying 嬴, Han's was Ji 姬).[89] That we have Zhao lineage members choosing to swear allegiance to the Han lineage leader clearly demonstrates individual political agency that disregards personal lineage ties.

An important qualification to make here is the reasonable conjecture that each individual covenantor represented some sort of family unit, as it seems unlikely that children took part, and we do not know if women were able to take the oath (for example, as widowed heads of a household). Covenantors might, for example, have been heads of households, thus representing the whole household. Alternatively, they may have been men over a certain age treated as a unit with their wives and children, even if living in a stem family with other adult males. Three tablets from pit T1K1, in which each covenantor is named as "Zhi's son X" (職子 [name]), do suggest grown sons covenanted separately from their father, although it is possible these sons already had their own separate nuclear families and were not all part of a stem family.[90]

This consideration of the unit represented by each covenantor is pertinent to the issue of the total number of people affected by this oath. This is significant when considering the degree to which this covenant encompassed different classes and multiple lineages. If all the pits with this oath type represent different groups of covenantors, then around 11,650 people took part. Even if pit WT1K14 was a reaffirmation of the WT1K1 covenant that took place three hundred days earlier (i.e., with the same participants, see n. 46), the number is still over seven thousand people (the number of tablets in T1K14 and several other pits with this oath). Even without considering the group represented by each covenantor, this is well over the maximum number of people one would expect for a single lineage before it splits.[91]

Based on Mark Lewis's analysis of households in the Warring States to Han, we can conjecture that, during the period of the covenants, family units generally had four or five to around eight members, depending on the number of generations and the married (and parental) status of the older son or sons within the household.[92] In the case of a nuclear family with only two parents and two or three young children, the father might, as discussed, represent this whole unit in the covenant ceremony, so one tablet would represent four or five people. In a stem family, with several adult males, perhaps those males covenanted separately (as suggested earlier), so three or four tablets might represent a household of around eight (e.g., a household with a father and two or three grown sons, along with other family members). These variables make it difficult to accurately estimate the total number of people represented by the basic oath of allegiance, but they give lower and higher estimates of between roughly twenty-three thousand to fifty-eight thousand people (fourteen thousand to thirty-five thousand if the two big pits represent the same group of people). Regardless of the precise total, these large numbers strongly support the view that participants in this oath included large numbers of non-elite individuals from multiple different lineages.

While the lineage affiliation of the covenantors was not a concern for the Han leader, he did identify those covenanting as belonging to at least two separate ranks. Distinguishing just between the slip-shaped tablets of finer stone and all other tablets used for the "Oath of Allegiance" (and assuming no repeat covenanting), of the roughly 11,650 covenantors who participated in the basic oath of allegiance, around 250 were of the higher rank, the remaining 11,400 were of the lower rank.[93] The two-way rank distinction was further emphasized by the use of certain pits for just one of the two ranks. Thus, two of the five pits in which this oath type was found only had slip-shaped tablets of the finer stone (T4K10 with 46 tablets, and T5K21 with 116), while two only contained gui-shaped tablets of the inferior stone types (T1K14 with around 6,250 tablets, and T4K9 with 702 tablets). Only pit T1K1 had both, with around 90 of the finer-stone tablets placed into the pit first, before approximately 4,450 other tablets.[94] We should also remember that pit T1K14, with over six thousand tablets, was the result of a covenant ceremony held three hundred days after that of pit T1K1. Given that no high-ranking covenantors took part in this later covenant, it perhaps reflects the success of the Han leader in attracting even greater numbers of the lower elites to swear allegiance to the new state, perhaps combined with the extension of the ritual to an even broader range of the populace.

We should further note that, while covenantors are treated as individuals, there is evidence that at least some were participating in the covenant as members of small kin-based groups. For example, in pit T1K1 we find a group of thirteen tablets prepared for individuals who share the lineage name Pan 鄱, and another group of twelve tablets with a shared lineage name Lei 雷. For each of the two sets, it appears that the tablets were placed in the pit together as a bundle and that one scribe wrote most, possibly all the texts.[95] So, here we seem to have two cases of related individuals from non-Han lineages (possibly Han lineage subbranches) acting as a small group to join the covenant, probably reflecting a subgroup within their own lineage.

This suggests that the continuing relevance of lineage ties at the social level could also play a role in political activity.

In summary, the archaic use of *de*, solely found in the two oaths related to ancestral sacrifice, reflects a Han lineage leader who, at the turn of the fourth century BCE, had a rigid and conservative view of the necessity of ancestral sacrifice and ritual for his own welfare and that of his polity. This contrasts greatly with the use of *de* in philosophical texts from this and the following period. While there are occasional references to *de* in this context in these philosophical texts, for example the *Laozi*'s very uncharacteristic linking of continuing ancestral sacrifices with the cultivation and extension of *de* throughout society (chap. 54), in general, *de* has been removed from the context of the lineage and ancestors, and it became a characteristic of the individual.[96] This, in turn, reflects the focus on the individual in the "Oath of Allegiance" from Wenxian. Thus we find a tension in these different oaths between traditional ideology and political change. The "Oath of Allegiance" is evidence for a general sociopolitical transformation in which the unified lineage was replaced by the individual and their nuclear or stem family unit as the basic building block in the political order. This correlates with, and perhaps helps explain, the intellectual changes traced earlier, which start to focus on *de* as a characteristic of the individual, removed from the context of extended lineage. The following section considers these points in the context of other evidence for sociopolitical and intellectual change during this period.

Related Evidence for Changing Ideas about *De*, Lineage, and the Individual

The traditional usage of *de* by the Han ruler, in the two oaths related to ancestral sacrifice, accords with observations made by Falkenhausen, based on analysis of other archaeological evidence, highlighting the conservative ritual outlook of the highest elites at this time. He argues that, during this period, while for the majority of the aristocracy the significance of the ancestral rites weakened, the highest elite, made up of rulers and leaders of the most powerful lineages, preserved highly conservative ritual practices.[97] A new "ordinary" assemblage of bronze vessels is seen in elite tombs, often made up of *mingqi* 明器 (small models of the vessels, rather than the full-size objects), reflecting a simplified set of ritual practices. In contrast, in the tombs of the highest elites, not only is this "ordinary" assemblage found but also a "special" conservative assemblage. The "special" assemblage uses full-size vessels of the highest quality, often executed in archaic styles. Falkenhausen suggests that the "special" assemblage served to bolster these elites' claims of legitimacy by demonstrating their links to "hallowed antiquity."[98] The use of the "special" assemblage in Jin during the period of the excavated covenants is evident from the extremely rich fifth-century BCE tomb of a Zhao lineage leader found at Jinshengcun 金勝村, Taiyuan 太原.[99] The insistence in the "Seeking Blessings" and "Prayers and Sacrifices" oath types that covenantors "pay due attention to their *de*" in support of the sacrifices of the Han leader corresponds to this emphasis on ancestral ritual evident from the "special" bronze assemblages.

Below this highest elite, however, simplification of the original aristocratic ranks diminished the significance of the lineage-based hierarchy. Falkenhausen describes a reduction in rank distinctions seen in tomb assemblages, and this seems to be broadly confirmed by the ranking we observed in the Wenxian Covenant Tablets.[100] We noted a minimum two-way distinction among the covenantors, with the ruler, and possibly his immediate ruling circle, assumed to belong to a separate rank with exceptional privileges. The evidence from tomb assemblages shows fewer distinctions among the lower elites, suggesting that the original aristocratic hierarchy had been reduced to a small number of ranks. A pertinent example is the Jin cemetery of Shangma 上馬, at Houma, Shanxi, in use from the ninth to fifth centuries BCE, and for which Falkenhausen describes a three-tiered hierarchy—ruler, aristocrat, commoner—and further suggests that the original aristocratic hierarchy itself also became less distinct and gradually merged with the commoner class.[101] Thus, the ranking we see in the Wenxian covenants corresponds to Falkenhausen's observation that "the most important social distinction was now between the rulers and the ruled, and no longer between the ranked and unranked members of a lineage."[102]

The covenant ceremony itself appears to be an example of the "downward spread of ritual privileges" that Falkenhausen suggests is reflected in the wide use of the "ordinary" assemblage in tombs.[103] In several oath types, including the "Oath of Allegiance," some individual tablets open with an additional phrase, variants of which include: "The *gui*'s command" (圭命); "The words of the *gui*'s command" (圭命之言); and "The *gui*'s command states" (圭命曰). The tablets, regardless of shape or stone type, are referred to as *gui* 圭 in these phrases, and their texts as *ming* 命, both terms associated with the traditional appointment ceremonies of the aristocracy. *Gui* were ritual objects, recorded in received texts as being presented to subordinates during appointment ceremonies marking the giving of land, office, decrees, commands, and so on. The term *ming* "charge" (or "command") is the name for these elite appointments. Its extended use in the Wenxian texts to refer to the oath of the covenant is also seen in received texts, where it generally refers to covenants imposed on subordinates by higher authorities, frequently with stipulations in the form of commands.[104]

We might, then, conjecture that, particularly in the case of the "Oath of Allegiance," the covenant was presented to the covenantors as a variety of the appointment ceremony, once the privilege of the aristocracy.[105] The suggestion being that, by swearing allegiance to the Han leader, they were formally becoming subjects, supporting him in his governing project, and receiving benefits associated with this. For those lower-ranking participants, this may have been a rare, possibly new experience of such ritual privilege. Joining in the covenant meant participation in a grand ritual ceremony at which, it is reasonable to assume, the Han lineage leader himself was present, along with other members of his elite entourage and administration, as well as ritual specialists overseeing the ceremony and sacrifices. The participants would have been aware that their personal name and the oath were written on a ritual *gui* tablet, even if many—surely the great majority in the case of the "Oath of Allegiance"—could not have read the text themselves, or possibly only their own name. They were perhaps able to see, or even hold, their personalized *gui* tablet, as the spirit was called on, and as they swore the oath. This accords with Lewis's point that such use of covenant "brought a new range of the population into the purview of the gods and spirits invoked to enforce them."[106] Given the huge number of participants in the "Oath of Allegiance," it seems reasonable to assume that many of them were members of the new class of the merged lower elites and commoners. This supports Falkenhausen's view that the downward spread of privileges "was tantamount to the elimination of the social distinctions originally implied by these privileges."[107]

On the one hand, then, the Wenxian oath types with *de* reflect the conservative ritual practices of the highest elites, as observed in the use of the "special" assemblage in their tombs. On the other hand, the two-way ranking of the covenantors, and the huge size of the covenanting group for the "Oath of Allegiance," are evidence of the weakening of these traditions among the lower elites and the spreading of these diluted ritual traditions to the commoner class.

The contrast between the Han leader's focus on lineage ancestral rites on one hand, and his reorganization of the political system to a non-lineage-based model on the other, may have been influenced by his awareness of

Jin's prior history. Jin Xian Gong 晉獻公 (Duke Xian of Jin) purged his own family in the seventh century BCE, and it was also traditional in Jin to send all ducal sons, apart from the heir apparent, out of the state. As a result, the main offices of Jin were held by individuals drawn from a number of other powerful lineages.[108] Inter-lineage conflict gradually reduced the number of these ministerial families and, by the middle of the fifth century BCE, only Han, Zhao, and Wei were left. These three lineages preserved a mutual peace, cooperating when necessary, as they focused on consolidating their own power. This ultimately led to the partitioning of Jin among themselves at the end of the fifth century BCE, leaving just a small ducal territory. Nevertheless, these lineages also experienced serious intra-lineage factional splits and warfare. Such conflict is recorded in the histories, but several of the excavated covenants provide firsthand evidence of such disunity in their use to delineate one lineage faction from another. The majority of the Houma covenants provide evidence for such a split within the Zhao lineage during the second half of the fifth century BCE: the covenant lord, head of the Zhao main lineage, is Zhao Jia 趙嘉, while the leader of the enemy camp is one Zhao Hu 趙弧, that is, a member of the same lineage leading a breakaway faction.[109] Similarly, at Wenxian, we find an oath type with eight enemies listed, four of whom have the lineage name Han.[110]

Aware of these dangers, the Han lineage leader wanted a strong lineage-based center to the new Han polity, presumably hoping to avoid the fate of the Jin ducal house. This would explain his insistence on participation in the Han ancestral sacrifices by a core group of subordinates, as evident from the "Seeking Blessings" and "Prayers and Sacrifices" oaths. At the same time, inter- and intra-lineage conflict in Jin had demonstrated the instability of a governing structure that gave significant power to ministerial families, and the unreliability of lineage ties as a basis for political loyalty. Han thus adopted the alternative form of political organization we see in the "Oath of Allegiance" at Wenxian. This gave the individual political agency, lineage affiliation was ignored as a qualification for joining, and the essential requirement was an oath of loyalty to the Han leader, taking precedence over all prior allegiances, lineage or otherwise.[111]

The use of Lord Yue, a mountain spirit, to sanction the oaths is further evidence of the move away from the ancestral cult in political organization. The oath types with *de* suggest a continued focus on lineage-based ancestral ritual by the Han leader himself. However, for the purpose of bringing together a diverse group of covenantors with ties to multiple different lineages, the lineage-neutral nature spirit, Lord Yue, was far more likely to be effective than a lineage-specific ancestral spirit. Lord Yue, from its elevated position, observed the activities of every individual within the geographical area of Jin, regardless of their lineage affiliation. This is an early example of the tendency for rites to local nature spirits to become more prominent as ancestral ties became less significant in political organization.[112] Further-more, the sanctioning spirit's punishment is limited to the individual and his direct male-descent line, not to the extended lineage. Therefore, it is the individual who is responsible for compliance with the oath, and the covenantors are considered equal in this respect, regardless even of rank.[113]

As analysis of the "Seeking Blessings" and "Prayers and Sacrifices" oaths demonstrated, this turning away from the lineage-based political order seems to have led to challenges for the Han lineage leader in maintaining the traditional ancestral sacrifices. Another excavated covenant text highlights a possibly related factor: the growing concept of private property. In the Houma "Confiscation Texts" (*nashi lei* 納室類), the key stipulations read as follows:[114]

> [Covenantor name] . . . 而尚敢或納室者, 而或聞宗人兄弟納室者, 而弗執弗獻, . . .

> [If the covenantor] . . . , furthermore, dares to seize property, or knows of lineage members who have seized property but does not apprehend them and turn them in, . . .

In discussing this oath type, Lewis argues that *shi* 室 here indicates "the lands and dependent followers of a noble."[115] Qiu Xigui 裘錫圭 suggests that this oath was a reaction to lineage members seizing the property of defeated aristocracy for themselves, rather than surrendering it to the Zhao lineage leader, and thus reflects a growing idea of private property.[116] Jin appears to have been at the forefront of several major reforms in administrative policies that contributed to this development, such as the development of the "county" (*xian* 縣). The county was governed directly by government-appointed offi-cials rather than lineages, so that people entered into a simple contractual relationship in which they were taxed and provided military service.[117] As a result, the right to farm land no longer entailed a whole series of further lineage-related obligations for these people. This led, Lewis suggests, to a de facto recognition of private ownership of land.[118]

We can conjecture, then, that in the Jin state of the late fifth century BCE this growing concept of private property, along with the introduction of taxation, and an increase in commerce and the use of money, was leading to a breakdown in the system of redistribution of resources through the traditional tribute system.[119] As a result, the Han leader may have found it increasingly difficult to secure the expected tributes for his sacrifices. One can imagine that sublineages in particular, already conceptually and possibly geographically distant from the main Han lineage, no longer felt inclined to make generous and ongoing tribute—of what they considered to be their own property—to supply the sacrificial activities of the main Han lineage. This would be felt all the more strongly by those non-Han lineage members now swearing allegiance to Han.

These last points remind us that, while the weakening of the traditional lineage-based political system is clear from the excavated covenants and received histories, it should be acknowledged that the lineage remained an important social and conceptual unit. The "Seeking Blessings" and "Prayers and Sacrifices" oaths demonstrate the lineage's significance to the Han lineage leader himself. We find lineage cemeteries dating to this period, ancestral worship continued, although more localized as sublineages grew distant from the original trunk, and the segmentary lineage-based social structure remained in place below the elite levels of society.[120] At the Wenxian site, we noted that tablets for the basic oath of allegiance were placed in the pits in bundles, and we identified two bundles representing groups of covenantors with the same lineage name, indicating that subgroups of lineages were acting as units, suggesting lineage-based communities. And we saw (n. 90) that, in enemy lists in the covenant texts, the minimal direct-patriline group is recognized as a basic unit, and this was probably also the unit threatened with destruction if the oath was transgressed.

At the same time, the philosophical texts previously surveyed are notable for the reduced significance they afford to the lineage, particularly in the context of *de*. While defining *de* differently to suit their own doctrines, they share the distancing of *de* from precisely the context of lineage and ancestral ritual clung to by the highest elite in the covenants and instead characterize *de* as an attribute of the individual.[121] The patrilineage does remain conceptually significant in the *Lunyu* and *Liude*, but as a basis for moral behavior.[122] The general tendency among the philosophers is to deemphasize lineage-based ancestral ritual and related aspects of *de*. The trend in the Ruist texts discussed herein (*Lunyu*, *Mencius*, *Liude*) is toward seeing ritual as primarily beneficial to the living, allowing individuals, not necessarily related to each other, to live together harmoniously.[123] The *Mencius*, by locating the potential for the growth of *de* (in the form of the four cardinal virtues) innately in every human heart, places the responsibility for that growth clearly with the individual.[124] The Daoist texts turn from lineage-based ancestral ritual toward individual mysticism and the possibility of personal divinization and transcendence through meditative self-cultivation techniques.[125] The *Neiye* also includes passages on diet, urging moderation to keep the body well balanced, indicating that maintaining health is now related to the individual physical self.[126] So, the sociopolitical changes evident in the covenant texts do appear to be reflected in developments in the treatment of *de* and related concepts in the philosophical texts from this and the following period. At the same time, these philosophical texts preserve certain aspects of *de*'s original meaning and usage that remained relevant, despite the changing sociopolitical context. The most conspicuous example of this is *de*'s continuing association with individual effectiveness in political rule and service. Government service was still a central topic for the philosophers and *de* was still very much applicable in this respect, preserving the bronze inscriptions' treatment of *de* as an essential quality in leaders and officials.

Coda

How successful the Han leader's attempts were to persuade his subordinates, by appealing to an archaic concept of *de*, to supply his sacrificial activities and secure blessings for himself and the state, we do not know. However, what is clear is that the reforms in political administration, discussed earlier and reflected in the oaths, particularly in the "Oath of Allegiance," went on to be widely adopted.[127] In the mid-fourth century BCE, less than fifty years after the Wenxian covenants took place, the state of Qin 秦 began to implement systematic reforms. These included abolishing the hereditary aristocracy and, as a result, bringing to an end the role of ancestral ties and rites in political organization.[128]

The late fifth, early fourth-century BCE Wenxian Covenant Texts provide evidence of a stage in the evolutionary process leading to these transformations. We see the Han ruler still bound to *de*'s connotations with lineage-based political service and ancestral ritual, requiring the covenantors to supply tribute for and engage in ancestral sacrifice to benefit him and his state. Yet, in many other aspects, the covenants reflect the breakdown of the traditional lineage-based political system, for example: the treatment of the individual as political agent; the extension of ritual privilege to great numbers of the merged class of lower elites and commoners, actively engaging them in the creation of the state; the mix of diverse lineage names among covenantors and enemies; the identification of lineage subgroups and minimal patrilineage units; the basic two-way ranking among covenantors; the decline in the tribute system and rise in the concept of private property; and the use of a territorial nature spirit to sanction the covenants. Such developments contributed to the development of what became, under the Qin, a centralized, institutionally homogenized state with a highly codified legal system (rather than ad hoc covenants) and a complex bureaucracy, overseeing an atomized and ranked population, with a state cult based on nature spirits.

The ancient concept of *de* as a lineage-based power had been so closely connected to its function of legitimizing aristocratic authority that its meaning had to change in order for the term to survive the Warring States breakdown in the lineage-based ritual and political order. This keyword, *de*, had too significant a pedigree to be abandoned and was instead adopted and adapted in multiple ways. This allowed *de* to retain relevance for different philosophical theories, reflecting a new political structure based not on the lineage but on the individual (and the family unit they represented).

Notes

1. Sarah Allan, *The Way of Water and Sprouts of Virtue* (Albany: State University of New York Press, 1997), 106.

2. Allan, *Way of Water*, 102, 107.

3. Raymond Williams, *Keywords: A Vocabulary of Culture and Society*, new ed. (New York: Oxford University Press, 2015), xxix.

4. The analysis on which this summary is based also referenced the following previous studies on *de*: Donald J. Munro, *The Concept of Man in Early China* (Stanford: Stanford University Press, 1969), 99–150; David S. Nivison, "'Virtue' in Bone and Bronze," "The Paradox of 'Virtue,'" and "Can Virtue Be Self-Taught?" (texts of lectures given in 1980) in *The Ways of Confucianism: Investigations in Chinese Philosophy*, ed. David S. Nivison and Bryan W. Van Norden (Chicago: Open Court, 1996); Vassili Kryukov, "Symbols of Power and Communication in Pre-Confucian China (On the Anthropology of De) Preliminary Assumptions," *Bulletin of the School of Oriental and African Studies* 58, no. 2 (1995): 314–33; Scott A. Barnwell, "The Evolution of the Concept of De 德 in Early China," *Sino-Platonic Papers* 235 (2013); Huaiyu Wang, "A Genealogical Study of De: Poetical Correspondence of Sky, Earth, and Humankind in the Early Chinese Virtuous Rule of Benefaction," *Philosophy East*

and West 65, no. 1 (Spring 2015): 81–124; Constance A. Cook, *Ancestors, Kings, and the Dao* (Cambridge, MA: Harvard University Asia Center, 2017); Joern Peter Grundmann, "Command and Commitment: Terms of Kingship in Western Zhou Bronze Inscriptions and in the *Book of Documents*" PhD dissertation, University of Edinburgh, 2018; Chao Fulin 晁福林, "Xian-Qin shiqi 'de' guannian de qiyuan ji qi fazhan" 先秦時期 "德" 觀念的起源及其發展, *Zhongguo shehui kexue* 中國社會科學 2005.4, 192–204; Zheng Kai 鄭開, *De li zhi jian* 德禮之間 (Beijing: Sanlian, 2009); Li Delong 李德龍, "Xian-Qin shiqi 'de' guannian yuanliu kao" 先秦時期 "德" 觀念源流考, PhD dissertation, Jilin University, 2013; Onozawa Seiichi 小野澤精一, "Toku ron" 德論, *Chūgoku bunka sōsho 2: Shisō gairon* 中國文化叢書 2: 思想概論, ed. Akatsuka Kiyoshi 赤塚忠 et al. (Tokyo: Taishukan, 1968), 151–84; Kominami Ichiro 小南一郎, "Tenmei to toku" 天命と德, *Tōhō gakuhō* 東方學報 64 (March 31, 1992): 1–59. For research on *de* in specific texts, see the relevant notes.

5. For specific references on dating issues, see notes for the separate texts in this chapter.

6. For a different interpretation of *de*, as a "consistent attitude" (or "commitment") "to the [Heavenly] norms," see: Munro, *The Concept of Man in Early China*, 100 and passim; Grundmann, "Command and Commitment," 307 and passim.

7. See examples in: Cook, *Ancestors, Kings, and the Dao*; Grundmann, "Command and Commitment." See also: Virginia C. Kane, "Aspects of Western Chou Appointment Inscriptions: The Charge, the Gifts, and the Response," *Early China* 8 (1982–1983): 14–28; Constance A. Cook, "Wealth and the Western Zhou," *Bulletin of the School of Oriental and African Studies* 60, no. 2 (1997): 253–94.

8. Kryukov, "Symbols of Power," 321. See also: Constance A. Cook, "Scribes, Cooks, and Artisans: Breaking Zhou Tradition," *Early China* 20 (1995): 241–77, see 247; Chao Fulin, "Xian-Qin shiqi," 199–200.

9. Kryukov, "Symbols of Power," 315–16; Grundmann, "Command and Commitment," chap. 3 and passim; Cook, *Ancestors, Kings, and the Dao*, 41 and passim; Cook, "Scribes, Cooks, and Artisans," 246–49.

10. For examples, see: Crispin Williams, "Interpreting the Wenxian Covenant Texts: Methodological Procedure and Selected Analysis," PhD dissertation, University of London, 2005, 321–22, 341–42.

11. The translation "awesome decorum" follows Cook in *Ancestors, Kings, and the Dao*, 52, 81–86, and passim. See also: Chao Fulin, "Xian-Qin shiqi," 199; Cook, "Wealth and the Western Zhou," 278.

12. Cook, *Ancestors, Kings, and the Dao*, 167. For examples, see: Cook, *Ancestors, Kings, and the Dao*, 167–95; Luo Xinhui 羅新慧, " 'Shuai xing zukao' he 'nei de yu ji': Zhoudai 'de' guannian de yanhua" "帥型祖考"和"內得於己": 周代 "德" 觀念的演化, *Lishi yanjiu* 歷史研究 2016.3, 4–20.

13. For *de* in the *Zuo zhuan*, see: Yuri Pines, "*De* 德 in the *Zuozhuan* 左傳," *Journal of Chinese Philosophy* 48, no. 2 (2021): 130–42. For the dating of the sources and compilation of the *Zuo zhuan*, see: Yuri Pines, *Zhou History Unearthed: The*

Bamboo Manuscript Xinian and Early Chinese Historiography (New York: Columbia University Press, 2020), 23–27.

14. Alan K. L. Chan, "Interpretations of Virtue (*De*) in Early China," *Journal of Chinese Philosophy* 38, no. 1 (2011): 134–50, see 143.

15. For *de* in the *Lunyu*, see: Xinzhong Yao, "*De* 德 Ethics in the Four Books," *Journal of Chinese Philosophy* 48, no. 2 (2021): 143–56; Li Delong, "Xian-Qin shiqi," 231–46. For the nature and dating of the *Lunyu*, see: E. Bruce Brooks and A. Taeko Brooks, *The Original Analects: Sayings of Confucius and His Successors* (New York: Columbia University Press, 1998), 4–9.

16. For *de* in the *Laozi* and *Zhuangzi*, see: Ellen Marie Chen, "The Meaning of *Te* in the *Tao Te Ching*: An Examination of the Concept of Nature in Chinese Taoism," *Philosophy East and West* 23, no. 4 (1973): 457–70; Roger T. Ames, "Putting the *Te* Back into Taoism," in *Nature in Asian Traditions of Thought*, ed. J. Baird Callicott and Roger T. Ames (Albany: State University of New York Press, 1989), 113–44; Philip J. Ivanhoe, "The Concept of *De* ('Virtue') in the *Laozi*," in *Religious and Philosophical Aspects of the* Laozi, ed. Mark Csikszentmihalyi and Philip J. Ivanhoe (Albany: State University of New York Press, 1999), 239–57; Erin M. Cline, "Two Interpretations of *De* in the *Daodejing*," *Journal of Chinese Philosophy* 31, no. 2 (2004): 219–33; Robert H. Gassmann, "Coming to Terms with *Dé* 德: The Deconstruction of 'Virtue' and an Exercise in Scientific Morality," in *How Should One Live? Comparing Ethics in Ancient China and Greco-Roman Antiquity*, ed. R. A. H. King and Dennis Schilling (Berlin: De Gruyter, 2011), 92–125, see 114–22. For the dating of the *Laozi*, see: William H. Baxter, "Situating the Language of the *Lao-tzu*: The Probable Date of the *Tao-te-ching*," in *Lao-tzu and the Tao-te-ching*, ed. Livia Kohn and Michael LaFargue (Albany: State University of New York Press, 1998), 231–53. For the dating of the *Zhuangzi*, see: *Early Chinese Texts: A Bibliographical Guide* (Berkeley: Society for the Study of Early China and Institute of East Asian Studies, University of California, 1993), 56–57; Liu Xiaogan, *Classifying the Zhuangzi Chapters*, trans. William E. Savage (Ann Arbor: University of Michigan Press, 1994), 1–46.

17. For *de* in the *Neiye*, see: Russell Kirkland, "Varieties of Taoism in Ancient China: A Preliminary Comparison of Themes in the *Nei Yeh* and Other Taoist Classics," *Taoist Resources* 7, no. 2 (1997): 73–86, see 77; Donald Harper, *Early Chinese Medical Literature: The Mawangdui Medical Manuscripts* (London: Kegan Paul, 1998), 119; see also: Harold David Roth, *Original Tao: Inward Training and the Foundations of Taoist Mysticism—Nei-yeh* (New York: Columbia University Press, 1999). The translation of *qi* follows Roth, *Original Tao*, 41. For the dating of the *Neiye*, see: Roth, *Original Tao*, 27, 187.

18. For *de* in the *Mencius*, see: Lee H. Yearley, *Mencius and Aquinas: Theories of Virtue and Conceptions of Courage* (Albany: State University of New York Press, 1990); Xinzhong Yao, "De 德 Ethics in the Four Books"; Li Delong, "Xian-Qin shiqi," 187–200. For dating, see for example: D. C. Lau, trans., *Mencius*, rev. ed.

(London: Penguin, 2004), x; Brooks, *The Original Analects*, 5–6, 9. For the argument that this text's (and the *Lunyu*'s) final compilation dates to the Han 漢 period, see: Michael Hunter, "Did Mencius Know the *Analects*?" *T'oung Pao* 100 (2014): 33–79.

19. For *de* in the *Liude* text, see: Chan, "Interpretations of Virtue (*De*) in Early China"; Scott Cook, *The Bamboo Texts of Guodian: A Study and Complete Translation*, vol. 2 (Ithaca, NY: Cornell University East Asia Program, 2012), 751–98; Gassmann, "Coming to Terms with *Dé*," 122–24; Constance A. Cook, "Which Comes First? *Dao* 道 or *De* 德: Evidence from the Guodian Manuscripts," in *Dao Companion to the Excavated Guodian Bamboo Manuscripts*, ed. Shirley Chan (New York: Springer, 2019), 117–38, see 132–34. For the dating of the Guodian tomb, see: Sarah Allan and Crispin Williams, eds., *The Guodian* Laozi: *Proceedings of the International Conference, Dartmouth College, May 1998* (Berkeley: Society for the Study of Early China and Institute of East Asian Studies, University of California, 2000), 118–19.

20. Robert Eno, *The Confucian Creation of Heaven: Philosophy and the Defense of Ritual Mastery* (Albany: State University of New York Press, 1990), 79–98; Michael Puett, "Following the Commands of Heaven: The Notion of *Ming* in Early China," in *The Magnitude of* Ming: *Command, Allotment, and Fate in Chinese Culture*, ed. Christopher Lupke (Honolulu: University of Hawai'i Press, 2005), 49–69; Ted [Edward] Slingerland, "The Conception of *Ming* in Early Confucian Thought," *Philosophy East and West* 46, no. 4 (1996): 567–81.

21. For *de* in the *Sande* text, see: Chan, "Interpretations of Virtue (*De*) in Early China"; Zhongjiang Wang, "Natural Order and Divine Will in *The Three Virtues*," in his *Order in Early Chinese Excavated Texts*, trans. Misha Tadd (New York: Palgrave Macmillan, 2016), 107–30. For dating of the Shanghai Museum slips, see: Liao Mingchun 廖名春 and Zhu Yuanqing 朱淵清, *Shangboguan cang zhanguo Chu zhushu yanjiu* 上博館藏戰國楚竹書研究 (Shanghai: Shanghai shudian, 2002), 3.

22. See, for example: Roth, *Original Tao*, 144–68; Edward Slingerland, *Effortless Action: Wu-wei as Conceptual Metaphor and Spiritual Ideal in Early China* (Oxford: Oxford University Press, 2003), 182–85.

23. The translation for *jing* follows Roth, *Original Tao*, 42.

24. Cook, *Ancestors, Kings, and the Dao*, 27, 146, and passim.

25. Yang Bojun, *Lunyu yizhu*, 129, 11.

26. Erica Fox Brindley, *Music, Cosmology, and the Politics of Harmony in Early China* (Albany: State University of New York Press, 2012), 90–91.

27. Allan, *Way of Water*, 105–06.

28. Chen Guying 陳鼓應, *Laozi jin zhu jin yi ji pingjie* 老子今註今譯及評介 (Beijing: Zhonghua, 1984), 178.

29. Chen Guying, *Laozi jin zhu jin yi ji pingjie*, 261.

30. Chen Guying, *Laozi jin zhu jin yi ji pingjie*, 312; Allan, *Way of Water*, 105.

31. Chen Guying 陳鼓應, *Zhuangzi jin zhu jin yi* 莊子今註今譯 (Beijing: Zhonghua, 1983), 157.

32. Allan, *Way of Water*, 50–53, 86–87, 105.

33. "Thus, like rushing water, *de*'s good example will flow [all the way] to the four seas" (故沛然德教溢乎四海), Yang Bojun 楊伯峻, *Mengzi yizhu* 孟子譯注, 2 vols. (Beijing: Zhonghua, 1988 [1960]), 167.

34. Allan, *Way of Water*, 104.

35. Allan, *Way of Water*, 106. As Allan notes, *jing* 精 is also used with this sense, and *de* and *jing* are equated in Daoist texts, supporting this interpretation.

36. See n. 12.

37. Yang Bojun 楊伯峻, *Lunyu yizhu* 論語譯注 (Beijing: Zhonghua, 1982 [1980]), 113.

38. Kai Vogelsang argues that this, and much of the *Lunyu*'s teaching, reflects the change, starting in the ninth century BCE, from a segmentary society, in which lineages were the key social units, to a stratified society in which the elites "transcended local and kinship borders." See: Kai Vogelsang, "Beyond Confucius: A Socio-historical Reading of the *Lunyu*," *Oriens Extremus* 49 (2010): 29–61, see 37, 44, and passim.

39. Chen Guying, *Laozi jin zhu jin yi ji pingjie*, 357. For the *Laozi*'s "ideal community" as a depiction of segmentary society, see: Vogelsang, "Beyond Confucius," 38.

40. For the initial short report of the site, see: Henan sheng wenwu yanjiusuo 河南省文物研究所, "Henan Wenxian Dong-Zhou mengshi yizhi yihaokan fajue jianbao" 河南溫縣東周盟誓遺址一號坎發掘簡報, *Wenwu* 文物 1983.3, 78–89, 102–05. The brief summary here is based on the full excavation report: Henansheng wenwu kaogu yanjiuyuan 河南省文物考古研究院, *Henan Wenxian Dong-Zhou mengshi yizhi* 河南溫縣東周盟誓遺址 (Beijing: Wenwu, forthcoming).

41. For this formulaic structure, see: Susan Roosevelt Weld, "Covenant in Jin's Walled Cities: The Discoveries at Houma and Wenxian," PhD dissertation, Harvard University, 1990, 353–54.

42. Henan sheng wenwu yanjiusuo, "Henan Wenxian Dong-Zhou mengshi yizhi yi-hao kan fajue jianbao," 82, 87–89.

43. Hao Benxing identified the name Qizhang as a match for that of Han Wu Zi (personal communication, September 2008). This name has only been found on a few of the small number of tablets from pit T1K3. See also: Crispin Williams, "Dating the Houma Covenant Texts: The Significance of Recent Findings from the Wenxian Covenant Texts," *Early China* 35–36 (2012–2013): 247–75, see 269–70. The graph I identify as the name Qu 取 was originally identified as the name of Han Buxin 韓不信, the Han leader in the early fifth century. See: Zhao Shigang 趙世綱 and Zhao Li 趙莉, "Wenxian mengshu de lishuo yanjiu" 溫縣盟書的歷朔研究, in *Xin chu jianbo yanjiu – di-er jie xin chu jianbo guoji xueshu yantaohui wenji 2000 nian 8 yue, Beijing* 新出簡帛研究·第二屆新出簡帛國際學術研討會文集 2000 年8月·北京, ed. Ai Lan 艾蘭 [Sarah Allan] and Xing Wen 邢文 (Beijing: Wenwu, 2004), 197–205. For my reanalysis, see: Wei Kebin 魏克彬 [Crispin Williams], "Wenxian mengshu T4K5, T4K6, T4K11 mengci shidu" 溫縣盟書T4K5, T4K6, T4K11盟辭

釋讀, *Chutu wenxian yu guwenzi yanjiu* 5 (2013): 280–363, see 293–96. The use in the covenants of—in the great majority of cases—only personal names corresponds to what was apparently the convention when addressing spirits. See: Li Xueqin 李學勤, "Xian-Qin renming de jige wenti" 先秦人名的幾個問題, *Lishi yanjiu* 歷史研究1991.5, 106–11. Unless otherwise stated, extrapolated BCE dates are taken from the *Cihai* 辭海 chronology; see Cihai bianji weiyuanhui 辭海編輯委員會, ed., *Cihai* 辭海 (Shanghai: Shanghai cishu, 1989), 5427–88.

44. Zhang Peiyu 張培瑜, *Zhongguo Xian Qin shi libiao* 中國先秦史曆表 (Jinan: Qi Lu, 1987); Zhang Peiyu 張培瑜, *San qian wu bai nian liri tianxiang* 三千五百年曆日天象 (Zhengzhou: Daxiang, 1997). The dates of the two covenants are exactly five sexagenary cycles (three hundred days) apart, supporting the suggestion they are from consecutive years, with the second covenant scheduled to occur at this presumably auspicious interval after the first.

45. In Hirase Takao's 平勢隆郎 tables, which list the reconstructed reign dates of several different scholars, four different years between 405 and 401 BCE are suggested for Jin Lie Gong's fifteenth year. See Hirase Takao 平勢隆郎, *Shinpen Shiki Tōshū nenpyō* 新編史記東周年表 (Tokyo: Tōkyō daigaku tōyō bunka kenkyūjo, 1995), 564.

46. Apart from the roughly 10,800 tablets in pits T1K1 and T1K14, several hundred examples of this oath were found in other pits, taking the total to around 11,650. In saying that this number of covenantors took this oath, I am assuming that the tablets in T1K1 and T1K14 represent two different groups of individuals. However, based on historical records of reaffirmations of earlier covenants (*xunmeng* 尋盟), we cannot rule out the possibility that pit T1K14 was a renewal, with the same participants, of the T1K1 covenant that had been carried out three hundred days previously. An analysis of the legible covenantor names from each pit—to determine whether there are enough repeated names to suggest this—has not been carried out. It is also assumed that, in pits in which all or the majority of legible tablets were of this oath type, those tablets on which the text was no longer legible had also been examples of this oath.

47. See, for example, discussion in: Pines, *Zhou History Unearthed*, 116–20.

48. If the analysis suggested here for the dates is correct, then Han Lie Hou was not yet using his own reign years (the first and the second) for the dating formula on the covenant tablets. This would correspond to the record of this period in the excavated *Xinian* 繫年, in which Han Lie Hou is treated as a Jin minister right up to his last mention, corresponding to around 395 BCE. His name is given as Han Qu with no title, and his troops are referred to as part of the Jin army (the recognition of Han, Zhao, and Wei by the Zhou king as regional rulers is also not directly mentioned). For translations of the relevant sections of the *Xinian*, see: Pines, *Zhou History Unearthed*, 231–41.

49. The names of the oath types were given by the processing team and indicate the main topic of the oath.

50. This is based on the number of tablets in pit T1K17 and assumes all illegible tablets shared this same oath.

51. All but one of the tablets with this oath type were found in pits T5K1 and T5K14, situated a meter or two apart. (A single example was found in T3K6.) Both pits contained about seventy-five tablets or large fragments, all of which are *gui*-shaped slate, apart from nine tablets of the finer stone (carbonatite) found in pit T5K1 (eight clearly slip-shaped, the other of indeterminate original shape). All the thirty-five legible tablets from T5K14 were of this oath type, but five of the thirty legible tablets in T5K1 were of two other oath types. It is assumed that all or the great majority of the illegible tablets were also of the "Prayers and Sacrifices" oath type. It is further assumed that each pit corresponds to two different groups of covenantors, although we cannot completely rule out the possibility that one of these two pits was a reaffirmation of the other. However, since the finer-stone slips, indicating a group of higher-ranking covenantors, were only found in one pit, this seems unlikely.

52. Henansheng wenwu kaogu yanjiuyuan, *Henan Wenxian Dong-Zhou mengshi yizhi*.

53. Since two pits were used for all but one of the "Prayers and Sacrifices" covenant tablets (only one pit including higher-ranked covenantors), this division may indicate some further distinction within this group of covenantors.

54. There are few legible covenantor names among both sets of tablets, and the majority use just the given name, so comparison of names between pits, to look for matching names, would be inconclusive.

55. Images of these two tablets have been previously published. For T1K17-129, see: Ai Lan and Xing Wen, *Xin chu jianbo yanjiu*, pl. 11. For T5K14-32, see: Wei Kebin 魏克彬 [Crispin Williams], "Wenxian mengshu WT5K14 mengshu bushi: shuo 'gong' zi" 溫縣盟書 WT5K14 盟書補釋: 說 "龏" 字, in *Chutu wenxian yu chuanshi dianji de quanshi—jinian Tan Pusen xiansheng shishi liang zhounian guoji xueshu yantaohui lunwenji* 出土文獻與傳世典籍的詮釋——紀念譚樸森先生逝世兩周年國際學術研討會論文集, ed. Fudan daxue chutu wenxian yu guwenzi yanjiu zhongxin (Shanghai: Shanghai guji, 2010), 99–129, see 128 (pl. 1). The transcriptions give the standard characters for the words I believe are represented by the original archaic graphs on the tablets. Punctuation is added and the transcriptions are laid out following the formulaic structure described earlier, that is: I. Name clause, II. Stipulations, III. Submission, IV. Imprecation. Detailed discussion of the identification and interpretation of specific graphs and phrases can be found in: Wei Kebin 魏克彬 [Crispin Williams], "Shuo Wenxian mengshu de 'ke shen qi de'" 說溫縣盟書的 "恪慎其德," in Ai Lan and Xing Wen, *Xin chu jianbo yanjiu*, 208–17; Williams, "Interpreting the Wenxian Covenant Texts"; Wei Kebin, "Wenxian mengshu WT5K14 mengshu bushi: shuo 'gong' zi"; Wei Kebin, "Houma yu Wenxian mengshu zhong de 'Yue Gong'" 侯馬與溫縣盟書中的 "嶽公," *Wenwu* 2010.10, 76–83, 98; Crispin Williams, "Early References to Collective Punishment in an Excavated Chinese Text: Analysis and Discussion of an Imprecation from the

Wenxian Covenants," *Bulletin of the School of Oriental and African Studies* 74, no. 3 (2011): 437–67; Crispin Williams, "Scribal Variation and the Meaning of the Houma and Wenxian Covenant Texts' Imprecation *ma yi fei shi* 麻夷非是," *Early China* 37 (2014): 101–79.

56. This tablet does not have the "=" symbol next to the graph indicating repetition, but it is found in most examples. For the identification of this graph, see: He Linyi 何琳儀 and Wu Hongsong 吳紅松, "Shengsheng shi xun" 繩繩釋訓, *Zhongyuan wenwu* 2006.1, 62–64. For further evidence supporting this analysis, see Wei Kebin, "Wenxian mengshu T4K5, T4K6, T4K11 mengci shidu," 341–42.

57. The last three characters are written on the reverse side of the tablet but, if comparing with the tablet image, note that above these characters there are several other unclear graphs that appear to be the standard opening phrase of the oath, suggesting that a scribe had started writing but then stopped and the tablet was reused later.

58. *Yin Zhou jinwen jicheng* 殷周金文集成 (Beijing: Zhonghua, 1984), vol. 5, no. 2812; Constance A. Cook and Paul R. Goldin, eds., *A Source Book of Ancient Chinese Bronze Inscriptions*, rev. ed. (Berkeley: Society for the Study of Early China, 2020), 77–79. Transcription: 丕顯皇考□公, 穆穆克明厥心, 慎厥德, 用辟于先王, . . .

59. *Yin Zhou jinwen jicheng*, vol. 5, no. 2836; Cook and Goldin, *A Source Book*, 178–79. Transcription: 穆穆朕文祖師華父, 聰□ (讓?) 厥心, 盂靜于猷, 淑慎厥德, 肆克龏保厥辟恭王.

60. For *zhongxin* 中心 as "innermost heart," see: Lisa Raphals, "Virtue, Body, Mind and Spirit in the *Shijing*: New Perspectives on Pre-Warring States Conceptions of Personhood and Virtue," *Journal of Chinese Philosophy* 48, no. 1 (2021): 28–39, see 35.

61. Grundmann, "Command and Commitment," 268. See also: Ke Heli 柯鶴立 [Constance A. Cook], "Zhuodai 'mingxin': yizhong tongzhi gongju" 周代"明心": 一種統治工具, in *Zhang Changshou, Cheng Gongrou xiansheng jinian wenji* 張長壽、陳公柔先生紀念文集, ed. Li Feng 李峰 and Shi Jingsong 施勁松 (Beijing: Chinese Academy of Social Sciences, Institute for Archaeology, 2022), 490–503.

62. While grammatically possible, this phrase cannot, in this context, mean that the covenantor is seeking the blessings of the lord. The "lord" here is the living leader of the Han lineage and blessings are received from spirits, not the living. Furthermore, the stipulations of the oaths always benefit the interests of the covenant lord, not the covenantors, so the beneficiary of the blessings must be the Han lineage leader. For further discussion, see: Williams, "Interpreting the Wenxian Covenant Texts," 329–35. For grammatical constructions of this type, see: Chiew Pheng Phua, "The Double-Object Construction in Archaic Chinese: A Preliminary Proposal from the Constructional Perspective," *Bulletin of Chinese Linguistics* 1, no. 2 (2007): 59–98.

63. *Yin Zhou jinwen jicheng*, vol. 1, no. 270.1; Cook and Goldin, *A Source Book*, 245–50, see 246 for the dating. Transcription: 余惟小子, 穆穆帥秉明德, 叙敷明型, 虔敬朕祀, 以受多福.

64. *Yue* 嶽 refers to lofty, often sacred mountains, so the spirit is the "Lofty Mountain Lord," and the name may specifically refer to Mount Huo 霍, also called Mount Taiyue 太嶽, a mountain in modern Shanxi, which textual evidence suggests was considered sacred in Jin. A comparable example of a nature spirit given a secular aristocratic title is the "Yellow River Earl" He Bo 河伯, well known from transmitted sources. For a full discussion, see: Wei Kebin, "Houma yu Wenxian mengshu zhong de 'Yue Gong'"; Williams, "Dating the Houma Covenant Texts," 261–69.

65. For this interpretation of the word *shi* 氏 as used in the covenants, see: Williams, "Early References to Collective Punishment."

66. Zhang Hequan 張鶴泉, *Zhoudai jisi yanjiu* 周代祭祀研究 (Taipei: Wenjin, 1993), 156–57, 175–80, and passim.

67. Lothar von Falkenhausen, *Chinese Society in the Age of Confucius (1000–250 BC): The Archaeological Evidence* (Los Angeles: Cotsen Institute of Archaeology, University of California, 2006), chaps. 8 and 9, and passim.

68. To confirm this, we would need to know the lineage affiliation of these covenantors. Unfortunately, the few names still legible on the tablets from this pit (WT1K17) are given names only, without the lineage name. Possibly they were all Han lineage members. Possibly some could have been from other lineages. All we can be sure of, concerning the relationship between these 155 covenantors and the Han leader, is that they must have held positions and responsibilities requiring them to participate in his ancestral sacrifices.

69. Pines, "*De* in the *Zuozhuan*," 134.

70. *Zuo zhuan* Xi 僖10.3: 神不歆非類, 民不祀非族 (Yang Bojun 楊伯峻, *Chunqiu Zuo zhuan zhu* 春秋左傳注, 4 vols., rev. ed. (Beijing: Zhonghua, 1995 [1990], 334); *Zuo zhuan* Xi 僖 31.5: 鬼神非其族類, 不歆其祀 (Yang Bojun, *Chunqiu Zuo zhuan zhu*, 487).

71. *Lunyu* 2.24: 非其鬼而祭之, 諂也 (Yang Bojun, *Lunyu yizhu*, 22). This and the previous two examples are cited in: Chao Fulin 晁福林, "Shi lun Chunqiu shiqi de zuxian chongbai" 試論春秋時期的祖先崇拜, *Journal of Shaanxi Normal University (Social Sciences)* 陝西師大學報(哲學社會科學版) 24, no. 2 (1995): 88–95.

72. One of the covenant pits at Wenxian also contained a sacrificial animal. Received texts describe sacrifice at covenanting ceremonies, as well as a part of the ceremony involving either smearing of blood on the lips, or possibly drinking of blood. The Houma Covenant Texts are almost all written in red ink, perhaps with the intention of symbolizing blood.

73. The issue of interpretation here is the graph I read as *gong* 供 "to supply." The corresponding graph in the covenant texts is a graphic variant of *gong* 龏, which, in bronze inscriptions, is commonly read as *gong* 恭 "to respect" in the sense of "to uphold," "to act in accordance with." This would be acceptable here, suggesting that the covenantors must attend to certain duties related to the prayers and sacrifices of the lord. However, the bronze inscriptions also sometimes write this same word with *gong* 共, but they also use *gong* 共 to denote the word *gong* 供 "to supply."

I suggest that the *gong* 龏 of the covenant texts might, then, also be denoting the word *gong* 供 "to supply." This word is commonly used in received texts in the context suggested by this Wenxian oath, as the quoted passage here shows. For full discussion, see: Williams, "Interpreting the Wenxian Covenant Texts," 305–13, 337–54; Wei Kebin, "Wenxian mengshu WT5K14 mengshu bushi: shuo 'gong' zi."

74. Chen Qiyou 陳奇猷, *Lüshi chunqiu xin jiaoshi* 呂氏春秋新校釋 (Shanghai: Shanghai Guji, 2002), 622–23.

75. Roel Sterckx, *Food, Sacrifice, and Sagehood in Early China* (Cambridge: Cambridge University Press, 2011), 27–29.

76. Tablets T5K14-3, T5K14-18, T5K14-40. In the excavated covenants, *de* is generally written with *zhi* 直 (as a phonetic loan) or 悳. The right sides of these three variant graphs are not very legible and it is possible one or two of the examples may have the heart component as well, that is, 惪.

77. *Shijing* Daya 大雅 Ji zui 既醉: 既醉以酒, 既飽以德 in Cheng Junying 程俊英 and Jiang Jianyuan 蔣見元, eds., *Shijing zhu xi* 詩經注析 (Beijing: Zhonghua, 1991), 813.

78. *Zuo zhuan* Xi 僖 5.8: 黍稷非馨, 明德惟馨 (Yang Bojun, *Chunqiu Zuo zhuan zhu*, 30). Cited in: Pines, "*De* in the *Zuozhuan*," 134.

79. Marcel Granet, *The Religion of the Chinese People* (New York: Harper & Row, 1975), 63.

80. Granet, *The Religion of the Chinese People*, 64.

81. See also: Zhang Hequan, *Zhoudai jisi yanjiu*, 194–214.

82. Zhang Hequan, *Zhoudai jisi yanjiu*, 232–48.

83. Falkenhausen, *Chinese Society in the Age of Confucius*, 297.

84. An image of this particular tablet has not previously been published, but for examples of this oath type on other tablets, see: Henan sheng wenwu yanjiusuo, "Henan Wenxian Dong-Zhou mengshi yizhi yi-hao kan fajue jianbao," 83–86, and pls. 5–8; Ai Lan and Xing Wen, *Xin chu jianbo yanjiu*, pls. 4–10.

85. The word *tu* 徒 often specified able-bodied men available for military action. It seems unlikely that covenantors were restricted to such a category, but this connotation might have been partially present given the context of inter- and intra-lineage and state warfare so common at this time.

86. The following discussion is partially based on: Crispin Williams, "Ten Thousand Names: Rank and Lineage Affiliation in the Wenxian Covenant Texts," *Asiatische Studien/Études Asiatiques* 63, no. 4 (2009): 959–89.

87. Susan Roosevelt Weld, "The Covenant Texts from Houma and Wenxian," in *New Sources of Early Chinese History: An Introduction to the Reading of Inscriptions and Manuscripts*, ed. Edward L. Shaughnessy (Berkeley: Society for the Study of Early China and the Institute of East Asian Studies, University of California, Berkeley, 1997), 125–60, see 138.

88. As will be discussed in more detail later, the excavated covenants frequently include names of enemies who share the same lineage name as the covenant lord

(i.e., enemies with the lineage name Zhao at Houma, Han at Wenxian), providing evidence of the breakdown of these lineages into warring factions.

89. Tablets of covenantors with the lineage name Zhao include: T1K1-1133 and T1K1-3606.

90. Tablets T1K1-2643, T1K1-2647, T1K1-2658. The tablets appear to have been written by the same scribe and the close numbering of the tablets suggests they were excavated as a group and thus originally had been placed in the pit together, further supporting the suggestion that the three covenantors were brothers. See: Williams, "Ten Thousand Names," 973–74. Note that the makeup of this unit would then differ from that of enemy units, which are listed in the oaths as "[enemy name] and his sons and grandsons" ([_] 及其子孫), or some variation of this formula, occasionally with additional consanguineous male kin added, for instance, paternal uncles and brothers. The *shi* 氏 threatened with destruction in the imprecation clause of the oaths may also refer to this basic group of the covenantor and any sons and grandsons. This minimal direct-patriline unit may, then, have been specifically targeted for punitive actions, as wiping out this group reduces the likelihood of acts of revenge and realizes the threat (directly stated in some oaths) to break the male-descent line. See: Williams, "Early References to Collective Punishment," 440–48, 453–54, and passim.

91. Based on Krisztina Kosse, Falkenhausen suggests a figure of two thousand to three thousand people for the maximum size of a lineage, after which it would have split; see Falkenhausen, *Chinese Society in the Age of Confucius*, 69, n. 65; Krisztina Kosse, "Group Size and Societal Complexity: Thresholds in the Long-Term Memory," *Journal of Anthropological Archaeology* 9 (1990): 275–303.

92. Mark Edward Lewis, *The Construction of Space in Early China* (Albany: State University of New York Press, 2006), 78–93.

93. A number of sandstone tablets were also found and the tablets were categorized during processing into five different shapes, suggesting the possibility of finer distinctions of rank. Nevertheless, the basic two-way distinction is further supported by the two pit types discussed here: one for high-ranking covenantors, one for all the rest.

94. These figures are based on a table prepared during processing, a version of which will be published in the excavation report: Henansheng wenwu kaogu yanjiuyuan, *Henan Wenxian Dong-Zhou mengshi yizhi*. Pit T3K6 also had a single legible example of this oath type (tablet T3K6-14).

95. Williams, "Ten Thousand Names," 975–81. Evidence for bundling in these cases is based on the closeness of the numbers assigned to the tablets during excavation. Diagrams of the tablets in situ were made for pit T1K14 (with over six thousand tablets) and show cases of small numbers of tablets (e.g., groups of ten to twenty) stacked together and facing the same direction, suggesting they were placed in the pit in bundles. With the general lack of lineage names appearing on the tablets, in most cases it will not be possible to determine whether such bundles

always reflect kin-based groups. See: Henansheng wenwu kaogu yanjiuyuan, *Henan Wenxian Dong-Zhou mengshi yizhi*.

96. Chen Guying, *Laozi jin zhu jin yi ji pingjie*, 273.

97. Falkenhausen, *Chinese Society in the Age of Confucius*. The summary here is based on chaps. 7, 8, and 9.

98. Falkenhausen, *Chinese Society in the Age of Confucius*, 365.

99. Falkenhausen, *Chinese Society in the Age of Confucius*, 351. This is particularly relevant to the excavated covenants as the tomb occupant is thought to be Zhao Yang 趙軮, who was the Zhao leader at the period of the earliest covenants found at Houma. For the excavation report, see Tao Zhenggang 陶正剛, Hou Yi 侯毅, and Qu Chuanfu 渠川福, *Taiyuan Jinguo Zhao qing mu* 太原晉國趙卿墓 (Beijing: Wenwu, 1996).

100. Falkenhausen, *Chinese Society in the Age of Confucius*, part 3, 290–400.

101. Falkenhausen, *Chinese Society in the Age of Confucius*, 127–61, 395–96. For the excavation report, see: Shanxisheng kaogu yanjiusuo 山西省考古研究所, *Shangma mudi* 上馬墓地 (Beijing: Wenwu, 1994).

102. Falkenhausen, *Chinese Society in the Age of Confucius*, 394–95.

103. Falkenhausen, *Chinese Society in the Age of Confucius*, 395.

104. For discussion of the use of the terms *gui* and *ming* in the Wenxian covenants, see Williams, "Interpreting the Wenxian Covenant Texts," 165–78.

105. Grundmann also makes this comparison; see Grundmann, "Command and Commitment," 232, 257–68.

106. Mark Edward Lewis, "Ritual Origins of the Warring States," *Bulletin de L'École française d'Extrême-Orient* 84, no. 1 (1997): 96, see also 73–98.

107. Falkenhausen, *Chinese Society in the Age of Confucius*, 395.

108. Melvin P. Thatcher, "A Study of the Nature of Political Power in China, as Revealed in the Activities of the Major Families, 636–403 B.C.," MA thesis, University of Washington, 1973, 50–61, 67–70; Barry B. Blakeley, "Functional Disparities in the Socio-political Traditions of Spring and Autumn China: Part III: Ch'u and Chin," *Journal of the Economic and Social History of the Orient* 22, no. 1 (1979): 81–118.

109. For examples of these covenants, see: Williams, "Interpreting the Wenxian Covenant Texts," 40–41; Weld, "The Covenant Texts from Houma and Wenxian," 140–48.

110. These are in the "Denounce [enemies]" oath type (*shengtao lei* 聲討類). For examples and paleographic analysis, see: Wei Kebin, "Wenxian mengshu T4K5, T4K6, T4K11 mengci shidu," 298–337.

111. See also: Mark Edward Lewis, *Sanctioned Violence in Early China* (Albany: State University of New York Press, 1990), 43–50.

112. A development that became more pronounced toward the end of the Warring States when, as Lewis states: "The transformation of the Chinese state from a league of cities under a theocratic dynasty to a great territorial empire was

marked by the shift of ritual primacy from the ancestral temple to cults devoted to Heaven and to major landscape features such as mountains." Lewis, *The Construction of Space in Early China*, 147. See also, for example: Constance A. Cook, *Death in Ancient China: The Tale of One Man's Journey* (Leiden: Brill, 2006), 43–46, 151, and passim; Andrew Meyer, "'The Altars of the Soil and Grain Are Closer than Kin' 社稷戚於親: The Qi 齊 Model of Intellectual Participation and the Jixia 稷下 Patronage Community," *Early China* 33–34 (2010–2011): 37–99, particularly 48–49.

113. In discussing the early Mohists' doctrine of uniform adherence to Tian's will (Tian *zhi* 天志), Brindley points out that this makes "each individual accountable for his or her actions through an equal method of punishment and reward. . . . Every individual is equally obligated to conform, irrespective of his or her family background or position in society." The use of Lord Yue as the sanctioning spirit in the covenants may reflect a similar concept. See: Erica Fox Brindley, *Individualism in Early China: Human Agency and the Self in Thought and Politics* (Honolulu: University of Hawai'i Press, 2010), 26.

114. Shanxisheng wenwu gongzuo weiyuanhui 山西省文物工作委員會, *Houma mengshu* 侯馬盟書 (Beijing: Wenwu, 1976), 39–40. This oath type does not include information that allows accurate dating, but other datable oaths from Houma reflect events from both the early as well as the second half of the fifth century BCE; Williams, "Dating the Houma Covenant Texts."

115. Lewis, *The Construction of Space in Early China*, 82.

116. Qiu Xigui 裘錫圭, "Cong jijian Zhou dai tongqi mingwen kan zongfa zhiduxiade suoyouzhi" 從幾件周代銅器銘文看宗法制度下的所有制, in *Qiu Xigui xueshu wenhua suibi* 裘錫圭學術文化隨筆 (Beijing: Zhongguo qingnian, 1999), 193–206.

117. Li Feng, *Early China: A Social and Cultural History* (New York: Cambridge University, 2013), 166–74.

118. Lewis gives an example from the excavated Yinqueshan 銀雀山 *Sunzi* 孫子 materials, describing how, in the fifth century BCE, Jin introduced policies that allocated land in exchange for a taxation on harvest. See: Lewis, "Warring States Political History," in *The Cambridge History of Ancient China: From the Origins of Civilization to 221 BC*, ed. Edward L. Shaughnessy and Michael Loewe (Cambridge: Cambridge University Press, 1999), 587–650, esp. 600.

119. For these developments, see: Hsu Cho-yun, *Ancient China in Transition: An Analysis of Social Mobility, 722–222 B.C.* (Stanford: Stanford University Press, 1965), 580; Falkenhausen, *Chinese Society in the Age of Confucius*, 409.

120. Falkenhausen, *Chinese Society in the Age of Confucius*, 382–85 and passim; Constance Cook, "Ancestor Worship during the Eastern Zhou," in *Early Chinese Religion: Part One: Shang through Han (1250 BC–220 AD)*, ed. John Lagerwey and Marc Kalinowski (Leiden: Brill, 2009), 237–79; Chao Fulin, "Shi lun Chunqiu shiqi de zuxian chongbai"; Zhang Hequan, *Zhoudai jisi yanjiu*, 232–48; Vogelsang, "Beyond Confucius," 37.

121. This corresponds to Erica Brindley's argument that aspects of individualism were an important theme for thinkers of the fourth century BCE. See: Erica Fox Brindley, *Individualism in Early China: Human Agency and the Self in Thought and Politics* (Honolulu: University of Hawai'i Press, 2010).

122. For example, in the *Lunyu* and *Liude*, it is the expected relationships between male members of the patrilineage that constitute the foundation of moral behavior, that is, filial piety (principally to one's father) and devotion to one's elder brothers (*xiaoti* 孝悌), for example, *Lunyu* 1.2 (Yang Bojun, *Lunyu yizhu*, 2). For the relevant *Liude* sections, see: Cook, *The Bamboo Texts of Guodian*, 786–88, 791.

123. Vogelsang, "Beyond Confucius," 46–50.

124. See also: Brindley, *Individualism in Early China*, 64–70.

125. Michael J. Puett, *To Become a God: Cosmology, Sacrifice, and Self-Divinization in Early China* (Cambridge, MA: Harvard University Asia Center, 2002), 109–17, 122–33, 165–67, 170–72, and passim; Brindley, *Individualism in Early China*, 55–63 and passim.

126. Li Xiangfeng 黎翔鳳, *Guanzi jiaozhu* 管子校注, 2 vols. (Beijing: Zhonghua, 2004), 947–48; Roth, *Original Tao*, 90–91. See also, for example: Paul U. Unschuld, *Medicine in China: A History of Ideas* (Berkeley: University of California Press, 1985), 67–73.

127. And, we might note, to be particularly associated with thinkers who were from, or had studied or worked in, the Jin successor states, which had started experimenting with aspects of these reforms relatively early on, for example, Shen Buhai 申不害, Shang Yang 商鞅, Li Kui 李悝, Shen Dao 慎到, and Han Feizi 韓非子.

128. See, for example: Lewis, "Warring States Political History," 603–16; Mark Edward Lewis, *The Early Chinese Empires: Qin and Han* (Cambridge, MA: Harvard University Press, Belknap Press, 2007), 30–50; Yuri Pines, Lothar von Falkenhausen, Gideon Shelach, and Robin D. S. Yates, eds., *Birth of an Empire: The State of Qin Revisited* (Berkeley: University of California Press, 2014), 24–32.

7

The Editing and Publication of
Ancient Books Written on Bamboo and Silk

LI LING

TRANSLATED BY CONSTANCE A. COOK

The publication of ancient bamboo and silk manuscripts typically involves four stages: discovery, preservation, editing, and dissemination. Each stage, no matter how tedious, is critical. Archaeologists and conservators handle discovery and preservation, while paleographers and presses handle editing and dissemination of data. The work conducted in the preliminary stages is realized through these latter stages. Having been involved with the preparation of reports on manuscript data, I would like to share my experiences and discuss best practices for publishing these important books.

Ancient Books Written on Bamboo and Silk:
Concepts and Terminology

In China, ancient books were written on bamboo and silk. They are a singular feature of Chinese civilization. In the following sections, I offer a brief analysis of what constitutes "bamboo and silk" (*jianbo* 簡帛) and "ancient books" (*gushu* 古書, alternatively *dianji* 典籍) and further discuss the distinction between "documents" (*wenshu* 文書) and "ancient books," as evident from excavated specimens.

Bamboo and Silk

There are three types of texts under this category:

1. *Jian* 簡 are slips of bamboo or wood, with which people are most familiar.

2. *Du* 牘 are tablets of bamboo or wood, of which bamboo tablets are rarer.

3. *Bo* 帛 are sheets of silk, which tend to date later than either slip or tablet manuscripts.

The *Lunyu* 論語, "Wei Ling Gong" 衛靈公 chapter, mentions how "Zi Zhang writes on a waist tie" (子張書紳), quite possibly a reference to a silk book.[1] The modern term *tushu* 圖書 refers to a book with illustrations and text, and in antiquity these media were associated closely with one another as well. There are only two repositories of silk manuscripts known thus far, those from Zidanku 子彈庫 and Mawangdui 馬王堆, and both sets include illustrations.[2] Although illustrations appear primarily on silk, some have been found on bamboo slips. These tend to be simple black-and-white line drawings, painted across adjacent strips, akin to illustrations on hanging screens or curtains, where the image is divided by lines—which is to say they are not as clear as those on silk. The Zidanku collection includes the illustration of the Spirits of the Twelve Months 十二月神圖 and of the Names of the Months 月名圖, for instance; the Mawangdui collection has many other examples besides.

The painting of images on silk was quite accomplished during the Han period. In the *Han shu* 漢書, "Yiwen zhi" 藝文志, as a rule works listed as *juan* 卷 were silk manuscripts and illustrations, whereas those listed as *pian* 篇 were bamboo-slip manuscripts, though they too incorporated a relatively large number of illustrations. Among the Mawangdui manuscripts, there are both *tu* 圖 (illustrations) and *shu* 書 (books, texts). A *tu* is predominantly pictures, for example, the Mawangdui *Dixing tu* 地形圖 and *Zhujun tu* 駐軍圖, or the pictures of cities, palaces, and graves found in this repository. It is not that writing is absent from these illustrations, only that it is used much more sparingly than in the other types of manuscripts.[3] *Shu* are different; they are primarily text, or as is the case with the Mawangdui *Yuzang tu* 禹藏圖 or the *Pinhu tu* 牝戶圖, illustrations supplement the text as a depiction of its content. Then there is a more mixed type, integrating text and illustration, such as the Mawangdui *Sangfu tu* 喪服圖 and *Taiyi jiangxing tu* 太一將行圖.

ANCIENT BOOKS

What is a *shu* or "book"? Discussions on the history of books in China often do not distinguish between writing and books; indeed, even just one verse can be called a book. This imprecision extends to the research of excavated manuscripts. Tsuen-hsuin Tsien, in *Written on Bamboo and Silk: The Beginnings of Chinese Books and Inscriptions*, followed a phrase from *Mozi* 墨子 to define a book: *shu yu zhubo* 書於竹帛 (written on bamboo and silk).[4] This is an important distinction. Throughout the world, a division is often drawn between the use of "hard" media versus "soft" media as writing supports. Generally speaking, in China inscriptions on metal and stone as hard writing required a knife for inscription; inscriptions on bamboo and silk, on the other hand, are soft writing, that is drawn with a brush. The two should not be confused. The study of writing on bronze and stone media is "epigraphy," and the texts on oracle bones, bronze vessels, and steles are "inscriptions," not "books." Only texts found handwritten onto bamboo slips and silk sheets are "books" proper, often called by Western scholars "manuscripts." Bamboo-slip manuscripts were bound into scrolls; silk-sheet manuscripts were either folded or rolled, akin to the two types of paper-made books popular later. Paper books are the descendants of silk books, and silk books are the descendants of bamboo-slip books, forming a single line of transmission. In fact, both paper and silk books imitated bamboo-slip manuscripts—the actual "book" (*shu*) of early China.

Books written on bamboo slips and silk sheets consisted of two different types: (1) public and private "administrative documents" (*wenshu* 文書), such as legal statutes, registers, personal letters, and divination records; and (2) treatises forming "ancient books" (*gushu* 古書), such as writings on humanistic and technical knowledge. Of course, by technical I am not implying "scientific" with its modern connotations. Technical knowledge at that time involved divination practices. Ancient books thus constituted, in part, manuals explicating these practices (cf. the administrative documents recording the divination acts themselves).

How do we distinguish "administrative documents" from "ancient books"? Administrative documents were archives, which is to say, files used for referential purposes and not reading. Ancient books were for reading, although not like modern publications, subject to the disputations of academics, forcing more and more footnotes—so that increasingly books too now are merely for reference and impossible to just read. Note that, in antiquity, the library was also an archive, and that documents and ancient books in fact overlapped in their usage. The royal archives would have included ancient books, while the historical annals record administrative documents such as imperial edicts or memorials submitted to the ruler.

EXCAVATED ADMINISTRATIVE DOCUMENTS

Documents found in the frontier regions at first derived primarily from China's arid northwest, at Han period sites such as Dunhuang 敦煌, Jiuquan 酒泉, Zhangye 張掖, and Wuwei 武威, located in modern-day Gansu 甘肅, Ningxia 寧夏, and the western part of Inner Mongolia.[5] The First Emperor of Qin 秦始皇, during his fifth tour of the realm, explored most of this northern region; it was a different situation for the south, where at best he reached the Yangtse. Nan Commandery 南郡 (literally "Southern" Commandery) was situated in the mid-Yangtse River valley, and in the past, travelers from Luoyang heading south inevitably had to pass through this territory. The only commandery south of Nan was that of Dongting 洞庭; the First Emperor did not travel any further south than that. When Han Wudi 漢武帝 campaigned against the Southern Yue, he dispatched troops from Yunnan 雲南, through Guizhou 貴州 and Hunan 湖南, to Jiangxi 江西; these areas represented the southern frontier during the Han. Although prior research into documents on bamboo and wood slips focused primarily on the northwest finds, recent discoveries in Hunan are garnering ever more attention.[6] Manuscripts dating from the Warring States Chu state, all the way up to the Three Kingdoms and Jin periods, have been discovered in this area. Indeed, the greatest quantity of material now comes from Hunan. It is noteworthy that the two sites where silk books were discovered, mentioned earlier, are also located in Changsha 長沙, Hunan. It is clear that the south is an equally critical region for our research into excavated documents.

In contrast to this, Central China has produced very few discoveries of administrative documents. Nothing has been found along the Yellow River or from Xianyang 咸陽; only a few from Chang'an 長安; and again nothing from Luoyang 洛陽, Zhengzhou 鄭州, or Shandong 山東.[7] Materials belonging to the central government have either been destroyed or simply have not yet been unearthed.

Excavated Ancient Books

Chu bamboo-slip manuscripts include tomb inventories, divination texts (often mistakenly called "prayer and sacrifice records" or *daoci jian* 禱祠簡), and other archival materials, which properly belong to the "administrative document" category and not the "ancient books" categories outlined earlier.[8] These are not, however, the only types of texts found on Chu manuscripts. According to the *Han shu* 漢書, "Yiwen zhi" 藝文志, bibliographic treatise, ancient books may be divided into six types: the six arts (*liuyi* 六藝, e.g., established Confucian classics), the philosophers (*zhuzi* 諸子), poetry (*shifu* 詩賦), military treatises (*bingshu* 兵書), calculations and arts (*shushu* 數術), and recipes and techniques (*fangji* 方技).[9] We may further differentiate the first three types as pertaining to humanistic knowledge, with the latter three types pertaining to technical knowledge. All six types are present among the Chu manuscripts.[10]

Qin bamboo-slip manuscripts include legal statutes and ordinances, hemerological daybooks, lists of distances for travel routes (*daoli shu* 道里書), and training manuals for officials (e.g., the *Wei li zhi dao* 為吏之道 series, which is akin to the later *Guanzhen* 官箴 works).[11] Among the Qin manuscripts, administrative documents are the most prevalent text type, but ancient books are not completely absent. The range of Qin ancient books we have found is much narrower than what was available during the Warring States. Following the categorization given in the *Han shu*, "Yiwen zhi," it appears that the first three types (humanistic knowledge), were restricted during the Qin, though not completely banned. As for what might be found in Qin tombs, the following speculation is perhaps warranted. Works on the six arts were banned in essence, but because Qin law exempted writings on medicine, divination, and agriculture, the *Changes* (*Yi* 易) could appear. The treatises of philosophers were banned and will not be found in Qin tombs. Chu rhapsodies (*fu* 賦) were popular during the Han; however, a rhapsody by Xun Qing 荀卿 is listed in the "Poetry" section of the "Yiwen zhi" catalog, while the entry *Various Rhapsodies of the Qin Era* (*Qinshi zafu* 秦時雜賦) likewise appears.[12] Thus, although Chu rhapsodies were not popular during the Qin, the poetic form of rhapsody was not banned at that time. Indeed, there is poetry among the Qin manuscripts acquired by Peking University.[13] As for military treatises, these sorts of manuals historically have been deemed as forbidden or secret knowledge, and even if they were kept privately, they never reached the popularity of hemerological and medical manuals. No military treatises have been found in Qin tombs. In fact, the only large batch of military writings archaeologically recovered, to date, are from the Han Yinqueshan 銀雀山 tomb.[14] Hemerological daybooks were the most popular of the calculations-and-arts-type texts during the Warring States, Qin, and Han periods,[15] while medical recipes were the most popular of the recipes-and-techniques-type texts.[16]

Han bamboo-slip manuscripts bear the greatest variety of texts, including more or less all six types listed in the "Yiwen zhi."[17] Of course, many changes took place between the Warring States and Han periods. For example, from the perspective of intellectual history, study of the classics eventually supplanted that of the philosophers, with Confucianism (Ru 儒) and Daoism (Dao 道) rising to prominence. Yin-yang 陰陽 ideology was associated with Confucianism, and Legalism (Fa 法) with Daoism, raising them to a secondary standing. Interest in the school of Names (Ming 名) and in Mohism (Mo 墨) met a precipitous decline.

At present, the study of administrative documents and ancient books already has formed two separate disciplines, each with their own field-specific research questions.

The Discovery and Publication of Manuscripts Over the Past Century

There is an old saying: "Mountains and rivers are numinous, the earth does not begrudge its treasures, in an age of peace and prosperity these treasures then will appear" (山川效靈, 地不愛寶, 盛世才出寶貝). Looking back over the past century however, it appears that this saying is actually backward.

At the turn of the century, around 1900, when the world was in crisis and the nation far from prospering, five great discoveries were made: Shang oracle bones from Yinxu 殷墟; Han slips from the northwest frontier; medieval Dunhuang scrolls; Ming and Qing archives of the Grand Secretariat; and various ancient scripts used by minority peoples. Different enumerations are sometimes given for the great discoveries of the early twentieth century, but in each case the Han slips always feature prominently. Furthermore, it should be noted that three of these discoveries—the northwest Han slips, the medieval Dunhuang scrolls, and the minority scripts—were made initially by "foreign devils on the Silk Road."[18]

The year 2000 marks the centennial anniversary of these five great discoveries, celebrating an era of discovery. Pian Yuqian 駢宇騫 and Duan Shu'an 段書安 offer a timely survey.[19] By the year 2010, twenty-eight provinces, cities, and autonomous regions have recorded finds of bamboo and wooden slips. They seemingly are everywhere. This includes most provinces in the north, except for Liaoning, Jilin, Heilongjiang, and Shanxi; most in the south, except for Shanghai, Zhejiang, Fujian, and Taiwan; and most in the southwest, except for Yunnan, Guizhou, and Tibet. This, all of a sudden! Who would have believed it! When I was a graduate student, bamboo-and-silk studies simply did not exist as a field. Now, however, it is all the rage among young scholars and has become one of the most fashionable academic fields. Due to the constraints of space, the following brief overview will discuss only thirteen key discoveries and their formal publications.[20]

DISCOVERIES BEFORE LIBERATION (1901–1949)

Prior to 1900, illustrations of "metal-and-stone" artifacts (*jinshi tulu* 金石圖錄) were primarily traced woodblock editions. Beginning in the twentieth century, however, photographic printing was employed. At this time, three discoveries deserve our special attention, for which I will list their publication details.

Dunhuang Han slips (1907, 1913–1915, 1920, and 1944):

Numerous Han slips have been unearthed near Dunhuang over the years, conveniently compiled in Gansu sheng wenwu kaogu yanjiusuo 甘肅省文物考古研究所, *Dunhuang Han jian* 敦煌漢簡 (Beijing: Zhonghua, 1991). The earliest discovery was made by Sir Aurel Stein in 1907, from sites along the Shule River basin 疏勒河流域, during his second expedition in Central Asia. These slips are now stored in the British Library. Luo Zhenyu 羅振玉 and Wang Guowei 王國維 conducted research on this repository, published as *Liusha zhui jian* 流沙墜簡 (Kyoto: Higashiyama, 1914; reprinted by Zhonghua in 1993). This publication effectively "opened the pass through the mountains" for the field of bamboo-and-silk studies in China, both for research on administrative documents and ancient books. Luo and Wang's study is still impactful today. For example, scholars follow their adoption of the term *lipu* 歷譜 (calendars and chronologies) to classify a text type among these slips (more on this later). Their research was based on Édouard Chavannes's material so, in fact, Chavannes's book began it all.[21]

"Old" Juyan Han slips (1908, 1930–1931):

The "Old" Juyan Han slips were discovered among the military fortifications of Juyan 居延, Zhangye Commandery 張掖郡, by the Sino-Swedish

Northwest Scientific Survey Team in 1930–1931.[22] The Institute of History and Philology, Academia Sinica, Taipei 臺北中央研究院歷史語言研究所, currently stores them. The earliest publications include (1) Lao Gan 勞幹, *Juyan Han jian—kaoshi zhi bu* 居延漢簡——考釋之部 (Nanxi 南溪, lithograph); and (2) Lao Gan, *Juyan Han jian—kaozheng zhi bu* 居延漢簡——考證之部 (Nanxi, lithograph). Later publications of note include: (1) Zhongguo shehui kexue kaogu yanjiusuo 中國社會科學院考古研究所, *Juyan Han jian jiayi bian* 居延漢簡甲乙編 (Beijing: Zhonghua, 1980); (2) Working Group on Wooden Slips, Institute of History and Philology, Academia Sinica 中央研究院歷史語言研究所簡牘整理小組, *Juyan Han jian bupian* 居延漢簡補編 (Taipei: Zhongyang yanjiuyuan lishi yuyan yanjiusuo, 1998); and (3) Jiandu zhengli xiaozu 簡牘整理小組, *Juyan Han jian* 居延漢簡 (Taipei: Zhongying yanjiuyuan lishi yanjiusuo, 2014–2017, in four volumes).

Zidanku silk manuscript (1942):

The Zidanku manuscript is the earliest silk-sheet manuscript unearthed in China and the first discovery of a relatively intact ancient book. It was collected initially by Cai Jixiang 蔡季襄 of Changsha 長沙 but was transferred in 1946 to the United States and is stored presently in the Smithsonian's Arthur M. Sackler Gallery (Washington, DC). Mr. Cai's self-published *Wan Zhou zenshu kaozheng* 晚周繒書考證 (Lantian 藍田: Self-pub., 1945; reprinted by Zhongxi 2013) was the first introduction to this newly discovered book and included a hand-drawing completed by his oldest son, Cai Xiuhuan 蔡修渙. Noel Barnard's monograph, *The Chu Silk Manuscript: Translation and Commentary*, published in 1973, includes infrared photographs.[23]

☙

Two of these three discoveries are primarily collections of administrative documents (with only sparse evidence of ancient books), while the third constitutes an ancient book. These are the foundational finds for our field.

DISCOVERIES FROM THE FOUNDING OF THE PRC TO THE CULTURAL REVOLUTION (1949–1966)

There are four main discoveries:

Changsha Chu slips (1951–1954):

The Changsha Chu slips were unearthed from sites in Hunan, such as Wulipai 五裡牌 and Yangtianhu 仰天湖. They consist primarily of tomb inventories (*qiance* 遣冊) and are the first discovery of Chu tomb inventories. Shang Chengzuo 商承祚, ed., *Zhanguo Chu zhujian huibian* 戰國楚竹簡彙編 (Jinan: Jilu, 1995) may be consulted for these finds.

Xinyang Chu slips (1957):

The Xinyang 信陽 Chu slips were unearthed in Henan and include not only a tomb inventory but also fragments of an ancient book, known as the *Shen Tudi* 申徒狄. The manuscripts were published in Henan sheng wenwu yanjiusuo 河南省文物研究所, *Xinyang Chu mu* 信陽楚墓 (Beijing: Wenwu, 1986). This is the first discovery of a Chu ancient book.

Wuwei Han slips (1959):

The Wuwei 武威 Han slips date to the end of the Western Han and include a copy of the *Yili* 儀禮, marking the first time a classic was discovered among our manuscripts. Chen Mengjia 陳夢家 was responsible for its editing; see Gansu sheng bowuguan 甘肅省博物館 and Zhongguo kexueyuan kaogu yanjiusuo 中國科學院考古研究所, eds., *Wuwei Han jian* 武威漢簡 (Beijing: Wenwu, 1964).

Wangshan Chu slips (1965–1966):

The Wangshan 望山 Chu slips from Hubei are different from the others. In addition to a tomb inventory, this repository included divination records. They are published in Hubei sheng wenwu kaogu yanjiusuo 湖北省文物考古研究所, *Jiangling Wangshan Shazhong Chu mu* 江陵望山沙塚楚墓 (Beijing: Wenwu, 1996). This is the first discovery of Chu divination texts.

Of these four repositories, three derive from the Warring States Chu region. They form the basis of research into Chu slips, together with the Chu silk manuscript. When these finds were made, understanding of Chu script was still in its infancy, with many of the graphs not yet recognized, but it was through research of these manuscripts that a foundation for our later expertise in Chu paleography was laid. The importance of the *Yili* version discovered at Wuwei cannot be emphasized enough, both because it is an ancient book of great length, but also because it represents the earliest discovery of one of the Five Classics.

DISCOVERIES DURING THE CULTURAL REVOLUTION (1966–1976)

The first major haul of bamboo-and-silk manuscripts was made during the Cultural Revolution. There is a saying popular in Hong Kong and Taiwan: China had two crucial cultural disruptions (*wenhua duanlie* 文化斷裂). The first was the May Fourth movement (*wusi yundong* 五四運動) and the second was the Great Proletariat Cultural Revolution (*wenhua dageming* 文化大革命). In fact, during the Cultural Revolution, while the editing of ancient books, translation of foreign literature, and archaeological work suffered from political persecution, the torch continued to be carried unabated. Under incredible pressure, China's mainland scholars accomplished much. For example, from 1974 to 1975, the Cultural Relics Bureau (Wenwuju 文物局) brought a selection of eminent paleographers to Beijing and, in the Red Building (Shatan honglou 沙灘紅樓) of Peking University, organized editing committees for the Yinqueshan Han slips, Mawangdui silk manuscripts, and, slightly later, for the Shuihudi 睡虎地 Qin slips as well. Their work compares to that done following the discoveries made in Confucius's Wall (Kong *bi* 孔壁) and at Jizhong 汲塚, serving still as a model for how to edit manuscript finds. Out of eighty-one scholars who first attended in 1948, only eleven fled to Taiwan (one-eighth of the mainland committee). Of the cultural relics that were transported south, there were 19,816 boxes, 72 packages, 15 items (*jian* 件), and 13 letters (*zha* 劄). Of the 13,427 boxes and 64 packages in the Palace Museum, only 2,972 boxes (about 14%) went to Taiwan.

Yinqueshan Han bamboo texts (1972):

Of the three volumes originally planned, only two were published by 2010. For the first volume, Wenwu Press released three editions: one in a traditional thread-bound, large-character format, another that was a more popular paperback edition, and finally a deluxe hardcover edition. The first two editions reflect the earliest stages of the work on the repository, while the deluxe hardcover edition reflect the final definitive version: Yinqueshan

Han mu zhujian zhengli xiaozu 銀雀山漢墓竹簡整理小組, *Yinqueshan Han mu zhujian (yi)* 銀雀山漢墓竹簡 (壹) (Beijing: Wenwu, 1985). The second volume, *Yinqueshan Han mu zhujian (er)* only recently saw publication (Beijing: Wenwu, 2010). This was the first time a large collection of ancient books was discovered among the same repository.

Mawangdui silk manuscripts (1973):

Of the six volumes originally planned, only three had been published by 2014 (vols. 1, 3, and 4). As with the Yinqueshan slips, Wenwu Press published three separate editions. The definitive hardcover editions are: Mawangdui Han mu boshu zhengli xiaozu 馬王堆漢墓帛書整理小組, *Mawangdui Han mu bo shu (yi, san, si)* 馬王堆漢墓帛書 (壹, 叁, 肆) (Beijing: Wenwu, 1980, 1983, 1985, respectively). More recently, photographs and transcriptions for the entire Mawangdui repository have seen publication in: Hunan sheng bowuguan 湖南省博物館 and Fudan daxue chutu wenxian yu guwenzi yanjiu zhongxin 復旦大學出土文獻與古文字研究中心, eds., *Changsha Mawangdui Hanmu jianbo jicheng* 長沙馬王堆漢墓簡帛集成 (Beijing: Zhonghua, 2014), in seven volumes. This was the second great find of ancient books.

Shuihudi Qin slips (1975):

The Shuihudi slips are predominantly legal texts and hemerological daybooks, but the find also includes the *Biannianji* 編年記 and *Wei li zhi dao* 為吏之道. The popular edition of the Shuihudi publication does not include the daybooks.[24] The definitive edition is: Shuihudi Qin mu zhujian zhengli xiaozu 睡虎地秦墓竹簡整理小組, *Shuihudi Qin mu zhujian* 睡虎地秦墓竹簡 (Beijing: Wenwu, 1990). This was the first discovery of a large repository of Qin slips.

༄

These three discoveries led to a surge of interest in bamboo and silk studies, with research into both administrative documents and ancient books seeing remarkable breakthroughs.

DISCOVERIES AFTER THE CULTURAL REVOLUTION (1976 TO 2000)

Following the Cultural Revolution, China "opened up" and implemented economic reforms. In the midst of this reform, there was "breaking of earth" everywhere, including looting and tomb robbery. This led to another great surge of bamboo-and-silk manuscripts. I feel greatly conflicted about this development—both joyful and sorrowful. My joy stems from the unprecedented richness of these materials; and yet, this rampant looting is likewise unprecedented and a cause for great sorrow. Skirting government oversight, looting by thieves has gotten completely out of control, like water bursting through the river dike; it is, in short, a cultural catastrophe, one unlike anything we have seen before in history.

During this period of time, so much has been discovered that I can only mention three of the more significant finds here, selected because of the direct impact they have had on our field.

Baoshan Chu slips (1986–1987):

The Baoshan 包山 Chu slips feature a tomb inventory, administrative records, and divination texts (similar to previous discoveries but in a much greater quantity here). See Hubeisheng Jing Sha tielu kaogudui 湖北省荊沙鐵路考古隊, *Baoshan Chu mu* 包山楚墓 (Beijing: Wenwu, 1991).

Guodian Chu slips (1993):

The Guodian 郭店 Chu slips consist of sixteen ancient books, including works such as *Laozi* 老子 and *Taiyi sheng shui* 太一生水. See Jingmenshi bowuguan 荊門市博物館, *Guodian Chu mu zhujian* 郭店楚墓竹簡 (Beijing: Wenwu, 1998). This was the first discovery of a large collection of Chu ancient books from the same repository.

Shanghai Museum Chu slips (1994 acquisition):

The Shanghai Museum (abbreviated Shangbo 上博) Chu slips consist of a rich variety of ancient books. The collection is still being published, but by 2011 nine volumes had been released in the series: Ma Chengyuan 馬承源, ed., *Shanghai bowuguan cang Zhanguo Chu zhushu* 上海博物館藏戰國楚竹書, vols. 1–9 (Shanghai: Shanghai guji, 2001–2011).

∾

The importance of these finds is manifest. First, after the discovery of the Baoshan Chu slips, there was a surge in the forgery of bamboo-slip manuscripts, with fakes of such a quality that they deceived eminent scholars, both domestic and foreign. Second, following the Guodian find, there was a surge in tomb robbery, which apparently led directly to the looting of the Chu manuscripts now preserved in the Shanghai Museum. Third, with the publication of the Shanghai Museum Chu slips, there was a surge in the purchase of bamboo slips in the illicit antiquities markets. The recent acquisitions made by Tsinghua University, Yuelu Academy, Peking University, Zhejiang University, and most recently Anhui University, among others, are all "rescued" looted artifacts.

Much like the year 1900, with the turn of the twenty-first century, we once again have embarked upon a new era marred by the rise of tomb robbery and forgery. I fear that future publications of manuscript finds will entail—at least in large part, if not entirely so—efforts to pick up the pieces left behind from these destructive acts.

Eight Issues for: the Editing of Manuscripts

Eight issues may be raised for the editing of reports on bamboo-slip and silk manuscripts, which deserve our close attention.

CLASSIFICATION OF MANUSCRIPTS (*FENLEI* 分類)

This is perhaps the greatest problem faced in the editing of these manuscripts. Currently, there are three standard practices, each with their own shortcomings:

Prioritization of important manuscripts:

In this approach, the seemingly most important manuscripts of a repository are prioritized over the others, by being placed at the beginning of a publication or released first, while those manuscripts deemed less important are treated afterward. The Yinqueshan Han slips demonstrate this approach. The military treatises, such as the two *Sunzi bingfa* 孫子兵法 (more on this later), were placed at the very beginning of *Yinqueshan Han mu zhujian* (*yi*). As a product of the "Criticize Lin, Criticize Confucius" (*pi* Lin *pi* Kong 批林批孔) era, when Legalism was esteemed and Confucianism derided, *Mawangdui Han mu bo shu* foregrounded the *Laozi* and Yellow Emperor manuscripts, by publishing them in the first volume, while conversely the

Zhou yi 周易 and its commentaries followed afterward. This approach to the classification of manuscripts is highly subjective, as the editors' judgments concerning the relative importance of given works will vary according to the dominant trends of the times in which they live.

Publish immediately upon collation:

Another approach is to not classify manuscripts in their presentation. In practice, this means to publish as soon as a given manuscript has been edited (irrespective of the status of other manuscripts in the collection, for which editing work may still remain). This is convenient for the editor, but not the reader. For example, the Shanghai Museum has adopted this methodology with their Chu slips. Volume after volume have been published, but they lack any obvious logic to their publication order. Manuscripts that originally were bound in the same scroll have been separated and published in different volumes; indeed, there is even a case where two different texts, written on the rectos and versos of the same bamboo slips, have been placed in different volumes. It is up to the readers to reassemble the original condition of these manuscripts.

Classify by content, present in traditional bibliographic order:

In this approach, manuscripts are classified and ordered following the categories established by bibliographic treatises such as the *Han shu*, "Yiwen zhi," and *Sui shu* 隋書, "Jingji zhi" 經籍志.[25] In *Liusha zhuijian*, Luo Zhenyu and Wang Guowei classify the ancient book fragments among the Dunhuang Han slips according to the "six essentials" (*liulue* 六略), as discussed in the *Han shu*'s "Yiwen zhi." This is a very traditional method. The medieval Dunhuang scrolls have been treated in a similar fashion. Wang Chongmin 王重民, in his *Dunhuang guji xulu* 敦煌古籍敍錄 (Beijing: Zhonghua, 1979), followed the "four categories" (*sibu* 四部) established by the *Sui shu*, "Jingji zhi." Although this approach appears to be orderly and principled, it does not reflect the state of the original bamboo-slip scrolls, nor does it provide transparency to the editing process, preventing other scholars from checking for mistakes.

Each of the three approaches just described has its own shortcomings, particularly the first two, though the third is problematic as well. When scribes wrote out these manuscripts in antiquity, they did not follow later traditions that classified texts into six or four divisions. Presenting collections in this anachronistic way is again highly subjective.

The ideal approach to classifying and then presenting manuscripts is to reflect the original as closely as possible. This is an ideal that, frankly, has yet to be realized. If we wish to reflect the original condition of the scroll, our best model to adopt is the structure of archaeological reports, where classification and presentation follows the materiality or typology of artifacts. For our manuscripts, this would entail following the length and type of slip, their notches, binding cords, and calligraphy, to accord with the original divisions in the scroll and the bound order of the manuscripts, as best as possible. This is not to say that content is ignored, only that it is considered following collation. A summary of the content may be conducted as a final step and listed for reference purposes. But it is only for reference and not a replacement for the work conducted in prior steps.

TITLE CONVENTIONS (*TIPIAN* 體篇)

Unearthed bamboo-slip manuscripts were part of personal libraries. For the most part, these personal libraries lacked overall book titles (that is to say, *dati* 大體 or *shuming* 書名, for multi-chaptered works) but rather titled individual treatises or tomes (the *pian* 篇).

Titling by text type:

Two approaches are employed for titling ancient books. One is to identify the manuscript based on its text type, and another is to use a more specific proper name. Regardless of which approach is adopted, if the manuscript is self-titled, then the intentions of the original compiler must be respected. Daybooks (*rishu* 日書) are examples of manuscripts titled based on their text type.[26]

Since they are found frequently among various Warring States, Qin, and Han tombs, the manuscripts are distinguished primarily by the name of the site where they were unearthed or by the institution that acquired them. Another interesting case concerns the *zhiri* 質日 calendars. As alluded to before, Luo Zhenyu and Wang Guowei adopted *lipu* 歷譜 as the name for this text type, but Marc Kalinowski argues that they should be called *liri* 曆日 instead.[27] In my opinion, it is best to follow the original self-titles given on the slips, even if they differ across manuscripts that are ostensibly of the same text type.[28] There are also the *yeshu* 葉書 manuscripts to consider, which are a kind of annal. In the past, scholars called them *dashiji* 大事記 or *nianbiao* 年表, but as there are now excavated examples self-titled *yeshu*, we should change our titling practices to reflect this original designation. In fact, *zhiri* calendars were used by officials as daily schedules (*richengbiao* 日程表).[29] Strictly speaking, these are administrative documents and should not be compared to ancient books. They are closer in nature to *lipu* than to the texts under the Five Agents (*wuxing* 五行) classification that concern the selection of auspicious times, such as the daybooks. *Rishu* (daybooks) are naturally matched to a calendar, and *zhiri* calendars do employ phrasing found in daybooks, but these were regarded as different types of texts in antiquity, and they therefore need to be distinguished clearly from one another by editors today. The *lipu*-type texts in the *Han shu*, "Yiwen zhi," may be classified as calendars (*lisuan* 歷算), of which there are genealogical records (*pudie* 譜牒) for varying temporal intervals (by generation, year, month, or day). Thus in a broader sense, *zhiri* calendars are a type of genealogical record, only they concern daily affairs; the *yeshu* may likewise belong to this larger classification.

Self-titling and invented titles:

When an ancient book is self-titled, that title may be located in various places on the manuscript, whether on its recto or verso, at the beginning of the text or upon its conclusion. Because verso titles appear on the back of a slip, often separate from the main text, they can be overlooked easily. Catalogs of "chapter" (*pian* 篇) titles have been discovered as well, but it is important to note that the titles listed do not necessarily relate to the manuscripts found among the same repository.[30] If a manuscript is self-titled, this should be used. Only when a self-title is not present must we then supplement it by adding in our own title for the manuscript. It is best to write the title within tortoiseshell brackets 〔 〕, as is the modern convention for supplementing missing content from a manuscript in the publication of paleographic data. Devising a proper name by which we may supplement a missing title for a manuscript requires extremely careful consideration. There are three basic methods: use the first words to the text; summarize the central meaning of the text; or borrow a usage found in the histories or other ancient books. Modern terminology must be avoided. Unfortunately, prior publications have at times supplemented missing titles with inappropriate names. This is a problem, because once the manuscript is printed under that title, it is referenced as such by other scholars and over time becomes ever more difficult to fix. For example, among the Yinqueshan Han slips, there are two versions of *Sunzi bingfa*, both belonging to the same family and called the same name. The *Han shu*'s "Yiwen zhi" differentiated them as being from Wu 吳 and Qi 齊, respectively: *Wu Sunzi bingfa* 吳孫子兵法 and *Qi Sunzi bingfa* 齊孫子兵法.[31] Today, however, scholars refer to them by titles different from one another, calling the first *Sunzi bingfa* and the second *Sun Bin bingfa* 孫臏兵法. In antiquity, it was common to title a text as Master X (*mouzi* 某子), but only rarely was a person's full name used (e.g., Sun Bin 孫臏). Furthermore, if we were to use this latter style as the title convention, then the Yinqueshan texts should be named: *Sun Wu bingfa* 孫武兵法 and *Sun Bin bingfa*. Take as another example the manuscripts in the Liye and Peking University collections of Qin slips that list distances for travel routes.[32] To call these *jiaotong licheng shu* 交通里程書 (books of traffic mileage) is anachronistic; the name *daoli shu* 道里書 (books of travel route distances) is more appropriate, as it accords with archaic terminology.[33] Bisyllabic words, such as *jiaotong* 交通 (traffic) or *licheng* 里程 (mileage, course) were rare in antiquity; simplicity is thus preferred when supplementing a missing title.

Slip Order

When arranging the slip order of manuscripts, in principle if the slips may be ordered definitively then do so, but otherwise we must not be too rigid in our slip placements. Young scholars today compete to find a flawless reconstruction that seamlessly connects each slip, but this sort of endless revision can be too rigid and lead to problems.

Clues for reconstructing slip order:

In the past when scholars arranged a manuscript's slip order, they relied predominantly upon the slip notches, binding cords remnants, features of the calligraphy, and the flow of textual content. Two other features are now recognized as important clues to slip order: slip numbering and verso lines. That bamboo-slip manuscripts may have numbered slips was known previously from the Wuwei Han *Yili* manuscript. I also came across this phenomenon later when editing the Shanghai Museum slips. More recently, we have found numbered slips prominent among the Tsinghua University and Peking University collections. The numbers are written consecutively on each slip and are located at either the very top or bottom of the slip, sometimes on the verso. They are a critical clue for how to order the slips in a manuscript. What we now call "pages" (ye 頁, previously written as ye 葉) must have evolved from these slip numbers, only they counted printed surfaces, not what was written in framed columns (reflecting the earlier slips). Another new discovery, made by a young scholar in 2010, has shown that many bamboo-slip manuscripts had carved or painted lines across the back of the slips.[34] These lines are often slanted and indeed may even reflect a "spiraling" cut around an original bamboo culm tube; slip order is suggested by fluidly reconnecting these angled lines.[35]

Identifying "connected groups":

In my research on the Guodian Chu slips, I have opted to think of slip order in terms of "connected groups" (*pinlian zu* 拼聯組).[36] "Connected groups" refers to those slips that may be joined to one another and, in doing so, bear coherent and complete textual content, leading to a high degree of confidence in their arrangement as a group. In recent publications, different styles have been adopted for the presentation of slip order. The editors of the Yinqueshan and Mawangdui Han manuscripts give interconnected transcriptions that are brought together as a complete text, while the Shanghai Museum editors only give the transcription for each Chu slip individually, creating a visual effect that isolates the slips and masks their relationship to one another. On the other hand, previously, with the Yinqueshan manuscripts, a number of the slips were damaged severely and are now only fragments. Since they could not be connected securely to the running texts, these pieces could only be placed at the end of the material, with the symbol ※ then used to designate the gap. This is a relatively safe method to use. Inspired by this, I would suggest that, if there is missing text between "connected groups," a space must be left to designate this. If connections are not apparent, or there is not enough evidence to support a tenuous connection between slips, it is better to publish them as separated. In other words, we should not force presentations of slip order where the entire manuscript *must* be connected, or conversely, where *every* slip is treated in isolation; rather, if groups of slips may be connected, then do so, but for those that cannot, leave them separated.

PHOTOGRAPHY

Photographs of slips should be presented in the artifact's original size and taken immediately following cleaning—preserving their moist freshness, like peaches just plucked from the tree. The dehumidifying process inevitably damages the slips to some degree, by either warping the shape of the slip or altering its coloring. Photographing the Shanghai Museum Chu slips was conducted after dehumidifying, which has led to some regret. Beforehand, both color filmstrips and black-and-white photographs were produced. For the publications, the color film was used, making the publication extremely valuable as unfortunately the film was later ruined. During my own editing work for this collection, I made cut-outs from the black-and-white photographs. These too are very precious, as they help supplement areas on the published slips that are unclear. It is a shame that these photographs were not also used to disseminate the slip data. With the formally published photographs, several issues deserve our consideration.

Black and white, color, and/or infrared:

In the past, color printing was expensive and therefore rarely used. If color photographs were published, generally only a few plates are presented, to serve as examples, but the rest of the collection is given, in its entirety, in black and white. Now it is possible to publish everything in color. If the writing on the slips is not entirely clear, infrared photographs may be appended. Yet it should be noted that infrared photography cannot pick up red colors and thus has its own limitations as a technology. For example, on the Tsinghua University and Peking University slips, many of the graphs, punctuation, and other symbols are written in red, rendering infrared less useful. As such, infrared photography cannot completely replace the use of color photography.

Placement of the transcriptions:

Should transcriptions be presented alongside the photographs of the slips, or placed in their own dedicated section of the volume? If transcriptions are to be presented alongside the photographs of the slips, then strict transcriptions (as opposed to interpretative) should be used, without additional punctuation (beyond what appears on the slip itself) or variant readings given.

Hand-drawings:

Should hand-drawings be produced for the slips and their writing? In the past, when photographs were of lesser quality, hand-drawings were appended to provide additional clarity. This is the case, for instance, with the Wuwei Han *Yili* manuscript, or with the Yinqueshan slips. The artists who produce these hand-drawings must understand paleography, which is rare. Even if a specialist is found, if they are only copying over what they see on the slips (without being involved in all the research that goes into editing these repositories), then inevitably mistakes will be made. It is my opinion that photographs are now of a high enough quality that hand-drawings are unnecessary.

Identifying notches:

It is also my suggestion that, in order to help identify where notches have been carved into slips, some form of symbol—such as small triangles—may be added to the side of the photographs, signaling their location. The location of notches and binding cords is critical to the editing process. Take for example the publication of the photographs of the Shanghai Museum Chu slips. First reduced-size photographs are presented (showing the entire slip on a single page), followed by enlarged photographs (where an individual slip is divided into multiple columns). The reduced-size photographs are too small, making it difficult to see the notches or binding cords. The enlarged photographs are too large, and the page layout is such that it is impossible to view a single slip as a whole; in order to reconstruct what the whole slip looks like, and garner a sense of where the notches and binding cords actually fell, the reader would need to fold, cut, and remount the image. Adding small triangles to signal where notches are located (on the photographs of the whole slips) could help resolve this problem.

TRANSCRIPTIONS

*Conversion into modern orthography (*liding 隸定*):*

When dealing with these paleographic sources, editors must convert ancient scripts, variant forms, or partial graphs into modern orthographic equivalents. How strict or interpretative they choose to make their transcriptions is a major question that must be answered. It is my belief that, if the graphs are commonly encountered in ancient or variant forms, recognized by most scholars, then it is appropriate to adopt a more interpretative transcription, with suitable explanation given in the prefatory guidance notes of the publication. If, however, it is a new way of writing a character, and there lacks a consensus on how to read it, then stricter standards must be upheld. For partial graphs (such as those on damaged slips), transcriptions may be given for orthographic components that remain, while the missing half is replaced with half of a square mark (e.g., □).

Variant readings:

A similar problem to the preceding is encountered with variant readings. To what degree should alternative readings be given as in-line supplements within the transcriptions? If the reading of a graph is uncertain, then as opposed to placing suggested readings as in-line supplements within the transcription, a footnote with more involved annotation is preferred.

*Repetition (*chongwen 重文*) and ligature (*hewen 合文*)*

Whether repetition or ligature punctuation should be preserved in the transcriptions or given in addition to in-line supplements (of the repeated/ split characters), or even simply removed, is another matter that must be carefully considered.

*Miswritten graphs (*cuozi 錯字*):*

Another issue that must be decided is how best to represent miswritten graphs. The miswritten graph can be placed in parenthesis ( ), with the corrected form following in tortoiseshell brackets 〔 〕, or angle brackets 〈 〉 may also be used.

Missing content:

To represent (indefinite) missing content in a manuscript, publications either use square brackets with a diagonal line running through it, or they use an ellipsis. My preference is for the latter. Both symbols represent the absence of content that could be multiple graphs in length. The square bracket with diagonal line, as a symbol, takes up the space of a single graph and is easy to confuse visually among the text in which it is embedded; the ellipsis, on the other hand, stands out more effectively.

ANNOTATIONS

The annotations given in the publications for the Yinqueshan Han slips and the Mawangdui silk manuscripts remain as exemplars still today. Successful annotations, in my opinion, are those that are concise and not overly wordy, providing reference to the most important materials without excessive speculation. A balance must be struck between gathering a variety of opinions and overloading the annotations with tedious details. The writing should be as concise as possible. There is no need to discuss every possibility or act as an arbitrator for the academic community. This is not a space for demonstrating the extent of one's knowledge; if more is left to be said, it is always possible to write a separate article. The objective here is to provide the most important materials for scholars to reference, in order to encourage new lines of research. I always say: "As an author, always be reading for someone else; consider yourself the first reader." If the annotations are too complex, you will not be able to bear them yourself. We must always think of our audience.

GRAPH INDEXES (*WENZIBIAN* 文字編)

Often times a graph index will be included as part of the publication of a manuscript repository. A number of decisions must be made on how best to create this index. For presenting the individual graphs within the index, photographs or hand-drawings may be used. Previously, hand-drawings were preferred, but now photographs are more commonly used. As discussed before, since photography today is of high enough quality, hand-drawings are no longer necessary. For organizing the index, it is perhaps still best to arrange the graphs according to the order of the 540 radicals listed in the *Shuowen jiezi* 說文解字.[37] Doing so allows for easier comparison with various other graph indexes of different time periods, since most recent publications have utilized the *Shuowen jiezi* order in their organization. What is extremely important, however, is that under each graph, examples are given for the word's usage. Furthermore, finding guides utilizing not only stroke number but also pinyin pronunciations should be included to aid users searching for a specific graph. Of course, the pronunciation of some archaic graphs is unknown, and therefore one can only offer a speculative reading.

BOOK SIZE AND FORMAT

When deciding on how best to present the photographs of the slips, whether at their original size or in clipped versions, both the length of the slips and the anticipated size of the book to be published must be considered. Using clipped versions of the slip photographs should only be a last resort. Slips that are too long to fit on a page may be treated individually instead. With the Yinqueshan and Mawangdui finds, the manuscripts were published in three editions: in thread-bound volumes, paperback, and hardcover. This is an approach that should be emulated in later publications. It is important to release popular editions as well. The Shuihudi Qin slips, for instance, published a popular edition with translations of the texts; this was a good first step.

Prior publications of bamboo-slip and silk manuscripts have—to varying degrees—left room for improvement, particularly in their editing and layout. A volume that truly conforms to archaeological standards, of which I dream, does not yet exist. With the preceding comments, it is my hope that we may begin to establish best practices for publishing manuscript data, a burden that I place now upon the shoulders of future editors and printing presses.

Notes

1. *Lunyu zhushu* 論語注疏 15.61 in Ruan Yuan 阮元 (1764–1849), ed., *Shisanjing zhushu* 十三經注疏 (1980; Beijing: Zhonghua, 1987 [rpt.]), vol. 2, 2517.

2. Hunan sheng bowuguan 湖南省博物館 and Fudan daxue chutu wenxian yu guwenzi yanjiu zhongxin 復旦大學出土文獻與古文字研究中心, eds., *Changsha Mawangdui Hanmu jianbo jicheng* 長沙馬王堆漢墓簡帛集成, 7 vols. (Beijing: Zhonghua, 2014); Li Ling 李零, *Zidanku boshu*, 2 vols. (Beijing: Wenwu, 2017); Li Ling, *The Chu Silk Manuscripts from Zidanku, Changsha (Hunan Province): Volume I, Discovery and Transmission*, vol. 1, trans. Lothar von Falkenhausen (Hong Kong: Chinese University of Hong Kong Press, 2020).

3. Maps can also be cast onto bronze plates or drawn upon wooden tablets. It is from these practices that the modern term *bantu* 版圖 is derived.

4. Tsuen-hsuin Tsien, *Written on Bamboo and Silk: The Beginnings of Chinese Books and Inscriptions*, 2nd ed. (Chicago: University of Chicago Press, 2013 [1962]). Ed. note: recent studies of *shu* by Sarah Allan include: "On Shu 書 ('Documents') and the Origin of the *Shang shu* 尚書 ('Ancient Documents') in Light of Recently Discovered Bamboo Slip Manuscripts," *Bulletin of the School of Oriental and African Studies* 75, no. 3 (2012): 547–57; *Buried Ideas: Legends of Abdication and Ideal Government in Early Chinese Bamboo-slip Manuscripts* (Albany: State University of New York, 2015).

5. Notable discoveries of administrative documents from China's northwest frontier include, for example: Gansu sheng wenwu kaogu yanjiusuo 甘肅省文物考古研究所, *Dunhuang Han jian* 敦煌漢簡, 2 vols. (Beijing: Zhonghua, 1991);

Jiandu zhengli xiaozu 簡牘整理小組, ed., *Juyan Han jian* 居延漢簡, 4 vols. (Taipei: Zhongying yanjiuyuan lishi yanjiusuo, 2014–2017); or most recently, Gansu jiandu bowuguan 甘肅簡牘博物館, Gansu sheng wenwu kaogu yanjiusuo 甘肅省文物考古研究所, Shaanxi shifan daxue renwen shehui kexue gaodeng yanjiuyuan 陝西師範大學人文社會科學高等研究院, and Qinghua daxue chutu wenxian yanjiu yu baohu zhongxin 清華大學出土文獻研究與保護中心, eds., *Xuanquan Han jian (yi)* 懸泉漢簡 (壹) (Shanghai: Zhongxi, 2019).

6. Notable discoveries from Hunan include, for example: Hunan sheng wenwu kaogu yanjiusuo 湖南省文物考古研究所, ed., *Liye Qin jian* 里耶秦簡, 2 vols. (Beijing: Wenwu, 2012, 2017); Changsha shi wenwu kaogu yanjiusuo 長沙市文物考古研究所, ed., *Changsha Zoumalou Sanguo Wu jian: Jiahe limin tianjia bie* 長沙走馬樓三國吳簡: 嘉禾吏民田家莂, 2 vols. (Beijing: Wenwu, 1999) and *Changsha Zoumalou Sanguo Wu jian: zhujian* 長沙走馬樓三國吳簡: 竹簡, 6 vols. (Beijing: Wenwu, 2003–2015); and more recently, Hunan sheng wenwu kaogu yanjiusuo and Yiyang shi wenwu chu 益陽市文物處, "Hunan Yiyang Tuzishan yizhi jiuhao jing fajue jianbao" 湖南益陽兔子山遺址九號井發覺簡報, *Wenwu* 文物 2016.5, 32–48.

7. See Zhongguo shehui kexueyuan kaogu yanjiusuo 中國社會科學院考古研究所, *Han Chang'an cheng Weiyang gong* 漢長安城未央宮 (Beijing: Zhongguo dabaike quanshu, 1996), 238–48; Wang Zijin 王子今, "Han jian Changan shiliao yanjiu" 漢簡長安史料研究, *Chutu wenxian* 出土文獻 2012.3, 237–90.

8. For instance: Hubei sheng Jing Sha tielu kaogudui 湖北省荊紗鐵路考古隊, *Baoshan Chu jian* 包山楚簡 (Beijing: Wenwu, 1991).

9. Wang Xianqian 王先謙 (1842–1918), ed., *Han shu buzhu* 漢書補注, *juan* 7 (*Han shu* 30.2) (Beijing: Zhonghua, 1983), vol. 1, 866.

10. For instance: Jingmen shi bowuguan 荊門市博物館, ed., *Guodian Chu mu zhujian* 郭店楚墓竹簡 (Beijing: Wenwu, 1998).

11. For instance: Shuihudi Qin mu zhujian zhengli xiaozu 睡虎地秦墓竹簡整理小組, *Shuihudi Qin mu zhujian* 睡虎地秦墓竹簡 (Beijing: Wenwu, 1990).

12. Wang Xianqian, *Han shu buzhu*, vol. 1, 892.

13. Beijing daxue chutu wenxian yanjiusuo 北京大學出土文獻研究所, "Beijing daxue cang Qin jiandu gaishu" 北京大學藏秦簡牘概述, *Wenwu* 文物 2012.6, 65–73.

14. Yinqueshan Han mu zhujian zhengli xiaozu 銀雀山漢墓竹簡整理小組, ed., *Yinqueshan Han mu zhujian* 銀雀山漢墓竹簡, 2 vols. (Beijing: Wenwu 1985 and 2010).

15. The Shuihudi repository, cited in n. 11, offers an example for the Qin period.

16. The Peking University Qin slips, cited in n. 13, include medical recipes, for instance.

17. The Han bamboo slips acquired by Peking University demonstrate this breadth of content, see: Beijing daxue chutu wenxian yanjiusuo 北京大學出土文獻研究所, "Beijing daxue cang Xi Han zhushu gaishuo" 北京大學藏西漢竹書概說,

Wenwu 文物2011.6, 49–56; and *Beijing daxue cang Xi Han zhushu* 北京大學藏西漢竹書, 5 vols. to date (Shanghai: Shanghai guji, 2012–2015).

18. Peter Hopkirk, *Foreign Devils on the Silk Road: The Search for the Lost Cities and Treasures of Chinese Central Asia* (Amherst: University of Massachusetts Press, 1980).

19. Pian Yuqian 駢宇騫 and Duan Shu'an 段書安, *Ershi shiji chutu jiabo zongshu* 二十世紀出土簡帛綜述 (Beijing: Wenwu, 2006).

20. For a recent survey in English of the latest manuscripts finds: Olivier Venture, "Recently Excavated Inscriptions and Manuscripts (2008–2018)," *Early China* 44 (2021): 493–546.

21. Édouard Chavannes, *Les documents Chinois découverts par Aurel Stein dans les Sables du Turkestan oriental*, vol. 1 (Oxford: Imprimerie de l'Université, 1913).

22. [Trans. note: This discovery is designated often as the "old" Juyan slips, to differentiate it from later finds from the region, which in turn are called the "new" Juyan slips. See: Zhang Defang 張德芳, ed., *Juyan xin jian jishi* 居延新簡集釋, 7 vols. (Lanzhou: Gansu wenhua, 2016)—CC].

23. Noel Barnard, *The Chu Silk Manuscript: Translation and Commentary*, Monographs on Far Eastern History 5 (Canberra: Department of Far Eastern History, Australian National University, 1973).

24. The editions of *Shuihudi Qin mu zhujian* 睡虎地秦墓竹簡 thread-bound in 8-*kai* size 八開線裝本 (Beijing: Wenwu, 1977) and paperback in 32-*kai* size 三十二開平裝本 (Beijing: Wenwu, 1978) both do not include the daybooks.

25. See Wei Zheng 魏徵 (580–643) and Zhang Yangdou 張映斗 (d. 1748), eds., *Qianding siku quanshu* 欽定四庫全書, Shi section 85, *Shui shu juan* 32–35.

26. *Rishu* is the self-title given on the Shuihudi Qin B (乙) daybook, Shuihudi Han daybook, Kongjiapo 孔家坡 Han daybook, and Peking University Han daybook. See, respectively: Shuihudi Qin mu zhujian zhengli xiaozu, *Shuihudi Qin mu zhujian*, 140 (photographs), 255 (transcriptions), though note that the slip is labeled 260 by mistake, with only the upper piece photographed; Hubei sheng wenwu kaogu yanjiusuo 湖北省文物考古研究所 and Yunmeng xian bowuguan 雲夢縣博物館, "Hubei Yunmeng Shuihudi M77 fajue jianbao" 湖北雲夢睡虎地 M77 發掘簡報, *Jiang Han kaogu* 江漢考古 2008.4, 31–37, pls. 11–16, see 35, on the verso of slip 82 of group C; and Li Ling 李零, "Beida Han jian zhong de shushu shu" 北大漢簡中的數術書, *Wenwu* 文物 2011.6, 80–83, see 80. Photographs of the Kongjiapo example are not yet published. The term *suanshu shu* 算術書 used by scholars to designate "calculations and arts texts" does not exist as an original title. The Yuelu Qin slips write *shu* 數 as a self-title, while the Zhangjiashan Han slips have *suanshu shu* 算數書. Chen Songchang 陳松長 calls this type of book a *shushu* 數書, which is perhaps most appropriate. See his: "Yuelu shuyuan suocang Qin jian zongshu" 嶽麓書院所藏秦簡總述, *Wenwu* 文物 2009.3, 75–88; Zhu Hanmin 朱漢民 and Chen Songchang 陳松長, eds., *Yuelu shuyuan cang Qin jian (er)* 嶽麓書院

藏秦簡 (貳) (Shanghai: Shanghai cishu, 2011), slip 1 (0956) verso, 1; Zhangjiashan ersiqi hao Han mu zhujian zhengli xiaozu 張家山二四七號漢墓竹簡整理小組, ed., *Zhangjiashan Han mu zhujian (ersiqi hao mu)* 張家山漢墓竹簡 (二四七號墓) (Beijing: Wenwu, 2001), slip 6 verso, 83, 249.

27. Marc Kalinowski, ed., *Divination et société en Chine médiévale: Étude des manuscrits de Dunhuang de la Bibliothèque nationale de France et de la British Library* (Paris: Bibliothèque nationale de France, 2003), 85–211. See also: Deng Wenkuan 鄧文寬, "Chutu Qin Han jiandu 'liri' zhengming" 出土秦漢簡牘 "曆日" 正名, *Wenwu* 文物 2003.4, 44–47, 51; Li Ling 李零, *Jianbo goshu yu xueshu yuanliu* 簡帛古書與學術源流, rev. ed. (Beijing: Sanlian shudian, 2008), 307.

28. During the Han, *zhiri* 質日 calendars were called *shiri* 視日 as well. The words *zhi* and *shi* both have the sense of "to inspect, examine, verify." See Li Ling 李零, "Shiri, rishu he yeshu—sanzhong jianbo wenxian de qubie yu dingming" 視日, 日書和葉書——三種簡帛文獻的區別與定名, *Wenwu* 2008.12, 73–80. Multiple different self-titles have been found on calendars, including *zhiri*, *liri*, and also *shiri*, which have complicated this debate. See Liu Lexian, "Daybooks: A Type of Popular Hemerological Manual of the Warring States, Qin, and Han," in *Books of Fate and Popular Culture in Early China: The Daybook Manuscripts of the Warring States, Qin, and Han*, ed. Donald Harper and Marc Kalinowski (Leiden: Brill, 2017), 57–90, especially "Daybooks and Calendars," 80–81.

29. *Yeshu* were the predecessors to *nianpu* 年譜 (biographical annals), while *zhiri* gave rise to *riji* 日記 (daily diaries). Chen Songchang refers to these calendars as *rishi* 日志 (daily records), which correctly identifies their function, in "Yuelu shu yuansuo zhang Qing jian congshu," 76–79.

30. For an example of such a catalog, see: *Yinqueshan Han mu zhujian (yi)*, 94 (photograph), 122 (hand-drawing), 154 (transcription).

31. Wang Xianqian, ed., *Han shu bushu*, vol. 1, 894. Note that the catalog drops *bingfa* 兵法 in the second title, but it may be supplemented.

32. Hunan sheng wenwu kaogu yanjiusuo 湖南省文物考古研究所, ed., *Liye fajue baogao* 里耶發覺報告 (Changsha: Yuelu, 2006), 196–204; Beijing daxue chutu wenxian yanjiusuo, "Beijing daxue cang Qin jiandu gaishu," 67–68.

33. *Jiaotong licheng shu* 交通里程書 was used to label the Peking University manuscript, in the online working report: "Beijing daxue chutu wenxian yanjiusuo gongzuo jiaobao san" 北京大學出土文獻研究所工作簡報三, October 2010, 4. The Liye editors offer a similar description of *diming licheng jian* 地名里程簡 (*Liye fajue baogao*, 196). For *daoli*, the word *dao* 道 stands for a travel route, and *li* 里 is a measurement of distance. This phrase is often seen in ancient books, with examples too numerous to list in full. See, however, the *Shiji* 史記, "Zhou Benji" 周本記, line: "This (Luoyi 洛邑) is the center of the realm, it is equidistant for (the lords from) four quarters to travel here and pay tribute" (此天下之中, 四方入貢道里均), with the last part rendered more literally: "From the four quarters, coming here to pay

tribute, the distances of the travel routes *daoli* are equal." Takikawa Kametaro 瀧川龜太郎, ed., *Shiki kaichū kōshō* 史記會注考證 4.40 (Taipei: Hongshi, 1977 [rpt.]), 74.

34. Sun Peiyang 孫沛陽, "Shanghai bowuguan zang Zhanguo Chu zhushu *Zhouyi* de fuyuan yu guaxu yanjiu" 上海博物館藏戰國楚竹書〈周易〉的復原與卦序研究, *Gudai wenming yanjiu tongxun* 古代文明研究通訊 Beijing daxue chendan gudai wenming yanjiu zhongxin 北京大學震旦古代文明研究中心 46 (September 2010): 23–26; "Jiance bei hua xian chutan" 簡冊背劃綫初探, *Chutu wenxian yu guwenzi yanjiu* 出土文獻與古文字研究 4 (2011): 449–62.

35. The spiraling line theory is raised, for instance, in Han Wei 韓巍, "Xi Han zhushu *Laozi* jianbei huahen de chubu fenxi" 西漢竹書老子簡背劃痕的初步分析, in *Beijing daxue cang Xi Han zhushu (er)*, 227–35. See also the discussion in Thies Staack, "Identifying Codicological Sub-units in Bamboo Manuscripts: Verso Lines Revisited," *Manuscript Cultures* 8 (2015): 157–87.

36. For example: Li Ling 李零, *Guodian Chu jian jiaodu ji* 郭店楚簡校讀記 (Beijing: Beijing daxue, 2002).

37. See Ding Fubao 丁福保 (1874–1952) and Dingwen shuju 鼎文書局, comp., *Shuowen jiezi gulin zhengbu hebian* 說文解字詁林正補合編 (Taipei: Dingwen, 1977).

8

The Philological Value of the Tsinghua Bamboo-Slip Manuscripts

ZHAO PINGAN AND WANG TINGBIN

TRANSLATED BY CONSTANCE A. COOK

Introduction

Thanks to a gift from an alumnus, Tsinghua University acquired a collection of Warring States bamboo slips in July 2008. In October, Tsinghua invited experts from Peking University, Fudan University, Jilin University, Wuhan University, Sun Yat-sen University, Chinese University of Hong Kong, National Artifacts Bureau, Institute of Chinese Culture Heritage, Shanghai Museum, and Jingzhou Museum to evaluate them. From their estimation, this cache of bamboo slips consisted primarily of books with varied and rich contents of critical importance to the study of China's ancient history and culture.

In March of 2009, the Tsinghua University Research and Conservation Center for Excavated Texts began the work of editing and reading these bamboo slips. There were 2,388 pieces in total, amounting to about 1,700–1,800 full slips after re-piecing and editing. Judging from the contents, the collection includes approximately seventy works, although as research progresses, this number could change.[1] For the sake of convenience, this collection of bamboo slips is

---

This chapter is based on Zhao Pingan 趙平安 and Wang Tingbin 王挺斌, "Lun Qinghua jian de wenxianxue jiazhi" 論清華簡的文獻學價值, *Dongyang gudian yanjiu* 東洋古典研究 74 (2019): 9–28.

referred to as the "Tsinghua slips." After the first stage of research, it became clear that most of the works among the Tsinghua slips may be classified in the "classics" or "histories" bibliographic categories. There are those already part of the Five Classics, such as *Zhou Wu Wang you ji Zhou gong suo zi yi dai Wang zhi zhi* 周武王有疾周公所自以代王之志, *Huangmen* 皇門, *Ji Gong* 祭公, and so forth. Others, such as *Xinian* 繫年 and *Chu ju* 楚居, are of high historical value. In addition, there are works of early fiction, such as *Chijiu zhi ji Tang zhi wu* 赤鵠之集湯之屋. This diversity of materials forces us to imagine what a mid-Warring States–period elite library must have been like. Table 8.1 lists

Table 8.1. List of published Tsinghua manuscripts between 2010 and 2023

2010	Vol. 1	*Yin zhi* 尹至, *Yin gao* 尹誥, *Chengwu* 程寤, *Baoxun* 保訓, *Qiye* 耆夜, *Zhou Wu Wang you ji Zhou Gong suo zi yi dai Wang zhi zhi* 周武王有疾周公所自以代王之志 (also known as *Jinteng* 金縢), *Huangmen* 皇門, *Zhai Gong zhi guming* 祭公之顧命 (also known as *Zhai Gong* 祭公), *Chu ju* 楚居
2011	Vol. 2	*Xinian* 繫年
2012	Vol. 3	*Yue ming, shang* 說命上, *Yue ming, zhong* 說命中, *Yue ming, xia* 説命下, *Zhou Gong zhi qinwu* 周公之琴舞, *Rui Liangfu bi* 芮良夫毖, *Liang chen* 良臣, *Zhuci* 祝辭, *Chijiu zhi ji Tang zhi wu* 赤鵠之集湯之屋
2013	Vol. 4	*Shifa* 筮法, *Biegua* 別卦, *Suanbiao* 算表
2015	Vol. 5	*Houfu* 厚父, *Feng Xu zhi ming* 封許之命, *Mingxun* 命訓, *Tang chuyu Tangqiu* 湯處於湯丘, *Tang zai Chimen* 湯在啻門, *Yin Gaozong wen yu sanshou* 殷高宗問於三壽
2016	Vol. 6	*Zheng Wu furen gui ruzi* 鄭武夫人規孺子, *Guan Zhong* 管仲, *Zheng Wen Gong wen Tai Bo* 鄭文公問太伯 (A 甲 and B 乙 versions), *Zi Yi* 子儀, *Zi Chan* 子産
2017	Vol. 7	*Zi Fan zi yu* 子犯子餘, *Jin Wen Gong ruyu Jin* 晉文公入於晉, *Zhao Jianzi* 趙簡子, *Yue Gong qi shi* 越公其事
2018	Vol. 8	*She ming* 攝命, *Bangjia zhi zheng* 邦家之政, *Bangjia chu wei* 邦家處位, *Zhi bang zhi dao* 治邦之道, *Xin shi wei zhong* 心是謂中, *Tianxia zhi dao* 天下之道, *Baqi wuwei wusi wuxing zhi shu* 八氣五味五祀五行之屬, *Yu Xia Yin Zhou zhi zhi* 虞夏殷周之治
2019	Vol. 9	*Zhi zheng zhi dao* 治政之道, *Chengren* 成人, *Naiming, yi* 廼命一, *Naiming, er* 廼命二, *Daoci* 禱辭
2020	Vol. 10	*Sigao* 四告, *Sishi* 四時, *Sisui* 司歲, *Xingcheng* 行稱, *Bingfang* 病方
2021	Vol. 11	*Wuji* 五紀
2022	Vol. 12	*San Buwei* 參不韋
2023	Vol. 13	*Dafu shi li* 大夫食禮, *Dafu shi li ji* 大夫食禮記, *Wuyin tu* 五音圖, *Yue feng* 樂風, *Wei tian yong shen* 畏天用身

the titles of the Tsinghua manuscripts, according to their year of publication and volume number.[2] Research on the Tsinghua slips published to date has inspired significant advances in many fields, including paleography, linguistics, history, philosophy, and so forth. In this chapter, we will focus primarily on the philological value of the Tsinghua bamboo-slip manuscripts.

Understanding Textual Transmission via the Analysis of Different Versions of the Same Text

Many scholars, in light of their varied research objectives, approach early Chinese manuscripts by dividing the materials into two larger types, those that are "ancient books" (*gushu* 古書) and those that are "administrative documents" (*wenshu* 文書). With the discovery of "ancient books" written on bamboo slips and silk sheets, we may now confirm Yu Jiaxi's 余嘉錫 (1884–1955) conclusion in his *Gushu tongli* 古書通例: "Individual chapters of ancient books circulated separately on their own" (古書單篇別行).[3] It is now well known that two Warring States–period manuscript versions already have been discovered of the "Ziyi" 緇衣 chapter to the *Liji* 禮記. The version from Guodian 郭店, Hubei, was written in Chu 楚 script and found together with other books in similar handwriting, such as *Wuxing* 五行, *Lu Mu Gong wen Zisi* 魯穆公問子思, and *Qiongda yi shi* 窮達以時.[4] The second version is in the Shanghai Museum collection, which is written in Qi 齊 script. It is found among the same cache as the *Kongzi shi lun* 孔子詩論, *Cao Mo zhi zhen* 曹沬之陣, *Rong Cheng Shi* 容成氏, *Zhou yi* 周易, *Cong zheng* 從政, *Jing Gong nüe* 景公瘧, *Tianzi jian zhou* 天子建州, and so forth.[5] It is therefore evident that individual chapters (*pian* 篇) of ancient books circulated on their own, and were copied and edited by various scholars for different reasons.

The Shanghai Museum has published nine volumes of bamboo-slip manuscripts, among which there are a number that have two versions of the same text (labeled A 甲 and B 乙 by the editors). This phenomenon was first seen with the Han-period Mawangdui silk manuscripts in the 1970s, with the two versions of the *Laozi* 老子. For convenience, they referred to the version with more archaic calligraphy as the A 甲 version, and the other as the B 乙 version.[6] The two versions preserve a number of differences in their use of loan words and grammatical particles. Furthermore, materials related to the *Laozi* also appear in the Guodian cache, separated by the editors into A 甲, B 乙, and C 丙. This is problematic, however, since each of these manuscripts has slightly different content and therefore should not be classified as A, B, and C. To date, the Shanghai Museum corpus has published duplicate versions of the following works: *Cong zheng* 從政, *Tianzi jian zhou* 天子建州, *Zhengzi jia sang* 鄭子家喪, *Junrenzhe hebi an zai* 君人者何必安哉, *Fanwu liu xing* 凡物流形, and *Cheng Wang wei Chengpu zhi xing* 成王為城濮之行.[7] After comparing the two versions of *Tianzi jian zhou*, Li Mengtao 李孟濤 argued that not only do they bear the same content, but also there is evidence of direct copying from an original.[8] In specific, *Tianzi jian zhou* A is a cleaned copy of *Tianzi jian zhou* B. Based on this observation, Li Songru 李松儒 compared how both individual characters and larger sections of text were written and pointed out that *Tianzi jian zhou* B was composed by two different scribal hands.[9] We see the same phenomenon with *Zhengzi jia sang* and *Fanwu liu xing* manuscripts.[10] On the other hand, *Cong zheng* A and B are both written in the same style and obviously copied by a single hand. From this, we can derive two models for textual transmission, with *diben* 底本 representing the original, and A and B the copies (note that in fig. 8.1 "A" and "B" are arbitrary editorial designations and not intended to express any inherent hierarchy).

The Tsinghua slips further advance our understanding of this sort of textual transmission. Ma Nan 馬楠 has noted that *Zheng Wen Gong wen Taibo* 鄭文公問太伯 A and B evidently were copied from different originals.[11] For example, the A version uses the graph *geng* 庚 to write both the words *kang* 康 (of *kangle* 康樂, happiness) and *tang* 湯 (of the name Shang Tang), whereas the B version writes them with the graph *kang* 康. Moreover, in placenames, the A version positions the *yi* 邑 element to the left side of graphs, while the B version places it on the right side. Where the A version writes *zheng* 爭, the B version instead writes *qing* 請.

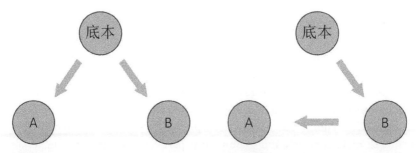

Figure 8.1. Models for Text Copying Based on the Shanghai Museum Slips. *Source:* Created by the author.

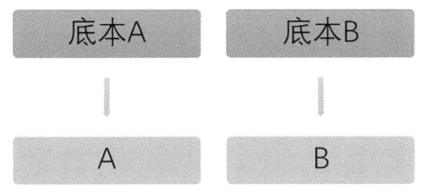

Figure 8.2. Model for Text Copying Based on the Tsinghua Slips. *Source:* Created by the author.

This model for text copying is similar to what was previously discussed for the Mawangdui *Laozi* A and B versions, but with the Tsinghua slips it is attested to far earlier materials. This not only deepens our understanding of how different versions of the same text came to be circulated; at the same time, it also encourages us to consider seriously the possibility for multiple originals (or ancestral editions) when discussing textual transmission during the pre-Qin era.

Different Regional Characteristics in the Early Transmission of Texts

Among previously unearthed manuscripts, a surprising amount of content appears to parallel materials from our received corpus of pre-Qin, Qin, and Han ancient books. Based on a comparison of these sources, researchers have completed significant exegetical work and now better understand the transmission processes governing pre-Qin texts. Yet previous finds have only provided us with a partial view of a much grander picture. The Tsinghua manuscript *Houfu* 厚父 offers a case in point, as it completely overturns these earlier ideas. In this section we will discuss these insights, through an analysis of the style of writing on this manuscript, along with its textual content.

First, it is clear that *Houfu* is written in a script type that does not belong to the Chu region. Paleographical analysis reveals that it is closer to the Jin 晉 script. On slip 8, in the phrase 皇天之政工, the graph *gong* 工

is written for *gong* 功 (merit), as is common in the Jin script.[12] This is seen often in the Zhongshan 中山 royal bronzes. For example, the inscription on the squared *hu* 壺 vessel writes *huanggong* 皇工 for *huanggong* 皇功; the inscription on the rounded *hu* vessel has *gong lie* 工烈 for *gong lie* 功烈; and on the *ding* 鼎 vessel, *ke you gong* 克有工 is used instead of *ke you gong* 克有 功.[13] It is scholarly consensus that the Zhongshan writing falls within the Jin script system.[14] In the Chu script system, both the graphs *gong* 玒 and *gong* 攻 were used to write *gong* 功. Examples among the Guodian manuscripts include *Laozi* C 老子, 丙, slip 2, in the phrase *cheng shi sui gong* 成事遂 玒 (功); *Taiyi sheng shui* 太一生水, slip 12, in the phrase *gu gong cheng er shen bu shang* 故玒 (功) 成而身不傷; *Qiongda yi shi* 窮達以時, slip 9, in the phrase *Zi Xu qian duo gong* 子胥前多玒 (功); and *Laozi* A 老子, 甲, slip 39, in the phrase *gong sui shen tui* 攻 (功) 遂身退.[15] In Qi 齊 script, *gong* 攻 is often used for *gong* 功 as well, while in Qin 秦 script, *gong* 攻 and *hong* 紅 are used for *gong* 功.[16] Thus, the *Houfu* manuscript's use of *gong* 工 for *gong* 功 represents a Jin feature. This is but one example of a number of similar cases in the *Houfu*. Due to space constraints, we cannot enumerate them all here, but we list a few in table 8.2. Note that the number in the leftmost column represents the slip on which the graph is found.[17]

There are, moreover, a few graphs on the *Houfu* manuscript for which regional affiliation is difficult to determine. Take for instance the graph 兔 on slip 1, 紫 on slip 2, 石 on slip 4, 羍 on slip 8, and 侷 on slip 13. Although we cannot entirely dismiss the possibility that these are in Qin, Qi, or Yan 燕 scripts, it is clear that there is a direct relationship between them and the Jin script system. If we consider the overall writing style and orthography employed throughout the *Houfu*, then we might say that these more ambiguous graphs either belong to the Jin script system or have been influenced by it. The fact that *Houfu* was written mainly in Chu script, yet still carried a strong Jin accent, suggests that the original on which this manuscript was based quite possibly was a Jin text.

Another consideration is that *Houfu* retains a remarkably archaic flavor. The graph 唯 on slip 7 is written 工隹, in which the right-hand element of *zhui* 隹 appears differently than elsewhere in *Houfu*, such as with 𢼄 and 𢽾 on the same slip. These latter examples are typical for Warring States–period scripts, but the graph 工隹 exhibits archaic characteristics. Compare, for instance, to the graphs of 工隹 (合集 *Heji* 36565) and 隹 (*Heji* 36567), from the Shang oracle-bone inscriptions.

On slip 8 of *Houfu*, the graph *xian* 憲 is written 憲, which is similar in its orthography to the graphs 憲, 憲, 憲, and 憲 from Western Zhou

Table 8.2. Comparison of Tsinghua *Houfu* writing to regional scripts

	Houfu	Jin Script	Other Script Types	Explanation
7	[script]	[script]	[script]	The Jin script system derived from Western Zhou bronze inscriptions.
3	[script]	[script]	[script]	The way graphs with the *you* 又 element as written derives from Western Zhou bronze inscriptions.
9	[script]	[script]	[script]	The graph *jing* 敬 is only abbreviated thus in Jin script.
3	[script]	[script]	[script]	In Jin script, the graph *xi* 夕 often includes an extra stroke.
3	[script]	[script]	[script]	In Jin script, the middle section of the graph *yan* 嚴 omits or has differing strokes.
5	[script]	[script]	[script]	In Jin script, the element *feng* 丰 in *bang* 邦 is placed on the left.

bronze inscriptions, without the bottom "heart" (*xin* 心) element.[18] It is only in Spring and Autumn–period bronze inscriptions that we begin to see *xian* written with the "heart" element.[19] By the Warring States, this is the predominant orthography, as we see for example on the Xincai 新蔡 slip A3.25, [graph], and B4.145, [graph].[20]

On *Houfu* slip 3, the graph for *wen* 聞 is written [graph]. This is the same as on slip 13 of the Tsinghua manuscript *Shifa* 筮法, which has [graph]. The graph is written in a slightly different manner on *Jinteng* 金縢, slip 10 (given as [graph]); *Rui Liangfu bi* 芮良夫毖, slip 3 (given as [graph]); and *Chu ju* 楚居, slip 13 (given as [graph]). They may appear similar, but a closer look reveals subtle differences in the style of the upper element, which can be traced back to Spring and Autumn–period bronze inscriptions, where it is written, for instance, as [graph] or [graph].[21]

It is worth noting that the graph [graph] on slip 5 of *Houfu* is written [graph] but read as *zhi* 治. This usage is also seen on the early Western Zhou Ke *gui* 舸簋 inscription, where the graph is written [graph].[22] In Warring States writing, when *zhi* means "order" (i.e., the opposite of *luan* 亂, disorder), it generally is written [graph], or shortened to either [graph] or [graph]. At the same time, the graphs [graph], [graph], or [graph] usually do not represent this *zhi*.[23] Thus, using [graph] to represent *zhi* must be an archaic usage.

Furthermore, *Houfu* preserves some features in its writing that are especially unique. Running thirteen slips in length, the *Houfu* manuscript is one of the shorter works that have been discovered among the extant corpus of Warring States unearthed manuscripts. Yet despite its limited size, the manuscript bears a number of graphs whose orthographies have never been seen before, offering new paleographic evidence for research into the history of the Chinese script. These new forms include, for example, how *yi* 彝 is written [graph] on slip 6; how *ming* 命 is written [graph] and [graph] on slips 2–3; and how, on slip 3, the word *cai* 𢦏 is written [graph], *yin* 禋 is written [graph], and *zhe* 折 is written [graph].

It is apparent from how *ming* 命 is written here that the copyist was sensitive to calligraphic artistry, making stylistic changes in the brushwork, while also maintaining the integrity of the graph. On slip 2 the word *qi* 啟 is written in two ways, [graph] and [graph]; on slip 4, the word *zheng* 政 is given as [graph], but on slip 8 it is instead written as [graph]; and on slip 10, the word *min* 民 is written [graph], while on slip 11 it is given as [graph]. This is the organic unification of what in calligraphy is called *wei* 違 (going against) and *he* 和 (harmonizing). In order to better observe this directly, consult the rearrangement to *Houfu* slip 2 shown in figure 8.3.[24]

Figure 8.3. Calligraphy of *Houfu* slip 2 (rearranged to read left to right, top to bottom). *Source:* Created by the author.

The scribe copying out the *Houfu* must have valued this text highly, a work that appears to have an early date of composition and had ancestral versions already in circulation. The present manuscript was based on a Jin original but copied using the Chu script. The scribe responsible for this manuscript acted in a highly authoritative and independent manner, and therefore was no ordinary scribe. It is thus possible that the *Houfu* manuscript was copied out personally by its owner. These are the sorts of hypotheses one may derive from paying attention to a manuscript's style of writing.

In regard to the textual content of the *Houfu*, there is one sentence that is particularly important. Slip 5 reads: "In antiquity, Heaven sent down (blessings) to the people below, setting up the myriad polities, creating rulers for them, and creating armies for them, so it was said: 'They help the God on High govern the people below'" (古天降下民, 設萬邦, 作之君, 作之師, 惟曰其助上帝𤔲下民). Similar language is found in *Mengzi* 孟子, "Liang Hui Wang, xia" 梁惠王下:

> The *Documents* state: "Heaven sent down (blessings) to the people below, creating rulers for them, creating armies for them, so it was said that 'they help the God on High to care for them.' In the

Four Quadrates, I am the one who must deal with cases of who are innocent of crimes or not. How can anyone under Heaven dare to trespass its will?" If the behavior of even one person under Heaven was cause for judgment, King Wu felt ashamed. This was the bravery of King Wu. With a single expression of anger, he settled the people below Heaven. Now (the present) king likewise settles the people below Heaven with a single expression of anger; the people only fear the king's unwillingness to express (the same) bravery."

"書" 曰: "天降下民, 作之君, 作之師, 惟曰其助上帝寵之. 四方有罪無罪惟我在, 天下曷敢有越厥志?" 一人衡行于天下, 武王恥之. 此武王之勇也. 而武王亦一怒而安天下之民. 今王亦一怒而安天下之民, 民惟恐王之不好勇也.

The reference to the *Documents* in this quote is to a lost chapter of the *Shangshu* 尚書, according to the commentary of Zhao Qi 趙岐 (108–201).[25] The received *Shangshu*, "Taishi" 泰誓 chapter, includes the lines: "Heaven aided the people below, creating rulers for them, creating armies for them, it is so they are able to match (the pattern) of the God on High and give favor and succor to the Four Quadrates. As to innocence or guilt, how dare I allow trespassing of its will?" (天佑下民, 作之君, 作之師, 惟其克相上帝, 寵綏四方. 有罪無罪, 予曷敢有越厥志?).[26] Previously, it was assumed that the "Taishi" chapter was a later forgery, with this sentence adapted from the lines in *Mengzi*. A comparison between the *Houfu* and *Mengzi* parallels reveals certain differences. One such difference is the inclusion or absence of the line "setting up the myriad polities" (*she wanbang* 設萬邦), which speaks to issues of textual integrity and the deeper cultural layers responsible for these texts. In the *Mencius*, after Heaven is said to have sent down blessings to the people below, a ruler and army are then set up for them. This seems to emphasize the people and their government as the most important factors in its political philosophy. The geopolitical concept of a "state," however, includes "territory" as another crucial factor, indeed it is even *the* necessary requirement for statehood. The words *bang* 邦 (polity) and *feng* 封 (land grant) are cognates, whose base meaning is the delineation of boundaries through the planting of trees, a concept directly related to "territory." By including "setting up the myriad polities" (*she wanbang*), the *Houfu* refers to territory, people, and government, incorporating all three of these factors; it moreover gives pride of place to territory, hinting that it is of the utmost importance. Yet in the *Mengzi*, "setting up the myriad polities" is shockingly absent. This suggests that changes occurred over the course of the text's transmission. Although we cannot confirm that *Houfu* is a lost chapter of the original *Shangshu*, it remains a definite possibility.[27]

Early Prefaces to the *Shu* (*Documents*) and *Shi* (*Odes*)

The most celebrated feature of the Tsinghua manuscripts, at least in regard to their content, is the great number of texts in the corpus associated with "classics" and "histories," especially those written in the same style as the *Shangshu*, for which there are many examples. It is a matter of habit for scholars now to refer to these works as *shu* writings as well. In pre-Qin ancient books, contextual information is commonly included before the main body of text, such as when the action took place and its historical background, as a sort of foreword or preface. Even if they are fewer than a couple dozen or several hundred words in length, these materials can be crucial to understanding the background to the text's composition, its content, and the intellectual orientation of the piece.

In our editing of the Tsinghua slips, we have discovered that, among the *shu* texts in our collection, there is an early *shu* preface (*shu xu* 書序). When compiling the *Fu Yue zhi ming* 傅說之命, we divided the materials into three parts (1 上, 2 中, and 3 下), because the content of each seemed to constitute independent and coherent pieces on their own.[28] Part 1 includes seven bamboo slips, part 2 has seven slips, and part 3 has ten slips (though it is missing its first slip). The last slip of each part bears the title *Fu Yue zhi ming* 傅說之命. Note that part 1 begins with a sentence reminiscent of the received *Shu* preface (slip 1): "It was the Yin king (Wu Ding) who was granted Yue from Heaven, a man in the employ of the Shizhong. The king commanded his hundred artisans to offer gifts when seeking out Yue among the settled peoples. It was an aide who obtained Yue at Fu Yan" (惟殷王賜 說於天, 庸為失仲使人. 王命厥百工像, 以貨徇求說於邑人. 惟弼人得說于傅 巖). The transmitted version for the *Shu* preface to the "Yue ming" reads: "Gao Zong dreamt that he obtained Yue and sent the hundred artisans to camp out and search for him in the wilds, (where) they obtained (him) in Fuyan. (Thus was) composed the *Yue ming*, in three parts" (高宗夢得說, 使 百工營求諸野, 得諸傅岩, 作 "說命" 三篇).[29] If we consider all three parts of the *Fu Yue zhi ming* materials among the Tsinghua slips as an integral whole, part 1 reads like an introductory outline. It narrates how Wu Ding sought out and found Yue, the details of their first meeting, Yue's attack on the Shizhong, Yue's physical features, the location of his settlement, and so forth.

Parts 2 and 3, on the other hand, contain the actual content of Wu Ding's "command" to Yue and serve as the main text. Part 2 begins (slips 1–2): "Yue came from Fuyan to reside in Yin. Wu Ding met him at the gate and escorted him into the ancestral shrine" (說來自傅岩, 在殷. 武丁朝 於門, 入在宗). After introducing the actors and the scene of the anecdote, the content immediately turns to the wording of Wu Ding's command to Yue. This structure parallels that of the proclamation (*gao* 誥), decree (*ming* 命), and injunction (*xun* 訓) chapters of the *Shangshu*. There are three places in the wording of Wu Ding's command that bear similarities to quotes of the *Shangshu*: the "Yue ming" chapter cited in the *Guoyu* 國語 chapter "Chu yu, shang" 楚語上, the *Liji* 禮記 chapter "Ziyi" 緇衣, and the *Mozi* 墨子 chapter "Shangtong, zhong" 尚同中.[30] Part 3 is structured around the line "The King said, 'Yue, . . .'" (王曰: "說 . . ."), which again is the same as the *Shangshu* proclamation, decree, and injunction chapters. And again, the last slip records the title *Fu Yue zhi ming* 傅說之命 (The Command of Fu Yue), confirming that this belongs to the main text of the "Yue ming" chapter. Part 2 mentions that Yue came from Fu Yan and resided in Yin, where he received Wu Ding's command; this repeats the narration given in part 1, where it is said that "(They) obtained Yue at Fu Yan" (slip 1), "Yue arrived, and gave his services to the Yin" (說來, 自從事于殷, slips 6–7), "the Yin king (Wu Ding) was granted Yue from Heaven" (slip 1), and so forth. We therefore propose that part 1 is actually the *Shangshu* preface to the "Yue ming" chapter.[31]

One lingering problem, however, is the fact that Tsinghua *Fu Yue zhi ming* 1 is too verbose to serve as a preface. Yet, we must also consider that in the *Liji* chapters "Wen Wang shizi" 文王世子, "Xueji" 學記, and "Ziyi," there are quotes from the "Yue ming" that do not appear in the Tsinghua *Fu Yue zhi ming*.[32] We cannot exclude the possibility that variant editions of the "Yue ming" circulated, yet it is perhaps more likely that these quotes are from lost content to the "Yue ming" that coincidentally did not happen to be preserved among the Tsinghua cache. Furthermore, despite its verbosity, *Fu Yue zhi ming* 1 is not an overly large text. Even though it accounts for about one-third of all the Tsinghua *Fu Yue zhi ming* materials, this does not discount it as a possible preface. Take for example the prefaces to the *Mao Shi* 毛詩, which are divided into the "Great Preface" (Daxu 大序) and the "Minor Prefaces" (Xiaoxu 小序).[33] The large paragraph before the ode "Guanzhu" 關雎 is understood as the "Great Preface" (which some scholars term the *Shi daxu* 詩大序). Taking this as a potential model, we might go so far as to call the Tsinghua *Fu Yue zhi ming* A the "Great Preface" to either the "Yue ming" chapter, or even the *Shangshu* (i.e., as the *Shu daxu* 書大序).

Following this discovery of a *Shu* preface, Yao Xiao'ou 姚小鷗 conducted further research into the *Rui Liangfu bi* 芮良夫毖 manuscript and noted that the text begins with around forty words that explain the background to the piece's composition. Yao argues that this functions like a "Minor Preface," with the main text proceeding afterward. Since the content is largely rhymed, and technical vocabulary used in the Zhou system of ritual music appears, such as the term *zhong* 終, the text may be classified as a *shi* (odes)-type work. As such, the opening sentences can then be seen as a preface to the *Odes* (i.e., *Shi xu* 詩序).[34] Yao's analysis is reasonable.

Our previous categorization for the *Rui Liangfu bi* was as a *shu*-type work. This was due to similarities in wording between it and *Shangshu* (*Documents*) texts (especially the instructional language of *xun* 訓 "injunctions" and *gao* 誥 "proclamations"), as well as the fact that the *Yi Zhou shu* 逸周書 has a chapter titled "Rui Liangfu" 芮良夫.[35] Yet it is also possible, as Yao argues, that the *Rui Liangfu bi* ought to be classified as a *shi*-type work. This impresses upon us the realization that the line separating *shi*- and *shu*-type works is not all that clear. For example, the *Zhanguo ce* 戰國策, "Qin ce, si" 秦策四, records Huang Xie 黃歇 telling King Zhao of Qin 秦昭王 that "the *Shi* states: 'The Great Wu residing far away did not cross the river'" ("詩" 云: "大武遠宅不涉").[36] In the *Shiji* 史記, "Chunshen Jun liezhuan" 春申君列傳, there is a similar quotation: "The *Shi* says: 'Great Wu went faraway to live and did not cross the river'" ("詩" 曰: "大武遠宅而不涉").[37] Curiously, the *Yi Zhou shu*, "Da Wu" 大武, includes the phrase "residing far away, without encroaching" (遠宅不薄), which must be related to the *Zhanguo ce* and *Shiji* lines, only slightly modified.[38] The *Yi Zhou shu* is a *shu*-type work, whereas the *Zhanguo ce* and *Shiji* both claim the line is a quote from a *shi*—a clear contradiction. Qing scholar Lu Wenchao 盧文弨 (1717–1795) noted that, in these cases, *shi* must be mistakenly written for *shu* ("詩" 必是 "書" 字之誤).[39] There is ample evidence, however, that in antiquity the two names were often confused in quotations.[40] With detailed analysis, it becomes obvious that if the instructional language rhymes, then it could be difficult to tell if a text ought to be labeled as either a *shu* or *shi* type.

The authorship of the prefaces to the *Mao shi* has been an enduring academic controversy in the study of the *Shijing* 詩經. Various theories have been raised in the past, from those that advocate for Zi Xia 子夏, for both Zi Xia and Mao Gong 毛公, or for Wei Hong 衛宏. The general consensus today is that the prefaces were written by different people at different times but edited with a heavy hand by Wei Hong during the Eastern Han (during the reign of Guang Wu Di 光武帝, 25–57).[41] If, by comparison, we understand that the Tsinghua *Fu Yue zhi ming* and *Rui Liangfu bi* preserve early examples of *Shangshu* and *Shijing* prefaces, respectively, then their significance cannot be overstated.

Clues to the Origins of Ancient Books

Some time ago, Li Ling 李零 raised two questions with regard to "ancient books" (*gushu* as opposed to *wenshu*, administrative documents) that deserve our close attention: In what period were ancient books first produced in China, and what were they initially like? Despite a lack of definite evidence, he suspected that the early books likely emerged from a "culture of scribal officials" (*shiguan wenhua* 史官文化), that is, the official scribes responsible for keeping records. The earliest such works in our received corpus, such as the *Shijing, Shangshu*, and the *Zhou yi* 周易, were culled from record offices and music bureaus, which is to say they originated in administrative archives.[42] The evidence from the Tsinghua corpus supports this hypothesis.

The Shang oracle bones and Western Zhou bronze inscriptions are often regarded as archives of administrative documents (*wenshu dang'an* 文書檔案). There is a unified rhetorical style in the majority of the recorded commands (*ceming* 冊命) in Western Zhou bronze inscriptions. They generally open with a record of the time and place, then introduce in order the *ceming* (recorded command of a new appointment) ceremony, the awarding of gifts, and the expressions of gratitude of the appointee toward the king. For example, on the Qinian Que Cao *ding* 七年趞曹鼎 (*Jicheng* 02783), it writes:

> It was the seventh year (of the king's reign), the tenth month, after the full moon, when the king resided in the Zhou Ban Hall. At dawn, the king ascended to the Great Chamber and Xing Bo escorted Que Cao in from the right, standing in position in the center of the courtyard facing north. (The king) awarded Que Cao black knee covers, a belt, and small bells. Que Cao clapped his hands together and bumped his head on the floor, daring to express gratitude for the grace of the Son of Heaven; (He) will use (the gift) to make a treasured caldron and to feast his compatriots.

唯七年十月既生霸, 王在周般宫. 旦, 王格大室; 邢伯入右趞曹,
立中廷, 北嚮; 賜趞曹緇韍, 回衡, 鑾. 趞曹拜稽首, 敢對揚天子
休, 用作寶鼎, 用饗朋友.

We find similar language at the end of the newly published Tsinghua manuscript *She ming* 攝命, on slip 32:[43]

> It was the ninth month, after the full moon, on a *renshen* day
> (9) when the king resided at Haojing, that he ascended to the
> Great Chamber and took up his position, and this part of the
> ceremony was completed. (Then) Shi Jie escorted Bo She in
> from the right and took up their position in the center of the
> courtyard facing north. The king called on Scribe Ren to record
> the command for Bo She: "So . . ."

唯九月既望壬申, 王在鎬京, 各於大室, 即位, 鹹. 士疌右伯攝, 立
在中廷, 北嚮. 王呼作冊任冊命伯攝: "虔."

The phrase "the king said: She . . ." (*wang yue: she* 王曰: "攝 . . .") occurs
many times throughout the *She ming* manuscript (e.g., slips 3, 4, 15, etc.).
The formulaic style and content belong to the *shu* type of instructional
language. If we placed slip 32 in the front of the manuscript, then *She
ming* would function just like *ceming* in bronze inscriptions, minus the
listing of gifts and expression of gratitude. It is well known that not all of
the Western Zhou *ceming* inscriptions record the ceremony in full as found
on the Qinian Que Cao *ding*. For example, the famous Mao Gong *ding*
毛公鼎 begins immediately with "The king thus said" (*wang ruo yue* 王若
曰).[44] There is thus no doubt that the *She ming* is the same type of text
as the *ceming* in bronze inscriptions. It is important at this point to note
that the bamboo slips bearing *She ming* are numbered, securing slip 32's
position at the end of the manuscript; it was definitely not at the beginning
of the manuscript, despite the fact that this is the formatting for *ceming*
bronze inscriptions. We thus have reason to speculate that the compiler of
this manuscript has edited the original text. What this therefore suggests is
that here a "document" originally from an administrative archive has already
begun to be transformed into an ancient book like the *Shangshu* classic.

A similar case is presented with the Tsinghua manuscript *Feng Xu zhi
ming* 封許之命, a record of the early Zhou establishment of the state of
Xu.[45] In addition to instructional language (as mentioned earlier), it lists
numerous gifts, many of which can be read according to the lists of similar

gifts in *ceming* inscriptions. Their mention, however, is inserted throughout the narrative of instruction, an editorial decision that must have been purposeful. Thus, to a certain degree, the *Feng Xu zhi ming* also demonstrates the transformation of a "document" (*shu*) into an ancient book.

The *Fu Yue zhi ming*, moreover, bears language reminiscent of that found on the Shang oracle bones: "We shall perhaps kill it? We should perhaps stop, do not kill it" (我其殺之? 我其已, 勿殺).[46] Yet upon comparison, the phrasing is not quite the same. The phrase seen on the oracle bones most akin to that in *Fu Yue zhi ming* is the statement: "Perhaps stop . . . do not stop" (其已 . . . 勿已), yet this is not exactly the same as the *Fu Yue zhi ming* line.[47] To account for this variation, our hypothesis is that the compiler of the *Fu Yue zhi ming* saw texts in the Shang language, but did not quite understand them entirely, and thus made the revisions found on this manuscript.[48]

In summary, the Tsinghua manuscripts support Li Ling's hypothesis that the *Shangshu* classic was compiled from edited archival documents. Guo Moruo 郭沫若 (1892–1978) expressed a similar idea as early as 1931, when he noted in his preface to *Liang Zhou jinwenci daxi tulu kaoshi* 兩周金文辭大系圖錄考釋: "There are already over three or four thousand inscriptions preserved on bronzes handed down through the ages. The fact that some of these are as long as five hundred words suggests that they could each be the basis of a chapter in the *Shangshu* . . . the *Shangshu* is the oldest catalog of bronze inscriptions" (傳世兩周彝器, 其有銘者已在三四千以上, 銘辭之長幾及五百字者, 說者每謂足抵 "尚書" 一篇 . . . "尚書" 為最古金文之著錄).[49] When Guo mentions inscriptions that "are as long as five hundred words," this is an obvious reference to the Mao Gong *ding*. Although the Bin Gong *xu* 豳公盨 in the Poly Museum (Baoli bowuguan 保利博物館) does not have the same formulaic language, it too resembles an ancient book. These long bronze inscriptions, together with the Tsinghua corpus *shu*-type texts, allow us to imagine the early origins of China's ancient books.

Rich Data on the Evolving Treatment of Historical Figures

The *Lunyu* 論語, "Ba yi" 八佾 chapter, records Confucius as saying: "I can talk about Xia ritual, but the Qi (state) is not enough to evince them; I can talk about Yin ritual, but the Song (state) is not enough to evince them. It is because their texts and worthies are lacking; should they be sufficient then I would be able to demonstrate them" (夏禮吾能言之, 杞不足徵也; 殷禮吾

能言之, 宋不足徵也. 文獻不足故也; 足則吾能徵之矣).[50] Among the Tsing-hua manuscripts already published, there are bountiful materials concerning Shang Tang's 商湯 minister, Yi Yin 伊尹. These texts greatly enrich our understanding of the evolving treatment of historical figures such as Yi Yin.

Previously, scholarship on Yi Yin depended upon the anecdotes contained within our received corpus of transmitted texts. Representative works include Cui Shu's 崔述, "Shang kao xin fulu *Yi Yin*" 商考信錄附伊尹; Chen Qiyou's 陳奇猷, "Yi Yin de chushen ji qi xingming" 伊尹的出身及其姓名, Du Zhengsheng's 杜正勝, "Zhanguo shidai Yi Yin shenfen de sanzhon xingtai" 戰國時代伊尹身分的三種型態, and so forth.[51] This research, however, was limited by the restraints of the textual corpus available to them, giving them only part of the picture. Among the Shang oracle bones, Yi Yin is mentioned in records of sacrifice and divination, but these data are fragmentary as well. The Tsinghua manuscripts thus shed important light upon research into Yi Yin, with such texts such as *Yin zhi* 尹至, *Yin gao* 尹誥, *Tang chuyu Tangqiu* 湯處於湯丘, *Tang zai Chimen* 湯在帝門, *Chijiu zhi ji Tang zhi wu* 赤鵠之集湯之屋; in fact, some scholars call them the "Five Yi Yin Texts" (*Yi Yin wupian* 伊尹五篇). Their discovery has served as a turning point, causing a wave of scholarship on Yi Yin in recent years, with remarkable results.[52]

At present, we are already able to sketch the contours of the Yi Yin tale, as it evolved from the Shang, through the Western Zhou, Spring and Autumn, and Warring States periods. Jing Lingling 荊玲玲 has produced a useful chart showing this: "Table on Yi Yin's Image in the Spring and Autumn and Warring States Periods."[53] In table 8.3 we cite its content in detail, with emendations.

From table 8.3, we can see that during the Shang and Zhou periods, representations of Yi Yin were multidimensional, with this figure serving multiple roles: that of cook, private servant, alcohol steward, worthy official, ancestral spirit, and so forth. Compared with the limited caricatures often given for historical personages previously, this amounts to a vast improvement. Tsinghua's "Five Yi Yin Texts," as well as the *Liang chen* 良臣 manuscript, corroborate the accounts given among the received corpus, satisfying Wang Guowei's 王國維 (1877–1927) call for a "dual-evidence approach" (*erzhong zhengju fa* 二重證據法).[54]

According to the *Shangshu* prefaces and the *Shiji*, "Yin Benji" 殷本紀 chapter, the instructional texts related to Yi Yin in the *Shangshu* include the "Yi xun" 伊訓, "Si ming" 肆命, "Cu hou" 徂後, "Xian you yi de" 咸有一德, and the three "Tai Jia" 太甲 chapters. Owing to textual parallels,

Table 8.3. Yi Yin's characterization from the Shang and Zhou periods

	庖廚 Cook	私臣/ 女師僕 Servant	小臣 Minister	酒保 Alcohol Steward	相/輔/ 三公 Aide	*神祖 Ancestor
*Oracle bones					*√	*√
Shuyi *zhong* 叔夷鐘			√		√	
Mozi 墨子, "Shang xian, shang" 尚賢上	√					
Mozi, "Shang xian, zhong" 尚賢中	√	√			√	
Mozi, "Sang xian, xia" 尚賢下		√	√		√	
Yin Zhi 尹至					√	
Yin gao 尹誥					√	
Tang chuyu Tangqiu 湯處於湯丘	√		√		√	
Tang zai Chimen 湯在啻門			√		√	
Chijiu zhi ji Tang zhi wu 赤鵠之集湯之屋	√		√			
Liang chen 良臣					√	
Zhuangzi 莊子, "Geng Sang-chu" 庚桑楚	√					
Heguanzi 鶡冠子, "Shi xian" 世賢				√		
Chuci 楚辭, "Tianwen" 天問	√				√	
Chuci, "Xi wangri" 惜往日	*√					

	庖廚 Cook	私臣/女師僕 Servant	小臣 Minister	酒保 Alcohol Steward	相/輔/三公 Aide	*神祖 Ancestor
Lüshi Chunqiu 呂氏春秋, "Zun shi" 尊師			√			
Lüshi Chunqiu, "Benwei" 本味	√					
Lüshi Chunqiu, "Zhi du" 知度	√		√			
Lüshi Chunqiu, "Jubei" 具備	√					
Lüshi Chunqiu, "Qiu ren" 求人	√				√	
Han Feizi 韓非子, "Nan yan" 難言	√					
Silk text *Jiu zhu* 九主					√	

Note: The issue of Yi Yin as a deity is complicated; see Chen Mengjia 陳夢家, *Yinxu buci zongshu* 殷虛卜辭綜述 (Beijing: Zhonghua, 1989), 363; Zhang Guangzhi 張光直, "Shang wang miaohao xinkao" 商王廟號新考 and "Tan Wang Hai yu Yi Yin de jiri bing zai lun Yin Shang wangzhi" 談王亥與伊尹的祭日並再論殷商王制, *Zhongguo qingtong shidai* 中國青銅時代 (Beijing: Shenghuo, dushu, xinzhi sanlian, 2013), 197, 233; Zhang Zhenglang 張政烺, "Shi ta shi—lun buci zhong meiyou canshen" 釋它示——論卜辭中沒有蠶神, *Guwenzi yanjiun* 古文字研究 1 (1979): 68–70; Yao Xiaosui 姚孝遂 and Xiao Ding 肖丁, *Xiaotun nandi jiagu kaoshi* 小屯南地甲骨考釋 (Beijing: Zhonghua, 1985), 64; Xiao Liangqiong 肖良瓊, "Buci zhong de Yi Yin he Yi Yin fang Tai Jia" 卜辭中的伊尹和伊尹放太甲, Guwenzi yanjiu 21 (2001): 14; Chang Yuzhi 常玉芝, *Shangdai zongjiao jisi* 商代宗教祭祀 (Beijing: Zhongguo shehui kexue, 2010), 399–408; Wang Tingbin, "Shuo 'Yi bin'" 說 "伊賓," *Zhongguo wenzi* 中國文字, n.s. 41 (2015): 243–47. Ed. note: Please also refer to Zhu Fenghan, "The Place of Yi Yin in the Shang Pantheon," chapter 1 in *Myth and the Making of History: Narrating Early China with Sarah Allan* (Albany: State University of New York Press, 2024).

some scholars claim that the Tsinghua *Yin gao* manuscript is in fact the real "Xian you yi de" chapter of the *Shangshu*.[55] According to the *Han shu* 漢書, "Yiwen zhi" 藝文志 bibliographic treatise, under the *Daojiao* 道家 (Daoist) category there is listed a *Yi Yin* 伊尹 text in fifty-one *pian* volumes, while the *Xiaoshou* 小說 (Tales) category lists a *Yi Yin* in twenty-seven *pian* volumes. Evidently, in antiquity, there were numerous texts which featured Yi Yin; what we see now is just the tip of the iceberg. The time is ripe for a complete collection of Yi Yin primary sources and scholarship.

Conclusion

The value of Tsinghua University's bamboo-slip manuscript corpus is multi-faceted. In this chapter, we have discussed briefly only the philological value, from five different perspectives. Despite the fruitful results already achieved by many scholars working on this collection, there are still many research questions that remain. With the publication of the remaining Tsinghua manuscripts, we anticipate that even more profound discoveries will be made.

Notes

1. Li Xueqin 李學勤, "Qinghua jian yu gudai wenxian" 清華簡與古代文獻, in Shoudu shifan daxue wenxuyuan 首都師範大學文學院, ed., *Yanjing luntan* 燕京論壇2013 (Shehui kexue wenxian Press 社會科學文獻出版社, 2015), collected in *Qinghua jian yu gudai wenming* 清華簡與古代文明 (Nanchang: Jiangxi jiaoyu 江西教育, 2017), 238.

2. Qinghua daxue chutu wenxian yanjiu yu baohu zhongxin 清華大學出土文獻研究與保護中心 and Li Xueqin 李學勤, eds., *Qinghua daxue cang Zhanguo zhujian* 清華大學藏戰國竹簡, 13 vols. (Shanghai: Zhongxi, 2010–2023). Publication is ongoing.

3. Yu Jiaxi 余嘉錫, *Mulu xue fawei: Gushu tongli* 目錄學發微: 古書通例 (Beijing: Shangwu, 2011), 267.

4. Jingmenshi bowuguan 荊門市博物館, *Guodian Chu mu zhujian* 郭店楚墓竹簡 (Beijing: Wenwu, 1998).

5. Ma Chengyuan 馬承源, ed., *Shanghai bowuguan cang Zhanguo Chu zhushu (yi)* 上海博物館藏戰國楚竹書 (壹) (Shanghai: Shanghai guji, 2001).

6. Guojia wenwuju guwenxian yanjiushi 國家文物局古文獻研究室, *Mawangdui Han mu boshu* 馬王堆漢墓帛書, vol. 1 (Beijing: Wenwu, 1980), 1.

7. Ma Cheng yuan, ed., *Shanghai bowuguan cang Zhanguo Chu zhushu: Cong zheng*, vol. 2 (Shanghai: Shanghai guji, 2002); *Tianzi jian zhou* A and B, vol. 6 (2007); *Zhengzi jia sang*, *Junrenzhe hebi an zai*, and *Fanwu liu xing*, vol. 7 (2008); *Cheng Wang wei Chengpu zhi xing*, vol. 9 (2012).

8. Li Mengtao 李孟濤, "Shitan shuxiezhe de shizi nengli ji qi dui luichuan wenben de yingxiang" 試探書寫者的識字能力及其對流傳文本的影響, *Jianbo* 簡帛 4 (2009): 400–02.

9. Li Songru 李松儒, *Zhanguo jianbo ziji yanjiu—yi Shangbo jian wei zhongxin* 戰國簡帛字跡研究——以上博簡為中心 (Shanghai: Shanghai guji, 2015), 416.

10. Li Songru, *Zhanguo jianbo ziji yanjiu*, 451, 491.

11. Ma Nan 馬楠, "Qinghua jian *Zheng Wen Gong wen Taibo* yu Zheng guo zaoqi shishi" 清華簡 "鄭文公問太伯" 與鄭國早期史事, *Wenwu* 2016.3, 84.

12. References to the *Houfu* manuscript will be given via slip number. These can be found beginning on: Qinghua daxue chutu wenxian yanjiu yu baohu zhongxin and Li Xueqin, *Qinghua daxue cang Zhanguo zhujian (wu)*, 2, 110.

13. Zhou Bo 周波, *Zhanguo shidai gexi wenzi jian de yongzi chayi xianxiang yanjiu* 戰國時代各系文字間的用字差異現象研究 (Beijing: Xianzhuang, 2012), 194.

14. Compare for instance the orthography on the Zhongshan Wang *hu* 中山王壺 against the writing on *Jicheng* 2451, 2590, and 1345.

15. Jingmen bowuguan, *Guodian Chu mu zhujian*, 9, 13, 27, and 6, respectively.

16. Zhou Po, *Zhanguo shidai gexi wenzi jian de yongzi chayi xianxiang yanjiu*, 193–94.

17. Zhao Pingan 趙平安, "Tantan Zhanguo wenzi zhon zhide zhuyi de yi xie xianxiang—yi Qinghu jian *Houfu* wei li" 談談戰國文字中值得注意的一些現象——以清華簡 "厚父" 為例, *Chudu wenxian yu guwenzi yanjiu* 出土文獻與古文字研究 6 (2015), collected in *Wenzi, wenxian, gushi—Zhao Pingan zixuanji* 文字, 文獻, 古史——趙平安自選集 (Shanghai: Zhongxi, 2018), 231–38.

18. *Jicheng* 9450, 2749, 10175, and 109.

19. *Jicheng* 262 and 268.

20. Henan sheng wenwu kaogu yanjiusuo 河南省文物考古研究所, ed., *Xincai Geling Chu mu* 新蔡葛陵楚墓 (Zhengzhou: Daxiang, 2003), 189 and 209, photographs pls. 79 and 154, respectively.

21. See for instance *Jicheng* 182, and the Wang Sun Gao *zhong* 王孫誥鍾 in Henan sheng wenwu yanjiusuo 河南省文物研究所, Henan sheng Danjiang kuqu kaogu fajuedui 河南省丹江庫區考古發掘隊, Xichuan Xian bowuguan 淅川縣博物館, eds., *Xichuanxiasi Chunqiu Chu mu* 淅川下寺春秋楚墓 (Beijing: Wenwu, 1991), 149.

22. Zhang Guangyu 張光裕, "Ke *gui* mingwen yu Xi Zhou shishi xinzheng" 牁簋銘文與西周史事新證, *Wenwu* 文物 2009.2, 55; Li Chuntao 李春桃, "Shuo Ke *gui* mingwen zhong de 'luan' zi" 說牁簋銘文中的 "亂" 字, *Fudan daxue chutu wenxian yu guwenzi yanjiu zhongxin wangzhan* 復旦大學出土文獻與古文字研究中心網站, December 17, 2010: http://www.gwz.fudan.edu.cn/Web/Show/1332.

23. For example, from the Shanghai Museum collection, see *Kongzi shi lun* 孔子詩論 22; *Neili* 內禮 10; *Ji Kangzi wenyu Kongzi* 季康子問於孔子 10; and from the Tsinghua slips, see *Huangmen* 皇門 11; and *Xinian* 繫年 93 and 100.

24. For the transcription, please see *Qinghua daxue cang Zhanguo zhujian (wu)*, 110.

25. *Mengzi Zhengyi* 孟子正義, in *Zhuzi jicheng* 諸子集成 series (1988; Shanghai: Shanghai shudian, 1991 [rpt.]), vol. 1, 68–69.

26. *Shangshu zhengyi* 尚書正義 11.68 in Wang Xianqian 王先謙 (1842–1918), ed., *Shisanjing zhushu* 十三經注疏 (1983; Beijing: Zhonghua, 1989 [rpt.]), vol. 1, 180.

27. Zhao Pingan, "*Houfu* de xingzhi ji qi yunhan de Xiadai lishi wenhua" "厚父" 的性質及其蘊含的夏代歷史文化, *Wenwu* 2014.12, collected in *Wenzi, wenxian, gushi—Zhao Pingan zixuanji*, 318–25.

28. *Qinghua daxue cang Zhanguo zhujian (san)*, part 2, 121–31.

29. *Shangshu zhengyi* 10.62, in *Shisanjing zhushu* (Beijing: Zhonghua, 1987), vol. 1, 174.

30. *Guoyu* 17.10 in Sibu beiyao edition (Taipei: Zhonghua, 1975 [rpt.]); *Liji zhengyi* 55.423, in *Shisanjing zhushu* (Beijing: Zhonghua, 1987), vol. 2, 1651, and *Mozi jiangu* 墨子閒詁 3, in *Zhuzi jicheng*, vol. 4, 51.

31. Zhao Pingan 趙平安, *Shizi Qinghua jian* Yue ming *de jiegou* 試析清華簡 "說命" 的結構, on the Qinghua daxue chutu wenxian yanjiu yu baohu zhongxin website 清華大學出土文獻研究與保護中心網站, posted May 7, 2013, later published in *Xinchu jianbo yu guwenzi guwenxian yanjiu xuji* 新出簡帛與古文字古文獻研究續集 (Beijing: Shangwu, 2018), 267–69.

32. *Liji zhengyi* 20.183, in *Shisanjing zhushu*, vol. 2, 1411; 36.293, in *Shisanjing zhushu*, vol. 2, 1521; 55.421, 423, in *Shisanjing zhushu*, vol. 2, 1649, 1651.

33. *Mao Shi zhengyi*, in *Shisanjing zhushu*, vol. 1, 261–64.

34. Yao Xiao'ou 姚小鷗, "*Qinghua daxue zan Zhanguo zhujian*, 'Rui Liangfu bi, xiao xu' yanjiu," "清華大學藏戰國竹簡, 芮良夫毖, 小序" 研究, *Zhongzhou xuekan* 中州學刊 2014.5, 145–47.

35. *Yi Zhou shu* 63, Sibu beiyao edition (Taipei: Zhonghua, 1980 [rpt.]), 9.1a–2b.

36. *Zhanguo ce*, Sibu beiyao edition (Taipei: Zhonghua, 1972 [rpt.]), 6.6b.

37. Takikawa Kametaro 瀧川龜太郎, ed., *Shiki kaichū kōshō* 史記會注考證78, *liezhuan* 18.7 (Taipei: Hongshi, 1977).

38. *Yi Zhou shu* 8, Sibu beiyao edition, 2.3a.

39. Huang Huaixin 黃懷信, Zhang Maorong 張懋熔, and Tian Xudong 田旭東, *Yi Zhou shu huijiao jizhu* 逸周書匯校集注, rev. ed. (Shanghai: Shanghai guji, 2007), 110.

40. Xu Renfu 徐仁甫, *Gushu yinyu yanjiu* 古書引語研究 (Beijing: Zhonghua, 2014), 114–28.

41. See for instance Ma Duanlin 馬端臨, *Wenxian tongkao* 文獻通考, vol. 178, "Jingji kao wu" 經籍考五.

42. Li Ling 李零, *Jianbo gushu yu xueshu yuanliu* 簡帛古書與學術源流, rev. ed. (Beijing: Shenghuo, dushu, xinzhi sanlian, 2008), 53.

43. *Qinghua daxue cang Zhanguo zhujian* (*ba* 捌 [8]), 2, 112.

44. *Jicheng* 2841.

45. *Qinghua daxue cang Zhanguo zhujian (wu)*, part 2, 117–23.

46. Li Xueqin first noticed this; see "Lun Qinghua jian *Yue ming* zhong de buci" 論清華簡 "說命" 中的卜辭, *Huaxia wenhua luntan* 華夏文化論壇8 (2012), republished in *Chushi Qinghua jian* 初識清華簡 (Shanghai: Zhongxi, 2013), 195–97.

47. *Heji* 6498.

48. Wang Tingbin 王挺斌, "*Yue ming* 'sheng er dushi' yu *Huanbao* 238 hao jiagu hedu" "說命" "生二牡豕" 與 "洹寶" 238 號甲骨合讀, *Zhongyuan wenhua yanjiu* 中原文化研究 2017.4, 128.

49. Guo Moruo 郭沫若, *Liang Zhou jinwenci daxi tulu kaoshi* 兩周金文辭大系圖錄考釋, 1.

50. *Lunyu zhengyi* 3, *Zhuzi jicheng*, vol. 1, 49.

51. See Cui Shu 崔述, *Cui Dongbi yishu* 崔東壁遺書 (Beijing: Zhonghua, 2013), 142–44; Chen Qiyou 陳奇猷, "Yi Yin de chushen ji qi xingming," *Zhonghua wenshi luncong* 中華文史論叢3 (1981): 111–17; Du Zhengsheng 杜正勝, *Gudai shehui yu guojia* 古代社會與國家 (Taipei: Yunchen wenhuashiye yifen LLC, 1992), 897–900.

52. Tian Xudong 田旭東, "Yin Zhi yu Yi Yin xuepai—yi chutu wenxian wei kaocha zhongxin" 尹摯與伊尹學派——以出土文獻爲考察中心, *Qinghua jian yanjiu* 1 (2012): 31–39; Huang Tingqi 黃庭頎, "Lun guwenzi cailiao suo jian zhi 'Yi Yin' chenghao—jianlun *Yin zhi, Yin gao* zhi 'Yin,' 'Zhi'" 論古文字材料所見之 "伊尹" 稱號——兼論 "尹至," "尹誥" 之 "尹," "執 (摯)," *Donghua Zhongwen xuebao* 東華中文學報 2012.5, 63–86; Liu Guozhong 劉國忠, "Qinghuajian *Chi jiu zhi ji Tang zhi wu* yu Yi Yin jian Xia" 清華簡《赤鵠之集湯之屋》與伊尹間夏, *Shenzhen daxue xuebao* 深圳大學學報 2013.1, 64–67; Song Zhenhao 宋鎮豪, "Tantan Shangdai kai guo mingchen Yi Yin" 談談商代開國名臣伊尹, *Chujian Chu wenhua yu Xian Qin lishi wenhua guoji xueshu taolunhui lunwenji* 楚簡楚文化與先秦歷史文化國際學術討論會論文集 (Wuhan: Hubei jiaoyu, 2013), 252–59; Zhao Shanshan 趙珊珊, "Qinghua jian *Yin zhi, Yin gao* xiangguan lishi wenti yanjiu" 清華簡 "尹至" "尹誥" 相關歷史問題研究, MA thesis, Tianjin shifan daxue 天津師範大學, 2013; Xia Dazhao 夏大兆 and Huang Deguan 黃德寬, "Guanyu Qinghua jian *Yin zhi, Yin Gao* de xingcheng he xingzhi—cong Yi Yin chuanshuo zai Xin Qin zhuanshi he chutu wenxian zhong de liubian kaocha" 關於清華簡 "尹至" "尹誥" 的形成和性質——從伊尹傳說在先秦傳世和出土文獻中的流變考察, *Wenshi* 文史 2014.3, 213–33; Du Yong 杜勇, "Qinghua jian yu Yi Yin chuanshuo zhi mi" 清華簡與伊尹傳說之謎, *Zhongyuan wenhua yanjiu* 2015.2, 31–43; Wen Haoyue 溫皓月, "Chutu wenxian yu zhuanshi wenxian zhi Yi Yin cailiao zhengli ji xiangguan wenti yanjiu" 出土文獻與傳世文獻之伊尹材料整理及相關問題研究, MA thesis, Jilin daxue, 2016; Li Shuang 李爽, "Qinghua jian 'Yi Yin' wu pian jishi" 清華簡 "伊尹" 五篇集釋, MA thesis, Jilin daxue, 2016; Jing Lingling 荊玲玲, "Xian Qin shiqi Yi Yin xingxiang de yanbian" 先秦時期伊尹形象的演變, *Chutu wenxian* 出土文獻 11 (2017): 184–93.

53. Jing Lingling, "Xian Qin shiqi Yi Yin xingxiang," 188–89. Asterisked entries in the table were newly supplemented by us, and we have also added a mark that was missing for the entry *Chu ci* 楚辭, "Xi wangri" 惜往日. The table title was also drafted separately.

54. Wang Guowei 王國維, *Gushi xinzheng: Wang Guowei zuihou de jiangyi* 古史新證——王國維最後的講義 (Beijing: Qinghua daxue, 1994), 2.

55. Namely, *Yin gao* bears the line *xian you yi de* (咸又 "有" 一惪 "德"), which is cited in the *Shiji* and then features prominently at the beginning of the received *Shangshu* chapter.

9

A Brief Look at the Shanghai Museum Manuscript "The State of Lu Suffered a Great Drought"

Scott Cook

Among all the Shanghai Museum manuscript texts, few have received as much scholarly attention as those entitled *Kongzi shilun* 孔子詩論 (Confucius's Discourse on the Odes) and *Zigao* 子羔, which respectively appear in volumes 1 and 2 of the published series.[1] As the latter text incorporates legends involving the miraculous births of dynastic progenitors and lends ideological support to the practice of abdication, it quite naturally has already been given extensive treatment by Sarah Allan, whose singular contributions to these subjects within the context of evolving debates over dynastic succession in early China have long enriched our field.[2] No less interesting, however, is a third text that may well have been bound together in a single physical manuscript with the other two: *Lu bang dahan* 魯邦大旱 (The State of Lu Suffered a Great Drought).[3] This text records two short conversations

---

This chapter is based largely on an earlier study of mine in Chinese, published as (Gu Shikao 顧史考) "Shangbo zhushu 'Lu bang dahan' pian jiqi xingcheng tansuo" 上博竹書《魯邦大旱》篇及其形成探索, *Jianbo* 簡帛 15 (2018): 17–30. That article, in turn, derived from a paper first presented on November 5, 2016, at the Beijing Forum 北京論壇 2016, held at Peking University 北京大學. The article has since been incorporated in my *Shangbo zhushu Kongzi yulu wenxian yanjiu* 上博竹書孔子語錄文獻研究 (Shanghai: Zhongxi, 2021), 293–311.

pertaining to what should be done in the wake of the great drought that has befallen the state: one between Kongzi 孔子 (Confucius, 551–479 BCE) and Lord Ai of Lu 魯哀公 (r. 494–468 BCE), and the other, a follow-up conversation, between Kongzi and his disciple Zigong 子貢 (Duanmu Si[/Ci] 端木賜, ca. 520–450 BCE). In its entirety, the text comprises only six strips of bamboo, the last of which ends with a text-end marker. The name of this text is given by the editors on the basis of its opening line.[4]

Given that the *Chunqiu* 春秋 records a "great rain-seeking sacrifice" occurring in the eighth month of autumn (秋八月, 大雩) in the fifteenth year of Lord Ai (480 BCE), Ma Chengyuan 馬承源 surmises that the drought ostensibly referred to in this text would most likely have taken place from the summer to fall of that year, just one year prior to Kongzi's death.[5] As scholars have long pointed out, however, arguably the most fascinating aspect of this text is that the entire story bears an uncannily close resemblance to one from the "Inner Chapters" of the *Yanzi chunqiu* 晏子春秋, including nearly verbatim repetitions within the dialogue, such that the two could almost be said to constitute different "editions" of the very same anecdote, save for the disparities in location and the main characters who comprise it.[6] Given this fact, the attempt to fix its precise temporal context in Lu would seem to be largely beside the point.[7] Of greater relevance is the fact that, along with the differences in personnel, there are also some subtle yet meaningful distinctions in content that, upon deeper reflection, point to interesting possibilities in the history of intertextual borrowing among different philosophical camps in the Warring States. Beyond this, though, a no less intriguing phenomenon—that should not be ignored—is the strategic similarities that this text would appear to share with *Zigao*, the text that, in all likelihood, it immediately preceded on the same manuscript. In order to get at these issues, let us begin with a transcription and brief analysis of the text itself.

Lu bang dahan: Transcription, Translation, and Analysis

Of the six strips comprising *Lu bang dahan*, only strips 3 and 4 are completely intact, though strip 6 is broken only after the conclusion of its text; strips 1, 2, and 5, on the other hand, are each missing portions that would likely have held around nineteen to twenty characters each. The strip order does not, however, appear to be in doubt, though whether strips 5 and 6 were in fact joined directly, or whether a missing strip might have originally intervened, remains open to question.[8] For the purposes of this chapter, I will keep textual endnotes to a minimum; for a more fully annotated transcription, I direct readers to my earlier article.[9]

▌ 魯邦大旱, 哀公胃 (謂) 孔= (孔子) 曰:「子不為我圉 (圖) 之?」孔
= (孔子) 含 (答) 曰:「邦大旱, 毋乃遊 (失) 者 (諸) 型 (刑) 與惪 (德)
虖 (乎)? 唯 (1) ‖ □□□□□□□□□□□□□□□□□□□□□[10]▌
之可 (何) 才 (哉)?」

The state of Lu suffered a great drought. Lord Ai asked Kongzi: "Will you not help me lay plans for dealing with this?"

Kongzi replied: "Is Lu's suffering of this great drought not in fact due to [your] erring in [the balance between the use of] punishments and virtuous deeds? For . . ."[11]

【Lord Ai asked】 ". . . , what should 【be done】 about it?"[12]

The ending of Kongzi's initial answer is missing, but the overall contours of his diagnosis of the central problem are clear enough. In response to the question of how to go about dealing with that problem, Kongzi then continues as follows:

孔= (孔子) 曰:「衆 (庶) 民智 (知) 敓 (/說) 之事鬼 (鬼) 也, 不智 (知)
型 (刑) 與惪 (德). 女 (如) 毋忘 (愛) 珪璧㫄 (幣) 帛於山川, 政 (正) 垫
(刑) 與 (2) ‖ □□□□□□□□□□□□□□□□□□□□□▌ [13]

Kongzi said: "The common people know only to serve the ghosts [and spirits] through the ritual of propitiatory sacrifice,[14] but they understand nothing of [the drought's relation to] punishments and good deeds. If you were to not be sparing in [your offerings of] jade vessels and fine silks to the mountains and rivers [at the same time that you] rectify your punishments and 【good deeds】 . . ."

【Lord Ai said:】 ". . ."[15]

At this point, we can only assume that Lord Ai gives some sort of brief, affirmative answer to this advice, after which point the narrative resumes with Kongzi's departure from court and encounter with his disciple:

■ 出，遇子贛 (貢)，曰：「賜，而 (爾) 昏 (聞) 菹 (巷) 迻 (路) 之
言，毋乃胃 (謂) 丘之含 (答) 非與 (歟)?」子贛 (貢) 曰：「否. 戜
(抑) ¹⁶崖 (吾) 子女 (如) 運 (重) 〔丌 (其)〕命 ₍丌 ₍其₎ ₎ 與 (歟) ¹⁷?
女 (若) 夫政 (正) 坓 (刑) 與惪 (德)，㠯 (以) 事上天，此是才 (哉)
■. 女 (若) 天〈夫〉毋炁 (愛) 珪璧 (3) ■ 㬎 (幣) 帛於山川，毋
乃不可₂?¹⁸

【Kongzi】 left and came across Zigong, whom he asked: "Si,
you have [no doubt] heard the word on the street [lately]. Do
[*you*] not in fact think that my response [to Lord Ai] was wrong?"

Zigong said: "No. But is it a matter of your giving great
weight to [Heaven's] mandate? If so, then to serve Heaven by
rectifying [the balance between] punishments and good deeds
is [surely] correct. As for not being sparing in [the offerings of]
jade vessels and fine silks to the mountains and rivers—is this
not in fact unacceptable?

This difficult section of text has puzzled scholars to no end, particularly regarding the sense in which Kongzi's opening question to Zigong
may have been intended. This, I believe, stems mainly from the fact that
the most intuitively natural way to read the line would be to take the
subject of the phrase centering on *wei* 謂 (say, think, consider) to be the
preceding *xianglu zhi yan* (word on the street)—which is precisely how all
commentators have heretofore taken it. But it makes no sense for there to
be any word on the street regarding the private conversation Kongzi had
concluded only minutes ago with Lord Ai. In fact, it works equally well
to take the *er* 爾 (or Si 賜, i.e., Zigong) as the subject of the phrase in
question—Kongzi presumably having just divulged the gist of his prior
conversation to him in the initial course of their own conversation, just
before the lines explicitly quoted here. Once we realize this possibility, the
entire dialogue suddenly makes much more sense—provided only that we
may understand Zigong's assumed disagreement with Kongzi's advice to Lord
Ai to somehow be related to his awareness of the "word on the street." It
may simply be the case that Zigong has heard the clamoring of the masses
for their ruler to conduct a propitiatory rain sacrifice, which Zigong, being
the rational disciple that he is, would certainly find objectionable. And this,
of course, he does, proceeding, after his initially deferential equivocation,
to offer his objections to the specific part of Kongzi's advice that calls for

generous sacrifice. Zigong then goes on to tear apart the argument for such sacrifice in the most cogent manner possible:

夫山, 石呂 (以) 為膚, 木呂 (以) 為民,[19] 女 (如) 天不雨, 石酒 (將) 虁 (焦) ₂, 木酒 (將) 死, 丌 (其) 欲雨或甚於我, 或 (又) 必寺 (待) 虍 (吾) 名 (命) 虍 (乎)?[20]夫川, 水呂 (以) 為膚,[21] 魚呂 (以) (4) ▌ 為民, 女 (如) 天不雨, 水酒 (將) 沽 (涸), 魚酒 (將) 死, 丌 (其) 欲雨或甚於我, 或 (又) 必寺 (待) 虍 (吾) 名 (命) 虍 (乎)?」

"For the mountains take rocks as their skin and trees as their people; if Heaven does not send down rain, their rocks will become scorched and their trees will die—[thus] their thirst for rain is perhaps greater even than ours, so why would they wait for our command [to induce rainfall]? For the rivers take water as their skin and fish as their people; if Heaven does not send down rain, their water will dry up and their fish will die—[thus] their thirst for rain is perhaps greater even than ours, so why would they wait for our command [to induce rainfall]?"

The logic itself, as far as it goes, is irrefutable, but there is clearly something Zigong as yet has failed to grasp, prompting some sort of lament from his Master:

孔 = (孔子) 曰: 「於 (嗚) 唇(呼)! (5) ‖ □□□□□□□□□□□□ □□□□□□▌ [22] 公剴 (豈) 不飯[23] 籾 (粱) 飤 (食) 肉才 (哉)? 殹 (抑) [24]亡 (無) 女 (如) 烝 (庶) 民可 (何)?」 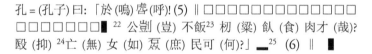[25] (6) ‖ ▌

Kongzi said: "Alas! . . . ,[26] would Lord [Ai] not [simply go on] stuffing himself with fine grains and meats? Or would you not make any efforts [at all] on behalf of the people?

There is clearly a strong rebuke in here somewhere, but regretfully much of the text is missing at a most crucial point. Based on what we know of Kongzi's philosophy from received texts and, moreover, the only thing that would make sense as a transition to the final lines, we can only assume that Kongzi is criticizing Zigong for his failure to account for the nature of humanity and the intrinsic importance of ritual to it, regardless of whether the ritual itself is efficacious in the literal sense.[27] Just as one should "sacrifice to the ancestral spirits as if they were present,"[28] Lord Ai should likewise generously sacrifice to the spirits of the mountains and rivers as if they, too, were listening. It is not that they would indeed send down rain at our beck and call, but it would nonetheless be a meaningful gesture of self-sacrifice on the part of Lord Ai; it would thus constitute an act in which the suffering populace could place its hope and trust, until the time when the drought might finally end. And, in the meantime, having been instilled with a greater sense of belief in the awesomeness of those spirits, Lord Ai may be given greater impetus to follow the second and more crucial part of Kongzi's injunction: the call to lessen punishments and increase virtuous deeds.[29] Should one follow Zigong's way of thinking and discourage the sacrifice on the grounds that it could not possibly produce any direct, tangible effect in ending the drought, one would only be encouraging Lord Ai to use the state's resources to continue stuffing his own face with fine grains and meats—and what good would that do the people?

Further Discussion:
The Text's Relation to *Zigao* and the *Yanzi chunqiu*

Stories involving "great droughts" and deliberations of the proper methods to deal with them are not at all uncommon among early Chinese texts. In some cases, the plot involves the ruler wanting to kill the shaman (*wu* 巫), invocator (*zhu* 祝), or astrologer (*shi* 史) in charge of sacrifices to the relevant spirits, to serve as a kind of sacrificial lamb to appease those unhappy spirits, with some enlightened minister then stepping forth to dissuade the ruler by presenting a clear and persuasive analysis of the situation. In one example, Zang Wenzhong 臧文仲 dissuades Lord Xi 僖 of Lu from killing a certain shaman both because, if Heaven wanted to kill him, it would not have given birth to him in the first place; and because Lord Xi would in any event be better served by simply placing his efforts on repairing city walls, rationing food, decreasing expenditures, and other practical measures designed to lessen the impact of the drought.[30] In another example, recounted as a story within another story, Lord Jing of Qi 齊景公 desires to personally perform a rain sacrifice (*ci* 祠) in order to relieve a great three-year drought; no sooner does he express this desire to perform it himself than Heaven sends down a great rain a thousand *li* square—which the teller of the story suggests was in fact due to Lord Jing's virtue toward Heaven and kind concern for his people (為有德於天而惠於民也).[31] The point of emphasis in each of these stories differs from that of *Lu bang dahan* in various ways, though they all retain certain common features. For our purposes, however, by far the most comparable story is a somewhat different one involving Lord Jing of Qi, found within the "Inner Chapters" of the *Yanzi chunqiu*.[32]

In this passage, the state of Qi has suffered a lengthy drought, and a diviner has determined the cause to lie with the spirits of the mountains and rivers. At this, Lord Jing summons his various ministers to inquire whether it might be appropriate for him to levy some taxes and make collections in order to "sacrifice to the Numinous Mountain" (*ci* Lingshan 祠靈山).[33] At first, none of the ministers respond, until Yanzi comes forth to tell Lord Jing: "It would be inadmissible! To sacrifice to it would bring no benefit" (不可! 祠此無益也), after which he provides, nearly verbatim, the same rationale we see Zigong giving in *Lu bang dahan*, stating, "For the Numinous Mountain inherently takes its rocks as its body and its grasses and trees as its hair . . ." Lord Jing then asks about sacrificing to the Earl of the Yellow River (*ci* Hebo 祠河伯) instead, and he naturally receives a comparable response, again more or less equivalent to the rest of Zigong's statement in our text: "For the Earl of the Yellow River takes its water as his state and its fish and turtles as his people . . . ," and so on. When further pressed for an answer on just what, then, the correct course of action might be, Yanzi responds by suggesting that Lord Jing should himself go out into the open countryside and dwell, exposed to the elements, for a while and thus share in the suffering with the mountain and river spirits (避宮殿暴露, 與靈山河伯共憂), upon which, if he is fortunate enough to receive a favorable response, it might just rain (其幸而雨乎). Lord Jing follows this advice, and, sure enough, after three days, Heaven sends down a great rain, allowing the people to plant their crops just in time, after which Lord Jing extols Yanzi for his ability to support the virtuous (其維有德).

The parallels with our text are clear, but we might first take note of the following main points of difference: (1) the drought takes place in Qi rather than Lu, and it involves Yanzi in dialogue with his lord, whereas Kongzi and Zigong are in dialogue with both their lord and each other; (2) Yanzi objects to the call for propitiatory sacrifice in almost exactly the same terms as does Zigong, and yet he is *also* the one who offers the final conclusion. Yanzi, therefore, essentially plays a combination of the roles that in our manuscript are separately performed by both Kongzi and Zigong; (3) Yanzi clearly states, "The sacrifice would bring no benefit," demonstrating that his attitude toward the matter is obviously different from that of Kongzi. At first glance, then, it might seem that the two versions of this otherwise closely comparable story betray a fundamental difference: the support, or lack thereof, of the main didactic character (Kongzi or Yanzi, as the case may be) toward the holding of the rain-seeking sacrifice.

A closer look, however, shows that the two versions are not so different after all in their fundamental outlook. In the end, Yanzi's proposal that Lord Jing himself should go out to dwell exposed in the open countryside for a while and, thus, share in the suffering of the spirits may yield a different sort of ritual gesture than the propitiatory sacrifice, yet it nonetheless remains a ritual act that likewise calls for an act of selfless sacrifice on the part of the ruler, in this case one that goes far beyond abstention from fine grains and meats. Even if this may merely be a symbolic act, it too would show the people that the ruler shares in their sufferings. Given that Yanzi does not, apparently, believe in the spirits' ability (or at least willingness) to control the rain, it may be entirely coincidental that just three days after Lord Jing's act of sacrifice, it does in fact rain. In any event, it remains clear from Lord Jing's final comments that, in the end, everything is contingent on the practice of virtue.

Given all this, what, then, accounts for the differences between these two versions of the story, and which preceded the other, and why were the changes introduced? A detailed demonstration of the evidence would go beyond the confines of this chapter, but there is a strong argument to be made that the *Yanzi chunqiu* version (or a close forerunner to it) in fact came first, given that, in terms of both the theme of the story and the particular logic of argumentation, it resonates quite closely with a number of other passages found in that same work. Here, let us just quickly note the example of the by-now well-known story of "Lord Jing Suffered a Protracted Illness" (Jing Gong gu 景公痼, aka "Lord Jing Suffered from Malaria," Jing Gong nüe 景公瘧), for which we now possess three different versions.[34] In brief, the story recounts how Lord Jing was suffering from a protracted illness of some sort for over a year, and, having sent an astrologer (*shi*) and invocator (*zhu*) to sacrifice to the spirits of the mountains, rivers, and ancestral temple, all to no avail, he summons Yanzi and a couple of other ministers to ask whether he should act on his desire to now execute the astrologer and invocator in order to appease the Lord-on-High. After the two other ministers tell Lord Jing that that would be just fine, Lord Jing then asks Yanzi for his opinion. In response to this, Yanzi first asks Lord Jing whether he believes that invocation is itself an efficacious act to begin with, and, upon receiving an affirmative response, Yanzi then proceeds to lay bare for him the absurdity of his logic—here according to the *Yanzi chunqiu* "Inner Chapters" version:

> If we take [invocation] to be beneficial, [it follows that] cursing [must] also be detrimental. My lord distances himself from those who would assist and refute him, blocking the path of loyal ministers so that words of remonstrance are not forthcoming. I have heard that, when close ministers are silent and distant ministers mute, the mouths of the masses can melt even bronze. At present, from Liaoshe on the east and from Guyou on the west,[35] there are certainly masses of people. Amid all the complaints and condemnations of the populace, many there are who curse you, My Lord, to the Lord-on-High. With an entire state cursing [but only] two men invocating, even the most skillful of invocators would be unable to succeed in the task. Moreover, should the invocators speak the truth of the matter plainly, they would [in effect] be disparaging My Lord, while, if they were to hide your faults, they would be deceiving the Lord-on-High. If the Lord-on-High is numinous, he cannot be deceived and, if he is not numinous, then to invocate [to him] would also [clearly] be of no benefit. I hope My Lord will carefully examine this. For otherwise, he would [end up] punishing the guiltless—[the same act] which brought about the downfall of the Xia and Shang dynasties.

> 若以為有益, 則詛亦有損也. 君疏輔而遠拂, 忠臣擁塞, 諫言不出. 臣聞之: 近臣嘿, 遠臣瘖, 眾口鑠金. 今自聊攝以東, 姑尤以西者, 此其人民眾矣. 百姓之咎怨誹謗, 詛君于上帝者多矣. 一國詛, 兩人祝, 雖善祝者不能勝也. 且夫祝直言情, 則謗吾君也; 隱匿過, 則欺上帝也. 上帝神, 則不可欺; 上帝不神, 祝亦無益. 願君察之也. 不然, 刑無罪, 夏商所以滅也.

Yanzi's logic is so impeccable that Lord Jing is left with no choice but to relieve the other two ministers of their duties and hand the reins of governance over to Yanzi instead—and within a month, miraculously, Lord Jing recovers from his illness.[36]

Not only does this story closely resemble the "great drought" story insofar as they both involve an appeal to the spirits to seek relief from some sort of calamity, drought or illness as the case may be, but the impeccable logic by which Yanzi goes about exposing the irrational absurdity of the ruler's intended course of action also reveals an undeniably close similarity between the two. While there are more than a few examples of such logical deconstructions in the *Yanzi chunqiu*, one would be hard-pressed to find anything even remotely similar among received texts of the Confucian tradition. This makes *Lu bang dahan* stand out as unique within early Confucian philosophical literature, and it suggests with high probability that the original dialogue on which it was based ultimately derived from "Yanzi materials" and was only later adapted into a Confucian context.[37]

If this is in fact the case, then to what purpose might this adaptation have been made? In seeking an answer to this question, we might first of all note how, in *Lu bang dahan*, the introduction into the dialogue of Zigong as a third person serves the function of making this a "teachable moment," one wherein Kongzi is able to more clearly offer a corrective to his disciple, a younger man who is wont to take the entirely rational part of the argument too far. Needless to say, this is a kind of criticism that Yanzi could never have offered to himself, even if he had wanted to. And, by leveling this critique on his disciple, Kongzi is able to lay primary stress upon the value of the ritual and its role in shaping human sentiments. It is not that Yanzi was not concerned with this human aspect—as discussed earlier, it is clear in his dialogue with Lord Jing that he was—but just that he was perhaps equally concerned with the absurdity of wasting resources on the ritual of the rain sacrifice. In *Lu bang dahan*, the criticism leveled at Zigong, who understood only the irrationality of the latter and had given virtually no thought at all to human sentiments, is not all that unlike Xunzi's 荀子 later criticism of the Mohists 墨家, who condemned all sorts of extravagant ritual expenditures outright, without giving any heed to the positive social values of such expenditures. This is not to suggest, however, that *Lu bang dahan* was purposely rewritten in a manner expressly designed to form a veiled criticism of some school of thought associated with the figure of Yanzi. A better way of thinking about the relationship between the two versions of the text, I would argue, is simply that the Confucians appropriated the story and adapted it in a way that would better manifest their own values. But, no matter how one chooses to look at it, the very existence of such a clear-cut case of "cross-school" literary adaptation already tells us much about the nature of intertextual dialogue within the Warring States philosophical context.

Finally, let us conclude this brief exploratory discussion by returning to the question of the relationship *Lu bang dahan* might have with its adjacent text, *Zigao*. The most striking aspect of *Zigao* is that it begins by having Kongzi essentially affirm the veracity of the miraculous birth stories passed down about the progenitors of the Three Dynasties. Initially, his endorsement of these legends is something of a shock to the reader who is accustomed to the image of Kongzi, as famously recounted in the *Lunyu*, as someone who never speaks of "anomalies, feats of strength, disorder, or the spiritual."[38] Why, then, would the Kongzi of this manuscript suddenly subscribe to such patent absurdities as women undergoing extraordinary encounters with Heavenly spirits to get impregnated with divine seed, eventually resulting in anatomically incredible births that produce sage children with miraculous capabilities? The answer, however, becomes clearer once we look at the text as a whole, given that most of the emphasis throughout is really on the ever-so-human Shun; and, as previous scholars have already pointed out, the miraculous birth stories are included simply to offset the extraordinary human accomplishments of this rare individual, who was able to achieve the incredible feat of having three literal "Sons of Heaven" serve him, all because of his own efforts in self-cultivation—coupled, of course, with the prerequisite that he encountered an enlightened ruler to promote him.[39] Thus in terms of emphasis, *Zigao* is really no different from any number of other Confucian texts that stress the need to first focus on one's self regardless of any external situation, and to study and practice in order to become the best possible person, because, given the right set of circumstances, there might hardly be any limits to what one could potentially achieve for the good of society as a whole. While the text is nonetheless striking for its having Kongzi accept the miraculous birth stories in the first place, what it achieves by this is a juxtaposition that places all the emphasis upon the work that one does after one is born and thus completely downplays the notion of inborn talent. After all, who has more going for them than the literal "Sons of Heaven"? And, yet, they are the ones who end up serving this man, Shun, who rose from obscurity almost solely on the basis of hard work and study.[40]

With minimal reflection, it should be immediately obvious that *Lu bang dahan* employs a similar tactic to achieve comparable ends. Whereas *Zigao* focuses on the value of self-cultivation and the need for perspicacious rulers with an eye for talent, *Lu bang dahan* places dual emphasis on the proper balance between punishments and virtuous deeds (i.e., focusing on virtue and keeping punishments to a minimum) and the need to rule in accordance with the people's affections. In order to drive forth their respective points of emphasis, however, both of these manuscript texts either affirm, or at least allow for, some sort of traditional ritual or spiritual belief that we might normally conceive of as "irrational," though in each case doing so purely for the purpose of manifesting some kind of higher Confucian principles—principles that are themselves otherwise wholly consistent with Confucian thought as we understand it from the *Lunyu* and other early texts of the received tradition. Whether or not it is more than just coincidence that these two manuscript texts were bound directly together is something we cannot determine with certainty,[41] but their simultaneous appearance is, in any case, remarkable, as the argumentative—or should we say pedagogical—strategy that they employ in common is in fact a highly unusual one among Confucian texts of the Warring States period. While these two texts ultimately may not reflect any radically different sort of Confucian beliefs from those to which we are already accustomed, they would certainly appear to exhibit a unique mode of presenting their beliefs in a way that might have been designed to accommodate or respond to the arguments of other philosophical camps that were being made at that particular point in time. Given this, their discovery has unearthed for us a wealth of new possibilities for better understanding the development of Confucian thought within the complex interplay of texts and ideas that characterized the intellectual history of Warring States China.

Notes

1. See Ma Chengyuan 馬承源, ed., *Shanghai bowuguan cang Zhanguo Chu zhushu*, vol. 1 上海博物館藏戰國楚竹書 (一) (Shanghai: Shanghai guji, November 2001), 3–4, 11–41, and 119–68; and *Shanghai bowuguan cang Zhanguo Chu zhushu*, vol. 2 上海博物館藏戰國楚竹書 (二) (Shanghai: Shanghai guji, December 2002), 4, 31–47, and 181–99. The transcription and annotations for both texts therein are those of Ma Chengyuan.

2. See Sarah Allan, "Not the *Lun yu*: The Chu Script Bamboo-Slip Manuscript, *Zigao*, and the Nature of Early Confucianism," *Bulletin of the School of Oriental and African Studies* (University of London) 72, no. 1 (2009): 115–51; and chapter 5 of her *Buried Ideas: Legends of Abdication and Ideal Government in Early Chinese Bamboo-Slip Manuscripts* (Albany: State University of New York Press, 2015).

3. See Ma Chengyuan, ed., *Shanghai bowuguan cang Zhanguo Chu zhushu*, vol. 2, 5, 49–56, and 201–10; the transcription and annotations for *Lu bang da*

han in that volume are also those of Ma Chengyuan. The physical dimensions of all three manuscript texts are exactly the same (roughly 55 cm in length, with notches for the top and bottom tying strings coming at around 8.6 and 7.9 cm from each end, respectively, with the middle notch halfway in between, about 19.5 cm from the others in each direction), and assuming they were all indeed bound together, the likely order of the three on the manuscript was: *Kongzi shilun, Lu bang dahan, Zigao*.

That *Zigao* came last is suggested by the fact that the lone title found on the back of any strip appears in *Zigao* strip 5, which, in Qiu Xigui's (and my own) reordering of the strips, most likely came as the third strip from the end. See Qiu Xigui 裴錫圭, "Tantan Shangbo jian *Zigao* pian de jianxu" 談談上博簡《子羔》篇的簡序, in *Shangboguan cang Zhanguo Chu zhushu yanjiu xubian* 上博館藏戰國楚竹書研究續編, ed. Zhu Yuanqing 朱淵清 and Liao Mingchun 廖名春 (Shanghai: Shanghai guji, April 2004), 1–11. For more on the ordering of the three texts within the proposed larger physical manuscript, see Li Rui 李銳, "Shilun Shangbo jian *Zigao* zhuzhang de fenhe" 試論上博簡《子羔》諸章的分合, in *Shangboguan cang Zhanguo Chu zhushu yanjiu xubian*, 85–96.

4. For further details, see Ma Chengyuan's introductory descriptions in *Shanghai bowuguan cang Zhanguo Chu zhushu*, vol. 2, 203, and *Shanghai bowuguan cang Zhanguo Chu zhushu*, vol. 1, 121.

5. Liao Mingchun also supports such a conclusion; see his "Shilun Chujian *Lu bang dahan* pian de neirong yu sixiang" 試論楚簡 "魯邦大旱" 篇的內容與思想, *Kongzi yanjiu* 孔子研究 2004.1, 8–15, esp. 9. Yang Chaoming 楊朝明 more conservatively holds only that the conversation would have happened during the six years of Lord Ai's reign when Kongzi was in Lu, that is, 484–479 BCE; see his "Shangbo zhushu *Lu bang dahan* guanjian" 上博竹書《魯邦大旱》管見, *Dongyue luncong* 東岳論叢 23, September 2002.5, 113–17.

6. The passage in question—to be discussed further later in this chapter—is entitled "Lord Jing Wanted to Sacrifice to the Numinous Mountain and Lord of the Yellow River in Order to Pray for Rain; Yanzi Remonstrated 景公欲祠靈山河伯以禱雨晏子諫," the fifteenth passage of the "Jian, shang" 諫上 chapter of the "Inner Chapters" of the *Yanzi chunqiu*.

7. This point is already well made by Cao Feng 曹峰 in his " *Lu bang dahan* chutan" "魯邦大旱" 初探, included in *Shangboguan cang Zhanguo Chu zhushu yanjiu xubian*, 131.

8. With Liao Mingchun, I find the former scenario much more likely; for Liao's take, see his "Shangbo cang Chujian *Lu bang dahan* jiaobu" 上博藏楚簡 "魯邦大旱" 校補, *Guji zhengli yanjiu xuekan* 古籍整理研究學刊 2004.1, 4–9, 8.

9. Refer to the *Jianbo* article mentioned in the footnote on the chapter opening page. The conventions employed in this transcription are as follows: " ‖ " represents the fragmented end of a broken strip, whereas "▮" represents the original boundary between two strips (whether intact or otherwise). Strip numbers are placed at the conclusion of each strip or strip fragment. Use of punctuation is a

follows: " () " denotes my adopted reading for any given graph; " ⟨⟩ " denotes the correction of what I presume to be a graphically erroneous character; " { } " denotes what I take to be either an accidental interpolation or displaced character; " [ ] " denotes either an accidentally omitted character or my correction of a displacement; "□" represents characters that are missing due to lacunae on the strips, the number of such empty squares corresponding strictly to my best guess of the number of missing characters; any text that appears within " 【 】 " represents my speculative reconstruction of possible missing text. Within the transcription proper, I limit such text only to what we can ascertain with relative certainty, relegating any further speculative text to the notes.

10. We could speculatively supply the missing text here along the lines of something like this: "型 (刑) 悳 (德) 皆當者, 天其佑之. 願君善圖 (圖) 之!」公曰:「若然, 則女 (如)."

11. A translation of my speculatively supplied text here would be: "Heaven assists those who find the appropriate balance between punishments and virtuous deeds. I hope My Lord will consider this carefully!' "

12. A more complete translation of my speculatively supplied text here would be: "Lord [Ai] asked: 'If that is so, then [what should] be done [about it?]'"

13. My speculative text here: "悳 (德), 則民酒 (將) 歸君而邦乃治矣.」公曰:「諾, 虐 (吾) 酒 (將) 厚祭之.」孔 = (孔子)."

14. The late Li Xueqin 李學勤 took *shuo* 說 to refer to the offering of words of prayer or invocation (*zhuci* 祝詞) during a sacrifice to the ancestors or deities; see his "Shangbo Chujian *Lu bang dahan* jieyi" 上博楚簡《魯邦大旱》解義, *Kongzi yanjiu* 孔子研究 1 (2004): 4–7. For a more elaborate exploration of what such a *shuo* ritual entailed, see Fan Limei 范麗梅, "Shangbo Chujian *Lu bang dahan* zhuyi" 上博楚簡 "魯邦大旱" 注譯, in *Shangboguan cang Zhanguo Chu zhushu yanjiu xubian*, 163–80. Alternatively, we could follow Luo Xinhui 羅新慧 in reading *duo* 敚 as is (= 奪), taking it as a kind of exorcistic ritual designed to remove a source of harm by either coercion of or appeal to the deities; see her "Cong Shangbo jian *Lu bang dahan* zhi 'duo' kan gudai de shenling guannian" 從上博簡 "魯邦大旱" 之 "敚" 看古代的神靈觀念, *Xueshu yuekan* 學術月刊 2004.10, 85–90.

15. The complete translation of my speculatively supplied text here would be: "good deeds, then the people would all adhere to you and the state would return to order. Lord [Ai] said: 'All right, I will sacrifice generously.'" The last character is likely a combined graph for "Kongzi," the subject of the narrative that resumes at the beginning of the next strip (next paragraph).

16. The editors read the particle 戝 as the phrase-ending particle 也; the late He Linyi 何琳儀 correctly took it as a phrase-head particle instead. With Yu Zhihui 俞志慧, I read it as 抑, but I decidedly do not follow him in seeing Zigong's reply as limited to just 否 and taking what follows from this 抑 onward as Kongzi's own further questioning (the 曰 that we would expect being omitted); rather, my interpretation concurs with that of Qiu Xigui, who more sensibly views it as Zigong's

qualified continuation of his own initial negative response. See He Linyi, "Hujian erce xuanshi" 沪簡二冊選釋, in *Shangboguan cang Zhanguo Chu zhushu yanjiu xubian*, 444–55; Yu Zhihui, "*Shangboguan cang Zhanguo Chu zhushu* (er) er ti" 上博館藏戰國楚竹書 (二) 二題, in *Shangboguan cang Zhanguo Chu zhushu yanjiu xubian*, 511–19; and Qiu Xigui, "Shuo *Lu bang da han* 'yi wuzi ru zhong ming qi yu' ju," 說 "魯邦大旱" "抑吾子如重命丌歟" 句, *Huaxue* 華學, vols. 9 and 10 (part 1) (Shanghai: Shanghai guji, 2008.8), 285–87.

17. A number of different explanations have been offered for this puzzling phrase, but none of them are particularly satisfying, and I shall not detail them here. My reading here in part tentatively follows that of Yu Zhihui, who takes 命其 as a mistaken inversion of 其命. I also tentatively follow Ji Xusheng in understanding 命 as 天命, Heaven's "mandate"; see his "Shangbo er xiaoyi (san): Lu bang dahan, fa ming bu ye" 上博二小議 (三): 魯邦大旱, 發命不夜, *Jianbo yanjiu wang* 簡帛研究網 (www.bamboosilk.org [www.jianbo.org]), May 21, 2003 (no longer accessible). With most (though not all) scholars, I follow the editor's reading of 運 as 重.

18. Yu Zhihui views what he sees here as Zigong's further response (to what he took to be Kongzi's follow-up question) to end at this point, taking what follows to once again be expressed by Kongzi (all the 曰 particles omitted); Hirose Kunio 廣瀨薰雄 and Mao Qing 毛慶 each authored further variations of this type of interpretation—all of which I find to be highly strained. See Hirose Kunio, "Guanyu *Lu bang dahan* de jige wenti" 關於 "魯邦大旱" 的幾個問題, *Wuhan daxue xuebao* 武漢大學學報 57, 2004.4, 507–10; and Mao Qing, "*Zhanguo Chu zhushu (er) Lu bang da han* shizi shiju xianyi" 戰國楚竹書 (二) "魯邦大旱" 釋字釋句獻疑, *Nantong shifan xueyuan xuebao* 南通師範學院學報 20, 2004.3, 154–57.

19. For 民, "people," the *Yanzi* version writes 髮 "hair," which, as Li Xueqin pointed out, makes for a more consistent analogy.

20. My reading of the first 虖 as 吾 and the second as 乎 accords with that of Chen Wei 陳偉; see his "Du *Lu bang dahan* zhaji" 讀 "魯邦大旱" 札記, in *Shangboguan cang Zhanguo Chu zhushu yanjiu xubian*, 115–20. I also follow him in reading 名 as 命, understanding this in terms of commanding by means of the propitiatory sacrifice. For more on this connection, see also Liao Mingchun, "Shangbo cang Chujian *Lu bang dahan* jiaobu" 上博藏楚簡 "魯邦大旱" 校補, *Guji zhengli yanjiu xuekan* 古籍整理研究學刊 2004.1, 4–9.

21. In place of 膚, "skin," the *Yanzi* version here has 國, "state"—once again yielding a more consistent analogy.

22. Here I would speculatively supply something like: "賜也, 而 (爾) 通乎天人之際, 而未能達乎民心. 女 (如) 不厚祭," for the roughly twenty characters that are missing here.

23. My reading of 飯 here follows that of Li Shoukui 李守奎 and others; see his "Du *Shanghai bowuguan cang Zhanguo Chu zhushu* (er) zashi" 讀《上海博物館藏戰國楚竹書》(二) 雜識, in *Shangboguan cang Zhanguo Chu zhushu yanjiu xubian*, 478–83.

24. I am reading 殷 as 抑 here, as serving to indicate an alternative decision to an unstated first choice of simply following along with Kongzi's advice to encourage the generous sacrifice. Liao Mingchun also reads 抑 here, but he takes it instead as a rhetorical question particle more or less equivalent to 豈.

25. The text ends here with a text-end marker followed by blank space; the lower half of this strip is missing.

26. My speculatively supplied text here would be translated as follows: "Si, you may understand the difference between the Heavenly and human realms, but you have yet to comprehend the hearts of the people. For should we not perform generous [rain] sacrifices, . . ."

27. As Liu Lexian aptly puts it: "Judging from the prior text, it seems that Kongzi might be criticizing Zigong for understanding only one-half of the equation, not comprehending Kongzi's intent behind advocating for the rain-seeking sacrifice" (據前文推測, 孔子可能批評子貢只知其一不知其二, 不懂得自己提出祭祀求雨的用心). See Liu Lexian 劉樂賢, "Shangbo jian *Lu bang da han* jianlun" 上博簡 "魯邦大旱" 簡論, *Wenwu* 2003.5, 62.

28. See the "Ba yi" 八佾 chapter (3.12) of the *Lunyu*: 祭如在, 祭神如神在.

29. Much of this is well summed up by the late Li Xueqin, who stated that, while "Heaven" and the "spirits" held no intrinsic "authority" 權 for Kongzi, Heaven still possessed for him a kind of "function for the entrusting of the human spirit" (精神寄託的作用); furthermore, that it is easy to see that "Kongzi's advice to Lord Ai to sacrifice to the mountains and rivers was merely in order to bring comfort to the masses, whereas his demand for Lord Ai to rectify punishments and good deeds was merely his taking advantage of the situation to offer a form of governmental admonition" (孔子建議哀公祭祀山川, 只是為了給民眾安慰; 而要求哀公正刑與德, 也不過是乘機在政治上進諫而已). See Li Xueqin's "Shangbo chujian *Lu bang da han* jieyi," 6–7. A similar assessment is offered by Liao Mingchun, "Shilun Chujian *Lu bang da han* pian de neirong yu sixiang," 9, 11. As Liao points out, Zigong is also seen as the main advocate for abandoning such rituals in the *Lunyu*, as in the famous passage from the "Ba yi" chapter (3.17), where "Zigong wished to do away with the ritual of sacrificing a sheep to welcome in the new moon" (子貢欲去告朔之餼羊), prompting Kongzi to declare, "You care for the sheep, but I care for the ritual" (爾愛其羊, 我愛其禮).

30. From *Zuo zhuan* 左傳, Lord Xi, year 21; see Yang Bojun 楊伯峻, *Chunqiu Zuo zhuan zhu (xiudingben)* 春秋左傳注 (修訂本) (Beijing: Zhonghua, 1990), 90–91. This same passage is also cited in Yang Chaoming, "Shangbo zhushu *Lu bang da han* guanjian," and Cao Feng, "*Lu bang dahan* chutan," 131–32.

31. See the *Xinxu* 新序, "Za shi" chapter 2 雜事卷第二, tenth passage; (Han) Liu Xiang 劉向; Shi Guangying 石光瑛 and Chen Xin 陳新, eds., *Xinxu jiaoshi* 新序校釋 (Beijing: Zhonghua, 2001), 219–22.

32. The passage in question is the fifteenth passage of the "Jian, shang" 諫上 chapter; for the full text, see Wu Zeyu 吳則虞, *Yanzi chunqiu jishi* 晏子春秋集釋

(Beijing: Zhonghua, 1962), 55–59. The same passage is also included in the "Bian wu 辨物" chapter of the *Shuoyuan* 說苑.

33. Given its parallel with the "Earl of the Yellow River" in the following, I take "Numinous Mountain" here to be a proper name rather than a general name for "the numinous mountains."

34. The version to be cited here occurs as the twelfth passage of the "Jian, shang" 諫上 chapter of the "Inner Chapters" of the *Yanzi chunqiu*. Another received version is found in the *Zuo zhuan*, Lord Zhao year 20, tenth month, a nearly identical account of which is repeated as the seventh passage of the seventh "Outer Chapter" of the *Yanzi chunqiu*. The third version is the Shanghai Museum volume 6 manuscript *Jing gong gu* 競公瘧. On the basis of how the 瘧 graph is written in the manuscript text, I have argued that it should be read as *gu* 痼 (protracted illness) rather than *nüe* 瘧 (malaria), and that the *nüe* of the *Yanzi* "Inner Chapters" and the *shan* 疝 of the *Zuo zhuan* (or *Yanzi* "Outer Chapters") should each, in turn, be seen as resulting from either a graphic misreading or graphic corruption of 痼/疝, as the case may be; for details, see my "Chuwen 'hu' zi zhi shuangchong yongfa: shuo 'Jing Gong "gu"' ji Miaomin 'wu "hao" zhi xing'" 楚文 "唬" 字之雙重用法: 說 "競公 '痼'" 及苗民 "五 '號' 之刑," *Guwenzi yanjiu* 古文字研究 27 (2008): 387–93. That article also appears as chapter 10 of my *Shangbo deng Chujian Zhanguo yishu zonghenglan* 上博等楚簡戰國逸書縱橫覽 (Shanghai: Zhongxi, 2018), 327–36. For my detailed analysis of the relationships among the three versions of this story, see the sixteenth chapter of the same book, "Cong chutu wenxian kan xian-Qin banben jian de guanxi: yi Qi Jing Gong bing jiu de gushi wei li" 從出土文獻看先秦版本間的關係: 以齊景公病久的故事爲例, 433–58.

35. That is, the entire expanse of Qi, as Liaoshe and Guyou lay at the westernmost and easternmost ends of the state, respectively.

36. See Wu Zeyu, *Yanzi chunqiu jishi*, 42–48.

37. By "Yanzi materials" I refer to that substantial body of texts and passages centering on Yanzi that, as we know from both the *Zuo zhuan* and a number of early Han excavated manuscripts, must have been in existence from at least the earliest years of the Warring States (and probably added to over the course of that period), long before the existence of any definite collection known as the *Yanzi chunqiu*. For further details, see Pian Yuqian 駢宇騫, *Yinqueshan zhujian* Yanzi Chunqiu *jiaoshi* 銀雀山竹簡《晏子春秋》校釋 (Taipei: Wanjuanlou, 2000 [rev. ed.]), 7; Zhang Xincheng 張心澂, *Weishu tongkao* 偽書通考 (1939 Shangwu yinshuguan facsimile edition; Shanghai: Shanghai shudian, 1999), 607–09; and (Qing) Yong Luo 永瑢 and Ji Yun 紀昀, eds, *Siku quanshu zongmu* 四庫全書總目 (Beijing: Zhonghua, 1965), "Histories" section 史部, *juan* 57, 514. Cao Feng, primarily because of the thematic similarities among certain passages and the "critical spirit" that such passages share, has also suggested the possibility that the text might have had its origins in Yanzi materials rather than Confucian ones; see his "*Lu bang dahan* chutan," 129–31.

38. See the "Shu er" 述而 chapter (7.20): 子不語怪, 力, 亂, 神.

39. See Qiu Xigui, "Tantan Shanbo jian 'Zigao' pian de jianxu" 談談上博簡 "子羔" 篇的簡序, in *Shangboguan cang Zhanguo Chu zhushu yanjiu xubian*; and Li Xueqin, "Chujian *Zigao* yanjiu" 楚簡 "子羔" 研究, *Shangboguan cang Zhanguo Chu zhushu yanjiu xubian*, 16.

40. For my own take on *Zigao*, and my own particular reconstruction and reading of the manuscript, see Gu Shikao, "Shangbo Chujian er *Zigao* pian xinbian ji gaishu" 上博楚簡二 "子羔" 篇新編及概述, in *Chutu wenxian yu Zhongguo gudianxue* 出土文獻與中國古典學, ed. Center for Excavated Manuscripts and Paleography, Fudan University 復旦大學出土文獻與古文字研究中心 and Tan Chin Tuan Council for Chinese Studies, Yale-NUS College 耶魯－新加坡國立大學學院陳振傳基金漢學委員會 (Shanghai: Zhongxi, 2018), 31–45. That article has also been incorporated in my *Shangbo zhushu Kongzi yulu wenxian yanjiu*, 270–90.

41. And we must hasten to add that the other text likely also included in the same larger physical manuscript, *Kongzi shi lun*, does not in any way reflect the features just discussed, nor does it bear any obvious relationship to the other two texts, other than simply insofar as they all involve Kongzi in some way.

10

An Introduction and Preliminary Translation of the *Jiaonü* (*Instructions for Daughters*), a Qin Bamboo Text

Anne Behnke Kinney

The Text

In the beginning of 2010, a grant from the Fung Sun Kwan Chinese Arts Foundation provided funding to Peking University to acquire a cache of unprovenanced Qin and Han bamboo texts comprised of some eight hundred strips, three hundred of which were inscribed with writing on both sides. The texts cover diverse subjects such as government, geography, literature, medicine, divination, and calendrics. One Qin text in this cache, given the title the *Jiaonü* 教女 (Instructions for Daughters) by Peking University scholars working on the slips, represents one of the earliest extant works in the Chinese tradition that focuses on women's morality. Professor Zhu Fenghan 朱鳳瀚, of Peking University's Department of History, has published the first preliminary transcription and study of the text.[1] Because a scholarly edition of the text and photographs of the strips had not yet been published, my English-language translation and study, which relies on Professor Zhu's work, is also preliminary.

The *Jiaonü* is comprised of 15 slips, each with approximately 51–61 graphs, totaling 851 graphs in total. Seven slips are undamaged, and the remainder have a few graphs missing at the bottom where a portion of the bamboo is damaged. The slips are 27.3–27.5 cm long, .5–.6 cm wide, and they were bound in three places, apparently after the text had been written. The text is mostly cast in couplets of four-character phrases with rhymes occurring at the end of the second line of the couplet.[2]

The *Jiaonü* is divided into two parts. The first half of the text, comprised of seven sections (including a brief opening statement that establishes a historical context), describes the behavior and bearing of the "good woman" or *shannü* 善女, while the second half, comprised of eight sections, describes the "bad woman" or *bushannü* 不善女. In its inclusion of both positive and negative role models, the text is reminiscent of another Qin excavated text, namely, the *Yu shu* 語書 (Speech Document), found at Shuihudi, as well as the traditionally transmitted text *Lienüzhuan* 列女傳, which reserves one chapter for negative exemplars.[3] The text is written in what may be called Qin clerical script (隸書 *lishu*), though the writing tends to be slightly cursive, and some characters are difficult to read.

The slips are dated to the period between 216 and 214 BCE.[4] But Zhu Fenghan also suggests that the *Jiaonü* itself may have been written before the establishment of the Qin empire because the text does not avoid the use of the First Emperor's personal name, and furthermore, uses the term *baixing* 百姓 (the hundred surnames) to refer to the common people rather than the later Qin-dynasty term *qianshou* 黔首 (the black-haired).[5] As will be discussed in this chapter, the subject matter of the text may also point to practices associated with Qin's social reforms recorded in the *Shiji*, but which have not been corroborated by archaeologically excavated materials.

The *Jiaonü* opens with God, that is, Di 帝, sending his daughter down to what is presumably Muye 牧野, the site of King Wu of Zhou's defeat of the Shang, and instructing her about the behavior of a good woman. The "good woman" of the *Jiaonü* is described in ways that differ little from descriptions of virtuous women found in later texts such as the *Lienüzhuan* (ca. 17 BCE) or Ban Zhao's 班昭 (32–92 CE) *Nüjie* 女誡 (Lessons for Daughters, ca. 72 CE).[6] Among these shared characteristics, the good woman of *Jiaonü* is an efficient worker; she complies with the wishes of her husband and his parents; she is not jealous; she is well groomed and proper in her behavior; and she is solemn and tranquil. She is occasionally described as the wife of an official (or at the very least of a man who works for an official) who makes a peaceful and happy home that slaves will not abscond from. One exception is the notion, "From ancient times, our forebears did not depend on the sages of former times" (自古先人不用往聖). This sentiment is in keeping with the views of the Qin statesman

Lord Shang (Shang Yang 商鞅, ca. 390–338 BCE) as expressed in *Shiji* 68, which suggest that each age has a system of morals and ethics specific to its time.[7] The description of the good woman in the *Jiaonü* also differs from the *Lienüzhuan* and *Nüjie* in that nowhere does the text discuss the duties of motherhood, or views on remarriage or widow chastity. The *Jiaonü* also does not explicitly mention suicide but enjoins the good woman to shield parents from humiliation even at the cost of her own life. Finally, while both the *Lienüzhuan* and *Nüjie* cite classical texts, the *Jiaonü* does not and summarizes its lessons in proverbial expressions cast in common speech. While the text addresses an audience with enough economic margin to include slaves in the household and lend money to acquaintances, some of the specific behaviors it mentions seem wildly out of keeping with those of an elite household. For example, the *Jiaonü* describes a woman who works as a shaman and one who is easily enamored with tradesmen. The lessons of the *Jiaonü* thus seem far more appropriate for the spouses and daughters of literate officials at the lower ranks of the bureaucracy, such as scribes and their assistants or other support staff to local officials.[8]

In contrast, the description of "bad women" often hints at an environment that allowed women a considerable degree of freedom in movement, some control of household finances, a large amount of time to themselves, and less scrutiny of their activities on the part of other family members. Gao Yizhi suggests that these conditions may point to the Qin state's measures to reduce household size (ca. 359 BCE) as recorded in the *Shiji* biography of Lord Shang. The biography cites laws that prohibited fathers and adult sons or elder and younger brothers from living under one roof.[9] However, if, how, and to what extent the Qin state implemented these rules remains open to question, since there is no archaeological evidence that corroborates the *Shiji* account. Records of Qin household registries unearthed at Liye 裡耶, Hunan, for example, reveal households that included more than one adult male. This text does not, however, provide conclusive evidence that, in Qin times, household size was not generally subject to reduction. For example, these families may have simply decided to pay the fine imposed on dwellings with more than one adult male. It may also be that such laws were less strictly applied in outlying places such as Liye, which was located in western Hunan and bordered present-day Chongqing County. Two additional sources are relevant. The Qin *Daybook A* 日書甲種 found at Shuihudi 睡虎地 mentions days that are auspicious for dividing households (*fenyi* 分異), but lack of context renders its meaning ambiguous.[10] The legal documents discovered in the Han-dynasty Zhangjiashan tomb no. 247, which show many consistencies with Qin legal texts, also suggest that households were in fact divided.[11]

It is important to note that the text's various descriptions of women are not meant to form a composite portrait of the good or bad woman but represent a catalog of various kinds of behaviors that applied to women in various living situations. For example, the text mentions the deference a married woman owes her parents-in-law and advises the daughter-in-law to offer them gruel in the morning and stew during the day when they are out of sorts. This reference may suggest that the wife in question lived with her husband's parents, though it is possible that the parents simply lived nearby and continued to exert control over their son's household. It is notable, however, that the text never mentions the husband's brothers' wives, that is, *zhouli* 妯娌, and may thus indicate a situation in which the husband's brothers and their families lived in separate dwellings. However, one passage in the section of the text that describes the "bad woman" is unambiguous about the family size of one particular individual: "That woman lives on her own and comes and goes serving as a spirit medium." This example is in keeping with the Qin texts found at Liye, which provide evidence of a woman's right to be named head of the household as an unmarried adult female or in the event of being widowed with no male heir or living parents-in-law.[12] Since other passages in this section of the *Jiaonü* mention the problematic relations between husband and wife, it is clear that the second half of the text covers the failings of women in a variety of domestic situations. Whether the subject is a single head of the household or married, in most instances the "bad women" of the *Jiaonü* seem to have very little supervision.

In contrast to the deeply evil and villainous women described in the final chapter of Liu Xiang's 劉向 (79–8 BCE) *Lienüzhuan*—women who are indifferent to the suffering and oppression of the common people, who torture the innocent, or ruthlessly exterminate any enemy who stands in the way—the "bad women" of the *Jiaonü* are far more relatable by dint of their more ordinary excesses and failings. The *Jiaonü* may indeed be our earliest glimpse of a social type that is missing in early texts—the not-so-bad bad woman.

For example, the bad woman "is unreserved in her jests with menfolk. She goes to sleep as soon as it is dark, but by midday she has not yet risen. She is unable to keep her residence clean but makes frequent visits to neighbors." This passage provides a fascinating glimpse of a woman who is free to wander about town, mingle and joke with men, and sleep as long as she likes with no authority figure to forbid such activities. Elsewhere in the text we are told, "At dawn she goes out to the neighbors and stays till dark. If a man looks at her, it causes her to smile with pleasure. She says, 'I am truly beautiful, the most (beautiful) in my village.'"

She also finds ways to misbehave at home: "When her husband is serving in office, he must come and go at the spur of the moment. But she is not happy about having to take care of business and delights in spending the day getting tipsy." It is possible that a government-mandated small household that included only one adult male may have inadvertently created a domestic situation in which the man of the house was too occupied with official duties to monitor or control what his wife was up to during the day.

References to the bad woman's mismanagement of money also point to her control over at least some portion of the household's finances: "As for the people she speaks to, she is especially enamored with tradesmen, buying their livestock, even oxen and horses. [When] her money has all been spent, she doesn't know what it's been used for. . . . As for the family's payment of household taxes, in the past, she has cheated in the amount she paid. But when she gives out loans, with regard to those who have not yet repaid her, she is small-minded and never forgets."[13] Given that she also seems able to manipulate figures to her advantage in tax payments, it is possible that she may have also possessed some rudimentary skills in writing and calculation, if only for the purposes of accounting and providing information required by the state. Even if she lacked writing skills, as Charles Sanft has demonstrated, "dictation is a legitimate form of composition," and evidence of a person's participation in a literate community.[14]

As paleographic evidence concerning Qin law continues to accrue, it is worth taking into account how various aspects of state policy might have affected the lives of women. It is especially the "bad woman" who gives us a new glimpse of womanhood in early China, one that looks beyond the larger-than-life exemplars of wickedness found in other texts to reveal how ordinary women might have dodged work or refused to conform to the expectations of their husbands and elders.

The *Jiaonü* also provides a new and valuable source on women's education in early China. It opens with a statement claiming that its lessons are directed by God (帝 *di*) to his daughter, indicating its use as an instructional text for women, though perhaps not exclusively. Occasionally it appears to address a male audience, for example, "With a wife like this, one will die early or become a beggar." It is therefore possible that its audience also included men who might have used it as a guide to choosing a wife or raising a daughter. The rhyming couplets, a common mnemonic device in entry-level educational materials, also points to its pedagogical function.

To date, the *Jiaonü* is the second earliest archaeological text dedicated to the instruction of women in the Chinese tradition. The oldest, a short and poorly preserved bamboo text dated to ca. 350–300 BCE, entitled *Jizi's Instructions for Women* 季子女訓, is concerned with the preparation of sacrificial food.[15] The two texts, the *Jiaonü* and *Jizi's Instructions for Women*, begin to give us some sense of the scope of pedagogical materials that focused on women. But women in pre-Han times may not have been limited to these kinds of simplistic didactic materials. In her book *Buried Ideas: Legends of Abdication and Ideal Government in Early Chinese Bamboo-Slip Manuscripts*, Sarah Allan speculates that there may have been women in the Warring States period whose studies were not limited to texts on women's work and morality. Allan argues that the Chu-script manuscripts in the Shanghai Museum may have come from the tomb of a woman.[16] Given the sophisticated nature of the texts in this collection, which includes works dealing with history, philosophy, poetry, and divination, if the tomb occupant was indeed female, she would have been highly literate. All of these sources provide valuable new insights into women's roles in early China. The publication of the *Jiaonü* and the ongoing discovery of new archaeological materials related to women and family structure should expand our somewhat limited understanding of this important facet of Chinese history.

Preliminary transcription and translation of the text of the *Jiaonü* follows.

Part One

1. (034)[17]

昔者帝降息女殷晦之X (野), 殷人將亡, 以 教其女曰: 凡善女子之方, 固不敢剛. 姻(因) 安從事, 唯審與良. 西東X (螽)若, 色不敢昌 (猖). 疾X (續) 從事, 不論 . . .

In the past, God sent down his own daughter to the Yin [site] Muye. When the people of Yin were about to perish, he instructed his daughter, saying,[18]

> "The rule of all good daughters,
> 凡善女子之方
> is that you must not dare to be overbearing.[19]
> 固不敢剛 (*kâŋ)

Maintain tranquility in all your undertakings,
姻(因) 安從事
[conducting yourself] only with meticulous care and virtue.
唯審與良 (*raŋ)

Whether in the east or west, be simple in demeanor;[20]
西東X (螽)若
in your bearing, do not dare to be insubordinate.
色不敢昌 (猖) (*thaŋ)

Be quick and productive in your work,
疾X (績) 從事
whether . . .
不論 . . .

2. (033)

[晦]明. 善衣 (依) 夫家, 以自爲光. 百姓賢之, 父母盡明. 疾作 (詐) 就愛, 如
阰 (妣) 在堂. 雖與夫治, 勿敢疾當. 醜言匿之, 善言是陽 (揚). 中 毋妒心, 有
(又) 毋奸腸, 亦從臣妾, 若□

[Lacuna] [your actions are obscured or] clearly seen.
□ [晦]明 (*mraŋ)

Be adept in complying with your husband's family,
善衣 (依) 夫家
and thereby reflect glory on yourself.
以自爲光 (*kwâŋ)

The common people will regard you as worthy,
百姓賢之
and your father and mother will both share in the luster [of
your reputation].
父母盡明 (*mraŋ)

Hate falsehood and cleave to love,
疾作 (詐) 就愛
as if one's deceased mother were in the hall.[21]
如 阰 (妣) 在堂 (*dâŋ)

Although you may manage things alongside your husband,
雖與夫治
do not dare to rush in to take charge.
勿敢疾當 (*tâŋ)

As for vile words: hide them,
醜言匿之

But fine words, these should be made known.[22]
善言是陽 (揚) (*laŋ).

Within, if you are without a jealous mind,
中 毋妬心
And moreover, without disloyal thoughts,
有 (又) 毋奸腸 (*draŋ)

Only then can you lead male and female slaves,
亦從臣妾
like [lacuna] . . .
若□

3. (032)

笑詇 (殃). 居處安樂, 臣妾莫亡. 今夫威公, 固有□ (嚴) 剛. 與婦子言, 弗肎 (肯) 善當. 今夫聖婦, 自教思長. 曰: 厓 (厓) 石在山, 尚臨中堂. 松柏不落, 秋尚反黃. 羊矢竝下, 或X (短) 或長. 水X (最)

. . . joyous and calamitous [events].
笑詇 (殃) (*ʔaŋ)

If a home is peaceful and happy,
居處安樂
No male or female slaves will abscond.
臣妾莫亡 (*maŋ)

Now if a husband's father and mother,
今夫威公
are indeed strict and firm,
固有□ (嚴) 剛 (*kâŋ)

[when] they speak to the wife [i.e., their daughter-in-law],
與婦子言
[they] will seldom be inclined to let her manage things.
弗胄 (肯) 善當 (*tâŋ)

The husband's sagely wife,
今夫聖婦
[thus] instructs herself to think long and hard.
自教思長 (*draŋ)

It is said, 'There are steep rocks on the mountain,
曰: 痓 (厓) 石在山
But they are still near a level place.
尚臨中堂 (*dâŋ)

Though pine and cypress do not shed [their greenery];
松柏不落
in autumn they turn yellow.
秋尚反黃 (*gwâŋ)

While all sheep pellets fall down,[23]
羊矢竝下,
some are [short] and some are long.
或 X (短) 或長. (*draŋ)

Water may be completely . . .
水X (最)

4. (027)

平矣, 尚有潰皇 (惶). 老人悲心, 雖惡何傷. 晨 爲之鬻, 晝爲之羹. 老人唯怒,
戒勿敢謗. 夫與妻, 如表與裏, 如X (陰) 與陽. 女子不作, 愛爲死亡. 唯愛大
至, 如日朝光.

calm,
平矣,
but there is still the threat of floods.'
尚有潰皇 (惶) (*wâŋ)

When elders are downcast,
老人悲心
Though bad-tempered, what harm is there?[24]
雖惡何傷 (*lhaŋ)

In the morning make them gruel,
晨爲之鬻
and during the day make them stew.
晝爲之羹 (*krâŋ)

If elders are angry,
老人唯怒
be cautious and do not dare to speak ill (of them).
戒勿敢謗 (*paŋh)

Husband and wife
夫與妻
are like coat and lining,
如表與裏
and like yin and yang.
如X (陰) 與陽 (*laŋ)

If a woman does not put forth effort,
女子不作
love will die and fade away.
愛爲死亡 (*maŋ)

As for how a great love is achieved,
唯愛大至
it is like the sun's brilliance at dawn.
如日朝光 (*kwâŋ)

5. (013)

男子之盧 (慮), 臧 (藏) 之心腸. 茀然更志, 如發幾 (饑) 粱. 莫 (暮) 臥蚤 (早) 起, 人婦恒常. 絜身正行, 心貞以良. 慎毋剛氣, 和弱心腸. 茲 (慈) 愛婦妹, 有 (友) 與弟兄, 有妻如此, 可與久長.

A man's concerns
男子之盧 (慮)

lay hidden in his heart.
臧 (藏) 之心腸 (*draŋ)

Quickly dispelling his worries,
茀然更志
is like giving grain to the starving.[25]
如發幾 (饑) 粱 (*raŋ)

Lying down at night and rising early
莫 (暮) 臥蚤 (早) 起
is the eternal principle of wives.
人婦恒常 (*daŋ)

Through the cleanliness of her person, the propriety of her
   behavior,
絜身正行
and the purity of her heart, she becomes good.
心貞以良 (*daŋ)

She takes care to avoid being overbearing,
慎毋剛氣
and is mild and yielding at heart.
和弱心腸 (*draŋ)

She is loving toward her sisters,
茲 (慈) 愛婦妹
and a friend to her brothers.
有 (友) 與弟兄 (*hwraŋ)

Possessing a wife like this,
有妻如此
[a man] can live [happily] for a very long time.
可與久長 (*draŋ)

6. (017)

有曰: 善女子固自正. 夫之義, 不敢以定. 屈身受令, 旁言百X (姓). 威公所
詔, 傾耳以聽. 中心自謹, 唯端與正. 外貌且美, 中實沈 (沉) 清 (靜). 莫親於
身, 莫久於敬. 沒

There is a saying:
有曰:
'A good woman firmly exercises self-restraint.
善女子固自正 (*teŋ)

What a husband considers to be right,
夫之義
she does not dare to judge.
不敢以定 (*têŋ)

She bows to receive his command,
屈身受令
and transmits it to the hundred surnames.[26]
旁言百X (姓) (*seŋh)

When her father- and mother-in-law issue decrees,
威公所詔
she inclines her ear and listens.
傾耳以聽 (*lhêŋ)

She carefully guards what is in her heart,
中心自謹
so that it is only proper and upright.
唯端與正 (*teŋ)

Her outer appearance is dignified and beautiful;
外貌且美
within she is solemn and tranquil.
中實沈 (沉) 清 (靜) (*tsheŋ)

[She] does not cling to her authority,[27]
莫親於身
[she] does not always behave in a formal manner.'
莫久於敬 (*kreŋh)

7. (035)

身之事, 不可曰幸. 自古先人, 不用往聖. 我曰共 (恭) 敬, 尚恐不定. 監所不遠, 夫在街廷. 衣彼口 (顏) 色, 不顧子姓 (甥). 不能自令, 毋怨天命. 毋詢父母, 寧死自屏.

The nature of life's end,
沒身之事
cannot be called a matter of chance.
不可曰幸 (*grêŋ?)

From ancient times, our forebears,
自古先人
did not depend on the sages of former times.[28]
不用往聖 (*lheŋh)

Daily we are respectful,
我曰共 (恭) 敬
but still fear the uncertainty of things [to come].[29]
尚恐不定 (*têŋ)

What we examine is not far away,
監所不邈
it is on our streets and in our courtyards.
夫在街廷 (*lêŋ)

If we wear clothes of a certain color,
衣彼□ (顏) 色
We do not compare them to that of our kin.[30]
不顧子姓 (甥) (*seŋh)

If we are unable to make ourselves good,
不能自令
We should not resent Heaven's decrees.
毋怨天命 (*mreŋ)

We should not disgrace our father or mother,
毋詢父母
preferring death to shield them [from such a lapse].
寧死自屏 (*bêŋ)

[Lacuna]
□

Part Two

8. (031)

告子不善女子之方, 既不作務, X[姿]義 (議) 不已. 口舌不審, 失戲男子. X (纔) 晦而臥, 日中不起. 不能清居, 數之鄰裡. 抱人嬰兒, 嘯人顛枲. 餔人飱將 (漿), 撓人淫□.

> I shall now tell you about the way of a bad woman.
> 告子不善女子之方
> She does not only not attend to her work,
> 既不作務,
> she also [lacuna] talks unrestrainedly without ceasing.[31]
> X[姿]義 (議) 不已 (*kə?)
>
> Her mouth and tongue are indiscreet,
> 口舌不審
> and she is unreserved in her jests with menfolk.
> 失戲男子 (*tsə?)
>
> She goes to sleep as soon as it is dark,
> X (纔) 晦而臥
> but by midday she has not yet risen.
> 日中不起 (*khə?)
>
> She is unable to keep her residence clean,
> 不能清居
> but makes frequent visits to neighbors.
> 數之鄰裡 (*rə?)
>
> She is fond of holding people's infants,
> 抱人嬰兒
> but tangles the hempen threads they spin.
> 嘯人顛枲 (*sə?)
>
> She'll eat their fermented gruel,
> 餔人飱將 (漿)
> and disturb them with her excess [lacuna].[32]
> 撓人淫□

9. (030)

入門戶, 文奇人忌. 甘語益之, 不X (知) 其久. 且而出鄰, 即到於晦. 男子視
之, 益粺 (埤) 笑喜. 曰: 我成 (誠) 好美, X (最) 吾邑裡. 澤沐長順, 疏 (梳)
首三X之. 衣數以之

[Lacuna] . . . when she enters [one's] home,
□入門戶
she glosses over what is strange and taboo to others.[33]
文奇人忌 (*gəh)

While she adds [to this] honied phrases,
甘語益之
she is unaware that she has stayed too long.
不X (知) 其久 (*kwəʔ)

At dawn she goes out to the neighbors,
且而出鄰
and stays till dark.
即到於晦 (*hməʔ)

If a man looks at her,
男子視之
it causes her to smile with even greater pleasure.[34]
益粺 (埤) 笑喜 (*həʔ)

She says, 'I am truly beautiful,
曰: 我成 (誠) 好美
the most [beautiful] in my village.'
X (最) 吾邑裡 (*rəʔ)

When washing her hair, she takes a long time to arrange it.
澤沐長順
When dressing, her hair, she rebinds it three times.[35]
疏 (梳) 首三 X (衿) 之 (*tə)

When dressing she makes multiple [changes] [lacuna].
衣數以之□

10. (029)

者, 意之父母. 良子有曰: 女子獨居, 淫與猒巫. 曰: 我有巫事, 入益X繀. 不級 (及) 凡X (盍), X [刋] 抿 (根) 惡兮. 環善父母, 言語自舉. 臣去亡,[36] 妾去之逋. 有妻如

She hides [these activities] from her father and mother.
意之父母

If a good person says,
良子有曰
'That woman lives on her own,
女子獨居
and comes and goes serving as a shaman.'
淫與猒巫 (*ma)

The woman responds, 'My work as a shaman
曰: 我有巫事
supplements my production of hempen thread.'
入益X繀 (*râ)

This [behavior] does not conform to the standard [way of doing things].
不級 (及) 凡X (盍)
How does this conform to the rules?[37]
X [遵] X [範] 惡兮 (*gî)

She rejects warm relations with father and mother,
環善父母
and her speech is full of self-vaunting.
言語自舉 (*klaʔ)

When a male slave flees,
臣去亡
the female slave leaves to abscond with him.
妾去之逋 (*pâ)

As for a wife like . . .
有妻如

11. (028)

此，孰能與居處. 不愛禾年，□豬盜之，有猷鳥鼠. 居處次善，從事毋屠(著).
居喜規 (窺) 望，出喜談語. 所與談者，大嫚行賈. 買其畜生，及到牛馬. 錢金

this,
此,
who could live with her?
孰能與居處 (*k-hla?)

She shows no concern for the harvest,
不愛禾年
and allows wild dogs and pigs to steal it,
□豬盜之
and even rats and birds eat their fill.
有猷鳥鼠 (*nha?)

Her household relegates goodness to an inferior status,
居處次善
and the nature of its activities are unclear.[38]
從事毋屠(著) (*dâ)

At home, she delights in looking out the window;
居喜規 (窺) 望
when going out, she delights in chatting.
出喜談語 (*ŋa?)

As for the people she speaks to,
所與談者
she is especially enamored with tradesmen,
大嫚行賈 (*kâ?)

buying their livestock,
買其畜生
even oxen and horses.
及到牛馬 (*mrâ?)

[When] her money . . .
錢金

12. (025)

盡索, 不賐 (知) 用所. 夫道行來, 客在於後. 不給歕食, 出入行語. 家室戶賦,
日奉起撟.貣(貸) 於人, 有未賞 (償) 者, 小器靡亡 (忘). 今此去, 或焦日, 或
歺 (朽) 雨者, 有妻如此,

    . . . has all been spent,
    盡索
    she doesn't know what it's been used for.
    不賐 (知) 用所 (*sraʔ)

    When her husband comes walking in,
    夫道行來
    with a guest following him,
    客在於後 (*ɦoʔ)

    she does not offer food or drink,
    不給歕食
    but comes out and begins chatting.
    出入行語 (*ŋaʔ)

    As for the family's payment of household taxes,
    家室戶賦
    in the past, she has cheated in the amount paid.
    日奉起撟 (*kauʔ)

    But when she gives out loans to others,
    貣(貸) 於人
    In dealing with those who have not yet paid (their debts),
    有未賞 (償) 者
    she is small-minded and never forgets.
    小器靡亡 (忘) (*maŋ)

    Going forward,
    今此去
    in hot weather or damaging rain,
    或焦日或歺 (朽) 雨者
    with a wife like this . . .

    有妻如此

13. (016)

苟勿去. 今夫不善女子, 不宵 (肯) 自計. 夫在官役, 往來必卒. 不喜作務, 喜歡
日醉. 與其夫家, 音越越剛氣 (氣). 街道之音, 發人請察. 夫 (021) 來旦到, □

> [lacuna] there will be trouble unless she is expelled.
> □ 苟勿去 (*khah)

> Now the bad woman
> 今夫不善女子
> is unwilling to plan for herself.
> 不宵 (肯) 自計 (*kĭh)

> When her husband is serving in office,
> 夫在官役
> he must come and go at the spur of the moment.
> 往來必卒 (*tsut)

> But she is not happy about having to take care of things,
> 不喜作務
> and delights in spending the day getting tipsy.
> 喜歡日醉 (*tsuts)

> In her dealings with her husband's family,
> 與其夫家
> her tone becomes increasingly loud and harsh.[39]
> 音越越剛氣 (氣) (*khəs)

> [If she hears sounds of activity] on the street,
> 街道之音
> she sends someone out to find out what's going on.
> 發人請察 (*tshrêt)

> If her husband returns in the morning [lacuna] . . .
> 夫 來旦到

14. (023)

必夕棄. 數而不善在前, 唯悔可X (擇). 衆口銷金, 此人所冑 (謂), 女子之敗.
見人有客, 數來數婙. 益粺 (埤) 爲仁, 彼沱 (池) 更瀯 (瀯). 效人不出, 梯以
塱外. 夫雖教之, 口羊 (佯) 曰若. 其□□

. . . by evening she will be expelled.
□必夕棄 (*khis)

When she has behaved badly several times before others,
數而不善在前
regret is her only option.[40]
唯悔可X (擇) (*dât)

[Indeed,] 'public opinion can fuse metal.'
衆口銷金
She is what people refer to as
此人所胃 (謂)
a complete disgrace among women.
女子之敗 (*brâts)

When she sees that others have guests,
見人有客
she keeps count [of each event]
數來數婕 (*rôk)
and in a flurry tries [to keep up with them].

But the more she tries to progress in virtue,
益粺 (埤) 爲仁
the more she muddies the waters.
彼沱 (池) 更澮 (濊) (*hwât)

If she tries to imitate another's sequestration,
效人不出
she'll find a ladder to spy [beyond the walls of her home].
梯以塱外 (*ŋwats)

Although her husband instructs her,
夫雖教之
she feigns agreement.
口羊 (佯) 曰若

But she [lacuna]
其□□

15. (022)

外. 直(值) 此人者, 不幸成大. 有妻如此, 蚤 (早) 死爲 X (匃). 今夫女子, 不肎
(肯) 自計, 以爲時命不會. 富者不可從, 貧者不可去, 必聽父母之令, 以因天命.

Outside . . .
外 (*ŋwats)

Meeting with this sort of person,
直(值) 此人者
bad fortune will proliferate.
不幸成大 (*dâs)

With a wife like this,
有妻如此
one will die early or become a beggar.
蚤 (早) 死爲 X (匃) (*kât)

Now these women,
今夫女子
are unwilling to plan for themselves,
不肎 (肯) 自計
considering that time and fate are misaligned.
以爲.時命不會 (*gôts)

The wealthy must not be pursued,
富者不可從
the poor must not be abandoned.
貧者不可去 (*khaʔ)

One must obey the commands of parents,
必聽父母之令
in order to accord with Heaven's will."
以因天命 (*mreŋ)

Notes

1. Zhu Fenghan 朱鳳瀚, "Beida cang Qin jian Jiaonü chushi" 北大藏秦簡
教女初識, *Beijing daxue xuebao* 北京大學學報 2015.2, 5–15. Photographs and full

transcriptions of the Peking University Qin strips have now been published, see: Beijing daxue chutu wenxian yanjiusuo 北京大學出土文獻研究所, ed., *Beijing daxue cang Qin jiandu* 北京大學藏秦簡讀, 5 vols. (Shanghai: Shanghai guji, 2023), with the *Jiaonü* in vol. 1.

2. For an illuminating analysis of another rhyming Han primer from the Peking University collection, the *Cang Jie pian* 蒼頡篇, see Christopher Foster, "Study of the *Cang Jie pian*: Past and Present," PhD dissertation, Harvard, 2017.

3. Shuihudi Qin mu zhujian zhengli xiaozu, 睡虎地秦墓竹簡 整理小組, *Shui-hudi Qin mu zhujian* 睡虎地秦墓竹簡 (Beijing: Wenwu, 1990), 13–16, strips 9–15.

4. Institute for Excavated Text Research of Peking University 北京大學出土文獻研究所, "Beijing Daxue cang Qin jian gaishu," 北京大學藏秦簡概述, *Wenwu* 文物 2012.6, 65–74.

5. See Institute for Excavated Text Research of Peking University, "Beijing Daxue cang Qin jian gaishu," 65–74. Also see Gao Yizhi 高一致, "Chu du Beida cang Qin jian Jiaonü," 初讀北大藏秦簡《教女》2015-08-13, http://www.bsm.org.cn/show_article.php?id=2285. The First Emperor's name, Zheng, is generally written as 政, though some argue that it was actually 正. See *Shiji* 史記 6 (Beijing: Zhonghua, 1982), 224, n. 4. In 221 BCE, the First Emperor changed the designation of the common people. See *Shiji* 6, 239. For more on this issue, see Robin D. S. Yates, "The Qin Slips and Board from Well No. 1, Liye, Hunan: A Brief Introduction to the Qin Qianling County Archives," *Early China*, no. 35/36 (2012/2013): 291–329.

6. On similarities between the *Jiaonü* and Ban Zhao's *Nüjie*, see Olivia Milburn, "Instructions to Women: Admonitions Texts for a Female Readership in Early China," *Nannü* 20 (2018): 169–97; and Chen Meilan 陳美蘭, "Zhong shi chen jing wei fan yu liang—Beida Qin jian Jiaonü tanlüe," 中實沈靜 唯審與良——北大秦簡《教女》探略, in Zhongguo wenhua yichan yanjiuyuan 中國文化遺產研究院, *Chutu wenxian yanjiu* 出土文獻研究 17 (2018): 178–93.

7. See *Shiji* 68, 2229; translated in William H. Nienhauser, ed., *The Grand Scribe's Records*, vol. 7 (Bloomington: Indiana University Press, 1994), 89. Also see Li Si's 李斯 (d. 208 BCE) views on using the past to criticize the present in *Shiji* 87, 2546.

8. See, for example, Anthony J. Barbieri-Low and Robin D. S. Yates, *Law, State, and Society in Early Imperial China: A Study with Critical Edition and Translation of the Legal Texts from Zhangjiashan Tomb No. 247* (Leiden: Brill, 2015), vol. 2, 1084–111.

9. Gao Yizhi, "Chu du Beida cang Qin jian Jiaonü." Also see *Shiji* 68, 2230–32; trans. in Nienhauser, *The Grand Scribe's Records*, vol. 7, 89–90: "Commoners with two adult males in their families who did not divide their household would have their military tax doubled. . . . After three years (350 B.C.). . . . Ordinances prohibited fathers and sons or elder and younger brothers from living under one roof" (民有二男以上不分異者, 倍其賦. . . . 居三年. . . . 令民父子兄弟同室內息者為禁).

10. See Wang Huanlin 王煥林, *Liye Qin jian jiaogu* 裡耶秦簡校詁 (Beijing: Zhongguo wenlian, 2007) (slips K43, K2/23, K5), 203–08. For the Qin *Day Book*, see Shuihudi Qinmu zhujian zhengli xiaozu 睡虎地秦墓竹簡整理小組, ed., *Shuihudi Qinmu zhujian* 睡虎地秦墓竹簡 (Beijing: Wenwu, 1990), 190 (strip 52). The legal documents discovered with Qin legal texts also suggest that households were in fact divided. See Barbieri-Low and Yates, *Law, State, and Society*, 2:803 (slip 343) from the Han-dynasty Zhangjiashan tomb no. 247, which shows many consistencies. Many thanks to Robin D. S. Yates for this reference.

11. See Barbieri-Low and Yates, *Law, State, and Society in Early Imperial China*, 2:803 (343).

12. See Chen Wei 陳偉, *Liye Qin jiandu jiaoshi (di yi juan)* 裡耶秦簡牘校釋 (第一卷) (Wuhan: Wuhan daxue, 2012), 32–33 board no. 8-19 (8-17), 370 board no. 8-1623 (8-1629).

13. For an example of the sort of taxes paid by households, see A. F. P. Hulsewé, *Remnants of Ch'in Law: An Annotated Translation of the Ch'in Legal and Administrative Rules of the 3rd Century B.C. Discovered in Yun-meng Prefecture, Hu-pei Province, in 1975* (Leiden: Brill, 1985), 23 [A3]. Ulrich Lau and Thies Staack, *Legal Practice in the Formative Stages of the Chinese Empire: An Annotated Translation of the Exemplary Qin Criminal Cases from the Yuelu Academy Collection* (Leiden: Brill, 2016), 192–95; and Anne Behnke Kinney, "Husbands and Wives in Qin and Han-Dynasty Bamboo Legal Texts," in "Family Relations in Chinese History," special issue *Journal of Chinese History* 6, no. 2 (2022): 225–45.

14. See Charles Sanft, *Literate Community in Early Imperial China: The Northwestern Frontier in Han Times* (Albany: State University of New York Press, 2019), 18, 71.

15. See Hubeisheng wenwu kaogu yanjiusuo 湖北省文物考古研究所 and Beijing daxue zhongwenxi 北京大學中文系, *Jiudian Chu jian* 九店 楚簡 (Beijing: Zhonghua, 2000), 141–45.

16. See Sarah Allan, *Buried Ideas: Legends of Abdication and Ideal Government in Early Chinese Bamboo-Slip Manuscripts* (Albany: State University of New York Press, 2015), 53–58.

17. Each section is numbered from 1 to 15; numbers in parentheses following each section header are slip numbers, following Zhu Fenghan. To display the rhymes clearly, I also display the text, broken down into what are largely couplets cast in four-character phrases, below each translated section. Empty boxes signify lacunae or illegible graphs; graphs in brackets that follow empty boxes indicate best guesses of editors. Loan words are placed in parentheses after the original graph; when there is no digital equivalent, the original graph is indicated by an X. I do not reproduce Zhu Fenghan's glosses and explanations unless I am in disagreement with him and urge readers to consult his essay for details. In the English-language translations, my interpolations are enclosed in square brackets. Passages that overlap from one numbered section/slip to the next conclude with ellipses.

18. Muye (here, the "wilds of Mu") was the site of King Wu of Zhou's victory over the Shang. See, for example, *Shiji* 3, 108.

19. An early Han bronze mirror inscribed with several lines of moral advice also uses the term 方 *fang* to describe a moral path or way: "The way/method of the gentleman, 君子 之 方 *junzi zhi fang*." See Xu Zhongwen 徐忠文 and Zhou Changyuan 周長源, eds., *Han Guangling guo tongjing* 漢廣陵國銅鏡 (Beijing: Wenwu, 2013).

20. This reading is based on that of Gao Yizhi 高一致, "Chu du Beida cang Qin jian Jiaonü." Gao cites the Qin-dynasty inscribed jade plate of Qin Yin 秦駰 (ca. 256–221 BCE) for similar text: 西東若卷. See Zeng Xuantong 曾憲通, Yang Zesheng 楊澤生, and Xiao Yi 肖毅, "Qin yuban wenzi chutan" 秦玉版文字初探, *Kaogu wenwu* 考古與文物 2001.1, 49–54. The word Zhu Fenghan originally interpreted as *zhong* (蠡/眾) he later identifies as *yao* 謠, rendering the line: "If rumors should arrive from west or east . . ." See Zhu Fenghan, "Beida cang Qinjian Jiaonü shiwen zaitan" 北大藏秦簡教女再探, in Chūgoku shutsudo shiryō takaku teki kenkyū 中國出土資料的多角的研究, ed. Yanaka Shin'ichi 穀中信一 (Tokyo: Kyuko-shoin, 2018), 311–22.

21. Gao Yizhi 高一致 who reads the graph as 妣 *bi* "deceased mother," rendering the line as "as if your deceased mother were present in the hall." See "Chu du Beida cang Qin jian Jiaonü." Zhu reads the graph as 陛 *bi* "steps for ascending the hall" and translates the line as "as if [ascending] a stairway to the hall." Zhu cites Duan Yucai's 段玉裁 note on 陛 *bi* in *Shuowen jiezi zhu* 《說文解字注》: " 自卑而可以登高者謂之陛." (Starting from a humble position and able to reach the heights is known as *bi* 陛). See Tang Kejing 湯可敬, *Shuowen jiezi jinshi* 説文解字今釋, 3 vols. (Changsha: Yue Lu shushe, 1997), vol. 3, 2102. Hu Ning 胡寧 cites the *Erya* to argue that 辟 *bi*, defined as 君 *jun* "ruler," is a better phonetic match; see "Beida Qinjian Jiaonü bushi jiuze," http://www.gwz.fudan.edu.cn/Web/Show/3170.

22. Gao Yizhi, reads this graph as is, that is, "illustrious." See "Chu du Beida cang Qin jian Jiaonü."

23. "Sheep pellets" (羊矢 *yangshi*) are sheep excrement. Zhu Fenghan reserves judgment on this phrase but considers the possibility that it refers to "sheep dates" 羊棗 *yangzao*. Mencius 7B, chap. 36, mentions 羊棗 *yangzao*. See translation in James Legge, *The Chinese Classics*, 5 vols. (Hong Kong: Chinese University of Hong Kong Press, 1970), vol. 2, 497–98. Guo Pu 郭璞 claims that the name comes from their resemblance to sheep excrement, according to his note in the *Erya* 爾雅, and that they are also called 羊矢棗 *yangshizao*. See Guo Pu, ed., *Erya Guo zhu* 爾雅郭注 in *Sibu beiyao* (Taipei: Zhonghua, 1965), vol. 28, *juan* 9, 6B. Furthermore, in his gloss on the ode "Yuan you tao" 園有桃, Zhu Xi 朱熹, in his *Collected Commentaries* 集傳 notes that 棘 *ji* are "short dates" 棗之短者 *zao zhi duan zhe*, in keeping with *Jiaonü*'s distinction of "long and short" goat pellets. See Hattori Unokichi, *Kanbun Taikei* (Taipei: Xinwenfeng, 1978), *juan* 5, 16. This sentence is one in a series of adages that seem to contrast striking or desirable features of various natural objects with their more

pedestrian or undesirable aspects: the majesty of grand vertical heights of mountain peaks, the endurance of pine and cypress, and calm conditions of water are contrasted with the lowliness of flat vistas and plains, the decline seen in yellowing pines, and the danger of floods. It is hard to see how "goat pellets" fit in this scheme, specifically, how a similar qualitative distinction arises in the comparison of long and short goat pellets. Construing the word *yangshi*, as "sheep dates," the contrast is formed by the easy access of all of them falling to the ground with the uneven quality of the dates.

24. Gao Yizhi suggests that this line be construed as "although the reason for the complaint may seem harmless." See "Chu du Beida cang Qin jian Jiaonü." This translation reflects Zhu Fenghan revised (2015) understanding of this sentence.

25. Gao suggests that 茀然 *furan* might be construed as 勃然 *boran* "quickly" and 幾梁 *jiliang* as 機梁 "releasable bridge": "She can change his mood as quickly as releasing a drawbridge." See "Chu du Beida cang Qin jian Jiaonü." On the releasable bridge, see Robin Yates, *Science and Civilisation in China* (Cambridge: Cambridge University Press, 1994), vol. 5.6, section 30, 364. Zhu Fenghan's (2015) update is in agreement with Gao.

26. Zhu Fenghan (2015) defines *baixing* 百X (姓) as all the surnames connected to the family.

27. Gao Yizhi interprets this phrase as "She is not overly self-regarding." See "Chu du Beida cang Qin jian Jiaonü." Also compare to *Analects* 17:7.

28. This sentiment is in keeping with the views of Lord Shang as expressed in *Shiji* 68. See *Shiji* 68, 2228–30.

29. Zhu transcribes the word *yue* 曰 "to speak" as *ri* 日 "daily." The text shifts to the first person here.

30. In pre-Qin times, the term *sheng* 甥 generally refers to affinal relatives: sons of paternal aunts, sons of maternal uncles, sister's husbands, sons of sisters, and sons of daughters. See Maria Khayutina, "Marital Alliances and Affinal Relatives (*sheng* and *hungou*) in the Society and Politics of Zhou China in the Light of Bronze Inscriptions," *Early China* 37 (2014): 15–38.

31. Zhu glosses this word as 姿 *zi* "manner" but later translates it as 恣意 *ziyi* "unrestrainedly."

32. Hu Ning supplies the word *yi* 意 for the lacuna, rendering the line: "She stirs up licentious thoughts." See http://www.gwz.fudan.edu.cn/Web/Show/3170.

33. Hu Ning renders this phrase as follows: "Her words match the sentiments of others." See http://www.gwz.fudan.edu.cn/Web/Show/3170, reading *qi* 奇 as 期 and 忌 as *ji* 惎/*zhi* 志.

34. Zhu Fenghan following Wang Tingbin 王挺斌, "Du Beida Qin jian Shan nüzi zhi fang xiaozha" 讀北大秦簡〈善女子之方〉小劄 (Fudan daxue chutu wenxian yu guwenzi yanjiu zhongxin wangzhan 復旦大學出土文獻與古文字研究中心網站, December 12, 2014), notes that the two words in the phrase 益埤 *yipi* both mean the same thing and thus suggests that the word 埤 *pi* is a loan for 俾 *bi* meaning 使 *shi* "to cause."

35. Zhu Fenghan (2015) changed his identification of the unknown graph from 衿 *jin* "to bind" to 缺 *que* "defective," rendering the line "She dresses her hair three times [but still finds it] unsatisfactory."

36. Since there are only three graphs in this phrase, one may be missing.

37. This sentence poses some difficulties. The first two words in this phrase are not found in the *Shuowen*. Zhu Fenghan at first suggested that the first word represents 刌 *cun* "to cut" and the second word, 挽 *wan*, means "to pull," rendering the sentence "This is like severing (the reins) of a cart—how can you expect to get anywhere?" In his 2015 articles Zhu suggests instead that the first word represents 遵 *zun* "follow" and the second 範 *fan* "standards."

38. The phrase *cishan* 次善 may also mean "substandard," and the entire sentence, "[The condition of] her household is substandard and there is no evidence of her having accomplished anything." Hu Ning construes the word *ci* 次 to mean "to compare" and the whole sentence as meaning something like "When compared to the households of the virtuous, there is no evidence of her having accomplished anything."

39. Zhu Fenghan suggests that the mark indicating the duplication of the word 越 *yue* is an error, noting the frequency of this specific error in Qin manuscripts and the disruption a second *yue* presents for the four-character phrasing. Gao Yizhi glosses the second 越 *yue* as 揚 *yang*. See "Chu du Beida cang Qin jian Jiaonü."

40. Reading 在前 *zaiqian* as it appears in *Analects* 9:10.1, that is, as a spatial rather than temporal term.

11

The Shape of the Text

Gu Prisms and Han Primers

CHRISTOPHER J. FOSTER

Introduction

In her latest book, *Buried Ideas*, Sarah Allan considers how the materiality of early Chinese manuscripts shaped many works in the received corpus.[1] The threat of missing or misplaced bamboo strips has long worried traditional and modern commentators alike.[2] Yet manuscript discoveries of the past century have inspired a more fundamental reappraisal of textual production from the Warring States to Han periods. These finds challenge assumptions about discrete author(s) in singular moments of literary genesis (and genius) who composed massive treatises, which were transmitted relatively faithfully to the

I am grateful for the help and advice of Dongsob Ahn, Mélodie Doumy, Maria Khayutina, Kim Kyung-ho, and Ondřej Škrabal in drafting this chapter. This research is affiliated with Yang Bo's 楊博 project, "Comprehensive Research on the Writing and Texts of the Peking University Collection of Qin and Han Bamboo-Strip Manuscripts" (北京大學藏秦, 漢簡牘文字, 文本綜合研究) (YWZ-J020), funded by the PRC Ministry of Education and State Language Commission. I first drafted the chapter when I was the Stanley Ho Junior Research Fellow in Chinese Studies at Pembroke College (Oxford) and completed it during a British Academy postdoctoral fellowship at SOAS University of London. As a disclaimer, the statements expressed herein are given in a personal capacity only. This work is not affiliated with my current position at the Library of Congress, nor does it reflect views endorsed by the Library.

present. An appreciation has grown for the textual fluidity present in early China.[3] We now are aware that shorter units of text circulated initially during the Warring States; this transmission occurred orally as well as in writing; anecdotes, proverbs, speeches, and so forth, constituted a shared wellspring of "building blocks" for literary production; and acts of composition, or rather (re)compilation, were multiple, continuous, and communal well into the Han.

How do we then explain the idiosyncratic appearance of many of our received works? In particular, Allan highlights the extensive length of certain received treatises, which were compiled into multiple chapters, often with heterogeneous materials, either loosely thematic in nature or lacking any clear organizational logic. Allan believes that transcription on silk sheets, as opposed to bound bamboo strips, played an important role. She argues that silk sheets accommodated for and stabilized longer, multichapter texts. Allan notes that "silk scrolls were lighter and could contain much more writing . . . [and] whether intended or not, the effect of writing manuscripts on silk scrolls was to formally set the text, clearly defining its scope, wording, and the sequence of its parts."[4] Movement between these mediums began already in the Warring States period but culminated with the deposit of silk scrolls in the imperial library during its reorganization in the late Western Han.[5]

Inspired by Allan's hypothesis, this chapter offers in her honor a meager observation of a similar nature: how the materiality of a certain strip format—that of the *gu* 觚 prism—helped shape Han scribal primers such as the *Cang Jie pian* 蒼頡篇 and *Jijiu pian* 急就篇. The chapter surveys references to objects called *gu* 觚 in antiquity, differentiating *gu* beakers (as drinking vessels) from *gu* prisms (as writing supports).[6] It then argues that popular adoption of *gu* prisms for study during the Western Han dynasty impacted later editions of the *Cang Jie pian* and the composition of the *Jijiu pian*. Long chapters were divided into smaller textual units to fit onto the prisms, and numerical titles replaced content-based titles. The effect of these changes was to stabilize the primers, when considered as a whole, fostering a stronger overall textual identity. Indeed, the very notion of a work "Cang Jie volumes" likely derived from this impetus, with the title *Cang Jie pian* anachronistically projected back onto earlier materials.

Gu Beakers as Drinking Vessels

In *Lunyu* 論語 6.25, Confucius cryptically quips: "A *gu* that is not *gu*-like . . . a *gu* indeed, a *gu* indeed!" (觚不觚觚哉觚哉!).[7] Many commentators, including the Han scholars Ma Rong 馬融 (79–166 CE) and Zheng Xuan 鄭玄 (127–200 CE), take *gu* here to be a ritual vessel, namely a "beaker" wine receptacle.[8] Ma explains: "This is a ritual vessel. If (the vessel holds) one *sheng* peck, then it is called a *jue* chalice; if (it holds) two pecks, then it is called a *gu*" (禮器也一升曰爵二升曰觚也).[9] Zheng concurs: "*Gu* is the name for a type of chalice, and it has a volume of two pecks" (觚爵名容二升).[10] Identifying *gu* as a beaker does not however explicate Confucius's statement, allowing for divergent interpretations. Zheng Xuan, for instance, believes Confucius was fashioning his own beaker but failed to finish the vessel properly, as he was lost in thought on other affairs. Confucius's exasperation with himself is intended as a warning: "If one's attention is not concentrated, then even when making a small vessel, the decorative finish will not be completed in time. How much graver will the consequences be for important matters?" (口所小器心不專一尚不時成況於大事乎?).[11] He Yan 何晏 (d. 249 CE) sees a political analogy in this line instead, with the pseudo-beaker a subtle critique of those who only rule nominally but do not truly grasp the proper way of governance.[12] Wang Su 王肅 (195–256 CE) however bemoans the loss of ritual decorum in the wanton drinking of Confucius's day.[13] Consensus on how to read this passage remains elusive even today.[14]

Early ritual compendia also treat *gu* as a type of wine vessel. In the *Yili* 儀禮, the *gu* beaker features prominently in scripts for hosting banquets (*Yanli* 燕禮) and archery matches (*Dashe* 大射).[15] The *Zhou li* 周禮 moreover states that the woodworker (*ziren* 梓人) makes drinking vessels, with "the *gu* three pecks in volume" (觚三升).[16] Mentions of *gu* in the ritual compendia, however, present complications. Zheng Xuan notes scribes occasionally mistook the character for *gu* with the graphically similar *zhi* 觚 "goblet" (a variant of *zhi* 觶).[17] He also mentions edition-level variants to the *Yili* that exchanged *gu* with either *zhi* or *jue* 爵.[18] Interestingly, the Han-period *Yili* manuscripts from Wuwei 武威 do write *zhi* as 觚 (akin to 觚), and differentiate the character for *gu* by means of a wood component, 柧.[19] Zheng's observation about edition-level variation is also confirmed.[20]

The precise volume of a *gu* beaker is contested. Ma Rong and Zheng Xuan describe *gu* as holding two pecks. The *Zhou li*, however, gives three pecks.[21] This is matched in the *Shuowen jiezi* 說文解字 definition: "Chalices used for drinking wine in district symposiums. One source says that *gu* are *shang* pitchers that hold three pecks . . ." (鄉飲酒之爵也一曰觴受三升者謂之觚 . . .).[22] Regardless, *gu* are commonly associated with other liquid receptacles. In the *Da Dai liji* 大戴禮記, Zengzi 曾子 warns that proper ritual decorum entails "grasping the *shang* pitcher, *gu* beaker, *bei* cup, or *dou* goblet, but not drinking to excess" (執觴觚杯豆而不醉).[23] The *Liqi bei* 韓勑

禮器碑 or *Ritual Implement Stele*, erected in 156 CE, offers another example: "Master [Han 韓] thereupon fashioned ritual implements and musical notations, with bells and chimes, strings and drums, *lei* water jars and *xi* used-water jars, [*shang* pitchers] and *gu* beakers, *jue* chalices and *lu* (i.e., *jue* 角) flagons . . ." (君於是造立禮器樂之音符鍾磐瑟鼓雷洗[觴]觚爵鹿 . . .).[24]

By at least the Eastern Han, the association of Confucius with *gu* beakers inspired a popular legend that Confucius could drink astonishing amounts of alcohol, thereby proving—or even enabling—his sagacity.[25] For instance, when Kong Rong 孔融 (153–208 CE) petitions against Cao Cao's 曹操 (155–220 CE) plan to proscribe alcohol, he argues: "If Yao rejected his thousand *zhong* jars (of wine), he could not have established lasting peace; if Confucius rejected his hundred *gu* beakers (of wine), he could not have sustained utmost sagacity" (堯非千鍾無以建太平孔非百觚無以堪 上聖).[26] Indeed, the phrases "a thousand *zhong* jars" 千鍾 and "a hundred *gu* beakers" 百觚 even became a poetic trope.[27] This legend also excited considerable criticism. Wang Chong 王充 (27–100 CE), in *Lunheng* 論 衡, refutes the theory that sagely virtue empowered Confucius to drink a hundred *gu* of wine. He concludes that "this is to be a wino, not a sage" (此酒徒非聖人也) and scolds believers of this legend for "falsely ordering Confucius a hundred *gu* beakers" (空益孔子以百觚矣).[28]

What was the shape of a *gu* beaker? Song antiquarian catalogs offer early identifications and portrayals of *gu* beakers.[29] These must be treated with caution, however, and views on the shape of the *gu* varied over the Song. Compare, for instance, the drawing of a *gu* in Nie Chongyi's 聶崇義 (fl. mid-10th c.) *Sanli tu* 三禮圖 (fig. 11.1),[30] with those in Lü Dalin's 呂 大臨 (1040–1092 CE) *Kaogu tu* 考古圖 (e.g., figs. 11.2a and 11.2b).[31] Lü's entry for Li Gonglin's 李公麟 vessel fortuitously quotes Li's justification for the piece's identification as a *gu*.[32] Li's methodology was twofold. First, he compared the volumes of extant vessels and matched them with the ratios prescribed for vessel types in classical texts. Second, Li sought parallels between features in the design and decoration of his vessel and the use of the word *gu* 觚 in ancient sources. For example, Li cites the line from the *Shiji* 史記 and *Han shu* 漢書, exclaiming how, when the Han arose, they "broke what was square and made it round" (破觚為圜), and muses that shaving off the flanges from his vessel would create a rounded belly.[33] The flanges, moreover, remind Li of the Phoenix Watchtower to the Han Palace, with "upper ridges where bronze birds perched" (上觚稜而棲金爵), as described in Ban Gu's 班固 (32–92 CE) *Liangdu fu* 兩都賦.[34] Finally, Li believes four elephants decorate the vessel's base and uses this to explicate the enigmatic *xianggu* 象觚 (elephant *gu* beaker) in the *Yili*.[35]

Figure 11.1. "*Gu* Beaker 觚," *Sanli tu* 三禮圖. After a 1680 edition of *Xinding sanli tu* 新定三禮圖 from the collection of the Harvard-Yenching Library of the Harvard College Library. *Source:* Nie Chongyi 聶崇義, Xinding sanli tu 新定三禮圖, in 20 *juan*, *Tongzhi tang* 通志堂, 1680 rare book, Harvard University, vol. 2, chap. "Xinding sanli paojue tu juan di shier" (新定三禮匏爵圖卷第十二), 18 (seq. 92). Available online: http://nrs.harvard.edu/urn-3:FHCL:4056721?n=92.

Figure 11.2. "*Gu* Beaker, (belonging to) Mr. Li of Lujiang" (觚廬江李氏), in two editions of *Kaogu tu* 考古圖. Both are from the collection of the Harvard-Yenching Library of the Harvard College Library. Figure 11.2a (left) is after an early Ming (1368–1464) edition of *Kaogu tu* 考古圖. Figure 11.2b (right) is after an eighteenth-century edition of *Yi Zhengtang chongxiu Kaogu tu* 亦政堂重修考古圖. *Source:* Lü Dalin 呂大臨 and Luo Gengweng 羅更翁, eds., *Kaogu tu* 考古圖, in 10 *juan*, early Ming [1368–1464] rare book, Harvard University, vol. 7 (self-titled *Kaogu tu di wu* 考古圖第乂), 21 (seq. 192). Available online: http://nrs.harvard.edu/urn-3:FHCL:4795446?n=192; Lü Dalin 呂大臨 and Yi Zhengtang 亦政堂, eds., *Yi Zhengtang chongxiu Kaogu tu* 亦政堂重修考古圖, 10 *juan*, in Huang Cheng 黃晟, *Sangu tu* 三古圖 (Tiandu: Huangshi Yi Zhengtang jiaokan ben, Qianlong renshen [1752]), vol. 22 (self-titled *Yi Zhengtang chongxiu Kaogu tu juan di wu* 亦政堂重修考古圖卷第乂), 25 (seq. 1431). Available online: http://nrs.harvard.edu/urn-3:FHCL:4909723?n=1431.

Chinese archaeologists today still employ the classification for *gu* beakers established by Li Gonglin's identification and Lü Dalin's catalog. Although this convention offers a practical workaround, it is problematic for several reasons.[36] Vessels shaped like figures 11.2a and 11.2b flourished during the Shang and persisted into the early Zhou, but largely drop out of the archaeological record thereafter.[37] Attempting to match Shang and early Zhou vessels to names in literature from the Warring States period or later risks anachronism. The literary associations Li draws between the word *gu* 觚 and his vessel's physical appearance are tenuous at best.[38] Recall also how classical sources contest prescribed vessel volume ratios, rendering Li's comparisons ineffective. On vessels identified today as *gu* beakers, inscriptions are rare and none self-identify as *gu* 觚.[39] In fact, the only vessel of this type carrying a self-identification is the Neishi Bo *tong* 內史亳同, which calls itself a *tong* 銅.[40] No vessels or items of other types self-identify as *gu* either.[41] Even if there were, naming practices could vary between artists or communities and change over time.[42]

Gu Prisms as Writing Supports

Let us return to *Lunyu* 6.25. Although most commentators identify *gu* 觚 here as a beaker, another interpretation has been raised—that Confucius speaks of a *gu* prism. Zhu Xi 朱熹 (1130–1200 CE), for one, acknowledged this possibility: "The word '*gu*' means 'ridge.' Some say that it is a drinking vessel, others say that it is a wood strip. In both cases, it is an item that has ridges" (觚棱也或曰酒器或曰木簡皆器之有棱者也).[43] In *Zhuzi yulei* 朱子語類, Zhu clarifies how multiple items were called *gu* in antiquity. He first likens the drinking vessel (*gu* beaker) to flower vases with "cornered" midsections. But there was also the writing support (*gu* prism), which he describes as "six-sided with delineated faces" (界方而六面).[44] Zhu Xi allowed that in *Lunyu* 6.25, Confucius may have intended a different type of "ridged" object altogether, namely a multisided writing support made from wood, what I call a "prism."[45]

In Han sources, the word *gu* 觚 can describe "prism-like" cylindrical objects, like a sword hilt: "If one grasps the hilt and raises the tip (of the blade) . . ." (操其觚招其末).[46] The phrase *caogu* 操觚 later comes to mean "grasping a (writing) prism," as a euphemism for drafting texts.[47] The use of prisms for writing appears in the *Shuowen* as well. Although the *Shuowen* glosses *gu* 觚 as a type of chalice, Xu Shen claims in the entry for *fan* 幡

(cloth): "This is a rag that young writers used to wipe off their *gu* prisms" (書兒拭觚布也).[48] Implied in this gloss is a close link between prisms and study.[49] This link is demonstrated again in the *Xijing zaji* 西京雜記, when Fu Jiezi 傅介子 (d. 65 BCE) "enjoyed his schoolbooks, but discarded his *gu* prisms" (好學書嘗棄觚) to pursue fame in the frontier.[50]

The strongest evidence that *gu* prisms were writing supports used in part for study derives from the opening lines of the primer *Jijiu pian*, which declares:

> For swift employ, this special prism is different from the many others. It lists out the characters for the names of various things and divides them into categories that are not mixed together. After using it for only a few days, you will indeed quickly get your way. Exert your energy to work on this, and you will inevitably have what you desire!

> 急就奇觚與眾異羅列諸物名姓字分別部居不雜廁用日約少誠快意勉力務之必有喜[51]

This opening mirrors that of its predecessor, the *Cang Jie pian*, which directly addresses young students working to become scribes.[52] The *Jijiu pian* is exceptional, however, in that it presumes a "special prism" 奇觚 for the text's writing support. Yan Shigu's 顏師古 (581–645 CE) commentary gives a detailed analysis:

> *Gu* were boards that served as schoolbooks. In some instances, they were used to record matters. They were made by shaving down wood (branches) and ought to be classified as a type of (writing) strip. When Confucius exclaimed about *gu*, he referred to this. As for their shape, some had six sides, others eight sides, all of which may be written upon. The word *gu* means "ridge." Since they had edges, (these prisms) thus were called *gu*. (The opening line) states that students should swiftly employ this special and fine prism, as its profundity separates it from ordinary books. In Ban Gu's *Rhapsody of Two Capitals*, he states: "(The palace's) upper *gu* ridges where bronze birds perched." Nowadays children's schoolbooks still are called informally "wooden *gu* prism chapters," a phrase passed down to us from antiquity.

觚者學書之牘或以記事削木為之蓋簡屬也孔子歎觚即此之謂其形
或六面或八面皆可書觚者棱也以有稜角故謂之觚言學僮急當就此
奇好之觚其中深博與眾書有異也班固兩都賦曰上觚棱而棲金爵今
俗猶呼小兒學書簡為木觚章蓋古之遺語也[53]

Yan highlights many of the associations explicated here: that *gu* were multisided wooden prisms; used for writing, and study in particular; named
after the prism's "ridges"; and conceivably the object Confucius exclaims
about in the *Lunyu*.

Among the Han manuscripts recovered in northwest China, the *Cang
Jie pian*, *Jijiu pian*, and other unidentified "character books" are often written on multisided cylindrical wooden sticks (fig. 11.3).[54] DHHJ 1972 (fig.
11.3b) even includes the *Jijiu pian*'s self-identification of "special prism"
奇觚. Scholars have labeled these pieces *gu* prisms, and utilize them and
similar-looking pieces to characterize this writing support, emphasizing their
"multisided" 多面 and "ridged or edged" 削棱角 features.[55] As with identifications of the *gu* beaker, however, we must exercise caution when labeling
any piece a *gu* prism.[56] Correlating Han artifacts with names found in Han
textual sources helps avoid the anachronism confronted with the *gu* beaker
case.[57] Yet the possibility of local naming conventions remain; standardized
naming must be proven and not assumed.[58] Unlike unique inscriptions
tailored for individual bronze vessels, DHHJ 1972's self-identification as
a "special prism" 奇觚 is not necessarily object specific. The *Jijiu pian*'s
opening lines appear on other media, without altering *gu* 觚 in its text.[59]
Michael Loewe, moreover, observes that many polygonal "rods" self-identify
as *xi* 檄 ("despatches"), though it is uncertain whether this names a writing
support, genre, or combination of both.[60] Characteristics associated with *gu*
in received texts, such as being multisided or ridged, also apply to pieces
disparate in shape from those in figure 11.3.[61] While acknowledging these
methodological difficulties, the pieces in figure 11.3 best match the description and function of *gu* prisms as found in our sources.

The majority of excavated *gu* prisms date to the Han.[62] A handful of
potential prisms date to the Warring States or Qin, but such discoveries are
rare. In all instances, these early pieces are either borderline cases (regarding
strip format) or not yet published in full.[63] It is possible *gu* were utilized
before the Han.[64] Pre-imperial writers clearly were capable of carving thicker
branches of wood into multisided writing supports akin to *gu* prisms. Preservation bias may also skew our data. Most Han *gu* prisms unearthed to
date derive from military installations in China's arid northwest, as opposed

Figures 11.3a–b. Examples of unearthed *gu* prisms bearing primers

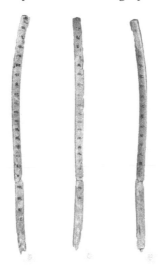

Figure 11.3a. *Source: Cang Jie pian* on JY 9.1A-C, after the images on the Academia Sinica Institute of History and Philology Juyan Han Strips Database website 史語所藏 居延漢簡資料庫, https://wcd-ihp.ascdc.sinica.edu.tw/woodslip/item.php?id1=H00390, under CC BY-NC-ND 3.0 TW.

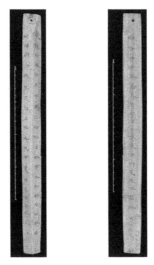

Figure 11.3b. *Source: Jijiu pian* on DHHJ 1972A-C, after images from the British Library International Dunhuang Project website (http://idp.bl.uk), © The British Library Board, Or.8211/1.

to the Warring States and Qin manuscripts finds, which largely differ in geography and archaeological context. That said, based on the current evidence, it was first in the Western Han that *gu* were adopted popularly as a strip format. Despite the invention of paper soon after, prism use appears to have persisted into the medieval period, while reaching the peripheries of the Chinese empires and beyond. Of special interest, in 1999 a *gu* prism (6th–7th c.) was found at Ponghwang-dong 鳳凰洞, Kimhae 金海, Korea; then again in 2005 another prism (4th–5th c.) was unearthed at the Kyeyang Mountain Fortress site 桂陽山城, in Inchŏn 仁川, Korea.[65] Both have lines from the *Gongye Chang* 公冶長 chapter of the *Lunyu*, which was one of the initial texts introduced to students in the classical curriculum. A similar prism (mid-7th c.) was discovered at the Tokushimaken Kannō-ji 德鳥縣 觀音寺 site in Japan in 1997, this time bearing the *Xue'er* 學而 chapter of the *Lunyu*.[66]

The content of Han *gu* prisms reveals how this writing support was used for a variety of purposes.[67] Yan Shigu's *Jijiu pian* commentary claims prisms either "served as textbooks" or "were used to record matters." The archaeological finds substantiate this basic division. Many unearthed prisms bear military dispatches, administrative documents, and private letters.[68] Others were utilized in study, whether as model "character books" (i.e., *zishu* 字書 like *Cang Jie pian* and *Jijiu pian*) that students viewed and copied from, or as the scrap pieces students practiced their writing on.[69] Wang Guowei 王國維 and others argue that *gu* prisms made ideal models for copying, since they could be stood on end and twisted, revealing and/or hiding content for study.[70] Others, such as Momiyama Akira 籾山明, emphasize how students could write their exercises on prisms instead.[71] Prisms have more writing surface and are easier to erase with a knife.[72] Yet writing is still confined to sides that approximate the dimensions of a *jian* strip, and the medium (wood) gives the same feel for brushwork. Prisms were also easier to fashion and could recycle discarded tree branches or parts otherwise unworkable for closely regulated strip formats, as a type of "scrap paper" in informal study.[73]

Influence of *Gu* Prisms on Textual Production of Han Primers

The adoption of *gu* prisms for study in the Western Han influenced the textual production of the scribal primer *Cang Jie pian* and, moreover, was fundamental in the composition of the subsequent *Jijiu pian* primer. To demonstrate this, let us first compare early and later editions of the *Cang Jie pian*.[74] According to the *Han shu* 漢書 "Yiwen zhi" 藝文志: "When the Han was founded, village teachers combined the three (earlier) texts of the *Cang Jie*, *Yuanli*, and *Boxue*, dividing each into sixty-characters chapters, in fifty-five chapters altogether. This combined text was the *Cang Jie pian*" (漢 書<興>閭里書師合蒼頡爰歷博學三篇斷六十字以為一章凡五十五章并為蒼頡 篇).[75] Excavated witnesses confirm that chapter length was indeed shortened at some point in the Western Han. Our earliest witnesses are the Fuyang Shuanggudui 阜陽雙古堆 and Peking University manuscripts, both of which date from the early to mid-Western Han.[76] The PKU manuscript is particularly important, as it is one of the most complete witnesses extant, and includes chapter titles and character counts, which clearly delineate the structure of this edition of the *Cang Jie pian*.[77] In the PKU *Cang Jie pian*, chapters vary in length, with counts ranging between 104 and 152 characters. The reconstructed "Shanglu" 賞祿 (Award Emoluments) chapter and partial "Han jian" 漢兼 (Han United) chapter, based primarily on PKU 1-11, follows:[78]

Shanglu → Han jian

{賞   賞祿賢知賜予分貸莊犯□強朋友過刻高喦平夷} [*]
祿   寬惠善志桀紂迷惑宗幽不識宧{穀}肆宜{益就}獲得 [PKU 1]
      賓勤向尚馮奕青北係孫褢俗狠鷺吉忌癒瘁癉痤 [PKU 2]
      疚痛遫欬毒藥醫工抑按啓久嬰但悁援何竭負戴 [PKU 3]
      谿谷阪險丘陵故舊長緩肆延渙奐若思勇猛剛毅 [PKU 4]
      便疌巧㔻景桓昭穆豐盈爨熾嬽𦱔蚂黑婐姍款餌 [PKU 5]
      戲叢書插顛顤重該悉起臣僕發傳約載趣遝觀望 [PKU 6]
      行步駕服遘逃隱匿往來眲睞   百五十二 [PKU 7]
漢   漢兼天下海內並廁胡無噍類菹醢離異戎翟給賓 [PKU 8]
兼   百越貢織飭端脩瀗變大制裁男女蕃殖六畜逐字 [PKU 9]
      顚魊觭嬴脮奐左右勢悍驕裾誅罰貴耐丹勝誤亂 [PKU 10]
      固奪侵試胡貉離絕冢辜棺柩巴蜀築竹筐篋籔筍 [PKU 11]
      {厨宰犓豢甘酸羹蔽 . . .} [*]

The *Cang Jie pian* appears among the documents discovered in China's northwest region. Although it is difficult to date these pieces with precision, Han military expansion into the Hexi Corridor began during Emperor Wu's reign and lasted into the Eastern Han.[79] These strips, therefore, mostly date later than the FY and PKU manuscripts. A *gu* prism from Juyan is of special interest:

第五　戲□書掩顛願重該□起臣僕發傳約載趣躁觀望　[JY 9.1a]
行步駕□遁逃隱[匿]往來眮睞漢兼天下晦内并廁　[JY 9.1c]
□□□類湆醢離異戎翟給賓佰越貢□[飭]端修法　[JY 9.1b]

This *Cang Jie pian* edition differs from that of the PKU witness. A chapter title, "Diwu" 第五 (Fifth), heads lines that straddle between what the PKU witness manifestly demarcates as two separate chapters.[80] Notably, this prism holds precisely sixty characters of base text, matching the Village Teachers edition described in the *Han shu*.

Additional evidence of sixty-character partitions to the *Cang Jie pian* exists in the shavings collected by Aurel Stein near watchtower T.VI.b.[81] On certain shavings, the final few characters of a given chapter appear just before the opening of that same chapter. In other words, the scribe copied a single chapter repetitively, most likely in study.[82] Such shavings often include a triangle or line mark signaling where the chapter ends and begins anew.[83] Imagine a student, copying from a model *gu* prism—with three sides, bearing a chapter in sixty characters, twenty characters per side—turning the piece, to view and copy one side at a time, returning back to the beginning. Time permitting, they may continue from the start without pause. This would produce the phenomenon where characters from the end of a given chapter are written just prior to characters from that same chapter's beginning.[84] YT 3382, YT 3543, YT 1921, YT 3248, YT 3254, YT 3675, and YT 2449 offer examples, for which please see the appendix to this chapter.

With YT 3382 and 3543, upon reaching *zuo* 座 (read *cuo* 座) the sixtieth character of the reconstructed "Award Emoluments" chapter, the scribe returns to the chapter's opening of *shanglu* 賞祿. YT 1921 has a mark after *zuo* 座 also, signaling a textual division, though it is unclear if the character afterward returns to *shang* or continues onto *chen* 疢.[85] Counting sixty characters further brings us to *xi* 戲, which is where JY 9.1 begins its "Fifth" chapter. Presuming "Award Emoluments" and "Han United" are consecutive chapters here, as in the PKU witness, then sixty characters after *xi* 戲 concludes with *fa* 法 (灋). This is where YT 3248, 3675, and 2449 add punctuation. On YT 3675 the scribe starts over with *xi* 虝 (戲), and both YT 3248 and 2449 preserve the right component of *xi* as well.[86]

It is clear that in the Western Han, a version of the *Cang Jie pian* had sixty-character chapters, which confirms the "Yiwen zhi" account of a Village Teachers edition.[87] Curiously, when parsing chapters, very little modification appears in the content; the text was simply split into smaller units. What motivated this rather mechanical editing? One theory, raised by Hu Pingsheng 胡平生, is that the *Cang Jie pian* included the *ganzhi*

干支 sexagenary cycle, which dictated sixty-character chapters.[88] Although practice writing of *ganzhi*, at times in archaic calligraphy, is found in the same caches as *Cang Jie pian* manuscripts, inclusion of the sexagenary cycle would break the strict rhyming pattern structuring the primer.[89]

Early on, however, Wang Guowei proposed that character books like the *Cang Jie pian* were written on *gu* prisms and therefore had short, but regular, chapter lengths.[90] Luo Zhenyu 羅振玉, upon examining unearthed specimens, suggests that three-sided *gu* prisms, with twenty characters per side, were the ideal format; and Lao Gan 勞榦 then raised JY 9.1 as proof.[91] The evidence introduced previously corroborates their hypothesis. Over the course of the Western Han, early editions of the *Cang Jie pian*, written on bound bamboo strips, had their longer chapters partitioned in rote fashion, at the same moment that *gu* prisms became popularized for study. It appears character books adapted to better fit their new material constraints.

This theory helps explain another difference between the PKU *Cang Jie pian* manuscript and Juyan 9.1 prism: title conventions. The PKU witness titles each chapter by means of the first two characters of that chapter's opening line, written horizontally across the upper margin of two strips. The following are preserved: "Shanglu" [賞]祿, "Han jian" 漢兼, "Kuocuo" 闊錯, "Bibo" 幣帛, "Tuokui" [拓]悝, "Jigou" 齎購, "Zhuan Xu" 顓頊, "Shiyu" 室宇, "Yunyu" 雲雨, "X Lun" □輪, and "Hebao" 鶡鴇. This title convention is attested on other Qin and Han bamboo-strip manuscripts.[92] It may also apply to the overall title of *Cang Jie pian*.[93]

Yet, on the JY 9.1 prism, the title is numerical: "Diwu" 第五 or "Fifth." I do not believe this was simply the idiosyncratic preference of the scribe.[94] With the PKU witness, multiple chapters were bound together, strip-by-strip, into a single roll, forming a cohesive whole. If model chapters were recorded on prisms, however, they likely circulated as individual pieces; a student could handle a single prism, and copy it repetitively, as suggested by the shavings listed in the appendix.[95] Using opening lines as titles provides no guidance for the relative ordering of chapters, however, whereas numerical titles allow students to place individual chapters easily within the larger text. This is important considering how the Village Teachers edition was compiled. Mechanically dividing earlier editions (with longer chapters) into sixty-character units, certain chapters in the Village Teachers edition not only disrupt the rhyme scheme but also separate vocabulary designed to be read together.[96]

Thus with the *Cang Jie pian* an earlier edition was altered to accommodate *gu* prisms in at least two ways: by dividing chapters into shorter lengths to fit one chapter per prism; and by adopting numerical titles to allow positioning isolated prisms within the text as a whole. Similar to Sarah Allan's hypothesis, I believe that switching between the media of bound *jian* strips and *gu* prisms helped stabilize the *Cang Jie pian* as a whole during the Western Han. The fact that the Village Teachers edition of the *Cang Jie pian* did not fundamentally alter the wording of the earlier PKU witness suggests that the content of the longer chapters to this edition was well established already. Yet it is possible that overall chapter order was once more fluid; the longer chapters of the PKU manuscript are themselves coherent units and could be easily rearranged within or removed from a bound roll.[97] The chapters in the Village Teachers edition cannot, due to the disrupted rhyme schemes and vocabulary clusters. Ironically, while this undermines the coherency enjoyed previously by the longer, individual chapters, it *improves* the integrity of the text as a whole, by necessitating a specific chapter order. With greater importance given to the positioning of chapters relative to one another, numerical titles offer more efficient guidance than content-based titles.[98]

The *Jijiu pian* offers a slightly different scenario, as it was composed with *gu* prisms in mind. According to the "Yiwen zhi," during Emperor Yuan's (48–33 BCE) reign, Shi You 史游 rearranged the *Cang Jie pian* into a new character book, known as the *Jijiu pian*.[99] Fukuda Tetsukuyi 福田哲之 argues that the *Jijiu pian* replaced the *Cang Jie pian* "on the ground" as the preferred character book for practicing writing almost immediately, at least among the military complex in the Han northwest frontier.[100] The opening lines of the *Jijiu pian*, as discussed before, reveal that this text was intended to be written on a *gu* prism, when it refers to itself as a "special prism" 奇觚. Among the *Jijiu pian* manuscripts unearthed thus far, DHHJ 1972 and 2356 are beautifully composed prisms that likely served as models for copying. With the *Jijiu pian* prisms, chapter lengths are again of approximately sixty characters and have numerical titles. In both its received and excavated editions, the *Jijiu pian* is divided in chapters sixty-three characters long, with lines consisting, for the most part, of three or seven characters.[101] This maps over nicely onto a three-sided prism, as shown on DHHJ 1972 and 2356, which record the first and fifteenth chapters, respectively.[102] Regarding title conventions, although the overall title of *Jijiu pian* given in the dynastic bibliographies still draws from the text's opening line, on both of our excavated prisms the chapter titles are numerical: "Diyi" 第一 (First) and "Dishiwu" 第十五 (Fifteenth).[103] Finally, it is possible the hole at the top of DHHJ 1972 allowed for the prism to be strung together with other pieces via a cord (forming a larger text); alternatively, the prism was attached to clothing (for transport) or slung from a post (for display in practice or storage).[104] Regardless, the prism is isolatable as an independent unit and likely was utilized as such.

Conclusion

During the Western Han, a fundamental transformation took place in the presentation of character books like the *Cang Jie pian* and *Jijiu pian*, when *gu* prisms began to be adopted as their preferred writing support in study. Adapting to the prism, the character books themselves were reconceived. The manuscript evidence reveals two changes in particular: the partition of chapters into shorter lengths and the adoption of numerical titles. These adjustments, though seemingly minor, allowed chapters to circulate more readily as isolated units, while paradoxically also buttressing chapter order and thereby fostering a stronger identity for the text overall.

Considering this strengthening of overall textual identity, the very idea of a work "Cang Jie Volumes" could be a late Western Han (or early Eastern Han) invention. The earliest mentions of the title *Cang Jie pian* are from this time, most notably with the *Shuowen jiezi* postface and *Han shu* "Yiwen zhi" catalog.[105] These two works position the *Cang Jie pian* as the successor of the (supposedly) Zhou period *Shi Zhou pian* 史籀篇, through which a lineage of "primary education" manuals sprung forth. In my opinion, this was an anachronistic projection of textual identity backward onto earlier materials, in an attempt to sort through China's written heritage and give order to a more miscellaneous corpus of scribal treatises and primers. When we examine the manuscript evidence, it is striking that our earliest witnesses for *Cang Jie pian* materials, the FY and PKU bamboo strips, lack content from the so-called opening chapter. This section begins with "Cang Jie created writing" (蒼頡作書), and probably inspired the title *Cang Jie pian*. Its simplistic vocabulary and narrative style, moreover, mark this opening as separate from the bulk of the text's other content, suggesting to me that it was a later addition. A comparison of the early Han *Shilü* 史律 (Statutes on Scribes) unearthed at Zhangjiashan 張家山 against the version of the same laws preserved in the *Shuowen* reveals a similar anachronistic projection could have occurred with the title *Shi Zhou pian* as well.[106] We must await further discoveries, however, to either bolster or disprove such claims.[107]

Early Chinese textual production did not occur in the abstract. As recent manuscript finds make abundantly clear, these texts were very much alive and tangible; in their production and consumption, all texts exist within a web of relationships that involve not only author(s) and audience(s) but also material writing supports and their physical handling. With her sensitivity to this aspect of early Chinese manuscript culture, Sarah Allan offers exemplary foresight and has led our field forward.

Appendix to Chapter 11

Transcriptions of the following shavings are based initially on, but modified from, those in *Yingguo guojia tushuguan cang Sitanyin suohuo weikan Han wen jiandu* and supplemented by: Wang Tao 王濤, Hu Pingsheng 胡平生, and Wu Fangsi 吳芳思, "*Yingguo guojia tushuguan cang Sitanyin suohuo weikan Han wen jiandu* buyi shiwen" 英國國家圖書館藏斯坦因所獲未刊漢文簡牘補遺釋文, *Chutu wenxian yanjiu* 出土文獻研究 15 (2016): 302–29, pl. 5–19; see also Bai Junpeng 白軍鵬, "*Yingguo guojia tushuguan cang Sitanyin suohuo weikan Han wen jiandu* de chubu zhengli yu yanjiu" 英國國家圖書館藏斯坦因所獲未刊漢文簡牘的初步整理與研究, *Zhongguo wenzi* 中國文字, n.s., 39 (2013): 187–216. Note that YT 2007 may also include a punctuation mark, followed by *shang* 賞, but the piece is too fragmentary for any positive identification.

Figures 11.4a–g are after from the British Library International Dunhuang Project website (http://idp.bl.uk), © The British Library Board, respectively: Or.8211/3382; Or.8211/3542; Or.8211/1921; Or.8211/3248; Or.8211/3254; Or.8211/3675; and Or.8211/2449.

Figure 11.4a. 庠雍座▲賞 [YT 3382].

Figure 11.4b. 雝座賞祿 [YT 3543].

Figure 11.4c. 瘁雝座▲□ [YT 1921].

Figure 11.4d. [飭]端脩法▲ [觥] [YT 3248].

Figure 11.4e. [脩]法▲觕 [叢]奢掩 [YT 3254].

Figure 11.4f. 脩法▲觕□ [YT 3675].

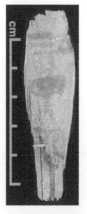

Figure 11.4g. 法■[觕] [YT 2449].

Notes

1. Sarah Allan, *Buried Ideas: Legends of Abdication and Ideal Government in Early Chinese Bamboo-Slip Manuscripts* (Albany: State University of New York Press, 2015), esp. 27–37.

2. See Yu Yue's 俞樾 entry on "bamboo and wood strips out of order" (簡策錯亂) in *Gushu yiyi juli* 古書疑義舉例, in *Gushu yiyi juli wuzhong* 古書疑義舉例五種 (Beijing: Zhonghua, 1983), vol. 6, 125–29; or from Western sinology, for example: Edward Shaughnessy, "On the Authenticity of the *Bamboo Annals*," *Harvard Journal of Asiatic Studies* 46, no. 1 (1986): 149–80.

3. Representative discussions include: Li Ling 李零, *Jianbo gushu yu xueshu yuanliu* 簡帛古書與學術源流 (Beijing: Sanlian, 2004), 198; William G. Boltz, "The Composite Nature of Early Chinese Texts," in *Text and Ritual in Early China*, ed. Martin Kern (Seattle: University of Washington Press, 2006), 50–78; Paul Fischer, "Authentication Studies (辨偽學) Methodology and the Polymorphous Text Paradigm," *Early China* 32 (2008–2009): 1–43; Lai Guolong, "Textual Fluidity and Fixity in Early Chinese Manuscript Culture," *Chinese Studies in History* 50, no. 3 (2017): 172–84; and Du Heng, "The Author's Two Bodies: Paratext in Early Chinese Textual Culture," PhD dissertation, Harvard University, 2018.

4. Allan, *Buried Ideas*, 35.

5. Also Lai, "Textual Fluidity," 178–79. On the imperial library project: Max Jakob Fölster, "The Imperial Collection of the Former Han and the Origins of Philology in China: A Study of the *Bielu*, *Qilüe* and *Han shu Yiwenzhi*," PhD dissertation, Universität Hamburg, 2016. Fölster discusses (e.g., 83–88) how Liu Xiang's editorial reports describe fixing certain texts initially on bamboo strips, and it is uncertain which texts had final versions copied onto silk sheets, complicating Allan's hypothesis. On Warring States texts as early imperial constructs, see also Matthias Richter's *The Embodied Text: Establishing Textual Identity in Early Chinese Manuscripts* (Leiden: Brill, 2013), 1–7; note Richter's caution against presuming the use of bamboo strips explains the composite nature and fluidity of texts in the pre-imperial period: "Manuscript Formats and Textual Structure in Early China," in *Confucius and the Analects Revisited: New Perspectives on Composition, Dating, and Authorship*, ed. Michael Hunter and Martin Kern (Leiden: Brill, 2018), 187–217.

6. For a brief Chinese introduction to the varied meanings of *gu*: Zhu Qixin 朱啟新, "Shuo 'gu'" 說觚, *Wenshi zhishi* 文史知識 2000.9, 65–68. On *gu* beakers in particular: Zhu Fenghan 朱鳳瀚, *Zhongguo qingtongqi zonglun* 中國青銅器綜論 (Shanghai: Shanghai guji, 2009), vol. 1, 243–50.

7. *Lunyu zhushu* 論語註疏, *Shisan jing zhushu* 十三經注疏 (Beijing: Beijing daxue, 2000), 6.88. Passage 6.25 does not appear in the Dingzhou 定州 or P'yongyang (DPRK) 平壤 Han witnesses, nor in the *Lunyu* fragments discovered among the Han strips from northwest China. We await publication of the Anhui University and Wangjiaju 王家咀 Warring States parallels, and the Haihun Hou 海昏侯 Han witness.

8. English translations of *Lunyu* 6.25 often render the word in pinyin, with or without further description (as a ritual vessel, drinking cup, etc.). I follow Sarah Allan's "beaker": *The Shape of the Turtle: Myth, Art, and Cosmos in Early China* (Albany: State University of New York Press, 1991), 134.

9. *Lunyu zhushu* 6.88.

10. Zheng Xuan's commentary to the *Lunyu* has been recovered from medieval Dunhuang and Turfan manuscripts. See: John Makeham, "The Earliest Extant Commentary on *Lunyu*: *Lunyu Zheng shi zhu*," *T'oung Pao* 83, no. 4-5 (1997): 260–99; Wang Su 王素, *Tang xieben Lunyu Zheng shi zhu ji qi yanjiu* 唐寫本論語鄭氏注及其研究 (Beijing: Wenwu, 1991). For a recompilation of Zheng's commentary via received citations, see: Zheng Jing 鄭靜, *Lunyu Zheng shi zhu jishu* 論語鄭氏注輯述 (Taipei: Xuehai, 1981), especially 105, 391.

11. Translation adapted from Makeham, "The Earliest Extant Commentary on *Lunyu*," 291. The Chinese text is a reconstruction, based on both Tang manuscripts and citations preserved in the *Taiping yulan* 太平御覽. Wang, *Tang xieben*, 71–72, nn. 138–39. That Zheng describes Confucius as "carving a beaker" (削觚) implies a malleable medium such as wood, as opposed to casting in bronze. See nn. 16 and 19.

12. *Lunyu zhushu* 6.88.

13. *Lunyu jijie yishu* 論語集解義疏, Congshu jicheng chubian 叢書集成初編, ed. Wang Yunwu 王雲五 (Shanghai: Shangwu, 1937), 3.80.

14. As one further example, Arthur Waley believes Confucius plays with the incongruity between the orthography of the character *gu* 觚 and the object it represents: "A horn-gourd that is neither horn nor gourd! A pretty horn-gourd indeed, a pretty horn-gourd indeed." Arthur Waley, trans., with introduction by Sarah Allan, *The Analects* (London: Everyman, 2000), 112. Like He Yan, Waley takes this incongruity as a political analogy. For a survey of English-language translations and interpretations, see: Wayne Alt, "Ritual and the Social Construction of Sacred Artifacts: An Analysis of *Analects* 6.25," *Philosophy East and West* 55, no. 3 (2005): 461–69.

15. For example, "The Master of Ceremonies washes his hands and the cup, goes up the steps, and raises a *gu* beaker to the principal guest . . ." (主人盥洗升媵觚於賓 . . .), *Yili zhushu* 儀禮注疏, *Shisanjing zhushu* 十三經注疏 (Beijing: Beijing daxue, 2000), 14.301 and 17.356, respectively. Translation adapted from: John Steele, *The I-Li, or Book of Etiquette and Ceremonial: Translated from the Chinese with Introduction, Notes and Plans* (London: Probsthain, 1917), vol. 1, 129 and 159.

16. *Zhou li zhushu* 周禮注疏, *Shisanjing zhushu* 十三經注疏 (Beijing: Beijing daxue, 2000), 41.1334.

17. *Yili zhushu* 15.325; *Zhou li zhushu* 41.1334.

18. For example, *Yili zhushu* 14.298 ("in the modern-script [edition], from this point onward, the *gu* beakers are all (written as) *jue* chalices" [今文從此以下觚皆為爵]).

19. Gansu sheng bowuguan 甘肅省博物館 and Zhongguo kexueyuan kaogu yanjiusuo 中國科學院考古研究所, *Wuwei Han jian* 武威漢簡 (Beijing: Zhonghua, 2005), for example, *Yanli* strips 17 (photographs pl. 11) and 39 (photographs pl. 13). On the Wuwei *Yili* wine paraphernalia: Zhang Guangyu 張光裕, "Cong xinjian cailiao tan *Yili* yinjiu li zhong zhi lisi ji suoyong jiuqi wenti" 從新見材料談儀禮飲酒禮中之醴栖及所用酒器問題, *Wenwu* 2013.12, 67–75; translated in "Terms for Wine Utensils in Drinking Ceremonies Referred to in the *Book of Etiquette and Ceremonial*, Based on Newly Discovered Materials," *Chinese Cultural Relics* 1 (2014): 287–302. Xu Kai 徐鍇 explains, "Originally this character [柧] was a phonetic loan for *gu* (with a horn component) 木 (read 本)" (此字假借觚字). *Shuowen xizhuan* 說文繫傳, *Yingyin Wenyuange Siku quanshu* 影印文淵閣四庫全書, vol. 223 (Taipei: Taiwan shangwu, 1983), 536a. Duan Yucai 段玉裁 likewise claims that "when *gu* (with horn component) became current, *gu* (with wood component) was abandoned" (觚行而柧廢矣). *Shuowen jiezi zhu* 說文解字注 (Shanghai: Shanghai guji, 1981), 268b.

20. The *gu* 柧 on *Yanli* strip 39 is one example where Zheng observes that "in the modern-script [edition], *zhi* is given [here] as *gu* beaker as well" (今文觶又為觚). *Wuwei Han jian*, photographs pl. 13; *Yili zhushu* 15.326.

21. Zheng Xuan believes *gu* is a mistake for *zhi* in the *Zhou li* here, and Jia Gongyan cites the *Han Shi* 韓詩 as additional support for the two peck volume. *Zhou li zhushu* 41.1334.

22. *Shuowen jiezi zhu* 187b. Primarily a dictionary of graphic etymology, *Shuowen* definitions must be treated with caution, as discussed in: Françoise Bottéro and Christoph Harbsmeier, *Chinese Lexicography on Matters of the Heart: An Exploratory Commentary on the* Heart *Radical in* Shuō wén jiě zì 說文解字 (Paris: École des hautes études en sciences sociales, Centre de recherches linguistiques sur l'Asie orientale, 2016), 2–4.

23. *Da Dai liji* 大戴禮記, D. C. Lau, ed., *Da Dai liji zhuzi suoyin* 大戴禮記逐字索引 (Taipei: Taiwan shangwu, 1993), 4.5/30/17-18.

24. Yan Kejun 嚴可均, ed., *Quan Shanggu Sandai Qin Han Sanguo Liuchao wen* 全上三代秦漢三國六朝文 (Shanghai: Zhonghua, 1958), vol. 1, 1005, *Quan Hou Han wen* 全後漢文 99.4. On reading *lu* as *jue*: Gui Fu 桂馥, *Zhapu* 札樸 (Beijing: Zhonghua, 1958), *juan* 8, *Han Chi bei* 韓勅碑, 268; and Wang Niansun 王念孫, *Dushu zazhi* 讀書雜誌 (Shanghai: Shanghai guji, 2014), vol. 5, *Han li shiyi* 漢隸拾遺 2535.

25. *Lunyu* 9.6 and 10.8 may have encouraged this myth as well. Roel Sterckx offers a comprehensive overview of Confucius's relationship to food and drink in *Food, Sacrifice, and Sagehood in Early China* (Cambridge: Cambridge University Press, 2011), "Cenat Confucius," 42–48, esp. 43–44, n. 156, for Confucius's legendary alcohol tolerance, covering the excerpts given later. On attitudes toward wine consumption in early China, see also: Poo Mu-chou, "The Use and Abuse of Wine in Ancient China," *Journal of the Economic and Social History of the Orient* 42, no. 2 (1999): esp. 139–45; Tak Kam Chan, "From Conservatism to Romanticism: Wine

and Prose-Writing from Pre-Qin to Jin," in *Scribes of Gastronomy: Representations of Food and Drink in Imperial Chinese Literature*, ed. Isaac Yue and Siufu Tang (Hong Kong: Hong Kong University Press, 2013), 15–26; Nicholas Morrow Williams, "The Morality of Drunkenness in Chinese Literature of the Third Century CE," in *Scribes of Gastronomy*, 27–44; and Roel Sterckx, "Alcohol and Historiography in Early China," *Global Food History* 1, no. 1 (2015): 13–32.

26. *Nan Cao gong biaozhi jiujin shu* 難曹公表制酒禁書, in Yan, *Quan Shanggu Sandai Qin Han Sanguo Liuchao wen*, vol. 1, 922, *Quan Hou Han wen* 83.8; and partial translations in: Williams, "The Morality of Drunkenness," 31–32; and Eva Yuen-wah Chung, "A Study of 'Shu' (Letters) of the Han Dynasty (206 B.C.–A.D. 220)," PhD dissertation, University of Washington, 1982, 496–98. Other early medieval accounts have Yao and Shun drinking the thousand jars and hundred beakers, while Confucius either has a limitless capacity for wine or cannot tolerate even one peck. For the former: Ge Hong 葛洪 and Yang Mingzhao 楊明照, *Baopuzi waipian jiaojian* 抱朴子外篇校箋 (Beijing: Zhonghua, 1997), vol. 1, *Jiujie* 酒誡, 588; and the latter: *Wei shu* 魏書 (Beijing: Zhonghua, 1974), 48.1088.

27. For example, Cao Zhi's 曹植 *Jiufu* 酒賦, in Yan, *Quan Shanggu Sandai Qin Han Sanguo Liuchao wen*, vol. 2, 1128, *Quan Sanguo wen* 14.2.8. In one amusing anecdote (from Master Huan [Ji]'s 環氏 *Wu ji* 誤紀, cited by Pei Songzhi 裴松之), Zhang Shang's 張尚 use of the phrase "a hundred beakers" offends Sun Hao 孫皓 (r. 264–280), by comparing him—the last emperor of Wu 吳—to Confucius, who did not rule as a king. This led to Zhang's arrest. *Sanguo zhi* 三國志 (Beijing: Zhonghua, 1964), 53.1247.

28. *Lunheng* 論衡, D. C. Lau, ed., *Lunheng zhuzi suoyin* 論衡逐字索引 (Hong Kong: Commercial Press, 1996), 25/105-106/25-14; translation aided by: Alfred Forke, *Lun-Hêng: Philosophical Essays of Wang Ch'ung, Translated from the Chinese and Annotated* (London: Luzac, 1907), part 1, 486–87. In the *Kong congzi* 孔叢子, Zi Gao likewise dismisses this legend about Confucius as having been "invented by a drunkard" (生於嗜酒者). *Kong congzi* 孔叢子, D. C. Lau, ed., *Kong congzi zhuzi suoyin* 孔叢子逐字索引 (Hong Kong: Commercial Press, 1996), 4.2/48/28.

29. Yunchiahn C. Sena, *Bronze and Stone: The Cult of Antiquity in Song Dynasty China* (Seattle: University of Washington Press, 2019), esp. chap. 2; Jeffrey Moser, *Nominal Things: Bronzes in the Making of Medieval China* (Chicago: University of Chicago Press, 2023).

30. Nie Chongyi 聶崇義, *Xinding sanli tu* 新定三禮圖, in 20 *juan*, *Tongzhi tang* 通志堂, 1680 rare book, Harvard University, vol. 2, chap. "Xinding sanli paojue tu juan di shier" (新定三禮匏爵圖卷第十二), 18 (seq. 92). Available online: http://nrs.harvard.edu/urn-3:FHCL:4056721?n=92.

31. Lü Dalin 呂大臨 and Luo Gengweng 羅更翁, eds., *Kaogu tu* 考古圖, in 10 *juan*, early Ming [1368–1464] rare book, Harvard University, vol. 7 (self-titled *Kaogu tu di wu* 考古圖第区), 21 (seq. 192). Available online: http://nrs.harvard.edu/urn-3:FHCL:4795446?n=192. Harvard's microfilm of the Chaling 茶陵 Chen

Yizi 陳翼子 1299 printing also bears this image. See also Lü Dalin 呂大臨 and Yi Zhengtang 亦政堂, eds., *Yi Zhengtang chongxiu Kaogu tu* 亦政堂重修考古圖, 10 *juan*, in Huang Cheng 黃晟, *Sangu tu* 三古圖 (Tiandu: Huangshi Yi Zhengtang jiaokan ben, Qianlong renshen [1752]), vol. 22 (self-titled *Yi Zhengtang chongxiu Kaogu tu juan di wu* 亦政堂重修考古圖卷第⊠), 25 (seq. 1431). Available online: http://nrs.harvard.edu/urn-3:FHCL:4909723?n=1431. Note Lü's musing in his authorial comment: "The *Lunyu* writes, 'the Master has said: a *gu* that is not *gu*-like . . . a *gu* indeed, a *gu* indeed!'—I suspect that this (vessel) is to what he refers" (愚按論語子曰觚不觚觚哉觚哉疑即此也).

32. On Li Gonglin's collection: Robert Harris, "The Artist as Antiquarian: Li Gonglin and His Study of Early Chinese Art," *Artibus Asiae* 55, no. 3/4 (1995): 237–80, esp. 261, for Li's comment on this *gu*, which I follow later. On the *Kaogu tu* and Lü Dalin's intellectual agenda: Jeffrey Moser, "The Ethics of Immutable Things: Interpreting Lü Dalin's *Illustrated Investigations of Antiquity*," *Harvard Journal of Asiatic Studies* 72, no. 2 (December 2012): 259–93.

33. *Shiji* 史記 (Beijing: Zhonghua, 2014), 122.3803; *Han shu* 漢書 (Beijing: Zhonghua, 1964), 90.3646. Both insert *er* 而 in the phrase. Translation after Harris, "The Artist as Antiquarian," 261, see also n. 68. Li calls the flanges *leng* 稜, perhaps an implicit nod to the *Shuowen* gloss of *gu* 觚 with *leng* 棱 (ridges): *Shuowen jiezi zhu* 268b.

34. *Hou Han shu* 後漢書 (Beijing: Zhonghua 1973), 40a.1341. The character given, however, is *gu* 觚, with other minor variants.

35. For example, *Yili zhushu* 14.299. The elephants are not depicted on figure 11.2a, and dubious for figure 11.2b. Robert Harris, in "The Artist as Antiquarian," believes the *Xuanhe bogu tulu* 宣和博古圖錄 depicts the same vessel with clear elephants' bodies (261), referencing "Shang si xiang *gu*" 商四象觚 (Four Elephant *Gu* Beaker of the Shang), though the decorative details and recorded dimensions vary from both figures 11.2a and 11.2b.

36. Zhu, *Zhongguo qingtongqi zonglun*, vol. 1, 243–50; and for a survey of theoretical debates over typology and nomenclature in Chinese archaeology: Anke Hein, "The Problem of Typology in Chinese Archaeology," *Early China* 39 (2016): 21–52.

37. E. Bruce Brooks and A. Taeko Brooks argue that Confucius is aware of this trend in *Lunyu* 6.25, comparing *ren* 仁 to this Shang vessel, with both woefully neglected in Confucius's time. They utilize a pun between *gu* 觚 and *gu* 孤 (orphan, lonely) to support this reading. E. Bruce Brooks and A. Taeko Brooks, *The Original Analects: Sayings of Confucius and His Successors* (New York: Columbia University Press, 1998), 36.

38. Later scholars, such as Chen Mengjia 陳夢家, pursue a similar approach. Chen, for instance, argues that the name *gu* 觚 relates to *hu* 弧 (arc, bending), reflecting the vessels' curving bodies with "bow-like" outlines. Surveyed in: Zhu, *Zhongguo qingtongqi zonglun*, 243.

39. This paucity of inscriptions could be due to the vessel's shape, with limited surface area on its interior. Edward Shaughnessy, *Sources of Western Zhou History: Inscribed Bronze Vessels* (Berkeley: University of California Press, 1991), 128. It might also be the consequence of shifting scribal habits. Maria Khayutina (personal communication) notes that self-identification with particular vessel names becomes prevalent only from the mid-Western Zhou, after the *gu* (as conventionally understood) faded in popularity.

40. This piece was not archaeologically excavated, warranting caution. The transcription of *tong* 銅 follows Ondřej Škrabal (personal communication, March 14, 2018). See: Wu Zhenfeng 吳鎮烽, "Neishi Bofeng tong de chubu yanjiu" 內史亳豐同的初步研究, *Kaogu yu wenwu* 考古與文物 2010.3, 30–33; Wang Zhankui 王占奎, "Dujin suili—Neishi Bo tong" 讀金隨禮——內史亳同, *Kaogu yu wenwu* 2010.3, 34–49; Li Xiaoyan 李小燕 and Jing Zhongwei 井中偉, "Yu bingxing qi ming 'zan' shuo—fuzheng Neishi Bo tong yu *Shangshu Guming* 'tongmao' wenti" 玉柄形器名 "瓚" 說——輔證內史亳同與尚書顧命同瑁問題, *Kaogu yu wenwu* 2012.3, 34–53.

41. A tag from a Han tomb in Yangzhou Pingshan Yangzhichang 揚州平山養殖場 may write *gu wei yi si* 觚笴一笥, though the transcription is contested: Li Junming 李均明 and He Shuangquan 何雙全, *Sanjian jiandu heji* 散見簡牘合輯 (Beijing: Wenwu, 1990), 102; cf. 104 (Hanjiang Huchang 邗江胡場 tomb 5,1066 *bao wei si* 鮑笴笥), and Yangzhou bowuguan 揚州博物館, "Yangzhou Pingshan Yang-zhichang Han mu qingli jianbao" 揚州平山養殖場漢墓清理簡報, *Wenwu* 1 (1987): 30. Škrabal also notes (personal communication, March 16, 2018) the name *gu* 鈲 (with metal component 金) appears, potentially as a loan for *fu* 斧 (axe), for example, Wu Zhenwu 吳振武, "Shi Pingshan Zhanguo Zhongshan wang mu qiwu mingwen zhong de 'gu' he 'siku'" 釋平山戰國中山王墓器物銘文中的 "鈲" 和 "私庫," *Shixue jikan* 史學集刊 1982.3, 68–69. Warring States tomb inventories may offer a fruitful avenue to analyze object names utilizing *gua* 瓜 as phonetic. Liu Guosheng 劉國勝, "Chu sangzang jiandu wenzi shicong" 楚喪葬簡牘文字釋叢, *Guwenzi yanjiu* 古文字研究 25 (2004): 364; Dong Shan 董珊, Xinyang Chu mu qiance suoji de taohu he muhu 信陽楚墓遣策所記的陶壺和木壺, *Jianbo* 簡帛 3 (2008): 29–39.

42. Hein, "Typology in Chinese Archaeology," 39–44, 49–51.

43. Zhu Xi 朱熹, *Lunyu zhangju jizhu* 論語章句集注 (Shanghai: Shijie, 1936), vol. 3, 25.

44. *Zhuzi yulei* 朱子語類, *Yingyin Wenyuange Siku quanshu* 影印文淵閣四庫全書, vol. 700 (Taipei: Taiwan shangwu, 1983), 696b. For prisms, Zhu quotes the phrase "gentlemen carrying *gu*" (操觚之士), which he dates to the Han. He also details how, in the Huaishang region, the lack of paper necessitated wood strips for writing and educating youths even in his day. Yet their prisms were rounded, deviating from ancient norms and realizing Confucius's complaint of "*gu* that are not *gu*-like."

45. Zhu Xi's influence is felt in Jesuit readings of the *Lunyu*, as seen in the *Confucius Sinarum Philosophus*, the first published Latin translation of the *Lunyu*,

where *gu* 觚 is rendered as a "square board" used for writing. Thierry Meynard, SJ, *The Jesuit Reading of Confucius: The First Complete Translation of the Lunyu (1687) Published in the West* (Leiden: Brill, 2015), 236–37, n. 37.

46. *Huainanzi* 淮南子, D. C. Lau, ed., *Huainanzi zhuzi suoyin* 淮南子逐字索引 (Hong Kong: Commercial Press, 1992), 9/78/2; John S. Major, Sarah A. Queen, Andrew Seth Meyer, and Harold D. Roth, with Michael Puett and Judson Murray, *The Huainanzi: A Guide to the Theory and Practice of Government in Early Han China* (New York: Columbia University Press, 2010), 327. Gao You 高誘 comments: "*gu* is a sword's hilt" (觚劍柎). Note also the cognate *gu* 觚 in *Zhuangzi* 莊子 for "a large or solid bone." *Zhuangzi* 莊子, D. C. Lau, ed., *Zhuangzi zhuzi suoyin* 莊子逐字索引 (Hong Kong: Commercial Press, 2000), 3/8/6.

47. For example, Lu Ji's 陸機 (261–303 CE) *Wenfu* 文賦: "He may have grasped the prism and dashed it off lightly, Or may have held the brush in his lips, [his mind] far in the distance" (或操觚以率爾或含毫而邈然). To this, Li Shan 李善 (d. 689 CE) comments: "A *gu* is a wooden board, in the past people used them for writing, like the *jian* strips used today . . ." (觚木之方者古人用之以書猶今之簡也). *Wenxuan* 文選 (Taipei: Yiwen, 1974), 246a; translation adapted from: Stephen Owen, *Readings in Chinese Literary Thought* (Cambridge, MA: Harvard University Press, 1992), 117. Ji Kang's 嵇康 (223–262 CE) *Nan Zhang Liaoshu ziran hao xue lun* 難張遼叔自然好學論 gives "grasp brushes and clutch prisms" (*caobi zhigu* 操筆執觚) instead in allusion to study. Yan, *Quan Shanggu Sandai Qin Han Sanguo Liuchao wen*, vol. 2, 1336, *Quan Sanguo wen* 50.6.

48. *Shuowen jiezi zhu* 360a.

49. For the use of *gu* prisms in study: Momiyama Akira 籾山明, "Xiaoyi, gu, shishu" 削衣觚史書, in *Yingguo guojia tushuguan cang Sitanyin suo huo weikan Han wen jiandu* 英國國家圖書館藏斯坦因所獲未刊漢文簡牘, ed. Wang Tao 汪濤, Hu Pingsheng 胡平生, and Wu Fangsi 吳芳思 (Shanghai: Shanghai cishu, 2007), 93–98; Wang Lunxin 王倫信, "'Gu'yu jiandu shidai de xizi cailiao" "觚"與簡牘時代的習字材料, *Jichu jiaoyu* 基礎教育 8, no. 6 (2011): 120–24.

50. *Xijing zaiji* 西京雜記, Zhongguo yeshi jicheng xubian 中國野史集成續編 (Chengdu: Bashu, 2000), 3.568–69.

51. Zhang Chuanguan 張傳官, *Jijiu pian jiaoli* 急就篇校理 (Beijing: Zhonghua, 2017), 5.

52. "Cang Jie created writing, and taught it to later generations. Young children, receive his instructions, and heed them with utmost care! Exert your energy to reading and chanting, doing so day and night without being excused. If you work to become a scribe, then you will tally records and govern. You will rise in the ranks and surpass the rest, distinguishing yourself as extraordinary. Even if, at first, the labor is toilsome, in the end you will inevitably have what you wish!" (蒼頡作書以教後嗣幼子承詔謹慎敬戒勉力諷誦晝夜勿置苟務成史計會辨治超等軼羣出尤別異初雖勞苦卒必有憙). Although the opening is reconstructed from multiple sources, JYX EPT 50.1 offers a nearly complete version. Zhang Defang 張德芳 et al., *Juyan xin*

jian jishi 居延新簡集釋, 7 vols. (Lanzhou: Gansu wenhua, 2016) [hereafter JYX]. My transcription here is interpretative and not strict.

53. Zhang, *Jijiu pian jiaoli*, 15.

54. For an example of the *Cang Jie pian* on a prism, see Jiandu zhengli xiaozu 簡牘整理小組, ed., *Juyan Han jian* 居延漢簡, 4 vols. (Taipei: Zhongyang yanjiuyuan lishi yanjiusuo, 2014–17) [hereafter JY], 9.1 on vol. 1, 28–29, and figure 11.3a. For the *Jijiu pian* on a prism, see Gansu sheng wenwu kaogu yanjiusuo 甘肅省文物考古研究所, *Dunhuang Han jian* 敦煌漢簡, 2 vols. (Beijing: Zhonghua, 1991) [hereafter DHHJ], 1972 on photographs pl. 185. For an unidentified character book on a prism, see DHHJ, 639 on pl. 138; or Zhang Defang 張德芳, *Dunhuang Majuawan Han jian jishi* 敦煌馬圈灣漢簡集釋 (Lanzhou: Gansu wenhua, 2013), 280–81. Wu Ran 吳然 surveys specimens of prisms in "Handai jiandu zhong de gu 漢代簡牘中的觚," MA thesis, Shoudu shifan daxue 首都師範大學, 2013.

55. Wang Guowei 王國維 cautions that the precise shape of *gu* prisms is uncertain, yet follows Yan Shigu's *Jijiu pian* commentary in imagining character books written on six- or eight-sided pieces. Hu Pingsheng 胡平生 and Ma Yuehua 馬月華 turn to archaeological finds to describe *gu* as cylindrical wooden rods, with three to eight leveled surfaces for writing. Wu Ran 吳然 further specifies that *gu* sides must be of the same approximate width and adjoining. Wang Guowei 王國維, Hu Pingsheng 胡平生, and Ma Yuehua 馬月華, *Jiandu jianzhi kao jiaozhu* 簡牘檢置考校注 (Shanghai: Shanghai guji, 2004), 66–69; Wu Ran, *Handai jiandu zhong de gu*, 4–5. Also: Zheng Youguo 鄭有國, *Zhongguo jianduxue zonglun* 中國簡牘學總論 (Shanghai: Huadong shifan daxue, 1989), 29–30; Lin Jianming 林劍鳴, *Jiandu gaishu* 簡牘概述 (Xi'an: Shaanxi renmin, 1984), 40; Pian Yuqian 駢宇騫 and Duan Shu'an 段書安, *Ershi shiji chutu jianbo zongshu* 二十世紀出土簡帛綜述 (Beijing: Wenwu, 2006), 53–55; and Cheng Pengwan 程鵬萬, *Jiandu goshu gezhi yanjiu* 簡牘帛書格式研究 (Shanghai: Shanghai guji, 2017), 15–7.

56. On the complexities of classifying writing supports: Thies Staack, "Single- and Multi-Piece Manuscripts in Early Imperial China: On the Background and Significance of a Terminological Distinction," *Early China* 41 (2018): 245–95.

57. This alleviates concerns over medieval claims that *gu* prisms have at least six sides (e.g., Yan Shigu and Zhu Xi), whereas most Han pieces are three- or four-sided. Cf. Xu Kai, *Shuowen jiezi xizhuan*, 536a on *gu* 觚: "Character books say a *gu* consists of three edge(d faces)" (字書曰三棱為觚).

58. On the relationship of *gu* to *yue* 籥 and *shan* 笘, as well as variants like *gu* 觚: Wang, *Jiandu jianzhi kao jiaozhu*, 66–67. See n. 64 in this chapter for *fang* 方.

59. DHHJ 2193 includes the *Jijiu pian* opening on a *du* 牘 board. Images available on the International Dunhuang Project website, idp.bl.org, as T.XXVIII.3. The opening is also painted on Eastern Han tomb ceilings, for example: Dingzhou shi wenwu guanlisuo 定州市文物管理所, "Dingzhou shi 35 hao Han mu qingli jianbao" 定州市 35 號漢墓清理簡報, *Wenwu Chunqiu* 文物春秋 1997.3, 35–37.

Practice writing and study transposed primers onto other strip formats, while the latter example is the use of the *Jijiu pian* as an alternative counting system.

60. Michael Loewe, "Some Notes on Han-Time Documents from Tun-Huang," *T'oung Pao* 50 (1963): 155–57; "Some Military Despatches of the Han Period," *T'oung Pao* 51 (1964): 335–54, especially 336, n. 1.

61. Consider the triangular "roof ridge" 屋脊-shaped pieces, for example: Hunan sheng wenwu kaogu yanjiusuo 湖南省文物考古研究所, *Liye Qin jian* 里耶秦簡 (Beijing: Wenwu, 2012), 8-762, vol. 1, photographs 110.

62. Wu Ran surveys approximately 150 different pieces that may be *gu* prisms, all from Han archaeological contexts, in *Handai jiandu zhong de gu*, 51–53.

63. Certain pieces—often called *gu* today—have multiple slanted faces on the recto but are otherwise level on the verso, forming a semicircular cross section, for example: *Liye Qin jian*, 8-1588, vol. 1, photographs 210; Hubei sheng wenwu kaogu yanjiu yuan 湖北省文物考古研究院 and Yunmeng xian bowuguan 雲夢縣博物館, "Hubei Yumeng xian Zhengjiahu mudi 2021 nian fajue jianbao" 湖北雲夢縣鄭家湖墓地 2021 年發掘簡報, *Kaogu* 考古 2022.2, 10–12 (figs. 17, 18). Akin to these are arc-shaped bamboo boards with multiple columns of writing, for example: Hubeisheng Jing Sha tielu kaogudui 湖北省荊沙鐵路考古隊, *Baoshan Chu jian* 包山楚簡 (Beijing: Wenwu, 1991), image pl. 121 (CXXI), 1; Sichuan sheng wenwu kaogu yanjiuyuan 四川省文物考古研究院 and Qu xian lishi bowuguan 渠縣歷史博物館, "Sichuan Qu xian Chengba yizhi" 四川渠縣城壩遺址, *Kaogu* 考古 2019.7, 792–93 (fig. 31); and the Western Han specimen from Jiangling Fenghuangshan 江陵鳳凰山, Wu Ran, *Handai jiandu zhong de gu*, 18. Reported but unpublished early *gu* include those from the Peking University Qin collection (M-015) and Tuzishan 兔子山 (J86:1): Beijing daxue chutu wenxian yanjiusuo 北京大學出土文獻研究所, "Beijing daxue cang Qin jiandu gaishu" 北京大學藏秦簡牘概述, *Wenwu* 文物, 2012.6, 69 (M-015); Tuzishan kaogudui 兔子山考古隊, "Hunan Yiyang Tuzishan yizhi fajue chengguo 湖南益陽兔子山遺址發掘成果," The Institute of Archaeology CASS website, March 24, 2014, http://kaogu.cssn.cn/zwb/xccz/201403/t20140324_3928891.shtml.

64. Wu Ran relies on questionable evidence, however, to argue for this in *Handai jiandu zhong de gu*, 10. In the Western Han Yinqueshan 銀雀山 strips, a fragmentary line of a military treatise urges: "On the eve of battle, write out a *gu* prism" (將戰書柧) (n.b. the variant *gu* 柧). Wu Jiulong 吳九龍, *Yinqueshan Han jian shiwen* 銀雀山漢簡釋文 (Beijing: Wenwu, 1985), 35–36, 0446. Wu Ran believes this text was composed in the generation prior. Wu further argues that the Shuihudi 睡虎地 *Qin lü shibazhong* 秦律十八種 mention of *fang* 方 (squared board) refers to *gu* prisms. Shuihudi Qin mu zhujian zhengli xiaozu 睡虎地秦墓竹簡整理小組, *Shuihudi Qin mu zhujian* 睡虎地秦墓竹簡 (Beijing: Wenwu, 1990), strips 131–32, photographs 25, transcriptions 50–51; cf. Staack, "Single- and Multi-Piece Manuscripts in Early Imperial China," 7, n. 17. On *fang* as *gu*, recall Zhu Xi's (n. 44) and Li Shan's (n. 47) comments. Li Xian's 李賢 (655–684 CE) *Hou*

Han shu commentary and Pei Yin's 裴駰 *Shiji jijie* 史記集解 gloss *gu* with *fang*. *Hou Han shu* 27.938; *Shiji* 122.3804. Luo Zhenyu 羅振玉 argued that three-sided *gu* prisms, such as DHHJ 1972, were made by splitting a rectangular *fang* board: Luo Zhenyu 羅振玉 and Wang Guowei 王國維, *Liusha zhuijian* 流沙墜簡 (Beijing: Zhonghua, 1993), 79–82; followed by Tsuen-Hsuin Tsien, *Written on Bamboo and Silk: The Beginnings of Chinese Books and Inscriptions*, 2nd ed. (Chicago: University of Chicago Press, 2004), 122.

65. Kim Kyung-ho, "A Study of Excavated Bamboo and Wooden-Strip *Analects*: The Spread of Confucianism and Chinese Script," *Sungkyun Journal of East Asian Studies* 11, no. 1 (2011): 72–74; Dai Weihong 戴衛紅, *Hanguo mujian yanjiu* 韓國木簡研究 (Guilin: Guangxi shifan daxue, 2017), 37–40, 240–41; Kongnip Changwŏn munhwajae yŏn'gu 國立昌原文化財研究所, *Han'guk ŭi kodae mokkan* 韓國의古代木簡 (Seoul: Yemaek ch'ulp'ansa, 2004), 144–49. For the excavation reports, Kim and Dai cite [not seen by this author]: Pusan Taehakkyo Pangmulgwan 釜山大學校博物館, "Kimhae Ponghwang-dong ch'ŏsŏpiji yujŏk" 金海鳳凰洞低濕地遺蹟, in *Pusan Taehakkyo Pangmulgwan yŏn'gu ch'ongsŏ* 釜山大學校博物館研究叢書 33 (Pusan: Pusan Taehakkyo Pangmulgwan, 2007), 1–93; and Yi Hyŏng-gu 李亨求, *Kyeyang sansŏng palgul pogosŏ* 桂陽山城發掘調查報告書 (Ch'ungch'ŏng-namdo Asan: Sŏnmun taehakkyo kogo yŏn'guso and Inchŏn Kyeyang-gu Office, 2008), respectively.

66. Kim, "A Study of Excavated Bamboo and Wooden-Strip *Analects*," 76–77; Tokushimaken Maizoo Bunkazai Senta 德島県埋蔵文化財センタ, ed., *Kannonji iseki (I): Kannonji iseki mokkan hen* 観音寺遺跡 (I): 観音寺遺跡木簡篇, *Tokushimaken Maizo Bunkazai Senta Chosa Hokokusho* 德島県埋蔵文化財センター調査報告書, No. 40 (Tokushima: Tokushimaken kyōiku iinkai, 2002), strip 77, 118–30 and front pl. 12, with accompanying article, esp. 193–204.

67. Wu, *Handai jiandu zhong de gu*, 20–42; also Xue Yingqun 薛英群, *Juyan Han jian tonglun* 居延漢簡通論 (Lanzhou: Gansu jiaoyu, 1991), 135–36.

68. Loewe, "Some Notes on Han-Time Documents from Tun-Huang," 155–57; "Some Military Despatches of the Han Period," 335–54. Of the 148 prisms surveyed by Wu Ran, Wu classifies 128 as administrative documents, with 5 others deemed practice writing on discarded administrative documents. *Handai jiandu zhong de gu*, 21.

69. Wu, *Handai jiandu zhong de gu*, 23–30. Separating prisms into "administrative documents" and "study materials" is not always straightforward. Consider the seven-sided Yumen Huahai 玉門花海 prism (DHHJ 1448), which bears a testamentary edict and personal letter. Although lacking repetition of characters or phrases, a hallmark of practice writing elsewhere, the incongruity of its texts, along with mistakes in handwriting, suggest the prism was produced during study. A similar dilemma arises when differentiating "models" from "exercises." Christopher J. Foster, "Writing Beyond Han Boundaries: A Scribal Primer at the Niya Site," in *Saved from Desert Sands: Re-discovering Objects on the Silk Roads*, ed. Imre Galambos and Kelsey Granger (Leiden: Brill, forthcoming). On strips used to study *Cang Jie*

pian and *Jijiu pian* more generally: Hsing I-tien 邢義田, "Handai *Cang Jie, Jijiu,* bati he shishu wenti—zai lun Qin Han guanli ruhe xuexi wenzi" 漢代蒼頡急就八體和史書問題——再論秦漢官吏如何學習文字, *Guwenzi yu gudaishi* 古文字與古代史 2009.2, 429–68.

70. Wang, *Jiandu jianzhi kao jiaozhu*, 69; Tsien, *Written on Bamboo and Silk*, 122; cf. Luo Zhenyu 羅振玉, *Liusha zhuijian*, 81–82, on the possibility certain prisms were laid down upon a surface instead. Some specimens have bottoms whittled to a point, for instance, DHHJ 639, which would prevent it from balancing on a firm surface. The point could anchor the prism into a soft surface, like sand, but with writing so close to the bottom, I question the feasibility of this, without obscuring the text.

71. Momiyama, "Xiaoyi, gu, shishu"; Wang, "'Gu' yu jiandu shidai de xizi cailiao," 120–24.

72. Momiyama thus associates "shavings"—thin pieces cut off from the wood's surface to erase text—with students practicing writing on prisms. For a collection of shavings: Wang Tao 汪濤, Hu Pingsheng 胡平生, and Wu Fangsi 吳芳思, eds., *Yingguo guojia tushuguan cang Sitanyin suo huo weikan Han wen jiandu* 英國國家圖書館藏斯坦因所獲未刊漢文簡牘 (Shanghai: Shanghai cishu, 2007) [hereafter YT].

73. Wang, "'Gu' yu jiandu shidai de xizi cailiao," 122–23.

74. Liang Jing 梁靜, *Chutu Cang Jie pian yanjiu* 出土蒼頡篇研究 (Beijing: Kexue, 2015), chap. 3, sec. 2, also published in "Lüli shushi ben *Cang Jie pian* diwu liu zhang de yanjiu" 閭里書師本蒼頡篇第五六章的研究, *Jianbo* 簡帛 2014.9, 281–86; Bai Junpeng 白軍鵬, "*Cang Jie pian* de liangzhong Han dai banben ji xiangguan wenti yanjiu" 蒼頡篇的兩種漢代版本及相關問題研究, *Wenxian* 文獻 2015.3, 41–49; Zhou Fei 周飛, "Chutu *Cang Jie pian* banben tantao" 出土蒼頡篇版本探討, *Chutu wenxian* 出土文獻 2016.8, 190–200.

75. *Han shu* 30.1721. The *Cang Jie* 蒼頡, *Yuanli* 爰歷, and *Boxue* 博學 supposedly were composed during the Qin dynasty, by Li Si 李斯, Zhao Gao 趙高, and Huwu Jing 胡毋敬, respectively. The *Han shu* "Yiwen zhi" reports the three works entailed twenty chapters in total.

76. Fuyang Han jian zhenglizu 阜陽漢簡整理組, "Fuyang Han jian *Cang Jie pian*" 阜陽漢簡蒼頡篇, *Wenwu* 文物 1983.2, 24–34; Zhongguo jiandu jicheng bianji weiyuanhui 中國簡牘集成編輯委員會, ed., *Zhongguo jiandu jicheng* 中國簡牘集成 (Lanzhou: Dunhuang wenyi, 2001+), vol. 14, 295–313, and vol. 18, 1655–74 [hereafter FY]. N.b.: Discrepancies exist in the data. For clarification: Christopher J. Foster, "Study of the *Cang Jie pian*: Past and Present," PhD dissertation, Harvard University, 2017, 145–46, n. 78. The Fuyang manuscript was entombed with Xiahou Zao 夏侯竈 (d. 165 BCE). For the Peking University manuscript: Beijing daxue chutu wenxian yanjiusuo 北京大學出土文獻研究所, ed., *Beijing daxue cang Xi Han zhushu* 北京大學藏西漢竹書, vol. 1 (Shanghai: Shanghai guji, 2015) [hereafter PKU]. The PKU manuscript is unprovenanced, which complicates its dating. The editors date the collection to the mid-Western Han, from Emperor Xuan's reign or

prior, and Zhu Fenghan believes the *Cang Jie pian* manuscript likely dates no later than approximately 100 BCE. On the dating: Zhu Fenghan 朱鳳瀚, "Beida Han jian *Cang Jie pian* gaishu" 北大漢簡蒼頡篇概述, *Wenwu* 2011.6, 59; with survey of arguments in Foster, "Study of the *Cang Jie pian*," 162, n. 197, and 183–85. It is possible content was composed earlier still: Bai, "*Cang Jie pian* de liangzhong Han dai banben ji xiangguan wenti yanjiu," 43. The FY and (presumably) PKU manuscripts come from burials in central China, whereas most witnesses of later *Cang Jie pian* editions were collected among watchtowers and forts along the Han northwest frontier (the Shuiquanzi 水泉子 and perhaps "Han board" witnesses being major exceptions). Differences in editions may reflect not just chronological developments but also their use "on the ground." For surveys of secondary scholarship on *Cang Jie pian* manuscripts: Foster, "Study of the *Cang Jie pian*," 61–169; Zhou Fei 周飛, "*Cang Jie pian* zonghe yanjiu" 蒼頡篇綜合研究, PhD dissertation, Tsinghua University, 2017, 1–18.

77. The FY manuscript is extremely fragmentary. Hu Pingsheng 胡平生 and Han Ziqiang 韓自強 note three strips bear significant empty space underneath the writing, implying a chapter break: FY C038, C056, and C061. "*Cang Jie pian* de chubu yanjiu" 蒼頡篇的初步研究, *Wenwu* 2 (1983): 38. Zhou Fei argues that there is also a chapter break at FY C041 and shows that C041, C056, and C061 all match content which concludes chapters in the PKU witness. Zhou moreover sees a punctuation mark on C044, which correlates to the beginning of a PKU chapter. "Chutu *Cang Jie pian* banben tantao," 196. N.b.: There is edition-level variation between the FY and PKU texts too. For example, the FY manuscript lacks the lines from PKU 8-9 on the subjugation of the Hu, Rong, Di, and Yue. The manipulation of this content is suspicious and may be a later editorial insertion with political implications.

78. Transcriptions follow Zhu Fenghan's strict readings, with slight modification. The opening lines, in {}, are not extant on the PKU manuscript. For their reconstruction: Zhang Cunliang 張存良, "*Cang Jie pian* yandu xianqin (yi)—Beida jian *Shanglu* zhang zhuibu" 蒼頡篇研讀獻芹(一)——北大簡賞祿章綴補, Wuhan daxue jianbo yanjiu zhongxin, November 24, 2015, http://www.bsm.org.cn/?hanjian/6532.html. The incomplete "Han United" chapter is extended, in {}, by FY C004 and SQZ C018 (n. 80 for reference). The PKU 1-11 verso lines show that this manuscript positioned "Award Emoluments" and "Han United" consecutively.

79. Dated strips in the Dunhuang and Juyan collections range from 111 BCE (DHHJ 1298) or 100 BCE (JYX EJT 4.107), to 152 CE (DHHJ 1447) or perhaps even 162 CE (JY 551.32). For an overview: Hu Yongpeng 胡永鵬, "Xibei biansai Han jian biannian ji xiangguang wenti yanjiu" 西北邊塞漢簡編年及相關問題研究, PhD dissertation, Jilin daxue, 2016.

80. Hsing I-tien classifies JY 9.1 as a model textbook, and not practice writing where titling could be idiosyncratic or absent: "Handai *Cang Jie, Jijiu*, bati he shishu wenti," 446. Other pieces write the lines that straddle between the PKU

"Award Emoluments" and "Han United" chapters consecutively without signaling a division, for instance, YT 2879, but lack punctuation or paratext signaling chapter identity. The Shuiquanzi 水泉子 *Cang Jie pian* offers a more complicated example, as this manuscript bears chapter character counts and does not include a count before the "Han United" opening line on SQZ C011, which accords with JY 9.1 and the Village Teachers edition. Zhang Cunliang 張存良, "Shuiquanzi Han jian *Cang Jie pian* zhengli yu yanjiu" 水泉子漢簡蒼頡篇整理與研究, PhD dissertation, Lanzhou daxue, 2015 [hereafter SQZ]. For SQZ C011 image: "Shuiquanzi Han jian qiyanben *Cang Jie pian* lice" 水泉子漢簡七言本蒼頡篇蠡測, *Chutu wenxian yanjiu* 出土文獻研究 2010.9, pl. 9, temp. 14; transcriptions after Hu Pingsheng 胡平生, "Du Shuiquanzi Han jian qiyanben *Cang Jie pian*" 讀水泉子漢簡七言本蒼頡篇, Fudan daxue chutu wenxian yu guwenzi yanjiu zhongxin, January 21, 2010, http://fdgwz.org.cn/Web/Show/1064. There is, however, evidence that character counts and/or chapter divisions were not recorded consistently in the SQZ witness, for example, C013 and C068. On this, also: Liang Jing, *Chutu Cang Jie pian yanjiu*, 90.

81. Recall Momiyama's association of shavings to *gu* prisms. On the location of these shavings: Zhang Defang 張德芳 and Hao Shusheng 郝樹聲, "Sitanyin dierci Zhongya tanxian suohuo Dunhuang Han jian weikan bufen ji qi xiangguan wenti" 斯坦因第二次中亞探險所獲敦煌漢簡未刊部分及其相關問題, in *Yingguo guojia tushuguan cang Sitanyin suohuo weikan Han wen jiandu*, 76–80.

82. Zhou Fei, "Chutu Cang Jie pian banben tantao," 199.

83. DHHJ 639 and DHHJ 562, both from Majuanwan 馬圈灣, offer intriguing examples of triangle marks. The former is a sixty-character unit on a four-sided *gu* prism, headed by the triangle. The latter has the triangle midway down a strip and also carries *jiu* 九 (nine) on its verso (a numerical title, strip label, practice writing, or something else?). It is unclear if either relates to the *Cang Jie pian* or another primer, for instance, on the former: Hu Pingsheng 胡平生, "Yingguo guojia tushuguan cang Sitanyin suohuo jiandu zhong de *Cang Jie pian* canpian yanjiu" 英國國家圖書館藏斯坦因所獲簡牘中的蒼頡篇殘片研究, in *Yingguo guojia tushuguan cang Sitanyin suohuo weikan Han wen jiandu*, 66–67.

84. On these shavings, the punctuation does not always fall at the top of the piece, with writing evident above them. In practice writing, the size, spacing, number of characters per column, and so forth, was not necessarily regulated, shifting the placement of the punctuation vis-à-vis the writing support.

85. Zhang Cunliang and Ju Hong 巨虹 suggest *chen*: Zhang Cunliang 張存良 and Ju Hong 巨虹, "*Yingguo guojia tushuguan cang Sitanyin suohuo Han wen jiandu weikan* bufen" 英國國家圖書館藏斯坦因所獲漢文簡牘未刊部分, *Wenwu* 2016.6, 79. Zhang Chuanguan's 張傳官 re-piecing of YT 1814+1809, in light of Zhang and Ju's transcription, could complicate the discussion: "Yingguo guojia tushuguan cang Cang Jie pian canjian pinhe shi ze" 英國國家圖書館藏蒼頡篇殘簡拼合十則, *Han yuyan wenzi yanjiu* 漢語言文字研究 2018.2, 114–15; accepted by Liu Wanling 劉婉玲, "Chutu *Cang Jie pian* wenben zhengli ji zibiao" 出土蒼頡篇文本整理及字

表, MA thesis, Jilin University, 2018, 139 and n. 2. The writing on these pieces, unfortunately, is mostly illegible.

86. Another example of this phenomenon pertains to the PKU *Zhuan Xu* 顓頊 (Lord Zhuan Xu) chapter, on PKU 46-52, the only complete chapter in the PKU witness. On YT 2674, punctuation precedes *zhuan* 顓 and the top of *xu* 頊. The characters before the punctuation are partial, but the first appears to be from 貝 and the second from 肉. The fifty-ninth and sixtieth characters of PKU "Lord Zhuan Xu" are *benda* 賁達; however, elsewhere in the YT shavings *da* is replaced with *tuo* 脫. Wang Ning 王寧, "Beida Han jian *Cang Jie pian* du zha (xia)" 北大漢簡蒼頡篇讀札 (下), Fudan daxue chutu wenxian yu guwenzi yanjiu zhongxin, March 7, 2016, http://fdgwz.org.cn/Web/Show/2747. As supplemental evidence, consider DHHJ 1836, where punctuation heads the lines following *benda*; and SQZ C077, where a character count follows *benda*.

87. DHHJ 1836 and base text of the SQZ witness attest to the Village Teachers edition on other media besides *gu* and shavings, namely, bamboo and wood strips. Note also that in 2019, a privately held *Cang Jie pian* manuscript was published. It writes one sixty-character chapter per board, in three columns of twenty characters, with numerical titles. The manuscript, however, awaits proper authentication. Liu Huan 劉桓, *Xin jian Han du Cang Jie pian Shi pian jiaoshi* 新見漢牘蒼頡篇史篇校釋 (Beijing: Zhonghua, 2019); Christopher J. Foster, "Further Considerations for the Authentication of the Peking University *Cang Jie pian*: With Brief Digression on the So-Called 'Han Board' Witness," *Early China* 44 (2021): 419–64; updating "Introduction to the Peking University Han Bamboo Strips: On the Authentication and Study of Purchased Manuscripts," *Early China* 40 (2017): 167–239.

88. Hu Pingsheng, "Yingguo guojia tushuguan cang Sitanyin suo huo jiandu zhong de *Cang Jie pian* canpian yanjiu," 67–68.

89. For example, DHHJ 2114; Hsing, "Handai *Cang Jie*, *Jijiu*, bati he shishu wenti," 462, nn. 37–38, and 465, n. 40, where Hu is said to abandon his hypothesis; Foster, "Study of the *Cang Jie pian*," 286–88.

90. Wang, *Jiandu jianzhi kao jiaozhu*, 67–69. Wang cites the "Yiwen zhi" on village teachers dividing the *Cang Jie pian* into sixty-character chapters, shows Yang Xiong's 揚雄 *Xunzuan* 訓纂 supplement also had sixty-character chapters, and uses Yan Shigu's *Jijiu pian* commentary to suggest six- or eight-sided prisms carrying eight to ten characters per side.

91. Wang and Luo, *Liusha zhuijian*, 77–78; Lao Gan 勞榦, "*Cang Jie pian* yu *Jijiu pian* wen" 蒼頡篇與急就篇, in *Juyan Han jian* 居延漢簡 (Taipei: Zhongyang yanjiuyuan lishi yuyan yanjiusuo, 1960), vol. 4, chap. *Kaozheng* 考證, 76.

92. For example, *Daozhe* 盜者 (Thieves) on Shuihudi Qin *Rishu* A 甲 69–70 (versos).

93. Recall the text opens with "Cang Jie created writing" (蒼頡作書), however no extant manuscripts are explicitly titled *Cang Jie* 蒼頡. Sun Xingyan 孫星衍, *Cang Jie pian* 倉頡篇, in *Congshu jicheng chubian* 叢書集成初編 (Beijing:

Zhonghua, 1985–1991), vol. 105, foreword, 1–2; Wang Guowei 王國維, "*Cang Jie pian* canjian ba" 蒼頡篇殘簡跋, in *Guantang Jilin (wai er zhong)* 觀堂集林(外二種), Ershi shiji Zhongguo shixue mingzhu 二十世紀中國史學名著 (Shijiazhuang: Hebei jiaoyu, 2001), vol. 5, 126.

94. Bai Junpeng agrees, as PKU chapter openings were often transposed in the Village Teachers edition, rendering content titles unhelpful: "*Cang Jie pian* de liangzhong Han dai banben ji xiangguan wenti yanjiu," 47; also Lin Suqing 林素清, "*Cang Jie pian* yanjiu" 蒼頡篇研究, *Hanxue yanjiu* 漢學研究 5, 1987.1, 64.

95. Yan Shigu's comment that medieval textbooks were still called "wooden *gu* prism chapters" (木觚章), supports this theory. If prisms were bound together, it was likely via a cord running through a single hole in the upper margin (e.g., potentially DHHJ 1972). N.b.: Luo Zhenyu wonders if the hole on DHHJ 1972 allowed it to be tied to another piece, restoring an original *fang* pair. *Liusha zhuijian*, 81–82; and n. 64 in this chapter.

96. For example, the chapter division between *cuo* 痤 and chen 疢 isolates the rhyme (completed by *kai* 欬) and separates vocabulary concerned with medical ailments.

97. Chapter order fluidity is difficult to ascertain for early *Cang Jie pian* editions. The "Yiwen zhi" hints at fluidity when it claims village teachers unified what was originally three separate texts (*Cang Jie, Yuanli,* and *Boxue*); however, the PKU "Award Emoluments" to "Han United" order is maintained in the Village Teachers edition, likely not a coincidence.

98. This is not to imply that chapter order was finalized with the Village Teachers edition. The *Han shu* "Yiwen zhi" and *Sui shu* 隋書 "Jingji zhi" 經籍志 document a long history of rearrangements, supplements, and commentaries to the *Cang Jie pian.* For example, Wang Yinglin's 王應麟 (1223–1296) *Jijiu pian* postface claims the *Cang Jie* concluded with the "Han United" chapter, Yan Zhitui 顏之推 (531–591 CE) seemingly quotes the "Han United" opening with additions, and the *Fashu yaolu* 法書要錄 describes those additions as being in the ninth chapter. For details: Foster, "Study of the *Cang Jie pian*," 57–58, n. 110.

99. *Han shu* 30.1721.

100. Fukuda, *Setsubun izen shogakusho no kenkyo,* esp. 136–54.

101. Four-character lines appear once in the opening, then again throughout the thirty-second chapter.

102. N.b.: The *Jijiu pian* rhyme schemes and vocabulary units still transect chapter divisions.

103. DHHJ 2185, which appears to be a *jian* strip, also has the title "Thirteenth" 第十三.

104. See n. 95 in this chapter.

105. *Shuowen jiezi zhu,* 758b; *Han shu* 30.1719–21. Also: *Lunheng* (Lau, *Lunheng zhuzi suoyin*) 39/186/6 and *Fayan* 法言, D. C. Lau, ed., *Fayan zhuzi suoyin* 法言逐字索引 (Hong Kong: Commercial Press, 1995), 2/4/27.

106. The Zhangjiashan *Shilü* describes how scribal students were tested on "the fifteen volumes" (十五篇), while the *Shuowen* labels this corpus as the *Zhou shu* 籀書 instead. Both the *Shuowen* postface and *Han shu* "Yiwen zhi," moreover, describe the *Shi Zhou pian* in "fifteen volumes." *Shuowen jiezi zhu* 758b; *Han shu* 30.1719; Zhangjiashan ersiqihao Han mu zhujian zhengli xiaozu 張家山二四七號漢墓竹簡整理小組, *Zhangjiashan Han mu zhujian [ersiqihao mu]* 張家山漢墓竹簡[二四七號] (Beijing: Wenwu, 2001), 203–04 (strips 475–76); Zhangjiashan ersiqihao Han mu zhujian zhengli xiaozu, *Zhangjiashan Han mu zhujian [ersiqihao mu]* (*shiwen xiuding ben*) 張家山漢墓竹簡 [二四七號墓] (釋文修訂本) (Beijing: Wenwu, 2006), 80–81; Anthony J. Barbieri-Low and Robin D. S. Yates, *Law, State, and Society in Early Imperial China: A Study with Critical Edition and Translation of the Legal Texts from Zhangjiashan Tomb No. 247* (Leiden: Brill, 2015), vol. 2, 1084–111, especially *Shilü* 2 (1092–1093); and Foster, "Study of the *Cang Jie pian*," chap. 4, sec. 4.2, 238–48.

107. The still unpublished Shuihudi 睡虎地 Han *Shilü* may shed further light on the title *Shi Zhou pian* among these statutes. For the latest report: Xiong Beisheng 熊北生, Chen Wei 陳偉, and Cai Dan 蔡丹, "Hubei Yunmeng Shuihudi 77 hao Xi Han mu chutu jiandu gaishu" 湖北雲夢睡虎地 77 號西漢墓出土簡牘概述, *Wenwu* 2018.3, 43–53.

12

Sanjiaowei M1

Hand Tools from the Grave of a
Hobbyist Woodworker?

CHARLES SANFT

Introduction

When Wang Chong 王充 (27–97 CE) wanted to make a point in *Lunheng* 論衡 about clerks whose engagement with text did not extend to classical learning, he drew an analogy to people who labored with their hands:

> Those able to hew and carve pillars and rafters I call woodworkers; those able to bore and drill grottoes and pits I call earthworkers; and those able to adorn and embellish documents and texts I call *scribeworkers*.[1] The learning of documentary officers concerns learning to handle documents. They should be classed with workers in wood and earth. How could they be measured alongside classicists?

> 能斲削柱梁, 謂之木匠; 能穿鑿穴坥, 謂之土匠; 能彫琢文書, 謂之史匠. 夫文吏之學, 學治文書也, 當與木土之匠同科, 安得程於儒生哉?[2]

My thanks to Shi Jie, who provided advice and articles that helped me in preparing this essay, and Huang Yiyun, who verified some of the numbers I use.

Although Wang Chong does not make this point, at least not explicitly, he may have meant this a bit more literally than it might appear. The work of early clerks could include the preparation of wooden writing media and thus the labor of making them. An extravagant Warring States grave at Xinyang 信陽 (Henan), in the former Chu 楚 region, shows this. It produced writing strips, clerk's knives, and woodworking tools in a case. An adze, a saw, and a number of different knives, along with a writing brush, formed a small kit for use in preparing strips and writing.[3] This reflects woodworking of a particular, limited sort. But Wang Chong's main interest was in the intellectual abilities of clerks, rather than their contact with sawdust.

Nowadays writers speak—with some complacency—of their work as *craft*.[4] But Wang Chong did not mean to compliment clerks by comparing them to handworkers. Just one step above the merchants (those dregs of the fourfold *simin* 四民 commoner community), skilled makers got little respect in early China. Influential writers of prose such as Jia Yi 賈誼 (201–169 BCE) singled out elaborate handicrafts for criticism, denigrating them as wasteful and harmful to society.[5] As Jia Yi put it: "The people of remarkable skills and frivolous facilities, the merchants and the mooches—their bodies are at ease and their minds grandiose, their intentions bent on unseemly gain and their actions licentious and extravagant" (夫奇巧、末技、商販、遊食之民, 形佚樂而心縣愆, 志苟得而行淫侈).[6] *Ouch.* Jia Yi's writing brush was as sharp as any clerk's knife.

Nonetheless, one need only look at examples of artisans' work, and thanks to the work of archaeologists we have many, to see the creativity and virtuosic abilities they could bring to bear. Wooden objects from Han-dynasty tombs are part of this. Han subjects whose trade was in a handcraft generally worked in an atelier, either a private or a government enterprise.[7] It takes little imagination to see how woodwork might be an outlet for the creative urges of someone whose primary job was something else, just as it can be today. In this chapter, I consider a man who appears to have been such a person, who had both an official position and an appreciation for working with wood.

Han grave M1 was one of the largest of the group of Warring States and Han graves at Sanjiaowei 三角圩, near Tianchang 天長 (Anhui). Its occupants were a man named Huan Ping 桓平 and a woman, presumably his wife, whose name we do not know. Huan Ping was an official and a man of some wealth. He was buried with bronzes and jades, as well as seals and writing implements, although no texts were recovered from the grave.

Incongruously, the Huans' grave also produced a lacquer toolbox that held an extensive set of tools for shaping wood: an axe, adzes, saws, drill bits, chisels, and other tools. The occurrence of this number of tools in the grave of someone who appears to have been an official is unexpected and unparalleled. While we will never know for certain, I suggest the tools were most likely in the grave because Huan Ping liked them.

The Grave

Workers repairing a dike at Zhujian Village 祝澗村, near Tianchang, on December 17, 1991, uncovered a number of coffins some two meters below the surface. After receiving notification of the find, local archaeologists and authorities acted quickly, excavating twenty-two graves within a couple of weeks. A few more graves were dug up in the spring of 1992 and a final pair in the summer of 1997, for a total of twenty-seven. They form the Sanjiaowei tomb group. Twenty-four of the graves produced burial goods of various quantities. The find was the subject of some articles soon after the discovery, but the preliminary archaeological report appeared only in 2010 and the full report in 2013.[8]

A substantial portion of the archaeological report treats the grave M1, which was one of the two largest in scale and which contained the most extensive burial array.[9] In structure M1 was a rectangular tomb chamber, with a north-south alignment and an access tunnel on the southern side. Inside the tomb was a single wooden vault (*guo* 槨) containing two wooden coffins (*guan* 棺) of equal size. The coffins were next to each other, with their heads to the south, on rollers that kept them off the floor. A dividing board within the vault created a single separate chamber at their feet. Based on the numbers of burial objects and unspecified traces of decomposed skeletal remains, the report authors reason that the coffin to the east is that of a male, that to the west of a female. Both coffins contained wooden head-covers (*touzhao* 頭罩), and that of the male was originally decorated with pieces of worked jade, which is also seen in other finds.[10] Both moreover contained bronzes; lacquerware; and objects of wood, horn, and jade. The coffin of the male additionally had in it iron implements, agate objects, and coins. The separate chamber at the foot of the vault contained grave goods in three layers: the first (top) consisting of bronze and lacquer items; the second, bronze, lacquer, and iron, with some of the bronze and iron pieces in lacquer cases; and the third layer of bronze and wood items, along with a smaller number of lacquer objects, some of which contained iron and stone items. Archaeologists did not find any pottery items in this grave.[11]

Sanjiaowei M1 produced nothing bearing a date, making periodization a matter of inference. The bronze mirrors and coins, in conjunction with the characteristics of the grave, however, provide enough information to reliably date the burial, by means of comparison, to the late Western Han period.[12]

The Contents of the Grave

M1 contained a large quantity of burial goods—the most of any grave in the group, and enough to make it a midsized burial among Han graves overall.[13] The array included sixty-two bronzes, sixty iron objects, ninety-three pieces of lacquerware, twenty-three wooden objects, ninety-two jades, seven pieces made from horn, and one agate object and one of another, unspecified stone.[14] A comprehensive discussion of the array would be otiose in this context, but there are some specific things that warrant mention. The seals that were in the grave are the most important of these. They establish the name of the male occupant as Huan Ping and show he was an official.

Three of the seals are bronze. One of them has a plain loop and an intaglio inscription reading "Vassal Ping" (*chen* Ping 臣平). The other two are a pair, each with a loop in the shape of a turtle. The inscriptions, one in relief and the other intaglio, both read, "The personal seal of Huan Ping" (Huan Ping *siyin* 桓平私印).[15] There was also an undecorated jade seal in the grave, with the inscription "The seal of Huan Ping" (Huan Ping *zhi yin* 桓平之印).[16]

A wooden seal (M1:41) from the grave indicates that Huan Ping held an official position. Its inscription reads, in relief, "Guangling huan ye" (廣陵宦謁). The first part is the name of the region of Guangling 廣陵, which was, except for a brief interruption, a princedom (*guo* 國) during late Western Han times.[17] The combination *huan ye* is not attested elsewhere. The authors of the archaeological report make the reasonable suggestion that this is a portmanteau abbreviation for the titles *huanzhe* 宦者 and *yezhe* 謁者. *Yezhe*, "internuncio," presents no problem. *Huanzhe*, however, usually denotes a eunuch, which seems out of place in the grave of a man and his wife. The report authors refer to records in *Han shu* 漢書 to interpret *huanzhe* as a reference to an official under the privy treasurer. They propose that Huan Ping was an official with responsibility for "taxes from mountains, seas, lakes, and swamps" (山海池澤之稅) and for "matters of receiving guests" (賓贊受事)—that is, his tasks combined those of the privy treasury with those of an internuncio.[18]

This interpretation is possible but is not fully satisfying. The uncertainty arises from the authors' treatment of *huanzhe*. Understanding *huanzhe*, and thus *huan*, as they do, relies upon taking *huanzhe* in *Han shu* as a term for a treasury official in contexts where it seems at least equally likely to denote simply a "eunuch" working in the treasury, rather than a specific official post. And since the grave M1 dates to the late Western Han period, it comes from the time when princedoms no longer had their own privy treasuries, at least according to received accounts.[19] It would of course be possible to take this seal as a piece of evidence for reconsidering those accounts, but that would call for more new information than is available. As such, I think a slightly different and more parsimonious explanation is in order.

I propose reading the graph 宦 differently than the report authors do, and not as "eunuch" (*huan*) but rather as "official" (*guan*, usually 官). This is not a transcription error: the photograph of the seal shows the graph to be a very clear 宦.[20] In the context of this grave, though, I suggest this character is a borrowing for *guan* 官, "official," an alternation that is attested in received sources.[21] The seal may thus be understood to say, "Official internuncio of Guangling." However one takes the inscription exactly, the general sense is clear. The seal is evidence that Huan Ping was an official in Guangling. That also fits with the relative wealth of his burial.

The Tools

The very first publications on the Sanjiaowei tomb group mentioned the unprecedented set of tools that archaeologists found in M1. The general types of tools were not unknown. What was new was the recovery of so many tools together in a set. I discuss the tools at length later. For now, it is enough to note that these examples came as a group, and many were very well preserved—to the point that some of the tools' edges and teeth were still sharp.[22]

Archaeologists knew this was a set, not just an accumulation, of tools in part because they were in a case—a plain lacquer toolbox (M1:263).[23] The toolbox was in the foot compartment on the east side, beneath the feet of the male. This is one of the reasons that I associate the tools with Huan Ping in this chapter. There were also knives in the male's coffin, and none in the female's. It is not impossible that the tools belonged to Huan Ping's wife, but it is unlikely enough that I will treat them as his.

The lacquer toolbox itself was damaged but mainly intact. It is rectangular and on a wood core, with straight sides and a flat bottom. The box consists of two parts, cover and body. The cover sits on top of the body, which it overlaps substantially but not completely. As a result, the case with the cover in place is 16.8 cm tall, even though the body is 14.7 cm and the lid 15.6 cm high. The other dimensions of the cover are 71.5 cm by 20.3 cm, and those of the body are 70.1 cm by 18.6 cm. The set consists of an axe-head; two adzes; a spade-shaped slick; a two-edged knife, mounted perpendicularly on its long handle; four saws; eleven chisels; four drill bits; a file; and an awl. There were also four lacquer containers, a wooden stand, and a flat grinding stone inside.

The tools in the box present a number of points for discussion. In many cases, their purposes are clear. There is, for instance, little question about what an adze or an axe is or does, although the design specifics of the examples remain of interest. In a few instances, the identity and/ or precise function of a particular item is uncertain. Some specific factors complicate historical discussions concerning tools, above all the basic lack of textual records.

Archaeologists in China have recovered many examples of tools dating back to earliest times.[24] But while labels are present in some cases (see, e.g., the following section), they are makers' marks and not descriptive. Nor do we have any extended discussion on the nature of tools in early sources. While tools occur in lexica, including Xu Shen's 許慎 (fl. ca. 100 CE) *Shuowen jiezi* 說文解字, the descriptions are general and the phrasings tend to be repetitive. Modern scholars often end up writing (and disagreeing) about classical terminology and modern analogues, which can serve to complicate matters rather than to clarify them. Subsequent discussion of a few of the tools will show what I mean.

What seems certain, however, is that this set of tools is complete from the perspective of use. Its contents would have enabled a skilled user to turn wood into a finished object, starting with fairly raw material and setting aside ancillary steps such as applying paint or lacquer, proper drying, and the like.

According to Sun Ji 孫機, prior to the emergence of the frame saw in China around the twelfth century CE, the saws in general use did not suffice for turning logs into boards. That process relied instead on splitting the wood by means of wedges and then shaping the resulting coarse boards with an adze. The adze work was followed with finishing by means of an edged tool called a *si* 鐁, then grinding with an abrasive stone. The plane was unknown in China at that point in history, and these latter steps served to smooth the wood.[25]

The items in the toolbox conform to this account and add detail to our understanding of the development of wood-finishing tools in China. The tools from Sanjiaowei M1 would suffice to create boards out of rough lumber—maybe even from standing timber, because of the presence of an axe-head. The only thing missing is a wedge, which may have decayed like some of the other wood items that seem to have been part of the original kit. The tools for constructing articles from those boards are present.

The Contents of the Toolbox

Axe and adzes

The head of an iron axe (M1:267) was in the toolbox. Rust had damaged it, and its handle was missing. The head is 13.2 cm long and bears the cast-in maker's mark "Huai, two" 淮二; the slightly curved edge is 8.8 cm wide. There is a socket on the back side of the axe-head, rectangular and shaped so that a two-part handle would insert into it (the intact handle of the adze M1:265 tells us more about this type of mounting).[26]

The toolbox also contained two iron adzes. The handle of one (M1:265) was substantially intact, although somewhat decayed. Its head, 6.8 cm long and with a cutting edge 7.9 cm wide, had a rectangular socket on the back. A wooden crosspiece 8 cm long was inserted into the socket and a 27 cm piece was inserted at a 90-degree angle into the crosspiece as handle. The craftsman who had made the handle carved it with a slightly offset grip and a protuberance at the end to counteract slippage. The second adze (M1:266) had its crosspiece still in place, although the vertical part of the handle was missing. Like the axe-head, it has the maker's mark "Huai, two." At 5.8 cm long, with an edge 5.6 cm wide, it is somewhat smaller than the other adze-head.[27]

Tools for smoothing wood

The history of the wood plane in China has been the matter of some dispute. Sun Ji dates the presence of the wood plane in China only to the Ming dynasty. Prior to that, the work of smoothing wood was accomplished with tools such as the two-edged, spearhead-shaped knife called a *si*, which I have already alluded to.[28]

He Tangkun 何堂坤 argued for the existence of the wood plane in the Tang period, but Sun Ji effectively refuted those assertions. The most important point in Sun's response is that the presence of wood that appears planed does not prove the existence of the tool.[29] Zhao Wucheng 趙吳成 has proposed, on the basis of deduction, the existence of a "proto-plane" (*qianqi bao* 前期刨) already in Han times. One aspect of that evidence is recovered wooden objects with tightly fitted sections and joints, including some that show smooth cuts of even depth in wood. Zhao also points to one perfectly preserved long wood shaving, of the sort that a plane produces, from an Eastern Han grave. These things, Zhao suggests, indicate the use of a tool more advanced than a knife.[30] Although Sun Ji has not addressed Zhao's argument directly in any of the publications I have seen, his response to He Tangkun (n. 30) applies here as well. The appearance of planing does not prove the presence of a plane, or proto-plane, however excellent the fit of the wood. The tools in this toolkit are in line with the idea that the wood plane did not exist at this point in time. Other tools filled that role.

The first of these tools from the box, tool M1:264, presents a bit of a puzzle.[31] It is shaped roughly like a miniature spade, with a flat, iron head 16 cm long and 10 cm wide, and a 23.5 cm wooden handle still intact. The report identifies it as a *chan* 鏟, which commonly means "spade" in both classical and modern Chinese. In his discussion of this identification, however, modern scholar Yang Yiping 楊以平 explains that the term had another sense in Han times and that this is what is functioning here. Yang cites definitions of *chan* from *Shuowen jiezi* and *Shiming* 釋名, both of which indicate an implement used for planing wood.[32]

The use of the term *chan* to denote two different tools—one for working in earth, the other for planing—seems likely to have resulted from the two different tools' similarities of shape. As Yang explains it, the woodworking *chan* was moved back and forth across a piece of wood to remove shavings and create a flat surface. The result was akin to that achieved by using a plane, just by a different means.[33] Yang's description seems to fit a kind of shipwright's chisel called a "slick" or a "slice," which is held in two hands and used for smoothing wood by the repeated removal of shavings.[34]

There was in the toolbox also another tool (M1:280) that seems to have had a plane-like function. It was intact and consists of a forged iron blade and a fairly long shank with a 90-degree bend and a socket on its end to fit a wooden handle. Thus, when the head was mounted for use, the blade was perpendicular to the wooden handle. The blade is curved on the outer side and straight on the inner side; both were sharpened, so that a user would be able to remove shavings from wood when both drawing and pushing the tool. Its overall length is 25 cm, 9.7 cm of which is handle; the blade is 9.1 cm long, 2.5 cm wide at its widest. The initial report identifies this tool as a *bo* 鈸, which usually refers to a small sickle for cutting grass. While the example from Huan's grave is for shaping wood, it is not the only example of a tool that developed from an agricultural implement. Yang Yiping points out, however, that having two sharp edges, rather than only one, sets this tool apart from a sickle in terms of form and use.[35]

Chisels

The eleven iron chisels in the toolbox are, like the saws and drills I will discuss later, clear indication that Huan Ping's assortment of tools is a proper set, with implements for various purposes. They differ in size and shape, reflecting the functions they had. All but one of the chisels has a socket to take a wooden handle; in six cases, those handles are still in place. The exceptional, socket-less example is a one-piece, all-metal construction (M1:278).

Four of the chisels are flat and of varying widths: 2.9 cm (M1:268), 2.55 cm (M1:269), 2.2 cm (M1:270), and 2.1 cm (M1:271). Two (M1:268 and M1:271) have their handles still in place.[36] Three of these flat chisels have sockets of nearly identical size (M1:269, M1:270, M1:271), in addition to being close to the same width. One might imagine that this was the most commonly used size of chisel and a woodworker would like to have several so as to be able to sharpen them all at once, then exchange them as they dulled during use to reduce interruptions.

The set of chisels includes gouges, shaped to expedite the removal of material. One of these is 2 cm wide (M1:273), missing its handle, and 0.2 cm deep. Another is slightly narrower at 1.7 cm (M1:272), with its handle intact, and 0.25 cm deep. There is also a chisel (M1:275) that the report describes as having a slight curve to its narrow 1.5 cm width edge.

The set also includes narrow chisels. Two of these (M1:274 and M1:276) are 1.2 cm wide, with flat edges. There are two additional narrow chisels with beveled cutting edges. One of these is the one-piece chisel I mentioned earlier (M1:278), the blade of which is .35 cm wide and formed from a single piece of iron, curled at the top to form a handle. The other is a chisel head (M1:277), sans handle, its edge .6 cm wide.[37]

Saws

The four iron saws in the toolbox, like the chisels, vary in form, suggesting a variety of applications. Two of them have metal blades that fit into channels in wooden handles, which resembles the design of a modern backsaw. The first of these (M1:281) consists of a wooden handle, which was shaped to fit the hand; the horizontal section of the handle, which held the blade, was damaged, and the blade is corroded. Enough of the teeth remain to determine they were an isosceles triangle shape. The saw's overall length is 23 cm, and the remaining section of blade is 13 cm long. The handle of the second backsaw (M1:282) was mostly missing upon excavation, with only a piece of the supporting handle section remaining. Its blade is 16 cm long, with triangular teeth that slant slightly. The serrated portion of the blade is a bit thinner than the rest, giving it a triangular cross section. A third saw (M1:283) is similar in design to a jab saw, in that its blade projects from the front of the wooden handle. This saw is 25 cm in total length, and its blade, 9 cm long, slants slightly upward. The teeth are heavily damaged and the handle is split.

The fourth saw (M1:291) is a bit puzzling. The report authors describe it as a toothless *xianju* 線鋸, literally, "wire saw," which usually denotes a small bowsaw with a thin blade, along the lines of a coping saw or similar tool.[38] The authors also say that this tool was formed from a long piece of metal, folded inward to make a narrow channel, the sides of which formed the saw's edge. The item had broken into six pieces, which together are 12.6 cm long.[39] I am uncertain about this tool. Saws without teeth, which cut through abrasion or other means, certainly exist, but the information in the report does not explain how this example would have worked and it is not evident from the description. There is also no indication of a bow to maintain tension and rigidity in use.

Drill bits

The toolkit contained four iron drill bits, three with three teeth and one with five teeth. While varying in size, all four bits have their teeth arranged similarly, with a longer one in the center and one or two additional teeth on each side. Two of the three three-tooth bits (M1:285 and M1:286) have more or less the same overall shape: both are four-sided bars of iron, 12.8 cm and 14 cm long, respectively; the latter had been broken. These two drill bits are slightly pointed on one end and slightly broader on the other, the latter being the location of the teeth. M1:285 is between 0.15 and 0.5 cm wide and 0.1–0.2 cm thick, while M1:286 is 0.1–0.3 cm in width and thickness. The other three-tooth bit (M1:287) is also four-sided but it tapers at both ends. It is 13.8 cm long, 0.15–0.3 cm wide, and 0.1–0.3 cm thick. The five-toothed drill bit (M1:284) is 18.5 cm long, with four sides and a square cross section. Rather than tapering only at the ends, as the others do, it is an elongated triangle shape, 0.4 cm wide at narrowest and 2.4 cm wide at the cutting end.[40]

Drills have a long history in China, going at least back to the Neolithic period, but archaeologists have recovered relatively few examples. There are two main ways to accomplish drilling using the early versions of the tool: either by rolling between the hands, or by using a simple apparatus to turn the bit by means of a cord or strap.[41] The report authors do not explain how the bits from M1 would have been used. The four-sided shape seems like it would have been uncomfortable to spin in the hands and I think they were more likely turned by means of a strap or cord, but there is no certain indication.

Additional tools

There were two other iron tools in the kit. One is a file (M1:279), similar in shape to a knife. The file is a 21-cm-long integrated whole, of which 12.6 cm is the blade, both faces of which have teeth, and 8.4 cm is the handle.[42] The report authors describe the other remaining tool as an awl (*zhui* 錐) (M1:288). It does not consist of a long point on a relatively small handle, as a modern awl generally does and other Han examples do.[43] This tool is an eight-sided block of wood some 6 cm long and 5.7 wide, from which a 1.1 cm iron point protrudes on one end.[44]

OTHER ITEMS IN THE TOOLBOX

The box containing the tools also held four lacquer cases.[45] There is no information about what they had originally contained. The first three cases were round in shape, lacquered black outside and red inside, with decorative motifs that combine bands and geometric shapes with irregular "clouds and air patterns" (*yunqiwen* 雲氣紋). One of these was a round container (M1:294), preserved only as a lacquer shell, with a bottom diameter of 10 cm and a height of 9.1 cm. The piece consists of a body and a lid, the latter with a carved dragon's head adornment. There were two other round containers (M1:292 and M1:293), which originally had handles, that were missing, although the objects were otherwise substantially intact. Both were round and flattened, with separate lids and made on wood cores. M1:292 was 10.8 cm high and had an upper diameter of 17 cm, a diameter at the base of 9 cm, and walls from 1 to 1.8 cm thick. M1:293 was similar: 10.7 cm high, 17 cm in diameter at top and 8.4 cm at bottom; its walls were also 11.8 cm thick. The fourth case (M1:295) is rectangular with a separate lid, 8 cm high in total, with its main part 16.9 cm by 10.5 cm. It was lacquered black inside and outside, without decoration, and has a short handle on one side.

The archaeologists recovered a wooden stand (M1:290) from within the tool case, as well.[46] Its top was intact, 31.4 cm long, 16 cm wide, and 1.4–2.2 cm thick. Its legs, although damaged upon recovery, were hinged to allow them either to raise the top surface to a height of 14.4 cm or to collapse against the bottom for storage.

Finally, there was a green-gray grinding stone (M1:263) in the case.[47] Rectangular in shape, it is 16.5 cm by 5.9 cm and 0.2 cm thick. The report authors identify its material as sandstone (*shashi* 砂石), which is a general designation.[48] They call the object a *daiban* 黛板, a stone for grinding black cosmetic powder (*dai* 黛), but also refer to "traces of ink" on the primary face, as well as other black marks and two rust spots.[49] The authors' terminology may be strictly correct, if unexpected in the context of this toolbox, or they may be thinking of something used to grind black pigment more generally. A final possibility is that this could be a sharpening stone for maintaining the edge of the tools.[50]

Explanations

The presence of a toolbox and extensive set of woodworking tools in grave M1 occasioned comment from the first. This is the first such find, and its placement in the grave of an official is surprising. The archaeologists describe the tools in great detail but do not attempt to explain their presence. There is no sure answer and nothing in the grave to say why these things are there. The work of interpretation is thus fraught.

I see a few possibilities. One is that this was simply a deluxe version of the kind of clerk's kit also seen in the grave at Xinyang, to which I referred at the start. This would then be something rare but not unknown. And while I cannot discount this possibility, it seems like it would fail to appreciate how different the Tianchang toolkit is, with its various tools in large sets. The inclusion of chisels of assorted sizes and shapes, bits for augering holes of various diameters, and saws of different sorts, suggests a greater variety of projects than the preparation of writing strips. The quintessential tool for working wooden strips, the clerk's knife, is also absent from this case, although present elsewhere in the grave.

Another possibility is that Huan Ping was by nature a collector. There was in fact another large lacquer case in the grave (M1:208), which contained one bronze and two iron daggers; seven iron swords; three iron spearheads; and eight iron knives, seven with ring pommels (*xiao* 削) and one with a curved handle (*dao* 刀).[51] This possibility, too, I cannot eliminate completely, but it seems to me unlikely. Swords, especially, had implications that do not mesh well with those of hand tools. Swords in early times were items of status and widely valued both for their intrinsic qualities and as collectibles.[52] Even if we consider these weapons as weapons only, their presence is not unexpected. Many bureaucratic careers in the early empire included military duties. That was not the case, at least not apparently, for the sort of woodworking that the Sanjiaowei M1 toolkit implies.

That brings me to the final possibility that I would like to consider, which is the one I referred to in the opening section, namely that Huan Ping liked woodworking. There is no way to really prove this. There are, after all, no texts in the grave to spell it out. Yet this possibility seems to me best to explain the characteristics of the tool set: its unique (to date) nature, which means it cannot have been a common article among burial arrays; its presence in the grave of a wealthy official; the completeness of the set, with tools for every stage of work; and the unadorned appearance of the tools, which befits implements for work rather than baubles for show. Whether Huan Ping did carpentry early in life and thus picked up the taste for it then, before his official career, or if he started later in life cannot be known.

From this grave and this set of tools, though, we can see Huan Ping in a way that would otherwise be impossible. He was not a particularly important person. But in his case, like others, archaeology gives us not only information about broad patterns but also glimpses into the human side of specific individuals who were not important enough to make it into received historical accounts. For Huan Ping, the human side included an abiding connection with working in wood.

Sarah Allan has written, "The accumulation of unspectacular data from smaller excavations is the foundation of archaeological research."[53] That applies also for historical research that draws upon archaeology. A find need not shake the scholarly world to be worth some closer consideration. The unspectacular has something to teach us, too.

Notes

1. My translation here follows the original in its use of a neologism. Whereas the terms "woodworkers" and "earthworkers" are ordinary language, "scribeworkers" is, as far as I can tell, a phrase of Wang Chong's own coining.

2. Huang Hui 黃暉, *Lunheng jiaoshi* 論衡校釋 (Beijing: Zhonghua, 1990), 12.552.

3. Sun Ji 孫機, "Woguo gudai de pingmu gongju" 我國古代的平木工具, *Wenwu* 1987.10, 71–73; Henansheng wenwu yanjiusuo 河南省文物研究所, *Xinyang Chu mu* 信阳楚墓 (Beijing: Wenwu, 1986), 64–67, 121.

4. For example, Stephen King, *On Writing: A Memoir of the Craft* (New York: Scribner, 2010).

5. Anthony J. Barbieri-Low, *Artisans in Early Imperial China* (Seattle: University of Washington Press, 2007), 36–44.

6. Qi Yuzhang 祁玉章, *Jiazi Xinshu jiaoshi* 賈子新書校釋 (Taipei: Zhongguo wenhua, 1974), 3.330–31 (*Gui wei* 瑰瑋).

7. Barbieri-Low, *Artisans in Early Imperial China*, 67–68, 114–15, and passim.

8. Yang Debiao 楊德標, "Anhui Tianchang faxian Han muqun" 安徽天長發現漢墓群, *Xiandai Zhongguo* 現代中國 1992.8, 51–52; Anhuisheng wenwu kaogu yanjiusuo 安徽省文物考古研究所 and Tianchangxian wenwu guanlisuo 天長縣文物管理所, "Anhui Tianchangxian Sanjiaowei Zhanguo Xihan mu chutu wenwu" 安徽天長縣三角圩戰國西漢墓出土文物, *Wenwu* 1993.9, 1–31; Anhuisheng wenwu kaogu yanjiusuo 安徽省文物考古研究所, *Tianchang Sanjiaowei mudi* 天長三角圩墓地 (Beijing: Kexue, 2013), 5–6, 324.

9. Anhuisheng wenwu kaogu yanjiusuo, *Tianchang Sanjiaowei mudi*, 8–163.

10. Shi Jie, private communication (April 4, 2018); and see, for example, Huaiyangshi bowuguan 淮陽市博物館, "Sayang Jiajiadun yihao mu qingli baogao" 灑陽賈家墩一號墓清理報告, *Dongnan wenhua* 1988.1, 63–64.

11. Anhuisheng wenwu kaogu yanjiusuo, *Tianchang Sanjiaowei mudi*, 8–12.

12. Anhuisheng wenwu kaogu yanjiusuo, *Tianchang Sanjiaowei mudi*, 401. The report refers to bronzes generally and also to lacquerware in the context of dating, but the arguments as presented rest upon coins, mirrors, and the grave.

13. Anhuisheng wenwu kaogu yanjiusuo, *Tianchang Sanjiaowei mudi*, 407–08.

14. This summary from Anhuisheng wenwu kaogu yanjiusuo, *Tianchang Sanjiaowei mudi*, 12.

15. Anhuisheng wenwu kaogu yanjiusuo, *Tianchang Sanjiaowei mudi*, 29–30 (M1:132, 159, 160); see also color pl. 11.

16. Anhuisheng wenwu kaogu yanjiusuo, *Tianchang Sanjiaowei mudi*, 154, 156 (M1:40); see also color pl. 26.

17. See Michael Loewe, "The Former Han Dynasty," in *The Cambridge History of China*, ed. Denis Crispin Twitchett and John King Fairbank (Cambridge: Cambridge University Press, 1986), 193, n. 152, and 199.

18. Anhuisheng wenwu kaogu yanjiusuo, *Tianchang Sanjiaowei mudi*, 142, 144, 395; color pls. 91–92. Titles here and later translated following Hans Bielenstein, *The Bureaucracy of Han Times* (Cambridge: Cambridge University Press, 1980), 8. For the *Han shu* texts the report authors cite, see, for example, Ban gu 班固, *Han shu* 漢書 (Beijing: Zhonghua, 1962), 19A.731–32; but see for comparison also Ru Chun's 如淳 commentary at *Han shu* 3.100.

19. Bielenstein, *The Bureaucracy of Han Times*, 47, 106.

20. Anhuisheng wenwu kaogu yanjiusuo, *Tianchang Sanjiaowei mudi*, color pls. 91–92.

21. Gao Heng 高亨, *Guzi tongjia huidian* 古字通假會典 (Jinan: Qi-Lu, 1989), 186.

22. Anhuisheng wenwu kaogu yanjiusuo and Tianchangxian wenwu guanlisuo, "Anhui Tianchangxian Sanjiaowei Zhanguo Xihan mu chutu wenwu," 31.

23. Anhuisheng wenwu kaogu yanjiusuo, *Tianchang Sanjiaowei mudi*, 62, 64, color pl. 44.

24. See discussion and examples in Li Zhen 李滇, *Zhongguo chuantong jianzhu muzuo gongju* 中國傳統建築木作工具, 2nd ed. (Shanghai: Tongji daxue, 2015), 225.

25. Sun Ji, "Woguo gudai de pingmu gongju," 71–73.

26. *Tianchang Sanjiaowei mudi*, 36 and figs. 23.1 and 2 on 37.

27. Anhuisheng wenwu kaogu yanjiusuo, *Tianchang Sanjiaowei mudi*, 36 and figs. 23.3, 4, and 5 on 37.

28. Sun Ji, "Woguo gudai de pingmu gongju"; Sun Ji, "Guanyu pingmu de baozi" 關於平木的刨子, *Wenwu* 1996.10, 84–85.

29. He Tangkun 何堂坤, "Pingmu yong bao kao" 平木用刨考, *Wenwu* 1996.7, 91–92; Sun Ji, "Guanyu pingmu de baozi."

30. Zhao Wucheng 趙吳成, " 'Pingmu yong bao kao' zai kao" "平木用刨考" 再考, *Sichou zhi lu* 絲綢之路 2000.1, 53–54; Zhao Wucheng 趙吳成, "Pingmu yong 'bao' xin faxian" 平木用 "刨" 新發現, *Wenwu* 2005.11, 72–74.

31. Anhuisheng wenwu kaogu yanjiusuo, *Tianchang Sanjiaowei mudi*, 36–37, 38 fig. 24.1, and 456.

32. Yang Yiping, "Tianchang Xihan mu chutu de mugong pingmu gongju kao" 天長西漢墓出土的木工平木工具考, in *Tianchang Sanjiaowei mudi*, 456, *Shuowen jiezi* (Beijing: Zhonghua, 1963), 295; Yang refers to commentary supporting his reading, which finds further support in *Hanyu dacidian*, s.v. "chan" 鑱; cf. also Tang Kejing 湯可敬, *Shuowen jiezi jinshi* 說文解字今釋 (Changsha: Yuelu shushe, 1997), 2016. Yang cites the *Shiming* definition without any further elaboration and I am unable to find the definition he has in the current version of that text; for the most likely

location for it, if it were there, see the "Explaining Implements" ("Shi yongqi" 釋用器) section, in Liu Xi 劉熙 (ca. 2nd–3rd c.), *Shiming* (Skqs. ed.), 7.1a–2a. Li Fang 李昉 (925–996) et al., *Taiping yulan* 太平御覽 (Song woodblock ed.; Taipei: Taiwan Shangwu yinshuguan, 1968 [rpt.]), 764.1b, however, incorporate the definition Yang Yiping cites and attribute it to *Shiming*. That may be Yang's proximate source.

33. Yang, "Tianchang Xihan," 456.

34. See R. A. Salaman, *Dictionary of Woodworking Tools c. 1700–1970 and Tools of Allied Trades*, rev. ed. (Newtown: Taunton Press, 1990), 143.

35. Anhuisheng wenwu kaogu yanjiusuo, *Tianchang Sanjiaowei mudi*, 37, 38 fig. 24.2, 456–57.

36. This statement follows the textual description given in Anhuisheng wenwu kaogu yanjiusuo, *Tianchang Sanjiaowei mudi*, 39–40, and the line drawings on 39. The images on color pl. 16, however, show all four with handles. I do not know whether the description and line drawings are inaccurate or if perhaps the photographs of M1:269 and M1:270 show them with replica handles.

37. Anhuisheng wenwu kaogu yanjiusuo, *Tianchang Sanjiaowei mudi*, 39–40, images on 39 and 41, color pls. 16 and 17.

38. This is according to the dictionary at https://tw.dictionary.search.yahoo.com, s.v. "xianju" 線鋸, and my image searches through Google.

39. Anhuisheng wenwu kaogu yanjiusuo, *Tianchang Sanjiaowei mudi*, 37–38; line drawings 38, color pls. 14 and 15.

40. Anhuisheng wenwu kaogu yanjiusuo, *Tianchang Sanjiaowei mudi*, 40–41, line drawings on 41, color pl. 15.

41. Li Zhen, *Zhongguo chuantong jianzhu muzuo gongju*, 186–88.

42. Anhuisheng wenwu kaogu yanjiusuo, *Tianchang Sanjiaowei mudi*, 41, 38, color pl. 17.

43. See Sun Ji, *Handai wuzhi wenhua ziliao tushuo* 漢代物質文化資料圖說 (Shanghai: Shanghai guji, 2012), 30–31.

44. Anhuisheng wenwu kaogu yanjiusuo, *Tianchang Sanjiaowei mudi*, 41, 38, color pl. 15.

45. Anhuisheng wenwu kaogu yanjiusuo, *Tianchang Sanjiaowei mudi*, 131–34, color pls. 76–77.

46. Anhuisheng wenwu kaogu yanjiusuo, *Tianchang Sanjiaowei mudi*, 139, 141, color pl. 36. The report is a bit confusing here, as the description does not specify that M1:290 was inside the wooden tool case M1:263. However, the list of items in the case on 63 indicates a stand was in the case. The chart listing all items recovered from the tomb on 400 also specifies that M1:290 was inside M1:263.

47. Anhuisheng wenwu kaogu yanjiusuo, *Tianchang Sanjiaowei mudi*, 162 (M1: 289), line drawings 156, color pl. 27.

48. Richard Scott Mitchell, *Dictionary of Rocks* (New York: Van Nostrand Reinhold, 1985), 175–76.

49. See *Hanyu da cidian*, s.v. "dai" 黛.

50. Compare discussion of sandstone and soft stone generally used for this purpose in Roy Underhill, *The Woodwright's Companion: Exploring Traditional Woodcraft* (Chapel Hill: University of North Carolina Press, 1983), 30; Roy Underhill, *The Woodwright's Shop: A Practical Guide to Traditional Woodcraft* (Chapel Hill: University of North Carolina Press, 1981), 64–65.

51. Anhuisheng wenwu kaogu yanjiusuo, *Tianchang Sanjiaowei mudi*, 62, 31, 33–36, 42–45.

52. See Charles Sanft, "Evaluating Swords: Introduction and Translation of a How-To Guide from the Han-Xin Period," *Early China* 39 (2016): 235.

53. Sarah Allan, introduction to *The Formation of Chinese Civilization: An Archaeological Perspective*, ed. Sarah Allan, Kwang-chih Chang, and Xu Pingfang (New Haven: Yale University Press, 2005), 5.

Afterword

Wandering Mt. Song, Chatting in Friendship: Exploring Mt. Song in Oracle-Bone Inscriptions

Qi Wenxin

Translated by Susan Blader

I have known Sarah Allan (艾蘭) since October of 1982, when I went to London to participate in a large Sino-British project to publish *Oracle Bone Collections in Great Britain.*[1] My task was to make rubbings of all the oracle bones. Previously, Professors Li Xueqin 李學勤 and Sarah Allan had already completed a comprehensive survey and listing of all oracle bones and related rubbings in British collections in England. For the next seven months, I worked in England, traveling to and fro between six cities and eleven public and private institutions, making rubbings of more than three thousand oracle bones. The work was extremely arduous, but Sarah gave me enormous support in this. It was from this time that we formed a profound and abiding friendship.

From 1984 on, Sarah came to China almost every year and, sometimes, twice a year; she became a familiar friend of Chinese scholars. Moreover, her research on early Chinese culture has been extensive and profound; her writings, brilliant and numerous. Her complete works have already been translated into Chinese and published, and have been welcomed by Chinese scholars.

Sarah has always been enthusiastic about exchanges between China and the West. Ever since she became Editor in Chief of *Early China*, she has made even more outstanding achievements in this area. For scholars, retirement means that you have even more free time to carry out research and writing; retirement is the "Second Springtime" in a scholar's life. We are very much looking forward to her next steps.

In October of 1984, Sarah Allan visited China for the first time. She was hosted by the Institute of History of the Chinese Academy of Social Sciences 中國社會科學院歷史研究所 for a stay of two months. From November 1st to the 10th, I accompanied her on an excursion to Henan 河南. Together we went to the Yinxu 殷墟 site in Anyang 安陽, Qi 淇, and Xun 濬 Counties, and then on to Zhengzhou 鄭州, Yanshi 偃師, Kaifeng 開封, and Loyang 洛陽, among other places. We visited museums and archaeological sites, where we interviewed archaeologists working there. We learned a great deal.

What was even more unforgettable was that we were in the presence of the magnificent, lofty Mt. Song (嵩山) and the grand surging Yellow River. I remember especially when, on November 4th, we fortuitously happened upon a grand temple fair at Mt. Song. There was a veritable sea of people in the square. Everywhere, the mass of worshipers and the crowds of tourists gathered together, admiring Mt. Song—maybe as many as two hundred thousand people. In front of the Mt. Song Temple, fragrant incense smoke swirled and rose upward. The worshipers fervently sang their prayers, pouring out their hearts' wishes. Being part of this greatly moving spectacle impressed us all with the antiquity of the ritual practice of worshiping Mt. Song.

Since antiquity, Chinese have believed in worshiping mountains and rivers. Mountains and rivers not only provide rich sources for life, they also provide protective barriers, safeguarding the economy and livelihood of the community. Furthermore, the ancients believed that the ruler received his mandate to rule from *tian* 天 (sky, heaven, nature) and that since the summits of tall mountains were naturally close to *tian*, where all spirits resided, here one could communicate with *tian* and understand *tian*'s will, ultimately providing protection and prosperity for the state. Transmission of this weighty historical tradition over time to posterity has been important since early antiquity.

In the "Fengshan" 封禪 chapter of the *Shiji* 史記, it is written: "The Son of Heaven makes sacrifices to the famous mountains and great rivers of the empire" (天子祭天下名山大川) and "The various lords sacrifice to the famous mountains and great rivers within their borders" (諸侯祭其疆內名山大川).[2] According to the *Shiji*, Shun 舜 of prehistorical times already "sacrificed to mountains and rivers" (望于山川) and performed hunting (*xunshou* 巡狩) rituals. Shun and other ancient rulers traveled to the "Five

Sacred Mountains" (Wu Yue 五岳) of the directions: East, Mt. Tai 泰山; South, Mt. Heng 衡山; West, Mt. Hua 華山; North, Mt. Heng 恒山; and Central, Mt. Song.[3]

Rituals of sacrificing to mountains evolved and changed over time. When Qin unified the empire, the government set up officers in charge of sacrificing in an orderly fashion to Heaven and Earth 天地, Famous Mountains 名山, Great Rivers 大川, and Ghosts and Spirits 鬼神. The comprehensive version of the rituals was set up during the reign of Emperor Wu of the Han dynasty (漢武帝). He famously performed the Feng 封 Sacrifice on Mt. Tai as part of systemized rituals to the Five Sacred Mountains and the Four Rivers (Si Du 四瀆).[4]

The middle peak of Mt. Song is a relatively independent mountain on the eastern side of the Qin Mountain Range (秦嶺). Its total area is 4,000 square kilometers; its highest peak is 1,440 meters. Mt. Song borders on the North China Plain, an ancient land that rose up thirty-five billion years ago. Replete with water resources, seven rivers flow from Mt. Song and converge into the Ying River (潁河). A branch of the Huai 淮 also originates from Mt. Song and joins others to feed the Yi 伊 and Luo 洛 rivers as well as the Yellow River. Thirty-eight kilometers north of the Yellow River stands Mt. Song, where there is abundant water and fertile soil, making this area very inhabitable.

Archaeological evidence has revealed that Mt. Song was the birthplace of a number of Paleolithic and Neolithic cultures. It is also the core area from which Xia, Shang, and Zhou civilizations emerged and spread. In the "Lu yu, shang" 魯語上 of the *Discourses of the States* (*Guoyu* 國語), it says: "The State is reliant on mountains and rivers" (國必依山川). The *Han shu* 漢書 explains, "Long ago, the Three Dynasties resided in between the Yellow and Luo Rivers, with Song prominent as the central peak, with the four other peaks each off in their own directions, and four rivers all on the east of the Mountain" (昔三代之居皆河洛之間, 故嵩高為中嶽, 而四嶽各如其方, 四瀆咸在山東).[5] This region of fertile soil and abundant water that was beside a high mountain was within the Shang royal domain; thus, the high mountain and great river upon which the Shang relied should be Mt. Song and the Yellow River.

There is ample evidence in oracle-bone inscriptions of the important positions that Mt. Song and the Yellow River had in Shang culture. This includes some 468 references to 𡉈, which we will argue should be read as Song, 嵩, and as many as 588 references to 河, which is identified as the Yellow River.[6]

We will first look at the debate over the graph 𝍝. Various interpretations have been raised. For instance, Luo Zhenyu 羅振玉 (1866–1940) explained it as *gao* 羔 (lamb).[7] Yu Xingwu 于省吾 (1896–1984) explained it as *ming* 冥 (dark).[8] Guo Moruo 郭沫若 (1892–1978) at first suspected that it was *hua* 華 (blossoming) and then interpreted it as Chuqiu 楚丘 (Chu Hill).[9] The classicist Sun Yirang 孫詒讓 (1848–1908) suggested early on that the Yin capital of Chaoge 朝歌 and the central sacred mountain (*zhong yue* 中嶽), Mt. Song, were within the Shang domain, so this character should be read as *yue* 嶽 (alternatively written as 岳), meaning a lofty or sacred mountain. This reading was then upheld by many of his followers and has been highly influential. However, their opinions differed about the identification of the sacred mountain. Qu Wanli 屈萬里 (1907–1979) preferred Mt. Taiyue 太岳山 and Zheng Jiexiang 鄭杰祥 further suggested Mt. Taihang 太行山. In fact, Sun Yirang already pointed out the centrality of Mt. Song, with its tall peaks, and the importance it must have held for the Shang.[10] Sarah Allan also suggested in *The Shape of the Turtle: Myth, Art, and Cosmos in Early China* that *yue* might refer to Mount Song.[11]

I would argue, however, that to interpret the graph 𝍝 as the common noun *yue*, giving the generic term "sacred mountain," is not quite accurate. The Shang oracle-bone inscriptions have a preference for calling geographic features by proper names, as opposed to using generic terms (e.g., "river," "mountain" . . .). For rivers, the proper names Huan 洹, Shang 滴, Huang 潢, Huai 淮 often appear, and notably He 河 is not a generic term (river) but refers to the Yellow River. Likewise, the graphs 𝍞, 𝍟, and 𝍠 are all written from the "mountain" 山 signifier, and while we no longer know their precise pronunciations or to which particular mountains they referred, they should be read as proper names. So too, the ancient graph 𝍝 ought to be read as a proper name, and not as the common noun *yue* or "sacred mountain." If we took *yue* as the name of a mountain, it would be Mt. Qian 岍山, which is also known as Mt. Yue 岳山. It is located in what is now the southwest part of Long County 隴縣, Shaanxi, which is unlikely for a mountain of such importance to the Shang.[12]

The oracle-bone graph 𝍝 is composed of the mountain signifier 𝍲 on the bottom, and the wavey shape 𝍳 on the top, which looks exactly like three mountain peaks. Mt. Song does in fact have three tall peaks: Taishi Peak 太室峰 on the east, Shaoshi Peak 少室峰 on the west, and Junji Peak 峻機峰 in the middle. The graph 𝍝 aptly portrays the three overlapping peaks of Mt. Song and in my opinion therefore should be regarded as a pictograph of Mt. Song, best read as *song* 嵩.[13]

In the Shang oracle-bone inscriptions, Mt. Song is a revered spirit. Like other spirits, it could send down blessings and calamities. For the Shang people, whose economy depended upon agricultural production, harmonious winds and timely rain were vital, as they determined the success or failure of crops. Believing that Mt. Song controlled rainfall and determined the annual harvest, the Shang therefore prayed and sacrificed to Mt. Song in a variety of ceremonies, for example: *wu* 舞 (Dance), *liao* 燎 (Burn), *qu* 取 (Extract), *zou* 奏 (Musical Performance), *jiu* 酒 (Ale), *di* 禘 (Pray), *gao* 告 (Announce), *you* 侑 (Gift), and *si* 祀 (Annual Sacrifice). Sacrifices of buffalo and sheep accompanied prayers. A special temple was erected, called Song Ancestral Hall 嵩宗 (*Heji* 30298).[14]

Mt. Song was also anthropomorphized, transforming from a nature spirit into a human spirit, and included among the ranks of the Shang "High Ancestors" (*gaozu* 高祖), receiving the same rites and sacrifices as High Ancestor Kui 高祖夒 (*Cui* 1), High Ancestor King Hai 高祖王亥 (*Heji* 32083), and High Ancestor River 高祖河 (*Heji* 32028). These High Ancestors are at times listed alongside one another on the same bone, and, further, the divination questions posed to each bear the same content. Some of the High Ancestors were lineage founders, whether distantly related by blood, or who led by virtue of their outstanding achievements; yet other High Ancestors were anthropomorphized nature spirits, such as the flowing waters of the great He 𠃌 (河) or lofty three peaks of Song 𡵂 (嵩).[15] These High Ancestors were clearly differentiated from the hierarchical spiritual pantheon that began with the founder Shang Jia 上甲. They were not given day names (i.e., *ganri* 干日), nor were they sequentially arranged. Hence, as Guo Moruo noted, it was only with Shang Jia that the historical period began. Prior to this was the realm of myth and legend.[16]

Among the oracle bones, a number of inscriptions bearing *song* 嵩 are records marked by a scribe (mainly engraved on a bone's socket, e.g., *Heji* 7322 臼), or alternatively reveal someone with a diviner status (e.g., *Bingbian* 94 正).[17] What this suggests is that, besides referring to Mt. Song as a spirit, in the oracle bones Song also appears as the name of a family, whose members served the Shang court in scribal positions, overseeing divinations, record keeping, and safeguarding the oracle bones. The family name of Song comes from their polity (*guozu* 國族), and this in turn was ultimately derived from the place where they resided—that is, forming a so-called *shi* 氏 "clan" name. Thus, the peoples who lived at the foot of Mt. Song were named after the mountain, as both a family and polity. The oracle-bone inscriptions also attest to the long-standing and close relations held between the Song and the Shang. That Song sent scribes to the Shang court must have been a prescribed obligation, with Song leaders or nobles either sent as envoys to inform the Shang about local conditions or as a type of hostage. The oracle-bone inscriptions supply additional evidence of frequent contacts between the Song and Shang as well (e.g., *Tunnan* 2107; 3107; and 4513+4518).[18]

In summary, the graph 𝖺 should be read *song* 嵩 and is a pictograph of Mt. Song. Mt. Song was seen by the Shang as an incomparably powerful mountain spirit, which eventually was anthropomorphized and, much like the Yellow River spirit He 𝄬, included among the High Ancestors. The people and polity who lived by Mt. Song, moreover, took their name from this mountain and were important to the Shang court. With the mentions of Song in the oracle-bone inscriptions, we can recover the earliest recorded tradition of sacred mountain worship. It is with deep pleasure that I remember experiencing this tradition with Sarah Allan.

Notes

1. Sarah Allan, Li Xueqin, and Qi Wenxin, eds., *Oracle Bone Collections in Great Britain / Yingguo suo cang jiagu ji* 英國所藏甲骨集, 2 vols. (Beijing: Zhonghua, 1992).

2. Takikawa Kametaro 瀧川龜太郎, ed., *Shiki kaichū kōshō* 史記會注考證 28 *shu* 書 6.7b (Taipei: Hongshi, 1977 [rpt.]), 497; compare *Liji zhengyi* 禮記正義 12.108, in Ruan Yuan 阮元 (1764–1849), ed., *Shisanjing zhushu* 十三經注疏 (1987; Beijing: Zhonghua, 1988 [rpt.]), vol. 1, 1336.

3. Takikawa, *Shiki kaichū kōshō* 1.35–36; compare *Shangshu zhengyi* 尚書正義 3.14–15, in *Shisanjing zhushu*, vol. 1, 126–27. The term *wang* 望 is defined in the *Zuo zhuan* as part of the "suburban sacrifices" (*jiao* 郊); *Chunqiu Zuo zhuan zhengyi* 春秋左傳正義 17.129, in *Shisanjing zhushu*, vol. 2, 1831.

4. Takikawa, *Shiki kaichū kōshō* 28 *shu* 6.80–81 (Taipei), 517–18. The term *feng* 封 as an altar built for sacrificing to *tian* is mentioned in reference to Mt. Tai in *Da Dai liji* 大戴禮記, "Bao zhuan" 保傳 48; Gao Ming 高明, ed. and commentary, *Da Dai liji jinzhu jinyi* 大戴禮記今註今譯 (1984; Taipei: Taiwan Shangwu, 1993 [rpt.]), 230. In the "Fengshan" (see n. 2 in this chapter), the Four Rivers are listed as the Yangtze, Yellow, Huai, and Qi 四瀆者江河淮濟也. For how these rituals become regularized *chang li* 常禮, see Wang Xianqian 王先謙, ed., *Han shu buzhu* 漢書補注 28b.8a (Beijing: Zhonghua, 1983), vol. 1, 553.

5. *Guoyu* 1.10b, *Sibubeiyao* (Taipei: Zhonghua, 1975). For the *Han shu*, see n. 4 in this chapter.

6. Yao Xiaosui 姚孝遂, ed., *Yinxu jiagu keci leizuan* 殷墟甲骨刻辭類纂 (Beijing: Zhonghua, 1989), 467–73, 488–96.

7. *Yinxu shuqi kaoshi* 殷墟書契考釋 (1916; Beijing: Wenwu, 2008 [rpt.]), 2, 28a.

8. *Shuangjian yi Yin qi pianzhi* 雙劍誃殷契駢枝 (Beijing: Daye, 1940), vol. 3, 7–11.

9. *Yin qi cuibian* 殷契粹編 (Tokyo: Bunkodo 文求堂, 1937), no. 73.

10. *Qiwen juli* 契文舉例 (1904; Beijing tushuguan, 2000 [rpt.]), vol. 1, 20.

11. Sarah Allan, *The Shape of the Turtle: Myth, Art, and Cosmos in Early Chin*a (Albany: State University of New York Press, 1991), 99.

12. Shi Weile 史為樂, ed., *Zhongguo lishi diming da cidian* 中國歷史地名大辭典 (Beijing: Zhongguo shehui kexue, 2005), 1269.

13. This new reading updates my prior work, especially: Qi Wenxin 齊文心 and Wang Guimin 王貴民, eds., *Zhonghua wenhua tongzhi: Shang Xi Zhou wenhua zhi* 中華文化通志: 商西周文化志 (Shanghai: Shanghai renmin, 1998), 103–04, 126–27.

14. *Heji* refers to Guo Moruo, ed., and Hu Houxuan 胡厚宣, ed. in chief, *Jiaguwen heji* 甲骨文合集, 13 vols. (Beijing: Zhonghua, 1978–1982).

15. For a more detailed discussion of the examples, see Qi and Wang, *Zhonghua wenhua tongzhi*, 103–07, 126–27.

16. Guo Moruo, *Buci tongzuan* 卜辭通纂 (Tokyo: Bunkodo, 1933), no. 362.

17. *Bingbian* refers to Zhang Bingquan 張秉權, *Xiaotun: Henan Anyang Yinxu yizhi zhi yi, di er ben, Yinxu wenzi, bingbian sanben* 小屯: 河南安陽殷虛遺址之一, 第二本, 殷虛文字, 丙編, 3 vols. (Taipei: Zhongyang yanjiuyuan lishi yuyan yanjiusuo, 1957–1972).

18. *Tunnan* refers to Zhongguo shehui kexueyuan kaogu yanjiiusuo 中國社會科學院考古研究所, *Xiaotun nandi jiagu* 小屯南地甲骨, 2 vols. (Shanghai: Zhonghua, 1980, 1983).

Contributors

Scott COOK is Tan Chin Tuan Professor of Chinese Studies at Yale-NUS College.

Christopher J. FOSTER is an independent scholar, formerly British Academy Postdoctoral Fellow at SOAS University of London.

HAN Ding 韓鼎 is Associate Professor of Archaeology and Museology at Henan University.

HAN Wei 韓巍 is Associate Professor of Ancient Chinese History at Peking University.

Anne Behnke KINNEY is Professor of Chinese at the University of Virginia.

LI Ling 李零 is Chair Professor of Humanities at Peking University.

LU Liancheng 盧連成 was formerly an archaeologist at the Institute of Archaeology, Chinese Academy of Social Sciences.

Colin MACKENZIE was formerly Curator of Chinese Art at the Art Institute of Chicago.

QI Wenxin 齊文心 was formerly Senior Research Fellow at the Institute of History, Chinese Academy of Social Sciences.

Charles SANFT is Professor of History at the University of Tennessee.

WANG Tao is Pritzker Chair of Arts of Asia and Curator of Chinese Art at the Art Institute of Chicago.

WANG Tingbin 王挺斌 is Associate Research Fellow in the School of Literature at Zhejiang University.

Crispin WILLIAMS is Associate Professor of East Asian Languages and Cultures at the University of Kansas.

ZHAO Pingan 趙平安 is Professor of History at Tsinghua University.

Index

administrative documents (*wenshu*), 165–68, 170, 173, 174, 178, 185n5, 193; on *gu* prisms, 268, 286nn68–69; received manuscripts as, 204. *See also* Wenxian Covenant Texts

Ai, Lord of Lu, xiii, 216–20

Allan, Sarah, ix, 305; on animal motifs, 29, 32; on *de*, xii, 119, 124, 125; and Mt. Song, 311–12; on *song* graph, 314; on transmission of texts, 259, 260, 272, 274; on women, 238

ancestral worship: and bird graphs, 2–4, 8–9; of High Ancestors (*gaozu*), 315, 316; lineage-based, xii, 120–47, 156n68, 160n112; sacrifices in, 220, 222, 228n14; and tribute system, 134–35, 136, 146, 147

ancient books (*gushu, dianji*), 188n33, 193; classification of, 175–77; definition of, 165–66; discoveries of, 168–75; excavated, 167–68; origins of, 204–6; prefaces to, 201; titles for, 177–79; types of, 163–65. *See also* manuscripts, bamboo and silk

Anhui University manuscripts, 175, 277n7

animal motifs: on Ba Bo vessels, 78–80; on Cheng Wang *fangding*,

63, 65, 66; on drinking vessels, 43, 44, 53; in Shang art, 10, 23–35; in wavy-band pattern, 110n10. *See also* birds

Anyang (Henan), 1, 26, 49, 74n11, 312; foundries at, 51, 52. *See also* Fu Hao tomb; Xibeigang

architectural motifs, xi, 23–35

artisans, 17, 201; bronze-working, 43, 51–54; woodworking, xiv, 293–94

Ba Bo (Elder Ba) bronze vessels, 77–117; animal motifs on, 78–80; dating of, 77–78; wavy band (*bodai*) pattern on, 80–81, 110n10

Ba clan, 102, 103, 104, 116n76, 116n81

Baicaopo (Lingtai, Gansu), 37–38, 39, 42, 47

Ban Gu, 262, 265

Ban Zhao, 234

Bang cemetery (Qucun), 103

Baoji (Shaanxi), 38–42, 44, 47, 51, 52, 53

Baoshan Chu bamboo strips, 86, 174

Beizhao Marquis of Jin cemetery (Jin Hou *mudi*), 103

Biannianji (Shuihudi Qin strips), 173

birds: and ancestral worship, 2–4, 8–9; on Ba Bo vessels, 80; on Cheng

birds *(continued)*
Wang *fangding*, 65; as deities, 4, 7, 17; on double bird drum (Senoku Hakuko Museum), 26, 29, 30; in oracle-bone inscriptions, 1–10; in Western Zhou period, 16–17. *See also* owls
Bo Kuo, 48
Bo Qin of Lu, 46
Boxue, 269, 287n75, 291n97
bronze artifacts: Allan on, x, 10; altar tables, 39, 40, 43, 51, 52; bells, 48; clan signs on, 37, 42, 46, 48, 49, 56n19; from Dahekou, 77–117; in Freer Gallery, 31–32, 34n24, 40, 65, 75n21; *gu* vessels, 260–64; *gui* vessels, 78–80; mountain *gui* (*shan gui*), 78, 80, 81, 83, 111n12; owl motif on, xi, 10–13; phoenix (*fenghuang*) motif on, 14; from Sanjiaowei tomb M1, 294–96, 305, 306n12; Sanxingdui face mask, 27; Shang, 10–13, 37, 42–43, 46–48, 49, 53–54, 68; Shang *vs.* Western Zhou, 63, 64, 65; and social structure, 141–42; weapons, 31, 38, 39, 43; Western Zhou, 13–17, 37–59, 63–65, 109n3; Zhongshan, 196. *See also* drinking vessels, bronze; Xiaoshuangqiao bronze architectural decoration
bronze artifacts, named: Ban *gui*, 52; Bin Gong *xu*, 206; Bo Hao *gui*, 85; Cheng Wang *fangding*, xi, 61–76; Cheng *xu*, 80; Chi *zun*, 83, 84, 111n15; Ci *zun*, 89; Da Bao *you*, 13–14; Da Yu *ding*, 49, 50; Dahe Human Face *fangding*, 30; De *fangding*, 67; Deer and Buffalo *fangding*, 64; Dian *gui*, 95–97, 99, 107, 108, 114n61; Doubi *gui*, 79; Elder Ba *gui*, 78, 79, 81, 83–88, 91, 95, 97, 98, 111n16, 112n35, 113n45; Elder Ba vessels, xii, 77–117; Elder Ba *xu*, 80–88, 91, 95, 97, 98, 111n12, 112n35, 113n45; Elder Ba (Shang) *yu*, 78, 113n43; Er Shu *gui*, 15; Fan *you*, 89; Guai Bo *gui*, 79; Hou (Si) Mu Wu *fangding*, 63–64, 65; Hou (Si) Mu Xin *fangding*, 64; Hu *ding*, 83, 84, 111n15; Hu *fangyi*, 39; Hu *gui*, 75n16; Ji Ning *zun*, 85; Jin *gui*, 95; Jin Hou Jin *hu*, 81; Jin Jiang *ding*, 97, 105, 106–7, 108, 109; Kang Hou Feng *fangding*, 67; Ke *ding*, 131; Ke *gui*, 198; Li *gui*, 42, 51–52; Liang Qi *hu*, 81; Lu *gui*, 81, 96–97; Mai *fangzun*, 15; Mao Gong *ding*, 205, 206; Marquis Cheng of Ying *xu*, 80, 81; Marquis of Jin *gui*, 78; Mi Shu Shi Cha *gui*, 83; Mian *gui*, 83, 84, 94, 95; Mian *hu*, 94; Mian *pan*, 94, 97, 99, 107; Mian *you*, 95; Mian *zun*, 83, 84, 95; Neishi Bo *tong*, 264; Neishi *xu*, 80; owl-shaped *zun* (Fu Hao tomb), 12–13; owl-shaped *zun* (Shen Zhai collection), 14–16; Peng Bo Cheng *gui*, 90; Qi *you*, 81; Qi *zun*, 81; Qin Gong *bo*, 132; Qinian Que Cao *ding*, 204–5; Qiu *pan*, 105; Ran *fangding*, 15, 44; Rong Sheng *zhong* bells, 105–6; Shi X *yan*, 68, 69; Shihu *gui*, 79; Shuyi *zhong*, 208; small owl *zun* (Sackler collection), 11; Song *ding*, 117n85; Song *gui*, 117n85; Tai (Da) Bao *fangding*, 65; tiger *you*, 31, 32; Wang Sun Gao *zhong*, 211n21; Wei *ding*, 85; Xian *gui*, 78; Xian Hou *li-ding*, 71; Xiao Chen Fou *fangding*, 68, 69; Xing Hou *gui*, 15; Yan Hou *yu*, 15; Yi *you*, 90; You *gui*, 78; Yu *ding*, 84; Yuanniao *hu*, 8–9; Zeng

Bo Qi *hu*, 108; Zhongshan Wang *hu*, 211n14; Zuoce Da *fangding*, 70, 71, 72

bronze inscriptions: *vs.* ancient books, 165, 204–6; bird graphs in, 8–9; on Cheng Wang *fangding*, 61–62, 63, 65–72; and covenant manuscripts, 120, 156n73; from Dahekou, 77–117; on drinking vessels, 37, 38, 40–44, 47–49, 51–53; on *gu*, 282n39; kings named in, 70–71, 72–73; on owl-shaped vessels, 14–15; and received manuscripts, 206; on Shang artifacts, 72–73; and Tsinghua manuscripts, 198; use of *de* in, 121, 131–33, 147

calendars, 169, 177–78, 188n28, 233; and salt production, 88, 97; and stem signs, 37, 128
Cang Jie, 269, 287n75, 291n97
Cang Jie pian (Cang Jie Volumes), xiv, 260, 265–73; bamboo-strip manuscripts of, 269–73, 287n76, 288nn77–78, 289n80, 290n87, 291n94, 291n97; chapter divisions of, 270–71, 273; chapter titles in, 271–72, 273; Shuiquanzi, 288n76, 289n80; sources for, 269; Village Teachers edition of, 269–70, 272, 289n80, 290n87, 291n94, 291nn97–98
Cao Cao, 262
Cao Mo zhi zhen (Shanghai Museum manuscript), 193
Changes (*Yi*), 167. See also *Zhou yi*
Changsha (Hunan), 18, 166
Changsha Chu strips (Hunan), 171
Cheng, King (Zhou), 15, 17, 50, 70
Cheng Wang *fangding*, xi, 61–76
Cheng Wang wei Chengpu zhi xing (Shanghai Museum manuscript), 194

Chijiu zhi ji Tang zhi wu (Tsinghua manuscript), 192, 207, 208
Chu, state of, 294; manuscripts from, 86, 166, 167, 170–72, 174; script of, 171–72, 193, 195, 196, 199, 238
Chu ju (Tsinghua manuscript), 192, 198
Chuci (Songs of Chu), 29, 208
Chunqiu, 216
Confucianism: in ancient books, 167, 168, 175; in *Lu bang da han*, xiii, 219–20, 224–26; and use of *de*, 119, 121, 126
Confucius (Kongzi): and *de*, 126; drinking habits of, 262, 280n26; on *gu*, 260–61, 262, 264, 265, 266; in *Lu bang da han*, xiii, 216–20, 221, 222, 224; on spirits, 225–26, 230n29
Cong zheng (Shanghai Museum manuscript), 193, 194
Cultural Revolution, 172

Da Dai liji, 261, 316n4
Dahekou (Yicheng, Shanxi), 77–117, 111n12
Daijiawan tombs (Baoji, Shaanxi), 40–42, 44, 51, 53
dao, 121, 123, 125, 126, 188n33
Daoism, 19, 147, 168; and *de*, 123, 124, 125, 126
daybooks (*rishu*), 177, 178, 187n26, 235, 290n92
Daybook A (*Rishu jia*, Shuihudi manuscript), 235, 290n92
de (inner power, virtue): changing meanings of, xii, 119–61; as hereditary power *vs.* individual virtue, 119–21; in received manuscripts, 121–26, 133–37, 141, 143, 146, 157n73; and water, 124, 125

Di people, 53, 99, 288n77
Die people, 52
divination: in ancient books, 165, 167; in Baoshan Chu strips, 174; and bird graphs, 2–10; diviner groups, 19n3; on sacrifices, 2–8; in Shuihudi Qin strips, 173; with turtle plastrons, x, 1–2; in Wangshan Chu strips, 171; on weather, xi, 2–3, 4, 7. *See also* oracle-bone inscriptions
Dixing tu (Mawangdui manuscript), 164
Dongxiafeng (Xia County), 93–94, 97, 113n50
double bird drum (Senoku Hakuko Museum), 26, 29, 30
Doujitai site (Baoji, Shaanxi), 47
drinking vessels, bronze, 37–59; from Dahekou, 78; manufacturing of, 51–54; Shang, 37, 42–43, 46, 47, 48, 49, 53–54; and social rank, 38–39, 41, 42, 43; and Zhou conquest of Shang, xi, 41–51, 52, 53
Du Yu, 91
Du Zichun, 87
Duan Yucai, 4–5, 85, 256n21
Duanfang, 40, 42
Dunhuang manuscripts, x, 166, 168, 169, 176, 278n10

E Hou, 41, 42, 43, 47, 53
Elder Ba, 82, 86–92, 98, 100, 102–4, 113n43, 115n65; tomb of, 78, 104. *See also* Ba Bo (Elder Ba) bronze vessels
Erligang period, 63, 93, 100
Erlitou culture, 93, 100
Erya, 256n21, 256n23

Fanwu liu xing (Shanghai Museum manuscript), 194
Feng Xu zhi ming (Tsinghua manuscript), 192, 205–6

filial piety, 9–10, 126, 161n122
Five Agents (*wuxing*), 178. See also *Wuxing*
Freer Gallery (Washington, DC) bronzes, 31–32, 34n24, 40, 65, 75n21
Fu Ding, 37
Fu Hao tomb (Anyang): bronze vessels from, 12–13, 14, 64, 72; jade figure from, 24–26; squatting figures from, 29, 30
Fu Jiezi, 265
Fu Yue zhi ming (Tsinghua manuscript), 201–4
Fuyang Shuanggudui manuscripts, 269, 273, 287n76, 288n77

Gaojiabao (Jingyang, Shaanxi), 49
Gong, King (Zhou), 78
government: and abdication, x, 215; Confucius on, 230n29; and *de*, 122–23, 124, 126, 147; and *gu* vessels, 261; and self-cultivation, 225–26
Grand Secretariat archives, Ming and Qing, 168
gu prisms, xiii–xiv, 259–92; evidence for, 264–68; excavated, 266, 267; and *gu* vessels, 260–64, 266; and Han primers, 268–73; received texts on, 266; shavings from, 270, 271, 274–76, 289n84
Guanzhen, 167
Guanzi, 121, 123, 124, 147
Guo Pu, 256n23
Guodian manuscripts, 85, 175, 180; *Laozi* in, 174, 193, 196; *Liude* in, 121, 123, 146, 161n122
Guoyu (Discourses of the States), 47, 202, 313
Gushu tongli (Yu Jiaxi), 193

Han, lineage and state of, 127–37, 143, 147; and Jin, 120, 128, 144–45;

leaders of, 128, 129, 138, 152n43, 153n48; oaths of allegiance in, 137–41; and Zhou, 128, 138, 153n48

Han dynasty: birds in, xi, 9; bronze artifacts from, 256n19; *gu* artifacts from, 266, 268, 282n44, 284n57, 285n62; legal documents from, 235–36; manuscripts from, 164–65, 168–70, 172, 173, 180, 184, 185, 193, 195, 231n37, 233, 259, 277n7, 282n41, 288n76; and Mt. Song, 313; primary education in, xiii–xiv, 260, 267, 268–73; salt monopoly of, 115nn66–68; southern frontier of, 166; tomb from, 296. *See also* Dunhuang manuscripts; Mawangdui; Sanjiaowei tomb M1

Han Feizi, 161n127

Han Feizi, 209

Han Lie Hou (Qu), 128, 129, 138, 153n48

Han Shi, 279n21

Han shu, 91, 209, 313; on ancient books, 164, 167, 176, 179; on *gu*, 262, 272, 273; and Huan Ping tomb, 296, 297; on primers, 269, 270, 291n98

Han Wu Zi (Qizhang), 128, 129

Han Xianzi, 101

He Yan, 261, 278n14

Hedong Salt Lake (Yuncheng, Shanxi), xii, 86, 87, 93, 97–99, 104, 108, 115n66, 117n93

Heguanzi, 208

Hengshui cemetery (Jiang County), 90, 102, 103, 104

Hou Han shu, 115n66, 117n93

Houfu (Houfu [Questioned by the King]; Tsinghua manuscript), xiii, 192, 195–201

Houma Covenant Texts, 120, 138, 144, 145, 156n72, 159n99, 160n114

Huaiyi peoples, 44, 46, 48, 53, 54, 108

Huan Ping, tomb of, xiv, 293–309; wooden seal of, 296–97; woodworking tools from, 294–95, 297–304

Huang Xie, 203

Huangmen (Tsinghua manuscript), 192

Hunan, 18, 166, 171, 186n6, 235, 236

individuality: and Mohism, 160n113; and private property, 136, 145–46, 148; and use of *de*, 120, 125, 126, 133, 136, 138, 141, 146–47, 148, 161n121

intertextuality, xiii, 216, 224, 226

Ji Gong (Tsinghua manuscript), 192

Ji lineage group, 45, 47, 48, 57n38, 116n76, 116n81

Ji Lu, 126

Jia Gongyan, 87, 279n21

Jia Yi, 18–19, 294

Jiaonü (Educating Women; Peking University manuscript), xiii, 233–58; translation of, 238–53

Jijiu pian (Swift Employ Volumes), xiv, 260, 265, 266, 267, 284n55, 284n59; chapters of, 272–73

Jin, state of, xii, 101–4, 106, 107, 108, 109; and covenant manuscripts, 120, 142, 144; and Han lineage, 120, 128, 144–45; reforms in, 145; script of, 196, 197, 199

Jin Hou Xiefu, 103

Jin Lie Gong, 153n45

Jin Xian Gong (Duke Xian of Jin), 144

Jinben zhushu jinian, 94

jing (vital essence), 124, 152n35

Jing, Duke of Jin, 101

Jing, Lord of Qi, 220–21

Jing Bo, 37, 38, 42, 44, 47
Jing Gong gu (Jing Gong nüe; Lord
  Jing Suffered a Protracted Illness;
  Shanghai Museum manuscript), 193,
  222–24, 231n34
Jing Lu, Elder, 83–84
Jing Nü, 94, 95
Jing Shu (Younger Jing), 82, 83–84,
  86, 88, 90–93, 97, 98, 103, 113n45
Jinteng (Tsinghua manuscript), 192,
  198
Jiu zhu (silk manuscript), 209
Jiuquan, 166
Jizhong, Confucius's Wall at, 172
Jizi's Instructions for Women, 238
Jucun (Jiang County), 102, 116n78
Jun District (Henan), 42
Junrenzhe hebi an zai (Shanghai
  Museum manuscript), 194
Juyan (Zhangye Commandery),
  187n22; gu prism from, 269–70,
  271; Han strips from, 169–70

Kang, King (Zhou), 49, 50
Kang Shu of Wei, 46
Kaogu tu (Lü Dalin), 262, 263
Kong Rong, 262
Kongjiapo Han daybook, 187n26
Kongzi shi lun (Shanghai Museum
  manuscript), 193, 215, 227n3,
  232n41
Kyeyang Mountain Fortress (Inchŏn,
  Korea), 268

Laozi: Guodian manuscripts of, 174,
  193, 196; Mawangdui manuscripts
  of, 175, 193, 195; use of de in,
  121, 123, 124, 125, 126, 141
legal documents, 173, 234–36, 237,
  254n9, 255n10
Legalism, 168, 175
Li, King (Zhou), 100, 104–5, 109

Li Gonglin, 262, 264
Li Kui, 161n127
Liang chen (Tsinghua manuscript),
  192, 207, 208
Liangdu fu (Ban Gu), 262
Lianshao Salt Pool (Lianshao lu), 98,
  114n63, 115n64
Licun (Qianshan County), 75n16
Lienüzhuan (Categorized Biographies
  of Women; Liu Xiang), xiii, 234,
  235, 236
Liji, 193, 202
lineage system: conflict in, 144,
  157n85, 157n88, 158n90; vs.
  individual, 120, 125, 126, 133,
  136, 138–39, 141, 146–47, 148;
  weakening of, 141–47; in Wenxian
  covenant tablets, xii, 119–48,
  152n38, 156n68, 158n93, 158n95
Lingshijingjie M1 (Shanxi), 49
Liqi bei (Ritual Implement Stele),
  261–62
Liu Xiang, 236, 277n5
Liude (Guodian manuscript), 121, 123,
  146, 161n122
Liujiacun (Fufeng District, Shaanxi), 42
Liye (Hunan), 235, 236
Liye Qin strips, 179
Loo, C. T. (Lu Qinzhai), 63
Lu, state of, 102; Ai, Lord of, xiii,
  216–20
Lu bang da han (The State of Lu
  Suffered a Great Drought; Shanghai
  Museum manuscript), xiii, 215–32;
  translation of, 216–20; and Yanzi
  chunqiu, 216, 221–24; and Zigao,
  215, 216, 225–26
Lü Dalin, 262, 264, 281n31
Lu Ji, 283n47
Lu Mu gong wen Zisi (Guodian
  manuscript), 193
Lu Wenchao, 203

Lunheng, 262, 293–94
Lunyu: on *gu*, 260–61, 264, 266, 268, 277n7, 278n10; on morality, 161n122; on rituals, 206–7, 230n29; on silk manuscripts, 164; on social structure, 152n38; on spirits, 225, 226; use of *de* in, 121, 122, 123, 124, 126, 134, 146; and Wenxian covenant manuscripts, 129
Luoyang, 41, 54, 68, 72, 166, 312
Lüshi chunqiu, 134–35, 136, 209

Ma Rong, 261
Majuanwan, 289n83
Mandate of Heaven, x, 19, 50–51, 218, 312; and *de*, 121–22, 123, 124
manuscripts, bamboo and silk, x, xii–xiii, 85, 163–89; annotations to, 184; classification of, 175–77; copying of, 194–95; discoveries of, 168–75; editing of, 175–85; excavated, xiii, 165–75, 273–74; format of publication of, 184–85; graph indexes to, 184; illustrations in, 164–65; looting and forgery of, 174–75; ordering strips in, 179–80; photographs of, 181–82, 184; received *vs.* excavated, xiii, 195–204, 207–9, 260; terminology for, 163–66; titles of, 177–79; tomb inventories, 171, 174, 282n41; transcriptions of, xiii, 182–83; transmission of, xii, 193–95, 260; types of, 165–66, 167
manuscripts, silk, 166, 209; *vs.* bamboo-strip, 164, 260, 277n5; from Mawangdui, 164–65, 172, 173, 180, 184, 185, 193; from Zidanku, 164, 170
Mao Gong, 52, 203
Mao Shi, 202–3
Mapo (Luoyang), 68

Mawangdui: silk manuscripts from, 164–65, 172, 173, 175, 180, 184, 185, 193; tomb No. 1 at, 9
medical manuscripts, 167, 168, 186n16, 233
Mencius (*Mengzi*): and excavated manuscripts, 199–201; use of *de* in, 121, 123, 124, 125, 146–47
military treatises (*bingshu*), 160n118, 167–68, 175, 179
Mo Bo Yi, 41, 42, 44
Mohism, 160n113, 168, 224
morality, 161n122, 233; and *de*, 123, 124, 126, 146
Mozi, 165, 202, 208
Mt. Song, 311–17
Mu tianzi zhuan, 94
music, 124, 203, 262, 315
Muye, battle of, 45–46, 48, 51

Names, school of (*Ming*), 168
Nan Gong, 47–48
Nangong Kuo, 48–49
Nanshunchengjie (Zhengzhou), 63, 64–65
Neiye (*Guanzi*), 121, 123, 124, 147
Neolithic period, 28–29, 32, 88, 303, 313
Nie Chongyi, 262
Nüjie (Lessons for Daughters; Ban Zhao), xiii, 234–35

oracle-bone inscriptions, ix, x, 311; as administrative documents, 204; *vs.* bamboo and silk manuscripts, 165; bird graphs in, 1–10; discovery of, 168; on Mt. Song, 313–16; rivers in, 313–14; on salt, 84–85, 93; and Tsinghua manuscripts, 196, 206; on Yi Yin, 207, 208
owls, 1–22; on bronze artifacts, xi, 10–13; as ill omen, 17–19; on oracle-

owls *(continued)*
    bone inscriptions, 4–10; in Western
    Zhou period, 13–17

Peking University manuscripts, xiii,
    167, 175, 179–81, 186n17, 187n26,
    188n33, 233–58, 273, 290n86. See
    also *Cang Jie pian*
Peng clan, 102, 103, 104, 116n76,
    116n81
Ping, King (Zhou), 107–8, 109
Pinhu tu (Mawangdui manuscript),
    164
poetry, 18–19, 29, 167, 208. See also
    Shijing
Ponghwang-dong (Kimhae, Korea),
    268
prefaces, xiii, 201–4
primers, Han, 260, 267, 268–73. See
    also *Cang Jie pian*; *Jijiu pian*
Puyang tomb 45 (Xishuipo), 29

qi (vital breath, energy), 123, 124
Qi, state of, 179, 206, 220–21,
    231n35; script of, 193, 196
Qicun (Fufeng), 75n16
Qin, First Emperor of, 166, 234,
    254n5
Qin, state of, 132, 147, 234–35; script
    of, 196, 234
Qin dynasty, xiii, 105, 148, 287n75,
    313; and *gu*, 266, 268; household
    registries from, 235, 236; legal
    documents from, 236, 237, 254n9,
    255n10; manuscripts from, 167–68,
    172, 173, 177, 179, 185, 186n16,
    187n26, 271, 290n92, 292n107. See
    also *Jiaonü*
Qinghua gongshe Youfangbao
    (Meixian), 75n16
Qingliangsi (Ruicheng), 93
Qiongda yi shi (Guodian manuscript),
    193, 196

Rhapsody of Two Capitals (*Liangdu fu*;
    Ban Gu), 265
Rhapsody on the Owl (*Pengniao fu*; Jia
    Yi), 18–19
ritual: Confucius on, 219–20, 226;
    and use of *de*, 120, 122, 123, 124,
    126, 146; Yanzi on, 221–24
Rong Cheng Shi (Shanghai Museum
    manuscript), 193
Rong peoples, 47, 52, 53, 99, 288n77
Rong Sheng, 106, 108
root metaphors, ix, 124, 125
Ru Chun, 114n63
Rui Liangfu bi (Rui Liangfu's
    admonition; Tsinghua manuscript),
    xiii, 192, 198, 203–4

sacrifices, 228n14, 315; and bird
    graphs, 2–8; Confucius on, 219–20,
    230n29; Yanzi on, 221–24
salt industry, xi–xii, 82–117
Sande, 121, 123
Sangfu tu (Mawangdui manuscript),
    165
Sanjiaowei tomb M1 (Tianchang,
    Anhui), xiv, 294–309; contents of,
    296–304; description of, 295–96;
    explanations of, 304–6; tools from,
    297–304
Sanli tu (Nie Chongyi), 262, 263
Sanxingdui bronze face mask, 27
scripts: Chu, 171–72, 193, 195, 196,
    199, 238; Jin, 196, 197, 199; Qi,
    196; Qin, 196, 234; regional, 168,
    196–97
self-cultivation, 147, 225; and *de*, xii,
    120, 123, 125, 126
shamanism, 220; and animal motifs,
    xi, 28, 29, 32; and women, 235,
    236, 248
Shang dynasty: bronze artifacts from,
    10–13, 37, 42–43, 46–48, 49,

53–54, 63–65, 68; *gu* vessels in, 264, 281nn35–37; High Ancestors (*gaozu*) of, 315, 316; and Mt. Song, 313–16; origin myth of, 8–9; owls in, 4–13, 14, 17, 19; salt industry in, 93–94, 115n67; shamanism in, xi, 27, 28, 29, 30, 32; Zhou conquest of, xi, 41–51, 52, 53, 223, 234. *See also* oracle-bone inscriptions
Shang Jia, 315
Shang Tang, 8, 194, 207
Shang Yang, 161n127, 235, 257n28
Shanghai Museum manuscripts, xiii, 174–76, 179–82; duplicate manuscripts in, 193–94; women in, 238. See also *Lu bang da han*
Shangma (Houma, Shanxi), 142
Shangshu (Documents), 107; and excavated manuscripts, 200–205, 213n55; prefaces to, 201–4; and Tsinghua manuscripts, 206; on Yi Yin, 207, 209; on Zhou conquest, 45–46, 49–50
Shao Gong Shi, 71, 72
She ming (Command to She; Tsinghua manuscript), xiii, 192, 205
Shen Bingcheng, 62
Shen Buhai, 161n127
Shen Dao, 161n127
Shen Tudi (Xinyang Chu strips), 171
Shi Shang, 41, 44
Shi Zhou pian, 273, 292n106, 292n107
Shifa (Tsinghua manuscript), 192, 198
Shigushan site (Baoji, Shaanxi), 39, 40, 42, 47, 51–53
Shiji: and excavated manuscripts, 203, 213n55; on *gu* vessels, 262; on Mt. Song, 312–13; on Qin laws, 234, 235, 254n9; on salt, 86, 87; on Yi Yin, 207; on Zhou, 45, 48, 91, 104, 188n33
Shijing (Odes), 8, 135, 204; on owls, 16–17; prefaces to, 201–4

Shilü (Statutes on Scribes), 273, 292nn106–7
Shiming, 300, 307n32
Shu Quan Fu, 41
Shuihudi Qin strips, 172, 173, 185, 187n26, 234, 235, 290n92, 292n107
Shuijing zhu, 87
Shun (Di Jun, Di Ku), 9, 225, 280n26, 312
Shuowen jiezi (Xu Shen), 258n37; on bird graphs, 4–5; and graph indexes, 184; on *gu*, 261, 264, 273; on salt, 85, 87; on tools, 298, 300
Shuoyuan, 231n32
spirit-man heads, 26–29, 32
spirits: Confucius on, 219–20, 225–26, 230n29; of Mt. Song, 312, 315; of nature, 130–32, 136, 138, 144–45, 148, 156n64, 160n113, 315; Yanzi on, 221–24; of Yellow River (He), 156n64, 221, 227n6, 316
Stein, Aurel, 169, 270
Sui shu, 176
Sun Hao, 280n27
Sunzi bingfa (Yinqueshan manuscript), 160n118, 175, 179

Tai Bao, 65
Taiqinggong tomb (Luyi, Henan), 41
Taiyi jiangxing tu (Mawangdui manuscript), 165
Taiyi sheng shui (Guodian manuscript), 174, 196
Tan Ji Jufu, 42
Tang chuyu Tangqiu (Tsinghua manuscript), 192, 207, 208
Tang dynasty salt industry, 116n75
Tang Shu Yu, 102
Tang zai Chimen (Tsinghua manuscript), 192, 207, 208
taotie motif, 10, 12, 14, 15, 23, 31, 38, 65

tian (heaven), 8, 9, 160n112, 199–
200, 245, 253, 316n4; and *de*,
121, 123–24, 125, 134–35; and
individuality, 160n113; sacrifices
to, 219, 220, 221, 230n29. *See also*
Mandate of Heaven
Tiangong kaiwu, 94, 97
Tianzi jian zhou (Shanghai Museum
manuscript), 193, 194
Tsinghua manuscripts, xiii, 175, 180,
181, 191–213; and ancient books,
204–6; copying of, 194–95; list of,
192; and manuscript transmission,
193–95; and received manuscripts,
201–4; regional characteristics of,
195–201; on Yi Yin, 206–9. *See
also Xinian*
Turfan manuscripts, 278n10

Waliucun (Zhengzhou), 41
Wang Chong, 262, 293–94
Wang Su, 261
Wang Yirong, 11
Wangshan Chu strips, 171
Wei, lineage and state of, 102, 128,
144, 153n48
Wei Hong, 203–4
Wei li zhi dao (Shuihudi Qin strips),
167, 173
Wen, King (Zhou), 14, 48, 124, 126
Wen, Marquis of Jin, 106, 107, 108
Wenfengta (Suizhou), 48
Wenfu (Lu Ji), 283n47
Wenxian Covenant Texts, xii, 119–61;
excavation and dating of, 126–29,
153nn44–45; numbers of people
represented by, 139–40, 153n46;
oath types in, 129–31, 142, 144,
146, 154n51; oaths of allegiance in,
120–21, 127, 129, 137–44, 146,
147; ranks represented by, 140–41,
142–43, 145, 148; and received

manuscripts, 121–26, 133–37, 141,
143, 146, 157n73; use of *de* in,
126, 129–37
women, 233–58; education of, xiii,
237–38; morality of, 233; social
status of, 235
wood: tools for working, 294–95,
297–304; writing strips of, 164,
166, 169, 185n3, 294, 305. *See also
gu* prisms
Wu, Duke of Quwo, 109
Wu, Emperor (Han), 115n68, 166,
269, 313
Wu, King (Zhou), 14–15, 44–51, 53,
71, 200, 234
Wu Dacheng, 11
Wu Ding (Shang), 2, 4, 8, 12, 201–2
Wu ji, 280n27
Wuguancun, 64
Wulipai (Hunan), 171
Wuwei manuscripts, 166, 171, 172,
179, 182, 261
Wuxing (Guodian manuscript), 193

Xi, Lord of Lu, 220
Xi Bo, 38, 42, 44, 47
Xia dynasty, 88, 223, 313; salt
industry in, 94, 115n67
Xiaoshuangqiao (Zhengzhou), xi, 23
Xiaoshuangqiao bronze architectural
decoration, 23–35; bird claws on,
29; elephant on, 24–26; feathers
on, 26–28; human-tiger-snake on,
29–32
Xibeigang (Anyang), 11, 29, 30, 73
Xie, King (Zhou), 107, 108
Xijing zaji, 265
Xincai (Henan), 106, 198
Xing Hou, 15
Xinian (Tsinghua manuscript), 107,
117n92, 153n48, 192
Xinyang (Henan), 171, 294, 304

Xiqing gujian, 11, 15
Xiqing xujian Jiabian, 11
Xizhangcun (Hubei), 41
Xizhangji (Wenxian, Henan), 126
Xu Shen, 4, 264–65, 298
Xuan, King (Zhou), 105
Xuanhe bogutu, 11
Xun, state of, 100–101
Xun Qing, 167
Xunzi, 81, 224

Yan, state of, 116n81
Yan Shigu, 265–66, 268, 284n55,
  290n90, 291n95
Yang Xiong, 290n90
Yangtianhu (Hunan), 171
Yangzishan M4, 41, 42
Yanzi, 221–24, 231n37
Yanzi chunqiu (Master Yan's Spring and
  Autumn Annals), xiii, 216, 221–24,
  227n6, 231n34
Yejiashan (Sui District), 41, 42, 47, 48
Yellow Emperor manuscripts
  (Mawangdui), 175
yeshu (*dashiji, nianbao*) annals, 178,
  188n29
Yi, Eastern, 44, 46, 53, 54
Yi Yin, 207–9
Yi Zhou shu, 203
Yijing (Changes), 167. See also *Zhou yi*
Yili: on *gu* vessels, 261, 262; in Wuwei
  Han strips, 171, 172, 179, 182
Yin gao (Tsinghua manuscript), 192,
  207, 208, 209, 213n55
Yin zhi (Tsinghua manuscript), 192,
  207, 208
Yinqueshan manuscripts, 160n118,
  172–73, 175, 179, 180, 182, 184,
  185, 285n64
Yinqueshan tomb, 168
Yinxu (Anyang, Henan), 1, 11, 12, 93,
  168, 312. See also Fu Hao tomb

Yin-yang philosophy, 168
Yu, state of, 38–39, 49
Yu Bo Ge, 38, 39, 42, 44
Yu Ji, 49
Yu Jiaxi, 193
Yu Kun, 40
Yu shu (Speech Document; Shuihudi),
  234
Yuanli, 269, 287n75, 291n97
Yue ming ([Fu] Yue's Command;
  Tsinghua manuscript), xiii, 192, 201–3
Yuelu Academy manuscripts, 175, 187n26
Yupian, 91
Yuzang tu (Mawangdui manuscript), 164

Zang Wenzhong, 220
Ze, state of, 41, 44
Zeng, state of, 47, 48, 109
Zeng Hou Jian, 41, 42, 43, 47
Zeng Hou Kang, 47
Zeng Hou Yu, 48
Zengzi, 261
Zhang Shang, 280n27
Zhangjiapo (Chang'an, Shaanxi), 84
Zhangjiashan Han strips, 187n26,
  235–36, 273, 292n106
Zhanguo ce, 203
Zhangye, 166
Zhangzhai Nanjie (Zhengzhou), 63
Zhangzi Kou, 41
Zhao, King (Qin), 203
Zhao, lineage and state of, 128, 139,
  144, 145, 153n48, 159n99
Zhao, Marquis of Jin, 106
Zhao Qi, 200
Zhao Wucheng, 300
Zhejiang University manuscripts, 175
Zheng Wen Gong wen Taibo (Lord
  Wen of Zheng Questions Tai Bo;
  Tsinghua manuscript), xiii, 192, 194
Zheng Xuan, 87, 261, 278nn10–11,
  279n21

Zhengzi jia sang (Shanghai Museum manuscript), 194

Zhou, Duke of (Zhou Gong), 15, 17, 44, 45, 46, 47, 50, 53, 70

Zhou, King (Shang), 47, 50, 51

Zhou dynasty: and bronze vessels, xi, 37–76; conquest of Shang by, xi, 41–51, 52, 53, 223, 234; and Han lineage, 128, 138, 153n48; and Jin, 128–29; lineage ties in, xii, 119–48; mandate of, x, 122, 123, 124; military elite of, 44–47, 49, 51–54; origin myth of, 14; and salt industry, xi–xii, 82–117; use of *de* in, 121–26, 133, 135. *See also* Cheng, King; Wen, King; Wu, King

Zhou li, 81, 87, 92–93, 261

Zhou shu, 135

Zhou Wu Wang you ji Zhou gong suo zi yi dai Wang zhi zhi (Tsinghua manuscript), 192

Zhou yi, 204; Mawangdui manuscript of, 176; Shanghai Museum manuscript of, 193. *See also Yijing*

Zhu Xi, 256n23, 264, 282nn44–45

Zhuangzi, 121, 123, 124, 125, 208

Zhujian Village (Tianchang, Anhui), 295

Zhujung tu (Mawangdui manuscript), 164

Zhuyuangou site (Baoji, Shaanxi), 38–39, 40, 41, 42, 47

Zi Xia, 203

Zidanku silk manuscripts, 164, 170

Zigao (Shanghai Museum manuscript), xiii, 215, 216, 225–26, 227n3

Zigong, xiii, 216, 218–20, 221, 224

Zuo zhuan, 91, 129; on state of Jin, 100–101, 102–3, 107; use of *de* in, 121, 122, 133, 135; on Yanzi, 231n34, 231n37; on Zhou conquest, 46, 47